Shifting Grounds

Shifting Grounds

Nationalism and the American South, 1848–1865

PAUL QUIGLEY

OXFORD
UNIVERSITY PRESS

OXFORD
UNIVERSITY PRESS

Oxford University Press is a department of the University of Oxford.
It furthers the University's objective of excellence in research, scholarship,
and education by publishing worldwide.

Oxford   New York

Auckland   Cape Town   Dar es Salaam   Hong Kong   Karachi
Kuala Lumpur   Madrid   Melbourne   Mexico City   Nairobi
New Delhi   Shanghai   Taipei   Toronto

With offices in

Argentina   Austria   Brazil   Chile   Czech Republic   France   Greece
Guatemala   Hungary   Italy   Japan   Poland   Portugal   Singapore
South Korea   Switzerland   Thailand   Turkey   Ukraine   Vietnam

Oxford is a registered trade mark of Oxford University Press
in the UK and certain other countries.

Published in the United States of America by
Oxford University Press
198 Madison Avenue, New York, NY 10016

Library of Congress Cataloging-in-Publication Data
Quigley, Paul, 1977–
Shifting grounds : nationalism and the American South, 1848–1865 / Paul Quigley.
      p.   cm.
Includes bibliographical references and index.
ISBN 978-0-19-973548-8 (hardcover : alk. paper); 978-0-19-937647-6 (paperback ; alk. paper)
1. Nationalism—Southern States—History—19th century.
2. Nationalism—United States—History—19th century.
3. Southern States—History—1775–1865.
4. Group identity—Southern States—History—19th century.
5. Regionalism—Southern States—History—19th century.
6. United States—History—Civil War, 1861–1865—Causes. I. Title.
F213.Q85   2011
975′.03—dc22   2011013391

For Mindy

Contents

Acknowledgments

THIS BOOK BEGAN as a doctoral dissertation at the University of North Carolina at Chapel Hill, an institution that has had a formative, enriching influence not only on this project but on much else besides. I am grateful to all my teachers and fellow students there, most especially to members of my writing group (Barb Hahn, Rose Stremlau, and Montgomery Wolf) and to my dissertation committee (William Barney, Fitz Brundage, Laura Edwards, Lloyd Kramer, and Harry Watson). Laura Edwards deserves special mention as someone who not only crossed the UNC-Duke divide but also went way above and beyond the call of duty in providing invaluable feedback and sage professional advice. She is an inspiration. Harry Watson, my doctoral advisor, has been a tremendous source of support all the way from my initial application to UNC to the present, offering guidance, encouragement, and astute commentary and criticism on my work. He is a terrific mentor.

North Carolina is pretty much impossible to beat as a place to do southern history, but I have been fortunate since moving to Edinburgh in finding fantastic students and colleagues. My fellow Americanists at the University of Edinburgh—Frank Cogliano, Alan Day, Fabian Hilfrich, Robert Mason, Mark Newman, and Rhodri Jeffreys-Jones—welcomed me into a supportive and vibrant community. Frank Cogliano in particular not only helped me with enthusiastic comments on a portion of this book but also sets the gold standard of academic leadership. It's hard to imagine what American history at Edinburgh would be without his dynamic presence. Beyond Edinburgh, in the course of writing this book I had the privilege of being part of two initiatives led by two exceptional U.S. historians, Don Doyle and Peter Onuf. Don Doyle's project "Secession as an

International Phenomenon," a model of interdisciplinary and transnational scholarly exchange, inspired me to continue placing southern history within broader contexts, while Peter Onuf's (and Peter Thompson's) symposium on "State and Citizen in Early America" encouraged me to think more about citizenship as a vital component of nationalism. Both experiences have enriched this book. Other scholars who have helped me by reading portions of the manuscript or related pieces of writing are Steve Berry, Owen Dudley Edwards, Drew Gilpin Faust, Joseph Glatthaar, Michael O'Brien, and two anonymous readers for the press. My editor, Susan Ferber, my copy editor, Ben Sadock, and their colleagues at the press have been an absolute pleasure to work with and have helped make this a better book. Worthy of special thanks are Bob Bonner and Susan-Mary Grant, each of whom generously read the final draft and provided valuable suggestions for some last-minute improvements. Proximity to Susan-Mary, a leading figure in U.S. nationalism studies, has been one of the fortunate consequences of my move to Edinburgh. She has been extraordinarily generous, providing help and encouragement in a number of ways.

For financial support I am delighted to thank the University of North Carolina at Chapel Hill (for the William R. Kenan, Jr. Fellowship, the George Mowry Dissertation Research Fellowship, and the Doris Quinn Dissertation Completion Fellowship), UNC's Center for the Study of the American South, the University of South Carolina's Institute for Southern Studies, the South Caroliniana Library, and the Virginia Historical Society. Most recently, a fellowship from the Leverhulme Trust combined with sabbatical leave from the University of Edinburgh's School of History, Classics, and Archaeology provided the luxury of a full year in which to expand my archival research and concentrate full-time on completing this book. I am also grateful to the staff of all the libraries and archives I used along the way, particularly Laura Clark Brown at the Southern Historical Collection and Elizabeth Dunn at Duke University's Special Collections. The *Journal of Southern History* allowed me to use parts of my article, "Independence Day Dilemmas in the American South, 1848–1865"; the *South Carolina Historical Magazine* permitted use of sections of "'That History is Truly the Life of Nations': History and Southern Nationalism in Antebellum South Carolina"; and the University of Georgia Press allowed me to use material from "Secessionists in an Age of Secession: The Slave South in Transatlantic Perspective."

Finally, I thank the people who have helped me in less direct, more profound ways to complete this book. My parents have been extremely supportive throughout, despite the inconvenience of distance that my academic life has necessitated. Alice took helpfully long naps as I wrote my dissertation and, as I was completing the book version, did not complain when our daddy-daughter dates sometimes involved the Civil War. I thank her most of all for those many moments of unalloyed glee we have shared, holding hands, running down hills, and discovering the world together. As for Mindy, it is impossible to thank her properly—impossible to calculate, let alone to repay, what this book and everything that goes along with it have cost her. She is my best friend, the only one whose judgment of this or anything else I do really matters, the one who keeps me right with the world and the world alright with me.

Shifting Grounds

Introduction

BETWEEN 1848 AND 1865, white southerners felt the grounds of nationhood shift beneath their feet. As the conflict over slavery led to secession and civil war, their allegiance was transferred from the United States of America to the Confederate States of America and back again. But it was not only formal political loyalties that changed. The intellectual and cultural grounds of nationhood shifted as well. White southerners were forced to engage more directly than ever before with the problems of nationalism: the problems of collective identity, of political loyalty and the responsibilities of citizenship, of what it meant to be a distinct nation, of why there should be nations at all. They would have been little surprised by the modern conceit of the nation as an invented or constructed artifact. The making and unmaking of nations was part of their daily lives.

Charles Fenton James, a Confederate soldier from Virginia, understood this viscerally. From the trenches near Richmond in February 1865, beleaguered not only by federal troops but also by desertions and desperation among his own comrades, James wrote to his sister with a prescription for Confederate success. In the process, he revealed an understanding of nationalism that was interwoven with the fabric of his life, and hers. The fate of the Confederacy, he told her, rested in the hands of all white southerners. "Let 'duty before pleasure' be the motto of all," he wrote. "There is work for all. There is a responsibility resting upon all and let no one shrink from meeting it." This appreciation of the responsibilities of citizenship was shaped by the lessons of other times and places. "Edmund Burke," he explained, citing the eighteenth-century British politician, "said that 'nations are never murdered but they sometimes commit suicide.' God forbid that we should be guilty of such folly. Nero fiddled while

Rome was burning. Shall it be said of our people that they exceeded Nero and fiddled and danced while the land was draped in mourning?"

James's reference to fiddling and dancing led him to the heart of the matter, as he went on to relate his broad understanding of nationalism to the particular case of his sister. Despite the ongoing state of war, she had been attending dances. This struck James as being not just inappropriate but downright dangerous. What, he asked, would happen if everyone spent their time attending dances? "Would it not be calculated to bring the curse of God upon us? . . . Both sacred and profane history will tell you of the wickedness of the people bringing the direct curses upon the nation. Why may it not be the case with us?" If his sister continued dancing, he implied, the fate of the nation, and of the men such as himself who were fighting on its behalf, would be imperiled. He left no doubt as to the gravity of this matter, warning her,

> When you desire to go to these dancing parties, first think of your responsibility, not only to your God but to your country and to your defenders. The people of the South have got to be worthy of freedom before they will get it. Every one has a duty to perform . . . and on the faithful performance of that duty depends the success of our cause. I hope that you, in the future, will be found doing yours.[1]

As James's admonition reveals, for white southerners of the Civil War generation, nationalism was above all else a problem—a political, intellectual, and emotional problem that demanded their careful attention. Most striking is his portrayal of a close relationship between the individual and the nation: every individual had a direct and powerful responsibility for the fate of the Confederacy. As he made clear, this was not merely an abstract responsibility but one that involved everyday life, behavior, and identity. When viewed through a religious lens, the morality of individuals' conduct—even apparently innocuous diversions such as dancing— carried national connotations. These connotations were inflected by gender, with James differentiating between men's duty to protect women and women's duty to deserve that protection by behaving virtuously. These connotations were also informed by comparative perspectives. This was evident in James's references to Edmund Burke and to the downfall of ancient Rome, and also, if less explicitly, in his understanding of nationalism as a burden—the assumption that shared hardship was the route to national fulfillment—which echoed a central premise of antebellum

American nationalism. Confederate nationalism, in this and in other respects, was based in no small part upon its American predecessor. In all these ways, James's letter reveals that southerners' encounters with nation, nationalism, and citizenship were embedded within existing patterns of thought and layers of identity.

SHIFTING GROUNDS EXPLORES the crisis of nationalism that white southerners confronted during the era of the American Civil War. In addition to causing the war, the long-standing North-South conflict over slavery also forced a rethinking of basic assumptions about national identity, allegiance, and the responsibilities of citizenship. As the problems of nationalism became more endemic and more urgent between 1848 and 1865, white southerners reached in three directions: outward, to their understandings of nationalism throughout the nineteenth-century transatlantic world; backward, to their long experience as American nationalists; and inward, connecting nationalism with their everyday lives and identities. This book follows them in all three directions.

Doing so allows for a deeper, more fully contextualized analysis of nationalism—as a concept—than previous studies have provided. Historians have, of course, long recognized the centrality of nationalism to the history of the Civil War. Traditionally they have been more interested in quantifying it than in understanding what it meant. They have debated whether Confederate nationalism was strong or weak, and whether it can really be said to have existed at all.[2] Recent scholarship has begun to move beyond the impasse of quantification and to see Confederate nationalism as a process rather than a static product.[3] Yet most historians continue to approach nationalism as a box—a rigid container which any given individual is either wholly inside or wholly outside—and have viewed the historian's principal tasks as describing the nature of the box and counting how many people were inside and how many outside. Instead, this work approaches nationalism as a variable and multidimensional concept that people relate to in different ways within changing contexts.

The "box" approach reflects a broader tendency to accept the overarching claim of nationalists themselves: that nationalism is the supreme form of legal allegiance and cultural identity in the modern world, and that because it is supreme it is unitary and indivisible. This may be true in strictly theoretical terms. Modern nation-states claim absolute authority within their borders: a monopoly on legitimate violence, the definition of right and wrong, control of the distribution of resources, and, especially with the policy of conscription, power over life and death. Nationalists also claim that nations—as cultural as well as political entities—form the ultimate object of emotional loyalty and cultural identity. Nations are supposed to be total, and most of us believe that they are. The fact that Confederate nationalism was so patently not a total phenomenon—it failed, after all, and was plagued by the dissent of both white and black southerners—has caused many historians to reject its very existence.[4] Even those who have taken Confederate nationalism more seriously have mostly seen it as an absolute form of allegiance. To continue with the box metaphor, there is a tendency to imagine white southerners in 1861 jumping out of a box marked "United States" and neatly into another box marked "Confederacy," and then back again in 1865. But allegiance and identity are far more complicated than that. Many white southerners remained loyal to the Union, and many more felt painfully torn between loyalties to America, to the South, to the Confederacy, to their individual states. These complexities can be overlooked if nationalists are taken at their word and nationalism is viewed as an absolute, indivisible form of allegiance.[5] *Shifting Grounds* therefore examines Confederate and American nationalisms within the same study, rather than treating them as completely separate subjects. In doing so it is inspired by scholarship on unionism in the Civil War South, which, unlike most scholarship on nationalism, has been sensitive to the existence of fine shades of loyalty that are contextual, relational, and changing.[6]

The grounds of nationhood were shifting throughout the transatlantic world in the nineteenth century, challenging widely held assumptions about political authority and collective identity, and altering the very map of Europe. This changing intellectual landscape across the Atlantic helped shape white southerners' own ideas about nationalism. At the risk of oversimplifying a complex process, nationalism at this time can be described as evolving from the liberal, inclusive, "civic" model embodied in the French and American Revolutions toward the conservative, exclusive, "ethnic" model that culminated in the fascism of the mid-twentieth century. The German philosophers Johann Herder and Johann Fichte, followed by other European thinkers, encouraged new definitions of the nation that centered on unique languages, cultures, and histories. Where nationalism had been cosmopolitan and universalistic, under the influence of romanticism it was coming to be parochial and particularistic. This rough transformation formed a crucial context for developments in the United States. At the same time, it is vital to note that nationalism was no more unitary in Europe than in the United States. Multiple and sometimes countervailing strands coexisted with one another, ensuring that nationalism would never mean quite the same thing to different people in different places and at different times. As the Hungarian writer József Eötvös commented amid the revolutionary fervor of 1848, "The great word 'nationality' blares out at us from every direction, but everybody wants to understand it differently."[7] This diversity renders comparisons between the American South and Europe less straightforward—yet, at the same time, considerably richer.

As Charles Fenton James's invocation of Edmund Burke and Nero suggests, when white southerners engaged with the concepts of nations and nationalism, they drew their own connections with other times and places. Looking to other examples, most commonly nineteenth-century transatlantic ones, helped white southerners to negotiate the crisis of nationalism that came along with the sectional conflict and the Civil War. Indeed, they had always thought about nationalism in broader perspective, throughout their long history as American nationalists. Northerners and southerners alike often placed the American nation in international context, whether they were celebrating its singular global mission as a beacon of universal liberty or striving to establish a cultural or ethnic nationalism along European lines.[8]

Although southern secession was to some degree a parochial, inward-looking movement, both before and after 1861 secessionists saw significant advantages in identifying their own cause with the powerful international force of nationalism. There were, of course, serious problems involved in this attempt. At first glance, secession and the Confederacy look very different from nationalism in places such as Hungary or Italy. How could a movement for political independence that was based on the apparently retrograde institution of racial slavery fit with a concept that elsewhere appeared to be so progressive? And how could southerners (or, for that matter, Americans in general) legitimately claim the same sort of ethnic and cultural distinctiveness that underpinned the Polish or the Irish movements? These incongruities, combined with the speed and apparent superficiality with which white southerners crafted their claim to nationhood, have caused much skepticism about the legitimacy of the South's nationalist claims. Yet even if these claims do not fit neatly into the normative template of nationalism, the fact that they were made—the fact that white southerners chose to cast their movement in the language of nationalism—surely warrants attention. Furthermore, recognizing the "invented," "imagined," and shifting nature of nationalism in Europe and elsewhere suggests a different place for the American South within the comparative picture. Rather than being the odd one out in an otherwise homogeneous group it begins to look like one more peculiarity in a whole host of peculiarities. If the American South did not possess a straightforward or "pure" nationalism, neither does anywhere else.[9]

In addition to looking outward to the wider transatlantic world, the crisis of nationalism also caused white southerners to look backward, to their experience as Americans prior to 1861. Existing works on Confederate nationalism have largely overlooked the fact that southerners' engagement with nationalism was an ongoing process that did not begin from nothing in 1861.[10] The prewar background is essential for understanding wartime nationalism. That is why this study begins in 1848, during the political conflict over slavery's expansion into lands acquired in the Mexican War, and examines white southerners' encounters with nationalism before the Confederacy came into existence.

In part, this involves an examination of the radical proslavery secessionists who had been arguing for southern independence for years. There were few southerners who gave more thought to the concept of nationalism than the prewar disunionists. Even so, theirs was only ever a minority opinion. For the large majority of white southerners, the nationalism they knew best before 1861 was not the separatism of the radicals but the American nationalism of the mainstream. Because the white South seceded in 1860–61 and fought a deadly war of independence, it is easy to assume that it had been following a separatist trajectory for some time.[11] In fact, many white southerners were keen unionists—albeit usually conditional unionists—right up to secession. Even those who did come to sympathize with the secessionist cause, whether in the 1850s or the 1860s, did not completely reject their Americanness. After the creation of the Confederacy, white southerners' long-standing identification with American national identity persisted. For some, this meant outright unionism. But for most it meant efforts to balance the new and the old, efforts to ground the new national identity in the remnants of the old. Not only did white southerners retain much of the content of their American nationalism—constitutional framework, political ideals and practices, heroes, revolutionary memory—but they also retained much of the conceptual apparatus as well. Thus, as Charles Fenton James captured so well, they continued to define the responsibilities of citizenship through the lenses of Christianity and republican political thought, conceiving of nationalism as a personal and collective burden, or what Daniel Webster famously called a "sacred trust." In defining Confederate nationalism, white southerners relied heavily on the nationalism they already knew.[12]

As they drew on their American past, they often did so with pained ambivalence. The fact that they had seceded from the United States clearly rendered their preservation of American nationalism problematic. How could they claim the national identity of a nation-state they had voluntarily left? If they retained the old national identity, how could they argue that the South was sufficiently distinct to warrant separate national status at all? White southerners resolved these problems in part by arguing that they were purifying and rescuing genuine American nationalism from errant northerners. But this was never quite enough. The dilemma of how Confederate nationalism related to its American predecessor—the problem of preserving the old while creating the new—would trouble white southerners throughout the era of the Civil War.

Often, white southerners stepped around this problem of continuity versus change, Americanness versus southernness, by emphasizing instead a different opposition: North versus South. As with many nations, Confederate national identity and its prewar antecedents were frequently defined negatively, against an external enemy, rather than positively, by publicizing the distinctive southern characteristics that warranted separate national status. Contrasts between nefarious northerners and noble southerners fueled southern separatism before 1861 and Confederate national identity thereafter.[13] This process often revolved around fear. Fear of northerners—their apparent differences and their apparent hostility—united white southerners in a shared community of victimhood and suffering.

Perceptions of shared suffering have long been recognized as a stimulus to nationalism. In the late nineteenth century, reflecting on his own country's defeat in the Franco-Prussian War, the French writer Ernest Renan observed that "suffering in common unifies more than joy does. Where national memories are concerned, griefs are of more value than triumphs, for they impose duties, and require a common effort."[14] Renan's words help explain why nationalism came to matter so much to white southerners. In their own time, they could see examples of perceived oppression generating nationalism in places such as Ireland, Hungary, and Italy. Since then, shared victimhood has been a crucial motivator of many nationalist movements, including postcolonial nationalisms in Asia and Africa.[15] The psychologist Joshua Searle-White has provided interesting

theoretical and comparative commentary on this phenomenon, arguing
that nationalist victimhood brings with it the moral high ground, sharpening the line between a good "us" and an evil "them." This insight illuminates the role of victimhood in southern ideas about nationalism during
the era of the Civil War.[16]

The theme of victimhood exemplifies a key premise of this book: that
nationalism thrives by traversing different areas of people's lives, crossing
boundaries between the historic and the everyday, the public and the private.[17] Victimhood encompassed white southerners' broadest intellectual
awareness of nationalism as a transatlantic concept as well as their most
personal identities and experiences. This is indicative of a more general
tendency. Although nationalism has become all but universal, connecting
individuals to global currents of thought and practice, it has flourished at
the same time in the most localized, intimate spaces. Although it has positioned itself as the supreme form of allegiance and identity in the modern
world, it has thrived not by eliminating other levels of identity and thought
but by subsuming them and intertwining with them. Hence *Shifting
Grounds* reaches not just outward and backward but also inward, into nationalists' ideas about personal life and identity.[18]

Particularly in the antebellum period, it was political and cultural
leaders who spoke and wrote most frequently about nationalism. With the
crises of secession and war, however, nationalism became an increasingly
immediate problem for white southerners from a wider range of social
backgrounds. They became increasingly likely to reflect on issues of national identity and citizenship, and increasingly likely to leave direct evidence of having done so.[19]

By 1865, countless southerners shared Charles Fenton James's visceral
understanding that nationalism does not exist in a discrete intellectual
compartment but is rather tightly interwoven with religious beliefs, with
ideas about what it means to be a man or a woman, with personal notions
of propriety, morality, and group identity. *Shifting Grounds* highlights gender, religion, and death and suffering as especially important bridges
between the individual and the nation. These bridges were acknowledged
most forcefully by nationalist leaders, but they gained stronger purchase
over time. Like other people across the world, white southerners increasingly defined their national identity in gendered terms.[20] Southerners also
shared with many other groups a belief that they had a special relationship
with God as a "chosen people," first as Americans and later as Confederates. Like religion, nationalism's widespread appeal lies partly in the way

it gives larger meaning to human life, suffering, and death, and the way it enables individuals to connect themselves to past and future generations. In the context of brutal war, nationalism came to matter more as it became a matter of life and death on the homefront as well as the battlefield.[21]

PRECISE DEFINITIONS FOR nationalism and related terms are notoriously elusive, so clarification is essential. The overarching concept *nationalism* refers to the modern notion that a given group of people, constituting a nation, ought to govern itself in a sovereign state. It is the conviction that each nation—a group of people with a distinctive identity, typically based on some combination of language, descent, history, cultural values, or interest—ought to be aligned with an independent unit of governance in the modern institution of a *nation-state*.[22] As historian Joane Nagel has observed, the concept contains two parts, one relating to action and the other to ideas: "Nationalism," as she puts it, "is both a goal—to achieve statehood, and a belief—in collective commonality."[23] Recent studies of nationalism in the Confederacy and elsewhere have largely been focused on cultural aspects of national identity, but the corollary political claim of sovereignty is what differentiates modern nationalism from other forms of group identity.

Nationalism is at its clearest when a person or group follows the concept to its logical conclusion, deciding that their nation is so deserving of political independence that they must pursue that independence by any means necessary, regardless of the obstacles. I refer to this extreme form as *active nationalism*. Active nationalism typically rests on carefully considered intellectual arguments designed to prove that the nation in question deserves independent status. It is often chauvinistic, relying on claims of the absolute superiority of "us" over "them," and the conviction that a given nation has a particular historical mission or destiny. And it often involves violence. The southern radicals who launched a movement for southern independence prior to secession are the most visible proponents of active nationalism. But this also inspired, at least to some degree, the many other white southerners who used nationalist ideas to justify their participation in the Confederate war effort. Moreover, unionists in the Civil War South were active nationalists too, committed as they were to the preservation of the United States as a legitimate nation-state.

Several other aspects of nationalism are also important to my analysis.[24] First, I use the term *the principle of nationality* to refer to the general conviction that the world is rightfully split into nations, each one clearly distinguished from the rest, and each one in control of its own affairs. Many people, including in the American South, have understood this separation to be divinely ordained. Eric Hobsbawm has demonstrated that the principle became particularly widely accepted in Europe in the middle decades of the nineteenth century.[25]

The problem raised by the general principle of nationality is the problem of how nations ought to be defined. What makes a nation a nation? How are the boundaries between them determined? Answers to this question normally rest on the concept of *national identity*. If the conventional rationale of nationalism is to align (or keep in alignment) a nation with a state, proving that a given group of people is a nation requires proving that they possess a national identity. Possible components of a national identity include race, language, religion, a shared history, an association with a particular territory, a more general cultural distinctiveness, and sometimes shared commitment to a specific political or economic interest. Above all, a national identity must validate the distinctiveness of its nation from all other peoples. Southern nationalists based their conception of southern national identity upon the institution of slavery, but also advanced arguments involving other criteria, particularly the notion of a unique southern "culture" or "civilization." While national identities can be benign phenomena, they often become more aggressively negative.[26] Such was the case with Confederate national identity, which white southerners defined in contrast to negative images of the North.

In addition to differentiation between the collectivities "us" and "them," nationalism involves ideas about how the individual relates to the nation, what obligations membership in a nation-state imposes upon individuals, and how personal and national identities shape one another. In discussing these issues, I use the term *citizenship*. This term obviously begins with the formal, legal system of mutual rights and responsibilities between individuals and the national government. It also encompasses more diffuse cultural and moral ideas that white southerners used to define individuals' status within the nation. This broader definition of citizenship can include white women, who were denied the legal status of full citizenship but who nonetheless forged for themselves important roles in the national communities of both the United and the Confederate States of America.[27] In both nation-states, citizenship took shape in a diffuse, collaborative process in which ordinary people as well as government officials influenced changing expectations about the mutual rights and responsibilities of citizens and government.

Consideration of these different aspects of nationalism highlights a vital premise of this study—that nationalism is not just one thing. There is no normal route to nationalism either for groups of people or for individuals. Nationalisms are ongoing, incomplete processes that hold different meanings and different experiences for different participants.[28] The Civil War–era American South is an extraordinarily rich place in which to explore this multiplicity. It offers the remarkable story of a new nationalism emerging as a variant of an existing one: a nationalism that began as a fringe movement but entered the mainstream, and was transformed in the process; a nationalism that was based on slavery but that helped inspire hundreds of thousands of nonslaveholders to willingly sacrifice their lives; a nationalism that derived legitimacy from the ostensibly antinational principle of states' rights; a nationalism that sought to retain the ideals of the nation whose institutions it had rejected. These multiple forms of nationalism, in short, are guaranteed to defy any prior expectations of what nationalism ought to be.

THE CHAPTERS THAT follow are arranged partly chronologically, partly topically. The first three consider discrete aspects of the antebellum era: American nationalism, southern nationalism, and the unraveling of white southern unionism. The remaining chapters turn to the Confederate period, one focusing on the formative months of Confederate nationalism in 1861 and the other on 1862–65, the years when war was fully underway.

The first chapter, "Foundations," analyzes how antebellum white southerners understood nationalism, both in abstract terms and in the case of the United States. Like their compatriots across the United States, white southerners were enthusiastic nationalists between the Revolution and the Civil War. They supported the divinely ordained separation of the world into nations, and although they felt Americans had a unique global mission as pioneers of democratic citizenship, they also sought to align their own nation with the emerging transatlantic model of romantic nationalism. They defined American national identity and citizenship with particular reference to Christianity, democratic political principles, and the commemoration of the American Revolution. While American nationalism was robust, it was not complete, fixed, or definitively moored to the Union. The problems of American nationalism, especially the structural problem of federalism, allowed the development of alternative visions of allegiance and identity.

This possibility was exploited by the small number of radicals who promoted southern independence prior to 1860. These early southern nationalists—politicians such as William Yancey and Robert Barnwell Rhett and cultural figures such as William Gilmore Simms—are the subject of the second chapter, "Dreams." The radicals forged a separatist movement that was based on the desire to preserve slavery. However, they expanded upon this simple material calculus to develop a broader argument for active southern nationalism. Inspired by European thought, they made romantic appeals to a distinctive southern identity based on specificities of place and culture. Inspired by American ideals, they contended that only southern independence could rescue the true legacy of the American Revolution and purify the true spirit of American nationalism. The radicals shared an acute frustration at the South's apparent victimization at the hands of an oppressive North. Indeed, the urgency of their crusade stemmed from their deeply emotional and personal perceptions of their region's victimhood.

The third chapter, "The Pinch," traces the South's road to secession. Most white southerners came to support secession not because of a positive embrace of the radicals' active southern nationalism but rather because their attachment to the Union could not withstand the pressures generated by northern opposition to slavery. The first secession crisis of 1848–51 revealed most white southerners to be conditional unionists: they dearly wished to remain in the United States, but only if slavery and the rights of the South were protected and respected within it. By the winter of 1860–61 the conditional unionism of the majority was dissolving. This dissolution was caused most directly by the political conflict over the expansion of slavery, but was also driven by perceptions that an American national community that had been imagined in affective terms—a community of brotherhood, friendship, even love—was being destroyed by northern betrayals. Yet even as the political bonds of Union were snapping that winter, many white southerners continued to feel strong loyalty to the United States, some of them opposing secession outright and many others feeling torn between their ties to the United States, to their individual states, and to their region. The transfer of allegiances was no simple matter.

After secession the problems of nationalism became more pressing still. Chief among them was the need to establish the Confederate States of America as a legitimate nation-state with a genuinely distinctive national identity and a government that wielded supreme power over its territory and residents. The fourth chapter, "Definitions," examines initial attempts in 1861 to define Confederate national identity and Confederate citizenship. Both of these emerged in the context of what white southerners already knew about nationalism: they were influenced by European models of nationalism and by both substantive and conceptual aspects of antebellum American nationalism. On the international stage and at home, southern nationalists crafted an argument for separate nationality that rested on assertions of fundamental North-South difference, the promise of a purified American nationalism, and appeals to the overlapping principles of nationality and self-government. Problems remained, however. Political and cultural leaders could not simply impose nationalism in precisely the way they chose, especially since significant numbers of southerners remained loyal, to one degree or another, to the ideas and the institutions of the United States. National identity and citizenship were works in progress, shaped by the competing agendas of a wide variety of southerners.

This continued to be true throughout the Civil War. After 1861, the development of Confederate nationalism was principally shaped by the determinative context of war. Chapter 5 demonstrates how war rendered nationalism and citizenship more urgent and more immediate issues in the lives of white southerners than ever before. To be sure, old patterns remained: southerners continued to feel ambivalence about the opposing pulls of the United and the Confederate States, and they continued to define their own distinctiveness in large part by vilifying their northern enemies. But the suffering of war infused nationalism and citizenship with new meanings and new urgency. The sense of shared victimhood that had always been so important was intensified by the passions of war, as the northern enemy came to seem even more menacing, even more subhuman, and even more different. And war's suffering, interpreted though a religious lens, sanctified that sense of shared victimhood, bringing the individual and the nation closer together in sacred bonds of blood sacrifice. Whereas for some white southerners the hardships of war consecrated Confederate nationalism, those same hardships drove others away from the Confederacy and back toward the United States. But for all white southerners—the die-hard Confederates, the intransigent unionists, and the large majority torn between the two—the problems of nationalism had come to matter more by 1865 than ever before.

I

Foundations

NATIONALISM IN THE ANTEBELLUM
AMERICAN SOUTH

WHITE SOUTHERNERS MARKED the Fourth of July, 1848, as they had
for decades, by coming together in cities, towns, and rural communities
to commemorate the American Revolution. They picnicked, they paraded,
they listened to speeches. Above all, they congratulated themselves on being principal members of what was surely the greatest country under the
heavens: the United States of America. Although 1848 marked the beginning of what we have come to call the Civil War era, white southerners'
celebrations of the Fourth of July that year suggest that they were little
aware of the fact.

In Greensboro, North Carolina, E. W. Caruthers, a clergyman and occasional historian, shared his reflections on American nationalism with an
audience of local students. After beginning with the truism that the United
States was an extraordinary nation, he went on to explain what he saw as the
main reasons for its greatness. First, he extolled America's defining political
principles. Unlike traditional nations, America's strength did not derive exclusively from a monarch or ruling elite: "Here," on the contrary, "it is the
people,—their freedom, their intelligence, their prosperity, their national
character, that are every thing." But the nation's strength was not exclusively
worldly. It derived directly from God. The United States held the distinction
of being the only nation since ancient Israel that had been founded principally to do God's work. "We are in fact," Caruthers said, "a nation of God's
own planting." In this combination of religious beliefs and political principles could be found the wellspring of American national identity. These
twin foundations of democracy and Christianity came together to generate

two important convictions. First, that the United States was an example, a beacon, to other nations around the world. Second, that each individual citizen bore a grave national responsibility. Thus Caruthers warned, "Whether we shall go on in our career of increasing prosperity and improvement must depend on the moral and religious character of the nation." The responsibilities of citizenship were especially critical at the present time, as America faced weighty challenges: excessive immigration; a material prosperity that could lead to the sins of pride, luxury, and vice; political partisanship; and, finally, the sectional conflict between North and South.[1]

E. W. Caruthers's sermon indicates the careful thought that he and many other white southerners gave to the concepts of nation, nationalism, and citizenship. As they did so, Caruthers and his contemporaries often connected their own circumstances to the wider world. This was just as true of southerners as it was of northerners. The distorting hindsight of the Civil War creates the impression that northerners were American nationalists while southerners were antinational sectionalists. But in fact, white southerners were active participants in American nationalism right up to the outbreak of Civil War.[2] Indeed, during the war antebellum American nationalism would became the major influence on the new Confederate nationalism, more so than the radical prewar separatism that is usually emphasized.

Nationalism necessitated reflection and debate in large part because it was then—as it continues to be—so capacious, amorphous, and inherently problematic a concept. Antebellum American nationalism, like all nationalisms, was unfinished, tentative, and fractured. E. W. Caruthers recognized a little, at least, of this. According to his understanding of Christian theology and democratic political principles, the maintenance of the American nation depended upon the moral and religious comportment of its members. If they erred, God would remove his favor. This was quite a responsibility, and, for the many Americans who shared Caruthers's logic, the fragility of their nation called forth continued effort, involving every aspect of their lives and behavior. Because national survival could not simply be assumed, the connection between citizens and their nation was conceived of as a vital and ongoing moral obligation. For antebellum Americans in the South as well as the North, nationalism mattered—it was worthy of careful reflection in the abstract, in the specific American case, and in broader international context. These reflections would prepare them well intellectually and culturally for the crisis of nationalism that came along with the Civil War.

The Principle of Nationality

According to the North Carolina newspaper editor and politician William Woods Holden, nationalism defined his century. "As the great idea of the eighteenth century was that of *union against tyrants*," he proclaimed in 1856, "so is that of the nineteenth century, *the independence of nationalities.*" And so it must have seemed. The American and French revolutions had established the basic truth that a people constituting a unique nation had the right to a national existence, in a national territory, with a national government. Latin Americans had followed, if less successfully, the thirteen colonies' lead in shaking off the yoke of colonialism and asserting national independence. In such apparently ancient countries as Britain, new ideas about citizenship and nationhood had prompted new political practices and cultural impulses. And across the European continent, faith in the irresistible might of nationalism fuelled new movements for independence or unification. German writers celebrated the character and spirit of a distinctive people whose shared culture warranted shared political existence. Giuseppe Mazzini campaigned to the same end in the Italian peninsula. In central and eastern Europe, legendary figures such as the Hungarian Lajos Kossuth struggled to realize their own, separatist visions of nationhood. With the revolutions of 1848, the twinned forces of nationalism and democracy shone brighter still, in Germany, Hungary, Ireland, and other places. Small wonder that from the vantage of mid-nineteenth-century North Carolina, nationalism appeared to define the century.[3]

In the eyes of most Americans who thought about such things, this was precisely as it should be. For antebellum southerners and Americans more generally, the principle of nationality—the separation of humankind into different nations with their own governments—was natural and divinely ordained. Just as it seemed obvious that the world ought to be divided into nations, it seemed equally obvious that it was God who directed that division. Nations were God's creatures, and national borders were sacrosanct. A reading in a schoolbook designed for southern students began with the pronouncement that "NATIONS are neither accidental nor arbitrary divisions of men. They exist by divine appointment, and are the product of natural laws as truly as families." Because "God divided to the *nations* their inheritance," the fortification of national distinctions and support of one's own nation were hallowed duties. As the lessons of world history proved, great nations were made great by the active support of their members, and it logically followed that "patriotism" was more noble than "cosmopolitanism and universal brotherhood."[4]

Like the principle of nationality, the responsibilities of citizenship were divinely ordained. Love for one's country was sacred. Speaking in a small southern town in 1860, the physician and local politician James G. Ramsay reflected on the causes of "patriotism." God had created man—nationalism was, in theory at least, a predominantly male affair—as a fundamentally "social being," Ramsay thought, which caused him to develop strong affections for those around him: first his wife, then his family, and eventually larger communities. As humans went on to create political communities and governments, the benefits incurred meant that man was "led, by an irresistible impulse, to love his government—the very soil upon which it is erected—its subjects, and all its essential auxiliaries." Accordingly, love of one's government and the land of one's birth were natural impulses evident throughout world history, from the Israelites and ancient Romans to "savage" Indians and "civilized" Europeans. "This love of Country," Ramsay believed, "is as universal as it is holy."[5]

Even if patriotism was a universal impulse, it seemed especially important in the United States, a nation that was thought to enjoy a special relationship with God. The clergy never tired of reminding their congregations of this relationship and the responsibilities it entailed. William Sparrow, a professor at a Virginia seminary, called attention to the religious foundations of American nationalism in an 1852 sermon. God was, in Sparrow's estimation, the God of nations. He had established the boundaries of the United States, and of all countries, and Americans ought to be grateful that he had blessed them with such a magnificent and spacious country, containing such bountiful natural resources. Americans should also give thanks to God for their political system, which was considerably more just than European equivalents. Emphasizing the link between religion and the responsibilities of each citizen, Sparrow concluded with the axiom, "He is the best patriot who is the best Christian."[6]

David Porter delivered a similar message to a Savannah congregation a few years later. Using as his text Psalms 33:12—"Blessed is the Nation Whose God is the LORD"—he began by expressing pleasure that this year, 1858, saw the Fourth of July falling on the Sabbath. He was thereby presented with a perfect occasion to remind his audience "of His overruling agency in the achievement of our Nationality," and to talk more generally about the connections between religion and government. Porter, like E. W. Caruthers, compared Americans to the ancient Israelites, God's original chosen people. He did not view the formal establishment of religion as a viable program in the United States, to be sure, but he, too, believed that Americans could retain God's favor by practicing piety on an individual level. Because the nation's health depended on keeping things right with God, and because keeping things right with God depended on individual actions, each individual had a powerful responsibility for the well-being of the nation. "Every man then in our nation," Porter said, "is an element of strength or weakness, just in proportion as he is virtuous or vicious, righteous or sinful, holy or corrupt." "If every citizen were *a true* Christian," then the United States would maintain God's favor and enjoy good health, but "one corrupt and wicked man, one rotten, crumbling stone, in this national edifice, is an element of weakness," with the potential to endanger the whole. Porter went on to reaffirm the judgment of William Sparrow: "The best Christian is the truest patriot."[7]

In contemplating the moral responsibilities of citizenship, Americans often invoked the concept of virtue.[8] The title of a graduation speech at the College of Charleston in 1848 summarized the consensus nicely: "National Stability dependant on National Virtue." It is difficult to imagine any opposition. In speeches and sermons, and elsewhere, this notion was constantly reiterated as a great truth. In the words of the South Carolina writer William Gilmore Simms, "It is the accumulation of personal character, that lays the great foundation of national renown. . . . The causes which make a nation triumph, have their roots in the successes of the citizen." Similarly, the clergyman Charles Taggart thought it was not "mere pulpit cant" but rather a worthwhile exercise to remind his Charleston congregation "that as all that gives permanent value to individual character is *moral* excellence, so the only true basis of *national* greatness is *moral* power." These connections between individual virtue and the fate of the nation carried the responsibilities of citizenship into the daily lives of individual Americans.[9]

A group of Virginians were told much the same thing by William Clark, another Independence Day speaker. For the good of the whole, he affirmed, individuals ought to live morally upright lives. Accordingly, and as many other public figures, both clergy and lay, would have agreed, Clark urged Americans to live moral lives and to train their children—the Americans of the future—to do the same. "The energy of a Government," he said, "does not repose upon the repulsion of foreign invasion or the subjection of lawless passion, but with its plastic though unseen hand moulds each rising generation to whom its destinies will in turn be committed." Ensuring that one's children lived virtuous lives was a vital national responsibility for citizens of a republic, since a republican form of government depended as no other on the continued virtue of its people. Clark believed that Americans were doing well, since the republican experiment was working. The most important ingredient for continued national success, he thought, was clear: "that each freeman of the land holds himself the *indispensable* guardian of his country."[10] Although Clark used the term "freeman," Americans often viewed the education of sturdy young republicans as primarily a female responsibility. Between the Revolution and the Civil War, the ideal of "republican motherhood" provided a prescriptive, gender-specific role for women in American politics, public culture, and nationalism. Because republicanism rested on civic virtue, thought to stem from a salubrious domestic life, and because domestic space was widely seen as female space, American women bore a grave national responsibility to instill in their children patriotic virtue.[11]

The lessons of history proved the importance of virtue to national survival. For South Carolinian Thomas Hanckel, the downfall of Rome showed that a republic's survival required "that no virtuous and intelligent citizen can rightly withdraw himself from public affairs, or can safely neglect his public duties." Otherwise, "the powers of the state . . . will be usurped by those who will abuse them"; they would be seized, that is, by tyrants and despots who would lead the republic to ruin. If history taught anything, thought Hanckel, it was that "the price of liberty is eternal vigilance."[12]

Lurking behind many such proclamations was anxiety that the current generation might not be up to the task, that the great American nation bequeathed to them by the founders might fail. Such uncertainty had been a constant theme of American nationalism from the beginning, reflecting an essentially pessimistic view of human nature, human history, and human destiny. In Daniel Webster's phrase, American nationality was a "sacred trust." Citizenship was a natural, spiritual responsibility, diligent attention to which was essential if Americans, both North and South, were to fulfill the promise of their great nation.

Democratic Citizenship and American Exceptionalism

The responsibility that Americans felt for their nation's health reflected a fundamental transformation in the relationship between individuals and their governments. Antebellum Americans recognized the importance of

democratic (or, as they would have preferred, republican) thought to nationalism. The rise of democracy in the Western world, embodied in the
American and French revolutions, was closely interrelated with the emergence of modern nationalism and citizenship. The phenomena were joined
most directly by the shared premise of popular sovereignty: the idea that
ordinary people as well as ruling classes had a stake in their political communities and ought therefore to have some control over their own governance. In the United States, visions of citizenship held that the nation and
its governance rested upon the individuals who made up "the people."[13]

This reflected a general shift in the nature of allegiance from traditional "subjecthood" toward modern "citizenship." Whereas in English
common law allegiance had been conceived as natural, perpetual, and hierarchical, modern citizenship has been conceived as being volitional and
horizontal. The citizenship that came along with the revolutions of 1776
and 1789 posited a perfectly equal status between all citizens, regardless of
their social status. Each citizen owed a set of clearly defined obligations to
the government, and in return each citizen could expect a range of political, social, and economic rights. The corollary of citizenship's internal
homogeneity is a severe sharpening of the line that separates insiders
from outsiders, citizens from aliens.[14] Of course, the universalist ideals of
citizenship were not matched by reality. Whereas in theory citizenship
creates two clear, rigid, and absolute categories of "citizen" and "alien,"
this has not always been the case in practice. The rights and responsibilities of citizenship have been gradated by race and gender, among other
factors. In the United States as in other countries, they have been complicated and contested, the product of political struggles between a variety of
social groups and individuals rather than the fiat of the central state.[15]
Despite these complications, the political ideals of modern citizenship
were powerful, and they reinforced the religious conviction that individual
citizens were responsible for the fate of the nation.

E. W. Caruthers emphasized the exceptional influence of "the *people*"
in appraising mid-nineteenth-century American nationalism. In doing so,
he tapped into a powerful vein of American thought. Earlier in the century, James Madison, one of the most influential political architects of the
United States, had given early expression to a belief that would come to be
axiomatic. "With a union of its citizens," he wrote in 1810, "a government
thus identified with the nation, may be considered the strongest in the
world, [owing to] the participation of every individual in the rights and
welfare of the whole." In an 1831 Independence Day speech, the South

Carolina planter and future professor Frederick A. Porcher similarly explained that the American political system produced a new kind of relationship between the individual and the nation. Whereas in the Old World notions of "country" began and ended with the monarchy or aristocracy, things were different in the United States, since "this country comprises every individual within its limits." In an 1842 speech, the future Georgia governor Herschel V. Johnson agreed that in the United States, because "all power emanates from and resides in the people," the government had to "impress every citizen with the identity between his own and his country's interest. Each must feel that he can promote *his own, only by* promoting the *public good*." Johnson compared the strength of citizenship in the United States with Old World countries like Ireland, where limited rates of suffrage and land ownership reduced individuals' attachment to their country.[16]

Just as individual citizens felt a grave responsibility for the welfare of the nation, so too did the nation as a whole feel an obligation to spread the benefits of democratic citizenship across the world. Just as religious and political values combined to generate conceptions of American citizenship that were anxious, inward-looking, and fixated on the responsibility of the individual to the nation, so too did they generate an optimistic, expansive vision of America's role in world history that magnified America's global responsibility.[17] Southerners no less than northerners were enthusiastic advocates of this exceptionalist vision of America's mission during the antebellum period. As they compared their own nation with others, they felt above all else proud to be Americans, citizens of what they believed to be the best country in the world. Thus John Taylor Wood, a nephew of Jefferson Davis's who was serving in the U.S. Navy in the late 1850s, wrote home to his wife from Turkey, "The more I see of other countries the more I love my own, we are favored above all the nations of the earth, as regards people, institutions, indeed everything that constitutes a nation."[18]

The conviction that America and its ideals were important to the rest of the world, already strong, was quickened by the European revolutions of 1848–49. One Georgia newspaper, introducing reports of these events, believed that they would be of obvious interest to Americans, since "it has been the example of the United States which has taught the oppressed of the old world that man is capable of self-government." Americans have never been modest about the significance of their nation's founding, but 1848 elevated national pride to new heights. On the floor of the U.S. Senate,

FIGURE I.I *Liberty Our Aim! Washington Our Example!* Edwin H. Brigham, Boston, ca. 1852. (Library of Congress.)

Georgian Herschel V. Johnson urged his colleagues to issue formal congratulations to the French people on the formation of their new republican government. Explaining that "the people of France are but exercising this great right which, for the benefit of mankind, was established by the struggles of our Revolution of Independence," Johnson argued that Americans were obligated to support "any effort, in any part of the globe, to overturn monarchies and despotism, and in their stead, to form governments based upon republican principles."[19]

Connections between the American and European revolutions were drawn even more insistently than usual as Americans celebrated the Fourth of July, 1848. As Nelson Mitchell, addressing an Independence Day crowd in Charleston, explained: "The American revolution, regarded merely as the division of one country from another was, comparatively, an ordinary occurrence among European nations, but considered as establishing the dogma that governments were to be the work of the popular will, it formed an era in the history of the world." Americans, in other words, had inaugurated the next stage of world history—the stage defined by the great truths of self-government and democratic citizenship—and everyone else was still trying to catch up. This belief reverberated across the South that day. In Richmond, anniversary celebrations portrayed the American Revolution as an inspiration to Ireland, France, and, ultimately, the rest of the globe. Virginians drank to such toasts as "Our Country, the cradle of Liberty: May her example be followed until the whole world is redeemed from the shackles of tyranny"; and "The Day we Celebrate. Americans hail it as their country's natal day. May all nations ere long date from it their political regeneration." The promise of the American Revolution—the promise of American nationalism and citizenship—was considered to be exportable.[20]

Some historians have rightly pointed out the limitations of such expansive idealism, especially in the South. Certainly, conservative opinion quickly soured on the perceived excesses of European radicalism. This sometimes involved sensitivity regarding slavery, particularly after France abolished slavery in the French West Indies. Indeed, this event had complicated Herschel Johnson's efforts to congratulate France. His speech irately referred to a northern senator's proposal to laud French emancipation as well as the new government, which prompted Johnson to wish that northerners and southerners could, "on this great occasion of national congratulation, harmonize as brethren of the same political family, and for once, forget all party distinctions and local prejudices." Sectional disputes over slavery compromised hopes for a consensual national stance on international affairs. Even without the problem of slavery, Americans became disillusioned with European revolutions as they evolved into more complicated and often more radical struggles after the spring of 1848.[21]

Even so, throughout the 1850s mainstream American—including southern—opinion continued to celebrate the international significance of American national ideals. The exporting of those ideals might not always be appropriate, but that did not change the fact that, in the right circumstances, they could flourish elsewhere. Reflecting on sectional dangers to the Union in 1850, for instance, one southern editor declared that the stakes involved were global. "The hopes of mankind" were with the Union, for "it is their Beacon, and its light has attracted the gaze of millions." In January 1850, New Orleans hosted a meeting in support of political refugees from the recent European revolutions, particularly the Hungarian independence movement. "It is the pride and the duty of every American

citizen," the meeting's resolutions announced, "to extend the hand of welcome to each and every patriot and exile whom foreign oppression has
forced to our land, to seek that freedom which is denied them at home."
Likewise, at a St. Patrick's Day celebration in Savannah, attendees toasted
not only Ireland, "*The Irish Patriots of '48*," and (of course) St. Patrick, but
also "*The Hungarian Refugees*," George Washington, and "*The United States
of America*—Our adopted country, the foe of monarchy, the nurse of liberty, the practical school of freemen, and the asylum of the distressed."
One man connected British and American politics with a toast to "*The
Union*—Procured in one hemisphere by fraud and corruption—may it be
repealed. Compacted in the other by compromise and concession—may it
be preserved." Southerners thus linked their own commitment to American nationalism with their support of other nationalist movements across
the Atlantic.[22]

The Fourth of July continued to call these connections to mind with
particular force. In 1852 a Fourth of July speaker in Kentucky effusively
touted the global significance of the Declaration of Independence:

> Nor have the effects of our Declaration been confined to North
> America alone. Touched by its magic wand, South America has
> lifted her lofty mountains above the convolving clouds of barbarism
> and slavery, and spread out her rich plains beneath the blazing sun
> of liberty. The cheering voice of freedom has circulated among the
> Empires, the Monarchies, the Aristocracies, the Dukedoms, the
> Princedoms, the Powers and the Dominions of the Old World; and
> institutions which have stood firm for centuries, have been con-
> vulsed as if heaved by the force of subterranean earthquakes.
> Throughout the civilized world a new impulse has been given to the
> doctrines of self-government and free institutions; and the mighty
> tide which has rolled against the relics of autocratic and feudal ages
> will continue to lash them until their iron features give place to the
> plastic moulds of republicanism.

This fulsome portrayal of the Declaration's significance captured a widespread confidence in the influence of American ideals on the rest of the
world.[23]

Yet most southerners, like most other Americans, remained ambiva-
lent. Holding up the United States as a noble example for the rest of the
world to follow was one thing. Actively helping others to follow that

example was quite another. In the mid-nineteenth century, as in other periods of American history, this distinction informed a mixed response to foreign revolutions: satisfaction that others were trying to imitate the American example combined with reluctance to get physically involved and cynicism about perceived excesses.[24]

In the early 1850s this ambivalence crystallized in attitudes toward Hungary. Americans had generally sympathized with the Hungarian independence movement in 1848 and 1849, a sympathy that persisted as late as 1851, when the Hungarian leader Lajos Kossuth commenced a fund-raising, consciousness-raising tour of the United States. But during the course of Kossuth's tour, American sympathy waned considerably. Here again, the ongoing sectional dispute over slavery caused problems. Abolitionists such as William Lloyd Garrison became disillusioned when Kossuth—whom they had assumed would support the liberation of American slaves as well as Hungarians—refused to ally himself openly with their movement, probably fearing for his reputation among conservative Americans, especially in the South. In spite of Kossuth's efforts to distance himself from the antislavery movement and align himself with states' rights, white southerners suspected that radicalism in one cause could too easily become radicalism in the cause about which they were coming to care above all else—the preservation of slavery. They too became increasingly hostile to Kossuth's pleas for American aid.[25]

Although American ambivalence toward foreign revolutions was partly driven by sectional politics, it also reflected general uncertainty about the extent and character of Americans' international responsibilities. Some observers explained this ambivalence cynically. One contributor to the *Southern Literary Messenger* wrote, "Our sympathy with the oppressed in Europe is emotional rather than founded on rational conviction, and having no root, it soon withers away." Other observers took American sympathy more seriously, but balanced it against the exigencies of active intervention in foreign affairs, the isolationist mandates of Washington and Monroe, and, occasionally, more theoretical ruminations on the right of intervention in other nations' affairs. A writer in the *Southern Quarterly Review*, in all likelihood then-editor William Gilmore Simms, opposed support for Hungary not only because of objections to the character of Lajos Kossuth (he did not even come close to meriting comparison with the great Washington, this reviewer thought) but also because of serious reservations about one nation "intermeddling" in the affairs of another. Rather than attempting to conquer the world by force, the United States ought to rely upon "the influences of honesty, truth and justice, of equal laws, liberal institutions, unfettered enterprise, unlimited commerce, and, above all, of perfect freedom of religious opinion and worship." By cultivating its status as a model, he went on, "the example of the United States, steadfastly presented, but not obtrusively or offensively thrust upon the attention of other nations, will exercise among them an incalculable power."[26]

Leander Cox, a U.S. representative from Kentucky, was troubled by these same problems, recording in his journal his own struggle with the rectitude of foreign intervention. Discussing Kossuth's calls for U.S. aid, Cox reflected at some length on the problems of nationality that lay at the core of this issue. Reporting that most Americans agreed with Kossuth that "every nation has a right to govern itself—and any interference with this right is a violation of the law of nations," Cox went on to ask, "How far should other nations interfere to prevent the dominion of one nation" over another? This was not an easy question to answer. Cox's solution rested on the difference between "national independence and individual liberty." Americans only had a duty to support struggles involving both goals, "so if Hungary only struggles to be free from Austria in a national point of view; but the people to remain under feudal oppression," as he thought was indeed the case, "it matters not to us." U.S. aid would only be warranted if a national independence movement sought to achieve freedom for its citizens as well as independence for the nation as whole. Although Cox did not spell it out, he clearly believed that only one type of independence movement was truly righteous—the type that simultaneously advanced the liberties of nation and individual, the type that advanced democratic citizenship—the type, in short, that sought to imitate Americans' own revolution.[27]

For many Americans, the Italian movement for independence, underway for several decades but rising to a crescendo in the late 1850s, fully qualified. Expressions of sympathy for efforts to overturn Austrian domination of parts of the Italian peninsula permeated newspapers, speeches, and

FIGURE I.2 Tintype of James Johnston Pettigrew. (Ruffin, Roulhac, and Hamilton Family Papers, Southern Historical Collection, Wilson Library, the University of North Carolina at Chapel Hill.)

private writings. Whereas most Americans limited their support to words alone, James Johnston Pettigrew, a wealthy young Carolinian, felt so strongly that he traveled to Europe to volunteer his services to the Italian independence movement. He got there too late to take part in the fighting, but his arrival on Italian soil prompted some revealing reflections on the character of the independence movement and its relationship to American national ideals:

> It was on the night of the 4th of July, 1859, that I crossed Mount Cenis, on the way to Turin. Though the precise date was a matter of accident, its associations were in happy unison with the object of the journey and the sentiments which prompted me. It was my birthday; but far more, it was the day that ushered into life my native land—a day ever memorable in the history of the world—not so much because it had added another to the family of nations, as because it had announced, amid the crack of rifles and the groans of expiring patriots, the great principle, that every people has an inalienable right of self-government, without responsibility to aught on earth, save such as may be imposed by a due respect for the opinions of mankind. Once more this great battle was to be fought, no longer in the wilds of the American forest, but on land renowned through all ages, and rendered sacred by recollections of intellect, art and religion.

Pettigrew offers a vivid expression of mid-nineteenth-century American idealism. The coincidence of his arrival on Independence Day provided dramatic proof of the similarities between the American and Italian independence movements. (Furthermore, he observed, both had benefited from French support.) The Italian crusade was so enticing because it combined the promise of advancing the distinctively American alliance of democracy and nationalism—fulfilling America's global mission—with the promise of reawakening Italy's noble past. In the eyes of Pettigrew and like-minded Americans, this was nationalism at its very best.[28]

As Pettigrew illustrates so well, antebellum southerners were fully engaged with the concepts of nationalism and citizenship. They saw the nation as a fundamental category that organized the world into discrete peoples, a category that was ordained by God and that ought to be upheld by all humans. Their own nation, of course, was exemplary insofar as each citizen held a grave responsibility for the moral health of the nation and that the nation as a whole was obligated to hold itself up as a model for the rest of the world. Southerners no less than other Americans were missionaries of nationalism and democratic citizenship.

Toward Romantic Nationalism

No matter how much they considered themselves a people apart, Americans could scarcely think about nationalism and citizenship without thinking about the wider world. They frequently positioned their exceptional nation at the forefront of human progress. Approached from different vantage points, though, the United States sometimes appeared to be either not exceptional at all or exceptionally retrograde in the character of its nationalism—a nation striving to catch up to foreign norms rather than setting the standard for others to follow.

Commentators have traditionally assumed that America has exemplified the "civic" model of nationalism: a liberal, inclusive phenomenon based on shared ideals and political values.[29] According to this model, allegiance and citizenship are volitional rather than natural or inherited, and individuals are free to enter or leave a given nation by accepting or rejecting that nation's core principles. Much of what we have seen so far supports this view. However, antebellum Americans were also developing other strands of nationalism that tended more toward the "ethnic" model: a more limited and exclusive phenomenon based on particularities of culture, place, ethnicity, and race. As much as Americans liked to think of their nationalism as being exceptional, it shared a good deal with the increasingly romantic, ethnocultural strands of nineteenth-century European nationalisms. Just as aspects of American national thought seemed available for export to Europe, so too were aspects of European romantic nationalism transferable to America. From Germans Johann Herder and Johann Fichte, Americans both North and South adopted the idea that each nation was defined by its own, unique national culture, comprising literature and other art forms, language, and ways of life. From French historian Jules Michelet, they took the notion that each nation had its own spirit, which resided in "the people." From Italian Giuseppe Mazzini and Hungarian Lajos Kossuth, they learned a faith in the absolute claim of place, and the certainty that genuine nations ought to be allowed to exist, in their own homeland, with their own government.[30] There was no one template of nationalism in mid-nineteenth-century Europe. But certain claims to national status and national identity were beginning to rise to the surface: claims of ethnicity, of distinctive cultures embedded in unique literatures and histories, of unique relationships with God. As Americans advanced their claims to nationality, they drew upon these emerging European norms.[31]

There were certainly limits to the importation of European concepts of nationalism. Americans could not claim a unique language as some European nationalists did, nor could they credibly claim a unique ethnic heritage. To be sure, there were some Americans, including some southerners, whose hostility to white immigrants stemmed in part from a desire to maintain an assumed ethnic purity. But most Americans envisioned their status as a sort of melting pot of a variety of European peoples.[32]

So blood or ethnicity did not determine membership in the American nation—not in the same way as it was thought to determine membership in ethnically based European nations. Yet even though U.S. citizenship was open to most white Europeans, it was largely closed to Native Americans and African Americans. This set American nationalism on a different trajectory than Latin American countries, where early-nineteenth-century revolutions created the new horizontal category of "Americanos," a category that included (in theory, though not always in practice) Latin Americans of different ranks and colors within the "sovereign people."[33] In the United States, however, the exclusion of racial minorities exposed the hypocrisy of white Americans' rhetoric of inclusive, ideals-based nationalism and open democratic citizenship, the category that was supposed to replace hierarchical subjecthood. For nonwhite Americans, this was patently not the case. The tone was set by the federal government's 1790 Naturalization Act, which offered a relatively easy path to American citizenship, but only for those with white skin. If modern citizenship demanded that every individual be sorted into the binary categories of citizen or alien, with no gradations in between, where then did racial minorities fit?[34]

Nineteenth-century Americans offered a variety of answers to these questions, often jumbled and contradictory, which together revealed more gradations, more shades of grey between citizen and alien, than was supposed to be the case. In the decades following the American Revolution, American courts moved toward what one scholar has termed the "denization" of African Americans: the placing of black people in a traditional legal category somewhere between citizen and alien, a category that afforded some basic rights but denied equal citizenship. Over time, white Americans excluded even more rigorously their black neighbors from

membership in the national community. Even northerners who were opposed to slavery and relatively sympathetic toward African Americans conceived of the American national community as being bounded by the
racial line of whiteness—a line that, thanks to developments in scientific
thinking, was becoming ever harder during the middle decades of the
nineteenth century. At the same time, American leaders deployed the
same body of newly aggressive racial thought to justify westward expansion and their "manifest destiny" to replace Native Americans as the legitimate inhabitants of the United States. The categories of race and nation
hardened simultaneously, even symbiotically, combining to create an emphatically white national identity. As historian Michael O'Brien has shown,
southern racial thought went much further than the narrow defense of
slavery; embedded in the broader transatlantic project of classifying peoples, nations, and other groups, race seemed from the vantage of the
South to be a "cosmopolitan idea."[35]

The culmination of this process of exclusion came with the Supreme
Court's *Dred Scott* decision in 1857. In addition to rejecting both the freedom of Dred Scott and the authority of the U.S. Congress to prohibit slavery in the territories, the court denied that *any* African American could
hold national citizenship in the United States. As the *New York Times* recognized, "This decision revolutionizes the Federal Government, and
changes entirely the relation which Slavery has hitherto held towards it.
Slavery is no longer local; it is national." The *Times* overlooked the fact that
Dred Scott nationalized not only slavery but also white supremacy. The two
were closely related, of course, but the latter had more far-reaching implications, demonstrating that the United States as a whole—not just the
slaveholding South—was a white nation that barred those with black skin
from the rights and the obligations of citizenship.[36]

Americans' racially exclusive citizenship was in certain respects similar to some European nations' ethnically defined citizenship and national
identity. White Americans claimed to subscribe to civic nationalist ideals
while practicing racial exclusions that resembled the ethnic nationalism
becoming more dominant across the Atlantic. Still, the fact remained that
Americans' vision of a racially exclusive citizenry was more open to a
range of white ethnicities than were most European nationalisms of the
day. There was no "American" ethnicity that could compare to, say, the
German ethnicity celebrated by Johann Herder.

The idea of a distinctive national culture, as opposed to a completely
distinctive national bloodline, appeared to be a more promising basis for

romantic American nationalism.[37] It was generally accepted that a nation's culture, its character, was reflected in its literature. So if America were a nation with a national identity of its own, then it should have a unique literature. For the first century or more of United States history, Americans exhibited a classic postcolonial anxiety that they did not measure up culturally to the Old World. They were notoriously sensitive to European scorn about the dearth of high-quality, distinctive literature in the United States. Calls to rectify the situation emanated most famously from New England— from Ralph Waldo Emerson, Margaret Fuller, and others of their ilk—but they came from southern literary figures as well. The Alabama writer Alexander Beaufort Meek, for instance, followed European thinkers in the belief that literature was the spiritual expression of a people. Accordingly, Meek thought, "The literatures of all other nations are entirely inadequate, unfit for Americanism. We must have a literature congenial to our institutions, to our position, to our great democratic faith." Such a literature was already being developed in the 1840s, when Meek wrote these words, and was based in his estimation on several key peculiarities of American life: the beauty of America's natural environment; the character of the ethnically mixed white American population; the American political ideals of equality and liberty; and, finally, the system of federalism, which minimized the potentially debilitating effects of centralized authority and promoted creative competition among different states and localities. All of this meant that even though American literature might not yet have reached the highest heights, its potential was great.[38]

In a review of Meek's work, William Gilmore Simms, the antebellum South's most prominent writer, lauded his intent and explication. The United States was still in its infancy, Simms conceded, but was nonetheless growing ready to claim for itself a strong and permanent national identity. "We have," he felt sure, "our own national mission to perform." In order to perform that mission, though, literary Americans had to understand the difference between writing *for* a people, which any skilled writer might do, and writing *from* a people, which required intimate knowledge and sympathies, and which alone could establish a true national culture. A nation's "poets and artists," he wrote, "to feel her wants, her hopes, her triumphs, must be born of her soil, and ardently devoted to its claims." Simms here gave voice to a central component of the romantic nationalism that was such a powerful force in mid-nineteenth-century Europe: the notion that a visceral attachment to a particular soil, land, or place generated powerful connections between individuals and their nation. This clearly contrasted with that important strand of American nationalism that emphasized individuals' voluntary connection to the American nation through ideas—a contractual acceptance of the principles of self-government, liberty, and equality. Simms revealed, then, an alternative strand of American nationalism, one based more on emotion and time-honored particularity of place than on reason and recognition of common principles.[39]

Southerners praised placed-based patriotism when they saw it in other countries. Thus a textbook used in southern schools reprinted a brief passage by Lajos Kossuth, a teary-eyed tribute to his primal devotion to the soil of his birth, to the national liberation to which he had devoted his life. Readers were clearly expected to sympathize with Kossuth, the personification of the nineteenth-century romantic nationalist.[40] James Johnston Pettigrew, the young Carolinian who travelled to Europe with the intention of fighting for Italian independence, found much to admire later in his travels in Spaniards' firm attachment to locality and country. "Like all Spaniards," he wrote of his guide, "he was jealous of his locality, and dwelt upon its peculiar beauties and excellencies—an amiable failing which is always agreeable to me, for I have never found one worth knowing who did not think his native land, all things considered, the first in the world." Such attachments, Pettigrew lamented, were out of vogue in the modern world. In his eyes, that rendered them all the more valuable. "Patriotism," he went on, "an attachment to, a preference for one's home, is still a virtue prolific of measureless good, and for its foundation rests upon enlightened prejudice. Of all nations, Spaniards have this sentiment most strongly developed. Every Spaniard believes that Spain, with all her faults, is, or can be made, the centre of the earth, and his own province the centre of Spain."[41] Pettigrew described exactly the kind of attachment to place that, in Simms' opinion, could produce a properly nationalistic sentiment and literature.

Like European nationalists, Americans believed that attachment to place was expressed in a nation's distinctive history as well as its literature, both important foundations of romantic national identity. As John Ward told the Georgia Historical Society in 1858, "A nation without history, is a nation without life." Because a sturdy history seemed such an indispensable component of a sturdy nation, the relative youth of the American nation was a matter of concern to some. The antebellum years saw considerable efforts to correct this, most prominently by Massachusetts historian George Bancroft, who advanced a celebratory nationalist interpretation of America's past, stressing the ideal of liberty as its central theme, in his multivolume *History of the United States*. Still, anxieties persisted. To New York lawyer George Templeton Strong, the nation's tender age aroused a desire for permanence: "We are so young a people," he wrote, "that we feel the want of nationality and delight in whatever asserts our national 'American' existence." Unlike European countries, he went on, America did not have centuries of tradition to bolster its national existence. "Hence the development, in every state of the Union, of 'Historical Societies' that seize on and seal up every worthless reminiscence of our colonial and revolutionary times." Although the first state historical societies originated in New England, the trend quickly spread south, and by the outbreak of the Civil War just about every southern state could boast a historical society of its own. Southerners saw a clear link between their state-level historical interests and their commitment to the United States as a whole. James P. Holcombe, for instance, expressed a commonly accepted belief when he advised members of the Virginia Historical Society that "it is essential to the unity and elevation of our national character" to look back periodically at the early history of the United States.[42]

Charlestonian Bartholomew Rivers Carroll believed history was especially vital to national identity and citizenship when it came to the rising generation. "When some Athenian youth inquired of Socrates, How they should become distinguished patriots and useful citizens" he told Citadel students in 1859, "the philosopher pointed them to the history of their country." The same, Carroll held, was true for young Americans such as the group gathered before him. History would be a critical resource no matter what profession they pursued—medicine, the law, politics, and just about any other occupation. "But the chief claim," he explained,

> that should impress itself upon us, is the agency, which history has in the formation of national character. If we would really stamp our country with a national peculiarity—if we would hold ourselves from the rest of the world—free and independent States, we should thoroughly study the institutions and principles which have made us what we are. This is what every State has done before establishing its nationality.[43]

For Carroll as for many Americans, history was a powerful substantiation of national identity, a crucial adhesive of national community.

Americans' best hope for a meaningful national past was, of course, the foundational event of their short history, the American Revolution.

Remembrance of the revolution lay at the center of antebellum American nationalism in the South as well as the North. This remembrance was so powerful because it fused together the core strands of American nationalism: the belief in America's unique global mission; the idealistic commitment to democratic citizenship; the conviction that Americans constituted a distinctive cultural community ordained by God and united by shared traditions; and the belief that individual citizens had a sacred duty toward their nation. The Revolution constituted America's "golden age": an idealized, even mythologized past of the sort that has been central to many modern nationalisms.[44]

Nationalist remembrance of the Revolution took place year-round, but was especially visible on national holidays such as February 22 (George Washington's birthday) and the Fourth of July. The Fourth was the day of the year when, according to countless reports, the American people forgot their differences and came together—symbolically, at least—in a unified celebration of their great nation. Many commentators at the time emphasized the simultaneity of the display of American nationalism on the Fourth of July: the fact that people in all parts of the country, from all walks of life, assembled in small groups and communities to enact their national identity and citizenship, in the consciousness that they were symbolically sharing the experience with countless unseen compatriots. As the anthropologist Benedict Anderson has observed, this concept of simultaneity has been a critical element of modern, mass nationalisms in general. Simultaneity enabled individual Americans, in Anderson's memorable description, to imagine themselves as part of a national community so large that no one could hope to meet even a fraction of their fellow citizens. Across the country, Americans rejoiced at the apparently amazing country they lived in, pointing to its impressive material resources, the wonderful progress it had made in the first decades of its existence, the glorious future it could look forward to. Most of all, they celebrated the political ideals that America purportedly stood for, and especially the great truth inaugurated by the American Revolution: the principle of self-government. Commemorating this great truth was the animating goal of the Fourth, and of American nationalism more generally.[45]

In this respect the Fourth embodied the political, civic elements of American nationalism. In theory anyone could demonstrate their Americanness by celebrating the nation's defining political values. In reality, of course, Independence Day celebrations were often exclusive events that reinforced existing power relations within communities by marginalizing groups such as women and African Americans, allowing them supporting roles at best. Independence Day celebrations had always been contentious events where groups with competing visions of American nationalism—the Federalists and Republicans in the early republic, abolitionists and slaveholders closer to the Civil War—advanced their own political goals against opposing groups, thereby repudiating the myth of consensual nationalism.[46] Furthermore, remembrance of the revolution frequently veered away from political and civic concerns toward the romantic strands of nationalism that were in the ascendant across the Atlantic, imbuing the nation's founding event with religious and cultural meanings that transcended the apparently political basis of U.S. nationalism.

The primary purpose of the Fourth was to celebrate the sacrifices of the revolutionary generation. Adulation of these sacrifices was a staple in newspaper editorials, speeches, and after-dinner toasts. One toast, given at an 1851 Independence Day celebration near Richmond, was dedicated to the Union: "The tears of patriots—the blood of martyrs, the trophies of war and the blessing of peace—our common glories and common sacrifices—all render it thrice sacred and hallowed." As the toast indicated, antebellum southerners recognized the primal, emotional power that tears, blood, sacrifice, and martyrdom could lend to nationalism. In the wake of the Mexican War, Fourth of July toasts came to include tributes to "the Heroes who have fallen in the Mexican War: A nation's hands have planted laurels on their graves, and a nation's tears will keep them fresh." But the martyrs at the center of American nationalism continued to be the patriots of 1776. A schoolbook published for southern students in the 1850s contained a reading that championed commemoration of the revolutionary martyrs: "Let their memories be eternally embalmed in our bosoms. Let the infants of all posterity prattle their fame, and drop tears of courage for their fate." Ensuring that the nation's founding martyrs lived on in Americans' memory, now and forever, was a fundamental concern of Americans in both the South and North.[47]

In this glorification of death sacrifice and the promise of immortality to national martyrs, American nationalism manipulated perennial human concerns about death and mortality in much the same way that religion did. The terms used to describe the concept—natural, holy, sacred—indicate that Americans conceptualized their responsibilities to their nation not just as a secular parallel to religious commitment and practice but as a system of belief inseparably interrelated with religion—to such a degree that nationalism itself demanded faithful piety. In America as in other modern nations, it would be impossible to understand the depth of nationalism's command of mass loyalties without understanding this religious dimension. Its widespread appeal can partly be explained by its formal imitation of several key elements of religion: ritualized holidays, sacred documents, and legendary heroes, as well as the overarching themes of death and immortality.[48]

In a similar way to Christians' use of the Sabbath and feast days to carry out important rituals and to rededicate themselves to the holy cause, antebellum Americans used national holidays to perform and uphold their nationalism. In 1860, on the occasion of George Washington's birthday, one Kentucky orator remarked that just as individuals celebrate birthdays and Christianity celebrates Christmas and Easter, so too was it important for nations to celebrate their own special anniversaries. This was part of what was described in the title of one speech as "the duty and obligations of American citizens."[49] The Fourth of July was often called "The National Sabbath." A newspaper editor in Tennessee, writing in 1850, asked, "Who does not rejoice that we have a day in which as American Citizens, we can meet each other, and renew our patriotic devotion by the recitation of the pledges of the life, estate and sacred honor, of those who made this day immortal?" He went on to draw the religion-nationalism comparison more explicitly: "To the christian, the Sabbath is a day peculiarly adapted to devotion—so this day serves to chasten and to purify the patriotism of the Nation." Other newspaper editors, as well as other public figures, encouraged Americans to celebrate the Fourth as a patriotic duty, just as the clergy might promote proper celebration of the Sabbath.[50]

By the late antebellum years, Independence Day celebrations had settled into standardized ritual forms: the ringing of bells and the firing of salutes, the mustering and parading of voluntary militia companies, civic processions, meetings of various voluntary associations, public prayer, speeches, and the reading aloud of the Declaration of Independence. The reading of the Declaration, whether in public or private, was to some degree analogous to Christians' reading from the Bible. A Mississippi editor informed his readers in July 1854 that it was "as strictly the duty of every citizen of this Republic, who enjoys civil and religious freedom, to read over this noble Declaration, upon this Sabbath of Liberty . . . as it is the duty of Christians to read a portion of the Old and New Testament upon the Christian Sabbath." Performing these duties was an important means of enacting one's citizenship.[51]

FIGURE I.3 *Design of the Washington National Monument to Be Erected in the City of Washington*, Charles Fenderich, ca. 1846. (Library of Congress.)

Like religions, modern nationalisms have often depended on messianic heroes. As Jesus Christ is the central figure of Christianity, George Washington was the central figure of antebellum American nationalism. While several revolutionary heroes were much celebrated in the antebellum years, it was Washington who loomed the largest in American national remembrance. The generations that followed the founders idolized "the Father of his Country" in textbooks, poems and songs, speeches, newspapers, and the like. Even neutrality toward Washington was rare, let alone enmity. One orator, speaking to a Savannah audience, concluded that it would be in "vain to eulogize the name of WASHINGTON, a name too grand for song, too sublime for eloquence"; no matter how much they praised him, it could never be enough. While much of this praise was secular, it not infrequently took on a religious tone. One clergyman, speaking in the United States Capitol in 1848, offered the ultimate acclaim, referring to this "one great man, who approached as near to the Saviour's precepts as man could approach."[52]

It is not surprising, then, that a group of women under the direction of South Carolina's Ann Pamela Cunningham joined together in an enterprise to purchase Mount Vernon, Washington's home, so that it could become something of a national shrine—the "Mecca of our country," as one visitor put it, a place where Americans from all parts of the country could congregate and rekindle "patriotism and brotherly love." Women's efforts to preserve this site revealed the possibility for female intervention in the supposedly male arena of nationalism, and they were universally praised for it. One southern poet proclaimed, "Still Honour be to Woman! she has shown / The loftiest patriotism earth has known," and pointed to Florence Nightingale and the Ladies' Mount Vernon Association as examples. Likewise, male orators held up the Mount Vernon movement as an example of women's distinctive capacity for selfless patriotism, even in a climate of political division. Supposedly removed from the practice of formal politics, women were immune to its corruptions; as one orator explained, "Woman's patriotism is love of country; man's patriotism is love of self, of party . . . it is left for woman to adore virtue . . . to love her country better even than life itself."[53] As in many other times and places, female roles in national affairs were constrained in theory yet could be fairly extensive in practice.[54]

An Alabama newspaper editor celebrated the Mount Vernon campaign in language infused with religious sentiment, explaining that "the burial place of Washington ought to be a holy sepulchre, where patriot-pilgrims may pay their homage. . . . The cause of 'Mount Vernon' is a sacred one, and it has fallen into holy hands." The editor went on to make the Jesus-Washington comparison more explicit, and to emphasize women's gendered national duties, pointing out that "Mary was earliest at the tomb of the Saviour, and our Marys have been first at the spot where sleeps the body of the Saviour of his country." Washington was, then, a Christ-like idol of American nationalism, a heroic founding figure whose supreme sacrifices deserved supreme veneration by women as well as men.[55]

Ironically, given the widespread assumption that their Revolution rendered them unique in world history, the way Americans celebrated their founding myth of the Revolution rendered them more similar to than different from nationalists across the Atlantic. Like their European contemporaries, mid-nineteenth-century Americans were coming to envision nationalism in cultural and spiritual as well as political ways; they conceived of citizenship not only as a rational, contractual relationship between the individual and the nation but also as a sacred cultural bond, embedding citizens in a sacred community that stretched back into a romanticized past and forward into a glorious future.[56] White southerners and other Americans were wide-ranging nationalists, defining the bounds of their nation and its citizenry using race, mythic pasts, and cultural particularities as well as inclusive political principles.

The Problem of Federalism

For all its strengths, antebellum American nationalism was—like all nationalisms—incomplete and troubled by inherent fractures. The most serious problems were generated by federalism. American federalism, which divides political authority between state and federal governments, has worked well in practice for most of the history of the United States. Yet it has represented a persistent challenge to nationalism, which rests on the principle that, whatever the nature of more localized levels of political authority, the authority of the nation must be supreme. Similar challenges resulted from regionalism in nineteenth-century Europe. As one European historian has explained, "By emphasizing that localism, regionalism, and nationalism coexisted, regional politics undermined what some historians have defined as the very essence of nationalism itself, at least nationalism of the ethnic variety: its claim to exclusivity, which turned it into the only legitimate focus of its citizens' loyalty."[57] For the same reason, in dividing political authority and the object of citizens' allegiance, American federalism subverted the central premise of modern nationalism: that membership in a nation is the ultimate form of belonging, in both cultural and legal terms.

Federalism worked so long as Americans were able to keep in alignment their various allegiances to locality, state, region, and nation. The
knowledge that the Civil War broke out in 1861 has made it difficult to
appreciate the capacity of southerners to harmonize their multiple allegiances. But for most of their history Americans from all regions have
been able to practice allegiance to these various communities without serious conflict.[58] In the antebellum years, most rejoiced in the system that
one South Carolinian described as "the sublime spectacle of a nation of
republics, each moving harmoniously in its own sphere, and constituting
together one glorious constellation." Federalism was credited with
enabling the United States to expand spatially while retaining its commitment to republican ideals and avoiding the perils of a behemoth state in
which centralized power led to consolidated tyranny. As historian Peter
Onuf has shown, a decentralized, federal nationalism had been actively
championed by Thomas Jefferson and other early republicans. Their vision persisted. In an 1857 address to an audience of students at the University of North Carolina, Henry Miller praised federalism for being able
"to keep together and harmonize conflicting interests and pursuits, and
better adapted to the expansion of the territory, and the enlargement of
the population." Others saw different advantages. Alexander Meek
believed that the diffuse governmental authority of federalism helped
stimulate the highest quality of literary production. The pride of belonging to a unit smaller than the whole country inspired Americans to
strive for excellence.[59]

For most white southerners, the flow of allegiances was clear: from the
local to the national. "I know it is very much the fashion now-a-days to
talk in swelling phrase of loving your country first and your State after-
wards," B. J. Barbour declared in 1854, "but I would reverse this process,
for I have ever felt that I should be a better American as I was a truer Virginian." Likewise, William Gilmore Simms believed that service to the
nation had to start locally. Because the United States was so large, contributions to its national literature—an undertaking of which Simms approved wholeheartedly—had to be carried out at a more local level. No
one could possibly comprehend the whole American nation in any work
of literature, but could only hope to portray a constituent part, and thereby
contribute a building block to national literature as a whole. Simms followed through on this belief in his own work, focusing on his native state
of South Carolina, and his native region of the South, with the aspiration
to strengthen thereby the cause of American literature. Describing one of

his own books as "local, sectional," Simms declared that "to be *national* in literature, one must needs be *sectional*."[60]

For William Gilmore Simms and many others, romantic attachment to land and soil stimulated the development not only of literary nationalism but also more localized identities as well. The various branches of identity and allegiance—local, state, regional, national—sprouted from the same seed. The Whig politician and diplomat William C. Rives explained to the Virginia Historical Society in 1847, "All our public affections take their origin in the small, but magic circle, which defines our home, and thence spread, by successive expansions, 'till they embrace and repose upon our country. The more intensely they glow at the centre, the warmer will their radiations be felt upon the circumference."[61]

Even as he drew such a perfectly ordered model of loyalty extending naturally and without diminishment from the local to the national, however, Rives expressed some concern that national allegiance might detract from appropriate fealty to the state—in his case, Virginia. W. W. Avery, a North Carolinian, was similarly uneasy that the federal-state balance in his own state was tilting perilously away from Raleigh and toward Washington, DC. He accordingly thought it important to attempt to inculcate "state pride" in the young men of North Carolina. Avery shared Rives's basic assumption:

> Love for the land of our birth . . . is one of the strongest instincts of our nature, and incites nobler actions, and induces greater sacrifices, than any other impulse of man's bosom. Love of birth-place and home, is developed simultaneously with those warm affections for parents—brothers—friends, that exist around the family hearth, and which, if cultivated, cluster ever after about the human heart.

Also like Rives, Avery thought that such affection extended outward, "until it comprises within its devotion the entire Government of the country we inhabit." But unlike Rives, Avery was gravely concerned that there was a finite quantity of patriotism, which meant that the further outward it spread, the thinner it became. Because "each successive enlargement of the circle of its sympathy weakens its intensity," the size of a country such as the United States presented a problem. Deriving from an immediate locality, how could patriotism reach the extent of the whole country—how could it underpin national citizenship—without becoming diluted to the point of nonexistence?[62]

Here Avery confronted a troubling problem of American nationalism. If attachments to national community derived from local attachments to place, how was the extent of the national community to be determined? Where should the boundaries be drawn? Why should a romantic-style commitment to the particularities of place substantiate a community defined by the borders of the United States rather than, say, the borders of Virginia or of Carteret County?

Because of federalism, the states had a strong claim to be the primary object of Americans' allegiance. Most Americans acquired citizenship status at the state rather than the national level. The majority of domestic political business was transacted at the state level. Intellectual organizations and educational institutions tended to be state-specific. State pride and identity were strong.[63] In some respects, it was Americans' relationships with their states more than with the United States as a whole that resembled European-style nationalism. Even so, the United States simultaneously held a strong claim on the allegiance of its citizens. These two claims normally coexisted in peace. But the nature of American federalism, with its problematical premise of divided sovereignty and allegiance, meant that loyalty to the state (and sometimes other, more local ties) was not always in alignment with national allegiance. Northerner Rufus Choate recognized this clearly. "It is," Choate wrote in the late 1850s, "the great peculiarity of our system . . . that the affections which we give to country we give to a divided object, the states in which we live and the Union by which we are enfolded. We serve two masters. Our hearts earn two loves. We live in two countries and are commanded to be capacious of both."[64]

Antebellum southerners spent a great deal of time contemplating the claims upon them of these two "countries," the state and the nation. Among the most persistent questions federalism raised were those involving the location of sovereignty and the relationship between individual Americans and state and federal governments. Ever since the writing of the Constitution, Americans had been debating whether or not it had created a unitary nation. While the dispute had taken a variety of forms, the basic disagreement was between the position that the Union was a sacred, unbreakable pact, and the belief that it was a political compact, one which the various states, retaining the sovereignty that had enabled them to make the compact in the first place, had every right to revisit, amend, and perhaps even withdraw from. Leading white southerners in the antebellum years were increasingly likely to support the last position. These unresolved problems enabled southern radicals to deny the existence of the United States as a nation by denying the status of the federal government as the rightful object of Americans' patriotism.[65]

The dispute took on momentous stakes during the nullification crisis of 1828–33. South Carolinians objected to two developments on the national stage. First, and most vociferously, they protested against the federal government's protective tariff policies, which discriminated against agricultural, staple-exporting southern states in favor of northern manufacturing interests. Second, they were increasingly anxious about the growth of northern antislavery sentiment and worried that a strong federal government might one day use its power over the states to hasten emancipation. The two concerns combined in a movement that set the authority of the state against that of the federal government. In 1832 a special South Carolina state convention decreed that unless circumstances changed the state would nullify the federal tariff law in February 1833, rejecting the legislative authority of Washington, DC. The showdown was set. Ultimately President Andrew Jackson—a slaveholder but also a strong nationalist when national power was being used for ends he favored—faced down the nullifiers. A compromise, enabling both the federal government and the nullifiers to save face, consisted of a reduced federal tariff along with a Force Bill affirming the supremacy of federal authority.[66]

These measures did not settle the matter with any finality. The crisis had crystallized opposing interpretations of the balance of power in American federalism, and these interpretations would continue to compete against each other. This dispute was reflected in the storied Webster-Hayne debates, in which Massachusetts senator Daniel Webster gave voice to an emerging vision of American nationalism as an organic, permanent, and supreme creed, against the state's-rights arguments of South Carolina's Robert Hayne. Even within South Carolina, the crisis had spawned what amounted to a new political party system that pitted nullifiers against unionists. These groupings persisted. James L. Petigru, a Charleston lawyer who would become well known as the state's most famous unionist during 1860–61, had been a strong nationalist during the nullification crisis as well. Writing to a friend in 1832, Petigru criticized John C. Calhoun, the most prominent nullification leader, saying that he "now stands altogether upon the allegiance—the exclusive and absolute allegiance of the Citizen to the State. There is no such allegiance and his declaration that there is no such thing as the American People, is unworthy of a citizen."[67]

The problem of federalism continued to generate heated debate among Americans—debate about the proper spheres of authority of the federal versus the state governments, debate about the nature of the allegiance that citizens owed to the individual states as opposed to the United States as a whole. In 1850–51 South Carolinians again set the authority of the state against that of the federal government, galvanized by the issue of slavery's expansion into the lands acquired as a result of the war with Mexico. This time South Carolina radicals went so far as to threaten secession—their state's complete withdrawal from the Union—and this time they were joined by like-minded separatists in other southern states. Again, southern radicals' efforts came to naught, thwarted by a combination of successful compromise on the national political stage and opposition from moderates within their own states. Their effort left in its wake not a final solution to the problem of federalism but rather a hardening of positions between nationalists and states' rights enthusiasts.

Southerners continued to struggle in personal as well as public life with the rival claims of nation and state. A particularly intriguing analysis of this problem came from Alfred Huger, the aging Charleston postmaster. Writing to a politician friend in the summer of 1860, Huger lamented the combustible state of public affairs. "My personal feelings are, as you know, National & Federal," he wrote; he felt loyalty both to the Union and to the state of South Carolina. Yet he differentiated between the nature of the two loyalties in a very revealing fashion. "My allegiance to So Ca, is natural, spiritual, & holy!" he wrote; "it lives in my affections, & it will die only, when my Heart ceases its pulsations! My affinity with this American confederacy is political, but made sacred by Every recollection that can be consider'd 'honourable'!" In other words, Huger's relationship to his state was a visceral, emotional one, charged with religious feeling, whereas his relationship to the American nation was based more on reason and political principle, enhanced by long association. (As a postmaster, it is worth noting, he was also an employee of the federal government.) In his case, dual allegiances to state and nation corresponded to the two different models of nationalism: the romantic and the particular versus the rational and the universal. Though not everyone responded to the problem of dual allegiance in the same way, Huger's insightful distinction between different kinds of allegiance clarifies the problem of American federalism.[68]

As southerners recognized, they were not the only people struggling with the problem of confederation, of the centralization versus the diffusion of power. One article in the *Southern Quarterly Review*, for example, reviewed German efforts to form a new confederation in 1848 but despaired of any ultimate success. In addition to noting the difficulties of setting stable boundaries for the proposed confederation, the author worried that the larger states, Prussia and Austria, would be disinclined to cede the authority that would be necessary to create any effective central power. Even so, this author did value federalism as a means of organizing political power, judging that it would be an effective framework in France, where the current political system centralized power excessively—and dangerously—in Paris. On this point other southerners agreed. James Johnston Pettigrew, for one, criticized French centralization, contrasting it with the American system in which the requirement "that every member of Congress should be an actual inhabitant of the State which he represents" fostered a healthy attachment to locality, an attachment that operated as a valuable counterweight to central power. Europe offered positive as well as negative examples. Pettigrew, in addition to admiring Spaniards' localized patriotism, was also taken with Spain's "States rights principle," which he believed was "profoundly ingrained in the Spanish heart—far more than in the United States. Though the foundation of their character be the same, the differences are striking, and are marked by the boundary lines of the provinces, which seem to be moral as well as geographical frontiers."[69]

Modern scholars have also noted the existence of multiple levels of Spanish loyalty and identity that were normally compatible, at least until the emergence of serious Catalan and Basque separatism in the late nineteenth century. Likewise, in places as diverse as Germany, Switzerland, and the Ottoman Empire, different levels of identity and often different levels of formal citizenship produced a complicated yet normally functional array of political responsibilities, identities, and loyalties. It was more often the case that these were contained within an overarching allegiance to a nation or empire than that they challenged the larger structure—witness Germany, where subnational political allegiances and cultural identities generally coexisted harmoniously with German nationalism both before and after unification in 1871.[70]

Historian Thomas Bender has used the apt phrase "federative crisis" to describe struggles over the distribution of political authority in countries across the mid-nineteenth-century world. In Latin America, for instance, the aftermath of the age of revolutions saw new challenges to national borders, generating instabilities that included secession movements in areas such as Mexico's Yucatán Peninsula. In many places, such as China, the Ottoman Empire, Germany, and Italy, the "federative crisis" eventually resulted in the centralization of political power in modern state forms, either newly created or significantly restructured. In other places, though, the solution was less straightforward. In 1867 the ongoing Hungarian nationalist movement secured not independence but increased autonomy in the Dual Monarchy agreement. That same year, the British Empire ceded limited sovereignty to Canada with dominion status. Within the United Kingdom itself, while many Irish partisans called for the limited sovereignty of "home rule," Scots settled for what one historian has called "Unionist nationalism," which reconciled pride in Scotland's unique culture with political fealty to London. Clearly there was no general solution to Bender's "federative crisis." Perhaps Americans could take some solace in the knowledge that their own messy and overlapping allegiances to different entities, their own assortment of forms of loyalty and identity, was redolent of similarly disordered arrangements around the world.[71]

ALTHOUGH THE PROBLEMS of nationalism were endemic, Americans were right—if not always for the reasons they would have cited—that their specific circumstances were distinctive. The exceptionalism of American nationalism derived in large part from the tension between lofty national ideals and actual practices. The American Revolution had supposedly ushered in the age of democratic citizenship, an age in which old hierarchies were broken down and replaced with the new horizontal, equal category of citizen. But it had not actually done so, leaving to post-Revolutionary Americans the challenge of sorting out those people, most notably African Americans, who did not fit into the category of citizen but whose presence could not be ignored. The American Revolution had supposedly instituted popular sovereignty, rendering the people—the nation—the supreme authority. Yet it had left undetermined the question of whether that sovereignty lay in the states or the federal government. Nationalist rhetoric everywhere rests upon the premise that sovereignty, the right of self-government, resides in a distinct community of people. By dividing sovereignty, American federalism neglected to define where the boundaries of sovereignty, and therefore the boundaries of national community, actually lay. Did South Carolinians enjoy a sovereignty—a nationality—that was independent of Pennsylvanians? How should Americans balance allegiance to state with allegiance to nation, and which ought to take priority? By the 1850s, the powerful bonds of an apparently distinctive American national identity, influenced by romantic nationalism in Europe, strengthened the sense of a united national community. Just as often, though, the bonds of blood, kinship, history, and attachment to place reinforced allegiance to the region, the state, or the local community.

This is not to say that American nationalism in the mid-nineteenth century was a fragile house of cards, ready to collapse at the first puff of disunionism. Rather, it had grown into a potentially strong framework. It was held up by the pillars of Christianity and the principles of democratic citizenship, which combined to connect individuals' everyday behavior with national responsibility. And it was fortified by historical associations, commitment to a global American mission, and the assumption of a distinctive national culture. White southerners in the antebellum years believed strongly in all of this, participating enthusiastically in the creation and the maintenance of American national identity.

However, the intellectual and cultural grounds of American nationhood were shifting. They were secured neither to the federal government nor to the national community of the United States. This did not make secession and the Confederacy inevitable, but it did make them possible. The problems of federalism, exacerbated by anxiety about the fate of the American experiment, opened up an intellectual space within which alternative conceptions of American nationality could develop.

2

Dreams

SOUTHERN NATIONALISM BEFORE
SOUTHERN NATIONHOOD

ALTHOUGH NATIONALISM WAS a shifting, unstable concept in the antebellum South, for the small number of committed secessionists, most of them proud residents of the exceptionally proslavery, exceptionally radical state of South Carolina, things could not have been much clearer. To these radicals, slavery and the civilization that had developed around it provided the South with a distinctive national identity. Such a distinctive national identity warranted—even demanded—political independence.

These ideas received forceful expression in Whippy Swamp, South Carolina, on the fourth day of July, 1855. Lewis M. Ayer, a planter and local politician charged with commemorating American independence, chose to do so by promoting the creation of "our Southern Confederacy." Ayer made the most of the date and the occasion it represented. Aligning the southern independence movement of the 1850s with the American independence movement of the 1770s, he argued that the North and the South were as different from one another as the colonies and England had been. In both cases, oppression at the hands of a central power mandated separation. Furthermore, in protesting the inferior status of white southerners within the American nation, Ayer drew international comparisons, including parallels with imperial subjects in India and Ireland. Southerners were being denied the fruits of modern citizenship that they had claimed in 1776 and were being pushed back toward the lowly rank of traditional subjecthood. Ayer insisted that they should strive to maintain their status. After all, "Who would not rather be a citizen of one of the free Cantons of happy little Switzerland than a subject of immense Russia?"

But why had the South become a lesser partner in the American nation? Why did membership in the United States entail oppression at the hands of the North? Ayer made no secret of the fact that it was slavery that made the South different from the North, nor of the fact that it was the North's increasing distaste for slavery that motivated his calls for national independence. Slavery, he claimed, had enabled the South to develop a superior civilization. If it were abolished, as proponents of northern "fanaticism" desired, Ayer predicted devastating upheavals in southern society, like those that had already happened in Jamaica. The way Ayer described the northern offensive reveals the intense emotions that fuelled active southern nationalism: "We stand like men, who, in the waste of a wide prairie, should see the wildfire circling them all around, leaping, rushing, careering along upon the deep dry-grass, and ever and anon caught up on the arms of a sweeping whirlwind, and lifted until its red flames lick the very clouds." If white southerners did not "set fire against fire," he cautioned, they would be "overwhelmed."[1]

This image of the white South being encircled by a "leaping, rushing" wildfire vividly captures the personal, visceral fears that drove the radicals toward the cause of southern nationalism. They were not alone in believing that slavery was the basis of southern society, that slavery made the South superior to the North, and that slavery was endangered by northern and even international assaults. These were common positions in the South. But the radicals were alone, before 1860, in the conviction that the proper response was immediate withdrawal from the Union and the establishment of an independent southern nation-state. The reason why they, and not others, made the progression from valuing slavery to believing that its preservation required national independence lay in their emotional response to northern opposition to slavery, which they perceived as a personal attack. Hence the potency of Lewis Ayer's wildfire metaphor.[2]

The radicals did not only formulate their program in emotional terms, however. They expended considerable intellectual energy on refining their ideas about nationalism, both in general terms and in the specific American and southern cases. As Lewis Ayer's references to the American Revolution indicate, the radicals grounded their argument for southern nationalism in their interpretations of American nationalism. They sought to claim not only the legacy of the revolutionary generation but also the conceptual apparatus of American nationalism, exploiting its tensions and its strengths. As Ayer's references to Ireland, India,

Switzerland, and Russia show, the radicals thought in comparative terms. Just as mainstream American nationalism was influenced by international, especially transatlantic ideas, so too was southern nationalism.[3] Although southern separatists have the reputation of having been rather parochial, in fact they tried to set their movement within broader intellectual and cultural frameworks.

The radicals espoused what I have termed active nationalism. They claimed that white southerners shared sufficient markers of national identity—deriving from but extending beyond their shared interest in slavery—to deserve political status as an independent nation-state. They advanced extensive, self-conscious arguments to support these claims, and believed that southern nationalism should achieve fulfillment by whatever means were necessary. They saw themselves as oppositional nationalist leaders in the same sense that Lajos Kossuth and Giuseppe Mazzini were. They saw themselves as agents of the inexorable nineteenth-century force of nationalism.

Slavery and Southern National Identity

It is generally accepted that the secession movement was driven by the desire to protect slavery. Proponents of southern independence were often explicit in pointing to slavery as the core of their national identity—the overarching characteristic that rendered the South truly distinct. "Our whole fabric of society," declared Frederick Porcher, a professor of history and belles-lettres at the College of Charleston, "is based upon slave institutions." For James Chesnut, the South Carolina politician and husband of the famous diarist Mary Boykin Chesnut, the particular form of the peculiar institution made the South unique not just in its own time but throughout world history: "It may be regarded as *our* characteristic." William Trescot, a South Carolina planter and diplomatic historian, agreed, explaining in 1850 that slavery had "developed the physical wealth of the country," had created "a civilization combining in admirable measure energy and refinement," and "informs all our habits of thought, lies at the basis of our political faith and of our social existence." Quite simply, southerners, Trescot wrote, "believe ourselves, under God, indebted to the institution of slavery—for a national existence."[4]

Slavery did not automatically necessitate a separate nationality for the South, however. There were many white southerners who valued slavery but who did not see secession as the best means of protecting it. After all, slavery had prospered in the Union for decades, and opponents of secession made a strong case that slavery was safer within the Union than out of it. Even though the progression was not an automatic one, proslavery did lead to southern nationalism when its ramifications were interpreted in certain ways. Secessionists cited three major consequences of slavery that necessitated southern independence. First, they argued that slavery generated different economic and foreign policy needs for the South. Second, around the same fundamental difference of the presence or absence of slavery, but ultimately transcending it, there developed the belief that the South possessed a distinct civilization, a distinct national identity, which it did not share with the North. Third—and most important in driving some supporters of slavery toward southern nationalism—was secessionists' tendency to take personally the North's hostility toward slavery. Believing "their" institution to be under attack, the radicals rallied to defend slavery, creating a potent sense of shared victimhood that provided a visceral stimulus for southern nationalism.

Slavery, according to proslavery thinkers, underpinned a unique society that was more conservative, more fair, and more stable than its free labor counterpart to the North—and, for that matter, than all other countries following a similar free labor trajectory. Though not an active secessionist in the 1850s, South Carolinian William J. Grayson strengthened such arguments for southern independence with his well-known poem "The Hireling and the Slave," in which he compared the civilization built on southern slavery with that built on free labor. Stressing the security and order that slavery provided for all members of slave society, including the slaves themselves, Grayson portrayed free society as an unstable system marked by inequality and misery. "Guarded from want, from beggary secure," he wrote of the slave, "He never feels what hireling crowds endure."[5]

Nor, Grayson might have added, could the slave vote—and therein lay another crucial aspect of the distinction that southern slaveholders' drew between their own society and those of the northern United States and Western Europe. Slavery, they believed, was an indispensable foundation of true republicanism. Only by preventing the lowest sectors of the population from voting could republican virtue be maintained. The best-known expression of this position came in an 1858 U.S. Senate speech by South Carolinian James Henry Hammond. Participating in the ongoing debate over whether slavery should be permitted in Kansas, Hammond asserted that southerners would be better off in the event of a separation. The great strength of the South's society and economy lay in the institution of slavery. "In all social systems," he declared, "there must be a class to do the menial duties, to perform the drudgery of life. . . . [This class] constitutes the very mud-sill of society and of political government; and you might as well attempt to build a house in the air, as to build either the one or the other, except on this mud-sill." So all societies—including the North—had to have a "mud-sill" class. Whereas at the North the "mud-sill" was of the same race as the ruling class, the South had "found a race adapted to that purpose." Whereas in the North members of the mud-sill were "equals in natural endowment of intellect, and they feel galled by their degradation," in the South slaves were called slaves and, because of the marker of race, there was no question that they could be considered even remotely equal to their masters. Importantly, Hammond pointed out, in contrast to the northern mud-sill, "our slaves do not vote," and therefore they presented no threat to political stability. But because members of the northern mud-sill were able to vote, and because the color of their skin rendered them desirous of full equality, they did present a threat—a serious one—to the stability of northern society and politics. As a result, Hammond saw dangers in the excessive democracy of the North that were absent in the South, thanks to the stability of slavery.[6]

Particularly stark iterations of this argument came from Hammond's fellow South Carolinian Leonidas Spratt, a lawyer and newspaper editor. Of all antebellum southern ideologues, Spratt was one of the most candid in his denunciation of democracy and equality. In a report arguing that the African slave trade ought to be reopened, Spratt claimed that "two distinct and antagonistic forms of society have met for the contest upon the arena of this Union." Whereas the northern form "assumes that all men are equal and that equality is right, and . . . is straining its members to the horizontal plain of a democracy," the southern form "assumes that all men are not equal, that equality is not right." Inequality, to Spratt's mind, was especially evident in the difference between the white and black races. Whereas the North disregarded this important fact, the South fully appreciated it, and had devised an excellent system—slavery—for enabling two races of such unequal capacities to live together in what Spratt saw as harmony. Although northern-style democracy and equality appeared to be the trends of their times, Spratt hoped that slavery and inequality would ultimately be vindicated as the best means of organizing a society. The lessons of history made him optimistic: pointing to ancient Greece and Rome, Spratt observed, "Whenever States have come to greatness they have exhibited the condition of unequal classes." He believed that southern inequality resulted in a better society than did the North's excessive equality and democracy.[7]

To its defenders, the labor-capital relations of slavery were far superior to those of free labor. Southern nationalists argued that this necessitated southern independence. The relationship of capital and labor, William Trescot explained, was the "basis of social and political life." Because the North and the South had such different labor-capital relations, they had "two individual and inconsistant [*sic*] systems both of representation and taxation." As southern nationalists never tired of complaining, the federal government's economic policies, specifically the protective tariff, privileged the commercially oriented North over the South and its agriculture-based economy. The two sections required different economic policies, which undermined political union between them. Thus the University of Virginia's Southern Rights Association proclaimed: "The one [section] is manufacturing and navigating, the other planting and agricultural. The interests of the one incline to monopoly and exclusion, those of the other to free trade and competition." Back in 1828–33, this same complaint, combined with anxieties about a possible federal assault on southern slavery, had produced the nullification movement in South Carolina. It would continue to fester in the subsequent decades, becoming a major strand of secessionism in 1850–51 and again in 1860–61.[8]

As Trescot explained, different economic profiles also dictated different foreign policy interests for the South and the North. Speaking with some authority, as a noted diplomatic historian who would later become assistant U.S. secretary of state, Trescot explained that the world was split into "those who produce cotton and those who manufacture it," and because the two regions lay on opposite sides of that line, each required a different set of relations with the rest of the world. The North was obviously the competitor of manufacturing countries such as Britain and hence adopted a stance of commercial rivalry toward them; but the interests of the South, as a supplier of such nations, entailed friendly relations. The economic and foreign policy needs of the slave-labor South and the free-labor North called for a political separation.[9]

Southern thinkers moved from arguments about the social, political, and economic connotations of slavery toward the assertion of a distinctive southern national identity that embraced the slaveholding South as a whole. For James Chesnut, different systems of labor produced different societies, cultures, and ultimately national identities. Southern slave-based agriculture promoted a stable and conservative civilization, while free labor, commerce, and manufacturing in the North generated a frenzied spirit of competition, selfishness, and recklessness. "These qualities," he went on, were "apt to become national, and shew themselves in politics and morals as in industry." Longtime southern nationalist Nathaniel Beverley Tucker, a professor at the College of William and Mary, agreed. In 1848 he wrote to a friend about how happy he was to live in the slave South. People in free labor societies tended to be mean-spirited and deceitful, he thought. The best explanation he could come up with rested on differences in the regions' economic systems: whereas southerners only had to worry about selling their crops once a year, northerners had to sell their products in dribs and drabs, all year round, which produced a constant and unhealthy acquisitiveness.[10] The key distinguishing characteristic of slavery rippled outward, then, shaping not only unique economic and political formations and interests but also unique patterns of behavior and value systems—in the parlance of the day, unique "national characters."

Victimhood: Personal and National

Above all else, the personalization of sectional difference explains why for the radicals a desire to protect slavery led to active southern nationalism. It begins to explain the sense of urgency in their arguments, and why this mattered so much. Although the straightforward material interest in slavery should not be underestimated, the fact remains that while there were many white southerners who valued slavery and wished to protect it, until 1860 there were relatively few who proceeded from there to advocate national independence. What made the situation seem so urgent to the radicals was a belief that attacks upon southern slavery were personal attacks upon them. Antislavery activism in the North and in Europe fuelled a sense of shared victimhood at the hands of a hostile and alien enemy. Merging political and personal fears, this drove the radicals to embrace southern nationalism as a means to simultaneously protect their region's peculiar institution and themselves as individuals.

Differences between the North and the South became ever more urgent as they moved into the realm of personal morality. William Gilmore Simms certainly believed that differing conceptions of personal moral behavior were important, going to the trouble of clipping a newspaper article entitled "Morals in Free States" and sticking it in his scrapbook.

"Really, we shall have to secede," the article began, "some time or other, from what are ironically termed the Free States, on account of their bad morals. . . . Not a mail reaches us but developes some new specimen of scoundrelism in those regions." The most noteworthy scoundrelisms were those involving women. Although southerners were known to get up to mischief every once in a while, they never heard of women being "dirked or bilked, butchered or beaten," as happened regularly in the North. Other southern partisans similarly recoiled at the apparent immorality of northerners, especially when the northerners in question were abolitionists. A correspondent of William Porcher Miles, for instance, worried that "continual intercourse with those Abolitionists will hurt any decent man," and, because they were so obnoxious, "the Halls of Congress are like a *dirty privy* [:] a man will carry off some of the *stink* even in his clothes." Themes of gender, morality, and the perception of disease all made sectional differentiation a more personal and therefore more urgent issue. Just like their contemporaries in countries such as England and Germany, southerners defined their own national community as "respectable," in contrast to their enemies' immorality and abnormality.[11]

The problem was, in part, one of political and economic power. As white southerners contemplated secession in 1850, Virginia law professor Nathaniel Beverley Tucker reminded them that the Union "is the old story of the Giant and the Dwarf: a partnership in which one gets all the profit, the other nothing but dry blows." Who would want to play the dwarf? South Carolina radical Robert Barnwell Rhett criticized the Union on similar grounds, complaining that "the bonds of the Union constitute the cords by which they propose to bind the victim to the altar." John C. Calhoun claimed that his proposed two-president system would "make the Union a union in truth,—a bond of mutual affection and brotherhood," rather than "a mere connection used by the stronger as the instrument of dominion and aggrandizement." This critique of the union had also been central to the nullification crusade. Thus the fiery nullifier Thomas Cooper had fumed in 1827, "We shall ere long be compelled to calculate the value of our union; and to enquire of what use to us is this most unequal alliance? . . . Is it worth our while to continue this union of states, where the north demand to be our masters and we are required to be their tributaries?" To nullifiers and later to secessionists, the Union of affection, sympathy, and brotherhood that had been envisioned by Madison and Jefferson's generation of Republicans had disappeared—if it had ever really existed at all.[12]

By the 1850s southern politicians were increasingly alarmed by their minority status within the Union. First, they watched the North drastically increase its population advantage over the South, which meant a steadily rising sectional disparity in the U.S. House. Later, by midcentury, the South saw the end of sectional equilibrium in the Senate, a serious threat. As the secessionist politician William Porcher Miles wrote to a colleague in early 1860, when one recognized that antislavery sentiment was in the ascendant at the North, one had to conclude that the South could never again be secure within the Union. Along with the threat to slavery, the increasing northern dominance of the federal government threatened to allow increased economic exploitation. Assertions of such exploitation were favorite devices of southern nationalists.[13]

In addition to political and economic power, the white South's "dwarf" complex involved territory. America's westward expansion and the recurring issue of whether new territories should be slave or free was central to the sectional conflict. As more and more of the new territory was declared off-limits to slavery, southern slaveholders felt increasingly beleaguered. In part, the territorial question simply reinforced their concerns about political power: the more new free states that were admitted, the greater the sectional imbalance in the Senate and the House would become. But it also produced a sense of being hemmed in, a feeling that was a crucial stimulant of southern nationalism. Nathaniel Beverley Tucker, for instance, attributed his own conversion to southern nationalism to bitter resentment of the South's territorial cessions in the Missouri Compromise. Other fire eaters, too, shared Tucker's and Lewis Ayer's deep fear of constriction.[14]

Southern resentment intensified after the Mexican War (1846–48) and the midcentury debate over what to do with the territories thereby acquired. Would these territories be slave or would they be free? Speaking in Charleston in 1849, William Porcher Miles lamented that "the blood shed in union against a common enemy by citizens of all parts of this confederacy, indifferently, has scarcely dried into the soil," but already "we of the South, who poured out our blood upon those battle-fields, at least as freely as the rest, are told that we must not set our feet upon that territory." In spite of their contributions to the national war effort, slaveholding southerners were being denied its benefits. William Gilmore Simms thought he detected a pattern. "One might say," he wrote to James Henry Hammond, "we have shown ourselves solicitous of nationality." Over the years, southerners had contributed much to the nation's wars, had sacrificed lives, property, and money, "and yet are denied the national securities, the national respect & sympathies, the protection of the national Aegis; every thing that should make a nation precious to our love, or valuable to our interest." The repeated frustrations of their territorial rights convinced southern nationalists that membership in the United States was no longer worthwhile.[15]

These perceptions that antislavery entailed territorial, political, or economic injustice to the South were powerful enough by themselves. But when combined and intensified by a psychological resentment against the northern-dominated federal government, they became even more potent. Southern nationalists tended to interpret the actions of the North and the federal government that they claimed it was coming to control as moral insults against themselves and their region. While complaining about southern slaveholders' exclusion from the territories, William Porcher Miles was clearly resentful of the moral slur that that exclusion represented: "We must be fumigated and purified from every Southern taint," he protested, "must pass through a sort of moral quarantine, before we can be allowed to enter the precincts of the free-soil paradise."[16]

The language of southern nationalists was full of prickly resentment of apparent insults from the North. One attendee at the Second Nashville Convention in 1850, for instance, complained that, on top of exclusion from the territories and infringement of property rights, northerners had added insults: "We have been harrassed [sic] and insulted, by those who ought to have been our brethren, in their constant agitation of a subject vital to us and the peace of our families. We have been outraged by their gross misrepresentations of our moral and social habits, and by the manner in which they have denounced us before the world." The implication was clear: white southerners could not remain in a national community with people who no longer acted like compatriots—"brethren"—but who instead threatened the personal realm, "the peace of our families." Likewise, Louis Wigfall complained that northerners were trying to restrict the slave South behind a wall of free states, and went on to emphasize how personally he and fellow southerners perceived northern insults: "You denounce us, degrade us, deride us . . . you tell us that we are degraded, that we are not your equals." The sense of outrage is palpable in all these statements, and it takes little imagination to see how such outrage could fuel a powerfully resentful southern nationalism.[17]

The feeling of an urgent personal stake in the well-being of the region propelled the radicals toward nationalism. Personal trauma, including the loss of family members and a sense of social isolation, likely contributed to feelings of anger and isolation that made the earliest southern nationalists particularly sensitive to apparent attacks upon the South. Nathaniel Beverley Tucker, for example, lost his mother at an early age and, according to one historian, projected anger derived from this and other losses onto the North. Writing to a friend in the 1840s, Tucker compared his alienation from his "country," to orphanhood: "Patriotism! I do believe, *if I had a country*, I could be a patriot—But I have none. I have tried to keep the pulse of Virginia beating—but it has stopt, & I am an orphan." William Gilmore Simms also lost his mother as an infant and faced what must have been a traumatic experience as a child when his father later sued for custody and the judge allowed the young Simms to decide between staying in Charleston with his grandmother or following his father to the Southwest. The child chose his grandmother and Charleston, but the decision seems to have haunted him, feeding into his literary alienation.[18]

In 1860, comforting a friend who had lost a child, Simms wrote, "I grew up without young associates. I grew *hard* in consequence, hard, perhaps, of manner; but with a heart craving love beyond all other possessions." It seems likely that Simms's craving played at least some part in his attraction to the idea of southern national independence. This is suggested, for instance, in one of Simms's poems which began,

> Oh, the sweet South! the sunny, sunny South!
> Land of true feeling, land forever mine!
> I drink the kisses of her rosy mouth,
> And my heart swells as with a draught of wine.

The next line of the poem read "She brings me blessings of maternal love." For Simms, the South seems to have fulfilled his craving for love in a number of ways.[19]

Nationalism held a similar appeal for other radicals, too. For all his successes, Edmund Ruffin remained something of an outsider. But secession provided him with what Michael O'Brien has called a "purposeful self." A particularly strong argument for the connection of personal to regional identity can be made in the case of William Lowndes Yancey. When Yancey's father died soon after his birth, his mother remarried, to a northern antislavery man, and Yancey's hatred for northern abolitionists seems to have been grounded in part in his resentment of his stepfather. In Yancey's case, southern nationalism also stemmed from the desire to defend southern honor, which in turn reflected a prickly and violent determination to defend his personal honor. Yancey was involved in several duels or near duels, and it is easy to see a correlation between his sense of personal and southern honor. Having murdered a man in an 1838 fight, Yancey was not only unrepentant but was proud of having acquitted his honor. "I have done my duty as a man," he wrote to his brother, "& he who grossly insulted me, lies now, with the clod upon his bosom." The dead man's blood, thought Yancey, should serve as a "warning to others who feel like browbeating a Yancey."[20]

Fulfilling one's "duty" as a man seems to have mattered to many other southern radicals as well. Their ideas and actions reveal that the imperatives of honor and masculinity moved back and forth between the realms of personal and southern identity. South Carolina unionist Benjamin F. Perry astutely described the leaders of southern separatism as "a set of young enthusiasts inspired with notions of personal honor to be defended and individual glory, fame and military laurels to be acquired." To some, the cause of southern nationalism offered a means by which to prove themselves. Thus there is a striking similarity in the rhetoric used to justify the "affairs of honor" that men like Yancey, Lawrence M. Keitt, and Louis Wigfall seemed drawn toward, and the rhetoric used to portray the South's need to defend itself against the aggressions of the North.[21]

Southern and personal honor were nowhere more dramatically joined, though, than in the notorious caning of Charles Sumner by South Carolina congressman Preston Brooks in 1856. When the senator from Massachusetts insulted not only Brooks's relative but also his state—and, by extension, the South—he blurred what little boundary might have existed between the personal honor that required Brooks to defend his kin and the group honor that required him to defend his state, his region, and slavery. His efforts were widely appreciated. Tributes echoed around the South. "Southern men, Southern States, and Southern Institutions, have been abused long enough," one newspaper editor wrote. "It has to be stopped by blows and blood." Brooks had, in the eyes of many southern partisans, acted as the defender of the whole South when he raised his cane in the Senate chamber. "In whipping Sumner you have *immortalized* yourself," wrote South Carolina governor J. H. Adams, and he expressed the hope that Brooks would "continue to *serve & honor* [his] country." Adams's prediction of immortality was prophetic, for when Brooks died the year after the caning incident, he was indeed celebrated as a martyr for the southern cause. "The South has lost the foremost sentinel in behalf of her institutions," mourned the Edgefield *Advertiser*. Likewise, a Georgia newspaper grieved, "Mr. Brooks passed from the field of duty with his armor on,—ready to the last to vindicate his native South against foes from without or traitors from within." As "citizens of a sister Southern State," they joined South Carolina in mourning its loss. In death as in life, Preston Brooks united self and would-be nation in a potent bond of violence, masculine honor, and blood.[22]

Although the connections that men such as Brooks and Yancey drew between themselves and the proposed southern nation were often emphatically masculinist, white women could develop similarly powerful personal bonds to southern nationalism. As the crisis of midcentury was gathering steam, for instance, the South Carolinian Louisa Cunningham bristled just as much as male radicals did at the aggressions of the North. If southerners only knew the extent of northern perfidy, she felt sure that secession would be immediate: "*At all and every hazard* we never can get along with them & our interests are too opposite to [theirs] and they have such a spirit of aggression for their own aggrandizement that I believe *it must, it will* end in disunion! *I am ripe for it!*" Cunningham clearly felt very personally the shame that the South would deserve if it submitted to northern aggressions. "*I shall hate my country*," she proclaimed, clearly meaning the South, "*if they yield.*"[23]

This was precisely what Elizabeth Rhett, wife of the fire-eating Robert Barnwell Rhett, ended up doing the following year. When the secession movement of 1851 failed, she was utterly crushed. "I declare to you," she wrote to her husband, "the shock has been so great to me, that I feel giddy, as if I had received a blow, I cannot think at all, & am bewildered. Has God indeed, forsaken our land"? She could not believe that after all her husband's efforts to redeem his people, they had disregarded him. Part of her frustration likely derived from sympathy for her husband's reverses, but her own personal investment in the cause is unmistakable. "My heart actually sickens," she complained, "at the prospect before us—what abject humiliation, what deep degradation is ours."[24]

Degradation and shame, inequality and submission—these were the watchwords of antebellum southern nationalism. In part, they were employed by the radicals as rhetorical devices with which to arouse their fellow white southerners to action. But they also provide a revealing window into the motivations of the radicals—into the reasons why they felt such a sense of urgency about the protection of slavery that they believed the only solution was national independence. The radicals were typical of most white southerners in their approval of slavery as a labor system and as a means of organizing race relations. What set them apart from the mainstream was the way that they interpreted northern and European hostility to slavery in intensely personal ways, believing these external assaults to be injurious not just to southern politics and economics but to their personal identities as well.

Southern Nationalism in the Atlantic World

Although the radicals' motivations were thus largely defensive, they did attempt to substantiate their argument for southern nationalism in more positive ways. These efforts were informed by what radicals already knew about nationalism and citizenship; in fashioning the argument for southern independence they drew on then-prevailing ideas about what made a nation a nation and why nations deserved political independence. As southern nationalists made their case, they reflected on the international context—especially the transatlantic context, since nationalism was becoming so dominant in mid-nineteenth-century Europe—and seized on those comparisons that appeared to offer support. In addition to bolstering their movement in general terms, presenting themselves as participants in the ascendant trend of nationalism might allow secessionists to counteract the stigma that slavery brought upon the American South.

From our perspective, the prominent success stories in nineteenth-century Europe were the unification movements in Germany and Italy. Given that southerners were trying to break up an existing union rather than forge a new one, the potential for comparisons with European nationalism seems limited. However, the separatist impulse was also robust in Europe. This was evident even in Germany and Italy, the prime examples of unification nationalism, both of which were faced in part with the problem of liberating territories from their current occupiers, most notably the Habsburg empire. But even more pertinent were the vibrant separatist nationalisms in Hungary, Poland, Bohemia, Norway, Serbia, Ireland, and (until it achieved independence in 1829) Greece. Most of these movements did not achieve fruition until the twentieth century, but in most cases they were already strong in the nineteenth.[25] Separatist movements, and European nationalism more generally, offered the promise of validation for southern secession.[26]

Secessionists sometimes identified themselves overtly with oppositional nationalist leaders in Europe. Thus William Lowndes Yancey, responding to charges that he was a "rebel," defiantly identified himself with other nationalist heroes battling colonial-style oppression: "Washington was a rebel! Lafayette was a rebel—and so was Tell and so is Kossuth—rebels against abuse of power; and welcome to us be the appellation received in defense of our rights and liberties."[27] In a speech of the late 1850s, Robert Barnwell Rhett looked toward Europe and saw "a bloody contest for the independence of nationalities." God had meant for there to be national differences, and a nation's right to independence was particularly strong when it was battling against a foreign occupier, as was the case in places such as Ireland, Poland, and Italy. "Let Italy be for Italy," he urged. Aligning his own nationalist cause with the others, Rhett argued that "the people of England and Ireland, Russia and Poland, Austria and Italy, are not more distinct and antagonistic in their characters, pursuits, and institutions, their sympathies and views, than the people of our Northern and Southern States." Such comparisons fit with the general American approval of certain foreign independence movements but gave it a special secessionist twist.[28]

Rhett was not the only southern radical to support the Irish struggle against an oppressive alien power. Indeed, the colonial condition was a powerful metaphor for southern victimhood at the hands of the North. "As the Catholics of Ireland were forced to feed a foreign faith," wrote one secessionist, "so we pay to pamper an avowed hostility." In the illustrious 1830 Webster-Hayne debates sparked by the nullification crisis, Robert Hayne compared the South's place within the United States to Ireland's exploitation within the United Kingdom: "The fruits of our labor are drawn from us to enrich other and more favored sections of the Union. . . . The rank grass grows in our streets; our very fields are scathed by the hand of injustice and oppression." Two decades later, in 1851, the editor of an Alabama newspaper likewise compared southerners to downtrodden European nationalists. The urgent issue for southerners was, as he put it, "whether they are to be free or slaves—whether they are to be subjugated as Ireland and Hungary—whether they are to be partitioned as Poland, or erect themselves into an independent State."[29]

So secessionists' comparisons with Europe frequently invoked the rhetoric of victimhood. Across the Atlantic, too, narratives of suffering stimulated separatist nationalisms. The Irish nationalist John Mitchel, who was energized by resentment at Britain's maltreatment of his country, is a case in point. Reflecting on his nationalist activism in a letter to an associate during the 1850s, he confessed, "I have found that there was perhaps less of love in it than of hate—less of affection to my country than of scornful impatience [that my country] suffered itself to be oppressed and humiliated by another."[30] Some of his contemporaries in Continental Europe shared similar motivations. Thus the nationalist Polish historian Joachim Lelewel, reflecting on the "purpose of the historian," thought it was to "study peoples, their sufferings and their wrongs." In the process he provided Polish nationalism with much of its emotional substance. Like his counterparts in the southern United States, Lelewel deployed international comparisons, appealing for the support of "Italians, Hungarians, Jews, Germans, and all other people denied their sovereignty and independence and living under foreign domination." The Czech historian František Palacký similarly stressed the historical wrongs inflicted upon his people by the Germans and the Magyars. From the Magyar perspective, though, *they* were the real victims: the 1849 Hungarian declaration of independence, written mostly by Lajos Kossuth, consisted of a long list of injustices that the Magyar people had suffered at the hands of outsiders. Similar claims of victimhood have infused many other nationalisms, including the pre-unification Italian independence movement and French nationalism following defeat in the Franco-Prussian War.[31]

Just as narratives of southern suffering echoed nationalist arguments across the Atlantic, so too did secessionists' emphasis on the distinction between nations and governments. This argument reflected a generally accepted differentiation between a government—the institutional apparatus of a nation-state—and a nation—a group of people who shared common interests, mutual affection, and a national identity. This distinction underpinned the principle of nationality that prevailed in both European and American thought, and it underpinned the movements of active nationalism—both separatist and unification—that swept nineteenth-century Europe. The basis of the claims of German, Hungarian, Italian, Irish, and other nationalists, after all, was that there existed iniquitous discrepancies between the nation (the people) and the unit of governance. Nationalists demanded that nation and government be aligned: "Every nation a state," as Mazzini memorably put it, and "only one state for the entire nation."[32] Baltimore's Brantz Mayer used this same distinction to explain what he saw as the failure of Mexico as a nation. In order for there to be a genuine "nation, in the true sense of nationality," he thought, its people "should be intimately united by bonds of interest, sympathy and affection. Such a nation may form a government, but it is difficult for a government to form such a nation." Clergyman Benjamin Palmer recognized a similar gap between nation and government in the case of the Jews, whom he described as "a people without a country—a nation without a Government."[33]

Southern secessionists recognized that European nationalists' talk of aligning nation with government bolstered southern nationalists' efforts to achieve the same goal. In an 1858 oration Lewis Ayer celebrated the ultimate, God-given right of sovereignty in each distinct people, and distinguished such divine sovereignty from temporary, artificial institutions of government. "Governments vanish as the shifting scenery of a stage," he explained, "but there is much permanency in a people." Because of this, in cases where "rights of sovereignty . . . are not recognized, or, at all events, properly appreciated," it was important to remedy the discrepancy. Ireland, Hungary, and Poland, he thought, were unfairly denied their rights to sovereignty and self-government, and ought to strive to secure those rights. Man-made governments were not infallible, Ayer concluded, and ought to give way to the natural rights of a people's sovereignty. The lesson for the United States was clear: two separate nations, North and South, should not be artificially coupled within a single government.[34]

South Carolinian William Porter similarly distinguished between a state—by which he meant a sovereign people, a national community—and the government under which they lived. "A State is something higher, more sacred and permanent than its government," he thought: "Surely, Government is the handiwork of man, but States and Nations are of God." In the case of the United States, he was convinced, the artifice of the federal government had been created by the people of the several states, acting as separate and sovereign communities: "Our system is Federal, and not National; . . . the Government is the offspring of the people of the States, and not of the people collectively." The founders had not intended the federal government to usurp the sovereignty of the states, to create a "consolidated" nation. America was no more a "consolidated" nation, he thought, than ancient Greece had been, or than England, Scotland, and Ireland were in 1860. States were the communities that enjoyed independent sovereignty, and states, not the Union, ought to claim the "primary allegiance" of each American. Indeed, the United States should not be thought of as a nation at all: "We have not now, and never had, a distinctive name as a nation, for 'America' is common to the whole continent on either side of the isthmus; and under the Constitution we are the same 'United States of America' that we were under the articles of Confederation." For Porter, the lack of a proper national name signified the larger consequence of American federalism: that the United States was no nation at all.[35]

Porter revealed a fundamental problem of southern nationalism. He rejected American nationality on the grounds not of a region-wide southern identity but of individual states' rights. Prior to 1861, secessionists often framed their movement in terms of national independence for the separate states. The constitutional argument for nullification had been formed at the state level, and states' rights continued to be a centerpiece of secessionist thought, culminating in the separate state secessions that took place in 1860 and 1861. There is no misinterpreting Nathaniel Beverley Tucker's statement that despite the federation of the United States, "Virginia is your country. To her your allegiance is due. Her alone you are bound to obey."[36] Southern secessionists very often cast their crusade in terms of states' rights and identity rather than an identity encompassing the South as a whole.

In an 1859 speech, William Henry Trescot observed, "If an American be asked abroad of what country are you, his first impulse is to answer, I am a New Yorker, a Virginian, a Massachusetts man, or a Carolinian, as the fact may be. Whatever his pride in his nationality, his home instincts and affections are bounded by State lines." In explaining the nature of allegiance to the state, Trescot saw its foundation in lifelong attachment to a specific place. "On every American heart," he said, "there is written the name of some locality, obscure, hidden away from the historians and geographers . . . the spot still around which all that is truly his life revolves." This might be the place where as a boy he had witnessed a public appearance of the governor, or where he had cast his vote as a young man—"the spot, in short, where local interests, acting on local affections, introduced him from boyhood into a sphere of higher activity." For Trescot then, the primal attachment to one's native locality, a classic foundation of romantic-style nationalism, attached him not to the United States, not to the South, but to the state of South Carolina.[37]

State-level identity and allegiance were further promoted by the legal framework of citizenship and the state-specific nature of most intellectual, educational, and political activity. Prior to 1861, attempts to present the individual southern states as European-style "nations" would in some respects have had more credibility than doing so for the South as a whole. Even so, secessionists ultimately recognized that presenting a multistate southern nation as the desired outcome of secession was more expedient, pragmatic, and likely to succeed than advocating a fragmentary collection of small independent states.

How did they make this argument? Asserting that the United States was not a nation was easy enough. So too was drawing surface-level parallels between secession and European nationalist movements. But what about the substance? What about the content of the distinctive national identity that was supposed to justify the South's claim of political independence? In answering these tough questions, secessionists unsurprisingly drew on European norms of national legitimacy. Like all Americans, white southerners were influenced by the romantic strands of nationalism that were becoming increasingly prominent in Europe. So when they set about adding substance to their claims that the South was a nation unjustly denied its rightful sovereignty, it was natural that these romantic strands of nationalism should provide, at the very least, some of the language with which they made their claims. Models of nationality existed, and the radicals tried to mold their cause to correspond with them.[38]

Ethnicity and culture were coming to be especially prominent features of European nationalism, especially the separatist nationalisms that southern secessionists liked to compare themselves to. In places such as Ireland, Bohemia, Hungary, and Poland, nationalist movements, their ideals inspired in part by the writings of Johann Herder, rested squarely on the claim of a unique and deep-rooted cultural community— within which ethnicity, language, and history were typically central features. In response to efforts by imperial powers to impose German or Russian as official languages, Czechs, Hungarians, and Poles celebrated and attempted to boost the use of their own national tongues. There were cultural revivals in Bohemia and Hungary. Young Irelanders such as Thomas Davis promoted language, medieval history, music, poetry, art, folklore—all proof that the Irish constituted a unique people with a noble past.[39]

History was especially important. John Hutchinson has emphasized that in these separatist nationalisms, "memories of former statehood, crowns and feudal constitutions provided a sense of historic nationhood."[40] But it took historians, of course, to create these histories and to endow them with political meaning. This is exactly what was undertaken by scholars such as Joachim Lelewel and František Palacký. Palacký devoted his life to archiving the primary sources of Bohemian history and to using those sources to construct a magnum opus, *The History of the Czech Nation*. He was dubbed the "Father of the Nation" for his efforts. Likewise, Lelewel authored numerous works of Polish historiography and history, including children's textbooks. As one of his biographers has put it, Lelewel "consciously used history to plead the Polish cause, to awaken national consciousness among the Poles."[41]

Did the American South have its own Joachim Lelewel? Could southern secessionists legitimately employ the mode of romantic nationalism—could they reasonably point to a distinctive ethnicity, language, culture, history? The short answer is no. But it is very revealing that southerners did sometimes try to cast their nationalism in this mold. They attempted, for instance, to invoke a distinctive southern ethnicity to bolster their cause. Such assertions typically rested on the claim that southerners were of a different ethnic stock than northerners. This stemmed, in most versions, from early migration to the American colonies. Whereas the Cavaliers of the English Civil War had settled in the South, their Roundhead enemies had settled in the North. Over the years, these ethnic differences had survived, fermented, and ultimately produced two separate nationalities. Here was an attempt, albeit a weak one, to fit the southern cause into the mold of European ethnic nationalism.[42]

Another possible ethnic-style basis for southern nationalism derived from the central foundation of the whole enterprise—racial slavery. As they sought to convince fellow southerners of the benefits of leaving the Union, secessionists sometimes cast the North-South difference in racial terms. Accusing northerners, and especially the "Black Republican Party," of advocating racial equality, white southerners contrasted the North's supposed racial "amalgamation" with their own dedication to racial purity and the unalloyed supremacy of the white race. This argument did not fit terribly well into the mold of European ethnic nationalism. For one thing, it claimed not so much that a shared ethnic identity made southerners unique, but rather that southerners were taking to its extreme a principle—white supremacy—that was then shared, to one degree or another, by most white Americans and Europeans. It gave southern nationalism a racial element but not an ethnic distinctiveness of the kind asserted by the Poles, say, or the Irish.

If ethnic distinctiveness was a stretch, what about a unique southern culture? Recognizing the importance of literature and culture to nationalism, southern partisans attempted to demonstrate—or, more often, to wish for—southern cultural independence. Indeed, the lack, or at least the weakness, of the usual "objective" markers of nationality, such as language, geography, or race, rendered claims of southern cultural distinctiveness especially crucial. James Chesnut took care to explain that the relative importance of the various criteria had changed over time. In the premodern and presumably less civilized world, simple differences of race or geography had been the most common dividers of nations. But humankind had progressed, and "under the civilization which rest[s] on moral and mental, rather than material elements," it was obvious that "character and condition, more than physical individuality," would distinguish nation from nation. Such a shift, of course, was most convenient to antebellum southern nationalists. Chesnut's fellow South Carolinian John McCrady proceeded from similar assumptions. "The fundamental ideas of the collective intellect of the Southern States," he believed, "are and must continue for a long period, entirely distinct from those of the collective intellect of any other people in Christendom"—and distinct most significantly from the North. Because North and South were "intellectually no longer one, but two distinct unities . . . they are in truth two distinct nationalities, and must probably, ere very long, constitute two distinct governments." Intellectual independence underpinned a unique national identity—which in turn mandated political independence.[43]

Because the South constituted a distinct intellectual community, thought McCrady, "the systems of education of other nations can never be adapted to the educational necessities of the South," and, therefore, "the greatest need of the South is a National Education." McCrady's declaration, issued in 1860, was one of a chorus of voices in the antebellum South calling for "A Southern Education for Southrons." These mostly resulted from fears that northern educational institutions and personnel would inculcate southern youth with antislavery opinions, but were often lent urgency by a broader fear of southern intellectual inferiority.[44] The University of the South was founded in the late 1850s, for both of these reasons. Leonidas Polk, who spearheaded the effort, also noted that state-level universities simply were not sufficient for a people who aspired to national independence; they "have not the claims nor the prestige of anything like nationality about them." Education was used to promote nationalism on both sides of the Atlantic. Jules Michelet used his chair in history and moral philosophy at the College de France to promote a nationalist interpretation of French history, and Heinrich von Treitschke, who was awakened to the cause of German nationalism as a student at the University of Bonn, went on to champion the crusade as a historian and university teacher himself.[45] In the American South, Nathaniel Beverley Tucker likewise valued his chair at the College of William and Mary because of the opportunity it gave him to proselytize to students. Though he did not publish much, he wrote to a friend, he did train young minds in his classroom, giving him "the satisfaction to believe that not one has ever left me, without being, *for the time*, a Southern man in feeling, and a

States-right man in conviction." And when he did write for the press, he did so for partisan publications such as the *Southern Quarterly Review*, in which, as he wrote, it would be his "constant aim to excite indignation resentment and scorn against our oppressors persecutors and revilers in the North."[46]

The campaign for a specifically southern educational system was not confined to higher education, nor was it confined to men. The Southern Education Society in Dalton, Georgia, was formed in response to northern hostility to slavery, and the resulting belief that southerners must actively defend their peculiar institution through a system of female as well as male education. After all, young women were destined to "become the mothers of sons worthy to inherit and qualified to defend our property and our institutions." The society aimed to ensure that southern women would prove equal to the task by publishing schoolbooks, establishing schools and colleges, and publishing a newspaper to publicize their efforts. Their ultimate aim was "to create a literature for the South, by the publication in the South of school books, bibles, hymn books, periodicals, and newspapers, and as far as practicable all other books and publications suited to or required by the public."[47]

These initiatives were part of a broader effort to establish southern literary and intellectual independence. William Gilmore Simms was at the forefront of this movement. In 1858 he ranked "the formation of our own opinion" as the foremost ingredient of genuine national independence. With Simms this was not just talk. In the early 1850s, planning to publish a volume of poetry which offered little promise of pecuniary gain, he took solace in the fact that such efforts constituted "one of the phases by which we are to secure home independence." Likewise, the Alabamian Alexander B. Meek, his fellow writer and southern partisan, wrote to Simms in appreciation of what was probably the same volume, which, Meek thought, "will form a fit *avant courier* for Southern Literature and Southern Publication." "I am convinced," he went on, "that we cannot have *Home* independence of any kind,—in Commerce, Manufactures, Politics, or what not, until we have a Home Independence of *Mind*."[48]

By the 1850s, Simms and others were issuing calls for southern literary independence that were similar to their earlier advocacy for American literary independence. Whereas in the 1840s both writers were promoting what Meek had called "Americanism in Literature," by the 1850s they both saw the value of romantic, place-based literature in specifically southern terms. Thus when Meek in 1857 repeated the familiar affirmations that "the poetry of a country should be a faithful expression of its physical and moral characteristics," and that "verse . . . is as much the genuine product and growth of a Land, as its trees or flowers," he did so in order to introduce a volume entitled *Songs and Poems of the South*, which included such offerings as "Come to the South" and "The Mothers of the South." Though Meek did not explicitly connect his writings to the cause of political independence, this was a classic example of place-based romantic poetry in the service of a putative national identity, and of how the conceptual framework of American nationalism could be transferred to a rival southern nationalism.[49]

There were similar efforts to claim a unique history for the South. Simms saw history in part as an adhesive ensuring southern unity, and in part as ammunition in the political struggle against the North. Thus he rejoiced when fellow southerners appeared to be taking an interest in their own history—especially when they transcended state lines and tried to make sense of the whole region's shared past—and, more commonly, chastised them when they did not. Other southern historians with secessionist proclivities agreed. In a secessionist pamphlet of 1850, William Henry Trescot argued that "history, in the action of its providential instinct," had produced fundamentally different peoples in the northern and southern United States. Beginning with the differences in the settlement of Plymouth and Jamestown, "the growth of the two great sections, radiated from different centres, diverged in different directions, were developed from different principles, and perfected through dissimilar experiences." Frederick Adolphus Porcher, a professor at the College of Charleston, later elaborated on the same premise. The founding philosophies of Virginia and New England were fundamentally different, he asserted: New England developed a tight-knit community ethos, whereas Jamestown quickly became a society of independent individuals. The nineteenth-century gulf between North and South was, according to Porcher, the direct result of a unique southern historical experience. Like their counterparts in Europe, southern nationalists responded to the political problem of uniting the South with the cultural argument of a shared southern historical experience, one sufficiently distinct from its northern equivalent to support a separate southern nationality.[50]

Despite the efforts of Meek, Simms, and others, the various strands of southern intellectual independence—appreciation of a shared history, a distinctive literature and art, and a southern education system—were hardly flourishing, even on the eve of the Civil War. Historical activity in the antebellum South was prosecuted most vigorously at the state level, with no significant regional initiatives until after the war. Neither Simms nor anyone

FIGURE 2.1   Edmund Ruffin. (Library of Congress.)

else wrote a pan-southern history or organized a South-wide historical society.[51] Nor did southerners successfully produce a recognizably southern
literary or artistic tradition that could underpin political independence. Part
of the difficulty stemmed from the attempt to tie a hazy romantic celebration of place and locale to a southern—as opposed to an American or a Virginian or a Charlestonian—political community. What value would one of
Simms's South Carolina neighbors have found in Meek's poetic celebration
of "The Homes of Alabama"? Southern nationalism, in other words, involved
the same problem of boundaries as did American nationalism: romantic

FIGURE 2.2 Giuseppe Garibaldi. (Library of Congress.)

ideas about place, culture, and peoplehood were only imperfectly fastened to
either the American or the putative southern national community.

The more serious problem, of course, was slavery. As southern nationalists well knew, the one thing that really did make the whole South
a distinctive unit was its peculiar institution. Without slavery there
would have been no reason to promote southern nationalism. But, as
they also knew, by itself slavery was a weak basis for securing unity
within the South or securing legitimacy as a genuine nation on the world
stage. Slavery also complicated the parallels secessionists drew between
themselves and European nationalists. For instance, although Edmund
Ruffin ranked the Italian nationalist Giuseppe Garibaldi among his
heroes, his admiration was necessarily limited. Garibaldi was much

FIGURE 2.3 John Mitchel; lithograph by N. Currier, ca. 1848. (Library of Congress.)

more liberal than Ruffin or any other southern secessionist, including on the all-important issue of racial slavery. Slavery would also have complicated any effort to compare secessionists with most other European oppositional nationalist leaders, such as Giuseppe Mazzini or Ireland's Daniel O'Connell.[52]

The one European nationalist with whom southern secessionists could identify with ease was the Irishman John Mitchel, in large part because he became a southern secessionist himself. Arrested by the British government for attempts to promote violent revolution in 1848, Mitchel was transported to Tasmania but escaped to the United States in 1853, first to New York City but later to eastern Tennessee, where he cofounded a newspaper called the *Southern Citizen* and became a staunch southern partisan. A long-standing supporter of American slavery, Mitchel saw parallels between Ireland and the South—both were rural societies unjustly oppressed by large, industrializing, foreign powers—and committed himself to the promotion of southern as well as Irish independence. Unlike most European nationalists, Mitchel valued slavery as a beneficial institution for white and black southerners alike, easily melding his ethnocultural vision of Irish nationalism with an appreciation for a southern nation built on racial inequality.[53]

As the example of Mitchel suggests, the character and success of any given nationalist movement was determined to no small degree by human thought and action. Although most European groups had a decidedly stronger case than the South for ethnic and cultural distinctiveness, this did not naturally or inevitably produce nationalism. Nationalism always required nationalists. In places like Italy and Germany, it arose more as a consequence than a cause of unification. Even the separatist movements that had more of a cultural or ethnic basis tended to rise to prominence as much because of politics and interests as the sentiment of nationality alone.[54] Hence those nationalists who based their claims on ethnicity and culture tended to ignore those features when they clashed with other priorities. This was true of the Czechs, the Poles, and the Hungarians, groups that demanded borders for their proposed nation-states that were determined more by historic political formations and pragmatic interests than by language or ethnicity. The figurehead of the Hungarian movement, Lajos Kossuth, was notoriously intolerant of the needs of non-Magyar minorities within lands that he claimed for Hungary. If the ostensibly all-important correspondence between the ethno-cultural nation and the unit of governance was not faithfully observed in the secessionist South, nor was it absolute in Europe.[55]

Recognizing this makes the strategies of nationalists on both sides of the Atlantic more comparable. Southern secessionists shared with their European counterparts the knowledge that nationalism does not simply happen; a successful nationalist crusade required organization, communication, and political action. Research on Italian nationalists Mazzini and Garibaldi has emphasized their commitment to consciousness raising and to publicity: they carefully cultivated their own reputations in order to advance their cause. To be sure, the extent of nationalists' commitment varied—there was no precise southern equivalent of Mazzini, for instance, who endured decades of impoverished exile, devoting his whole life to his cause.[56] Even so, southern secessionists approached their mission in comparable ways. Stretching back to nullification, southern radicals had pressed their case using pamphlets, newspapers, and political associations old and new. Just as Italian nationalists had associations such as the Carbonari, Young Italy, and the Italian National Society, secessionists had the Bluffton Boys, Southern Rights Associations, the League of United Southerners, and, finally, the 1860 Association. In commenting on the League of United Southerners, William L. Yancey famously stressed the importance of deliberate political activism, writing of the need to "organize committees of safety all over the cotton states. . . . We shall fire the southern heart—instruct the southern mind—give courage to each other, and at the proper moment, by one organized, concerted movement, we can precipitate the cotton states into a Revolution."[57] It is easy to imagine such words emanating from Dublin or Prague. There were other transatlantic commonalities, too. Just as Germans tried to negotiate national unification at the Frankfurt Assembly in 1848–49, southerners came together at the Nashville Conventions of 1850 with similar goals—and a similarly dissatisfying outcome. Just as the Young Ireland group had *The Nation*, Robert Barnwell Rhett acquired control of the *Charleston Mercury* to disseminate his message. The forms and techniques of southern nationalism— the political and intellectual activism, the narrative of suffering, the arguments about cultural distinctiveness—were firmly embedded in transatlantic nationalism.

Secession and the American Revolution

Secessionists drew their most powerful comparisons not with European nationalisms but with American nationalism, especially as represented in the American Revolution. They took great pleasure in aligning their proposed southern revolution with the earlier American Revolution. This was a long-standing technique. Nullifiers and their opponents had all laid claim to the heritage of the American Revolution, with each side claiming that their path more accurately conformed to the founders' project. Such claims persisted beyond the nullification era. In staking their claims to the memory of the American Revolution, southern secessionists staked their claim to American national identity itself.

Particularly during the first secession crisis of 1850 and 1851, radicals used the Fourth of July and other occasions of revolutionary commemoration to draw parallels between their own struggle against the federal government's oppression and the colonists' struggle against British tyranny. In an 1851 Fourth of July address, South Carolinian John Richardson held up the revolutionary generation's example of standing up courageously for one's principles—an example that he thought should be replicated with secession. David F. Jamison, a planter who would go on to preside over South Carolina's secession convention, agreed that southerners should follow their ancestors' example, warning of the consequences of not doing so: "If the people of the South shall submit to a worse than colonial subjection to the States of the North, that revolution will have been achieved for them in vain. All celebrations of the day of Independence will then be over with us." In other words, only by standing up for their rights—even if it meant secession—could white southerners preserve the true spirit of the Fourth of July and the American Revolution.[58]

The parallels that southern supporters of slavery drew between themselves and the revolutionary generation have surprised many subsequent commentators. How did a nationalist movement based on slavery portray itself as the heir of a revolution apparently founded on freedom?[59] Part of the answer lies in the way Americans had always separated white freedom from black slavery in different intellectual compartments or imagined the former to rest upon the latter.[60] The answer also lies in the particular ways that southerners remembered the Revolution and the Declaration of Independence, and the particular ways that they applied the lessons of the past to the present. They were especially likely, for instance, to emphasize the Constitution—a proslavery document, William Holden informed a North Carolina audience in 1856—as the outcome of the Revolution.[61] Even the Declaration, though, could be used to support the slave South, so long as it was used in the right way. Because the extent to which the Declaration and the American Revolution stood for freedom and equality has always been open to interpretation, southern secessionists could emphasize those aspects that suited their needs and overlook those that did not.

Foremost in the latter category was the apparent assertion of human rights contained in the Declaration's second paragraph: the "truths" that "all men are created equal; that they are endowed by their Creator with certain unalienable rights; that among these are life, liberty, and the pursuit of happiness." Though this section of the Declaration has symbolized the meaning of the American Revolution for many Americans, this was not at all the case for southern nationalists, nor for proslavery southerners in general. Their American Revolution did not offer the promise of equality for all. Edmund Ruffin, for instance, thought that "the indefensible passage in the Declaration of Independence" was "both false & foolish." The eccentric Virginian George Fitzhugh was more specific in his critique: "We agree with Mr. Jefferson, that all men have natural and inalienable rights. . . . We conclude that about nineteen out of every twenty individuals have 'a natural and inalienable right, to be taken care of and protected, to have guardians, trustees, husbands, or masters." The other one in every twenty people, according to Fitzhugh's reinterpretation of the Declaration, had the right to rule over the rest and enjoy true liberty.[62]

Nor, according to southern nationalists, was the formation of the Union an important part of the Revolution's legacy. Thus Lewis Ayer reminded his audience which aspects of the Revolution they ought to cherish and which they ought not:

> The great act of Washington in dissolving in blood, the accursed union of government between the American Colonies and Great Britain, should be held up to our admiration and imitation, rather than the wreck and refuse of that government which he established for our use and protection, but which is about to be wrested to our ruin.

Here was an interpretation that southern nationalists could use. "The act of Union," Ayer went on, "was but a mere business transaction." In other words, there was no mysterious American nationalism at work in the American Revolution; the fact that the era concluded with a federation of the states was the result of a simple calculation of interests. The great lesson of the American Revolution was that humans no longer needed to blindly trust in their government: the essence of the movement was the great truth of self-government, and if a particular government was not working, it ought to be replaced with another. The revolution's great achievement lay in dismantling rather than building up, and once southerners recognized this great truth, "soon would the aspiring shout for a Southern Confederacy wake the welkin with its gladsome note." Rather than romantic strands of nationalism, this line of argument rested on the politically oriented, sovereignty-based strands that had been prominent during the late-eighteenth-century age of revolutions. The radicals seemed happy to deploy either type of nationalism—or both.[63]

Secessionists invoked the all-important distinction between nation and government in arguing that the revolutionary generation had created only a government, not a real nation. One of the earliest devotees of an independent South, law professor Nathaniel Beverley Tucker, wrote to a friend in 1836, "We delude ourselves by continuing to think of the U.S. as a Country instead of a mere creature of convention." As he would explain in following years, the founders had created not a nation but a loose confederation. Although the forces of "centralism," had been present, the forces of "federalism" had been stronger, strong enough to block the use of "the word National" in the U.S. Constitution. Hence the United States was a dissolvable compact rather than a permanent nation. Other southern partisans agreed, rejecting the idea that the United States was a "consolidated" nation (the word "consolidated" elicited more repugnance in these circles than any other, except perhaps for "Yankee"). Reflecting in the 1840s on the consequences of the American Revolution, William Gilmore Simms concluded that "the common cause did not make us a common family. . . . The ligaments which now chiefly bind us together, are those of our political union." William Henry Trescot employed a different metaphor to similar effect. He compared the revolutionary-era colonies-cum-states to "the immense masses of ice which sometimes congregate in northern seas, floating in such immediate contact that they must close into one compact body" or face the risk of crashing together. Even so, the founders had really only created a government, not a nation, since "it was impossible that a nation could be made in one generation." After all, "national love must be a matter of feeling, not reason," and even though "reason" had enabled Americans to construct a government, the deficiency of "feeling"—which persisted even in the late 1840s—rendered genuine nationhood elusive. The United States, both Simms and Trescot held, was a "political union" based on "reason," and did not constitute a "common family" based on "feeling." Their terminology echoes the distinction between "civic" and "ethnic" models of nationalism. While the United States had succeeded in establishing the former, according to these southern writers, there was little evidence of the strength of the latter.[64] This notion that the United States had never been a real nation infused southern nationalists' remembrance of the American Revolution.

Selective remembrance offered political gain. Just as Thomas Macaulay in England and various liberal historians in mid-nineteenth-century France promoted current political concerns by stressing the moderate aspects of their respective countries' revolutions, so too did southern nationalists' political needs shape the way they remembered the achievement of American independence. Rather than a radical initiation of democracy, the Revolution could be seen as an ideologically conservative act intended primarily to resist repression—"more a separation of States," as Thomas Hanckel put it, "than a social and political revolution." Minimizing the democratic potential of the Revolution, William Trescot asserted that American independence "introduced into history a new power, not a new principle." The revolutionary generation, he explained, "sheltered no wild sentiment, fostered no mischievous principle of universal democracy"; rather, they "conducted a revolution with the caution of a lawsuit." By emphasizing the principle of self-government and the conservative dimension of the American Revolution, while minimizing the democratic radicalism that could—if desired—be seen in the Declaration, southern nationalists were able to draw credible parallels between themselves and the Founders.[65]

As part of their effort to lay claim to the mantle of the American Revolution in the present, southern nationalists called attention to what they saw as the South's unappreciated contributions to the War of Independence itself. Their endeavors spawned heated disputes. Once again, William Gilmore Simms was in the vanguard. Simms's displeasure with an 1848 book written by Massachusetts's Lorenzo Sabine, which emphasized the high proportion of loyalists in South Carolina, inspired an acerbic two-part review. "A waste of goodly type and paper," *The American Loyalists* had, according to Simms, been quite wrong in its claims that northern troops were more patriotic than southern (in fact, he thought, northerners had been motivated more by money than by patriotism) and that battles in the South had been won by the valiant troops of New England. Accepting the high proportion of loyalists in his state, Simms attributed this to the foreign-born population, and to the fact that South Carolina had no substantial material motivations for rebellion. Indeed, these factors only made his state's hefty contribution more admirable. Simms joined his fellow southerners in insisting that, once the facts were known, "the deeds and sacrifices of Carolina, and of the whole South, will bear honorable comparison with those of any part of this nation."[66]

Simms was here trying to right the historical record. Yet he also fully understood that conflicts over historical interpretations carried much political weight in such a charged sectional situation. Writing to his friend James Henry Hammond late in 1848, Simms advised him to read the first part of the review, "if you would see, how I have carried the war into Yankeedom, & furnished an argument, much needed, to our politicians." As the politicians took up this very argument, the dispute over contributions to the Revolution spread to the floors of both branches of the United States Congress. In fact, it was an element of the 1856 dispute between senators Andrew Butler and Charles Sumner that led to the caning of Sumner by Butler's relative Preston Brooks. Part of the honor that Brooks was trying to defend concerned proper recognition of his state's contributions to the Revolutionary War. Indeed, Simms wrote to Sabine that "Sumner properly owes his cudgeling to you!" Soon after, South Carolina's southern-rights supporter Lawrence M. Keitt used the occasion of his resignation from the U.S. House to rebut claims that his own state's revolutionary record was less honorable than New England's. Explicitly criticizing Sabine's book, Keitt reiterated Simms's earlier arguments, contending that "Massachusetts embarked in the Revolution for water-falls, spindles, and merchant craft; South Carolina engaged in it for the royalty of mind." Though Keitt's complaint was at the level of individual states, it was clearly part of the larger conflict that pitted the whole North against the South. The contention that southerners had played such an important role in the fighting of the revolution strengthened the argument that they more properly represented its spirit in the present day.[67]

George Washington's memory, too, could be claimed for regional as well as for national ends. One Charleston orator, for instance, referred to Washington as "the Great Southerner," and urged that his example ought to be followed by the present generation of southerners—especially because the North had so patently failed to do so. No less a figure than John C. Calhoun complained about misuse of Washington's memory, stating that "we have a right to claim [Washington] as an illustrious Southerner, for he was a southern man—a southern planter—and we do not intend that he shall be taken out of our hands."[68]

It was a South Carolina woman, Ann Pamela Cunningham, who led the attempt to preserve Mount Vernon, and Cunningham's mother, at least, wished zealously to guard the southernness of the whole endeavor.

Writing to a potential collaborator, Louisa Cunningham described how on a recent trip her "heart swelled with emotions" upon coming into the vicinity of Mount Vernon. The effort to save the national shrine was particularly urgent in her mind because of the possibility that the property might otherwise "fall, into the hands of the Yankee speculator." Her prejudice against northerners extended even to those northern women who desired to assist in the enterprise. It had been suggested that part of the name of the organization be changed from "the Ladies of the South" to "the American Ladies," but Louisa Cunningham was dead set against the idea. "Let it be all South," she wrote—"The grave of Washington lies in Southern Soil—let it be solely and wholly ours."[69]

These insistent assertions of their ownership of the revolutionary heritage suggest that, rather than abandoning their existing American national identity, southern nationalists were attempting to define a new nation within the parameters of the old, striving to render the sacred remembrance of American nationalism's "golden age" specifically southern. While they sought a political separation from the United States, they did not intend a wholesale rejection of the idea of America. In 1857 one Charleston orator emphasized that withdrawing from the Union would not mean rejecting America but rather rescuing it from those who had perverted its real promise: "If that hour of final dissolution comes, then let us claim as our portion the Star Spangled Banner . . . *rescue it from apostate hands*, and . . . rededicate it to a more enduring Southern Union." William Trescot similarly believed that secession would renew the promise of America. In 1850, he predicted that, in the event of political separation, "the experiment instituted by our fathers will receive its highest illustration." The southern nation would be more American than the United States. Not that Trescot wanted to deny southerners' gratitude to the Union. But all the same, he concluded, "It has achieved its destiny. Let us achieve ours."[70]

The Southern Future

But what was the South's destiny? What was the end goal of all of this nationalist rhetoric and argument? What, in the estimation of prewar southern nationalists, did the future hold for an independent South? This was a crucial question for any nationalist in the nineteenth-century world. After all, nationalism's deep emotional appeal lay in its ability to connect individuals with sacred communities and transcendent purposes within time past, present, and future. To southern nationalists, one thing was certain: an independent future would be a magnificent one. "If this un-holy union could be severed," thought Frederick Porcher, "if we could be left to ourselves, to work out our own destiny, we see no reason why we should not equal the moral greatness of any people in history."[71] Most ar-guments for southern nationalism concluded with a similarly rousing—and usually a similarly vague—vision of the South's national future.

Some antebellum nationalists did, however, take the time to elaborate a little more fully on exactly what would be so wonderful about southern independence. Edmund Ruffin and Nathaniel Beverley Tucker wrote pre-dictive novels presenting their visions of what an independent South would look like, and how it might come into being. Ruffin, Tucker, and other southern nationalists hinted at the content of those visions in a va-riety of other writings as well, which together make possible a composite picture of what the proposed southern nation actually looked like.[72]

The most consistent characteristic of the southern nation they envi-sioned was its internal unity. In view of constant southern division on how to respond to the sectional crisis, the unity of the South understandably was a sensitive point to southern nationalists.[73] They were suspiciously insistent that an independent South would be a united South. One seces-sionist implied that southerners would be practically identical: "Asking the same political privileges—needing the same political protection—their communities resting on the same basis—their laws the same—their language, tastes, sympathies, the same—homogeneous in every thing that pertains to their political, civil or social relations." The actual substance of southern homogeneity and unity were typically skipped over in these kinds of statements. But when specifics were introduced, slavery loomed large. Outlining a novel he planned to call "A Century Hence," Virginia politician John C. Rutherford envisioned "a united confederacy held firmly together by the conservative influence of slavery." Others, too, pre-dicted that the national unity that the United States lacked would be pro-vided in the new nation by southerners' shared stake in racial slavery.[74]

Rutherford also decided he would "make the South profit and the North suffer by a dissolution of the Union" in his novel. Assertions of the prosperity that awaited an independent South ran through just about all southern nationalists' predictions of the future. After all, such assertions followed logically from the conviction that the South was currently exploited economically by the North. As one Virginia secessionist predicted, "A degree of prosperity, greater than the world has ever known, would await us in a separation from the selfish and contemptible horde that have fattened on our bounty till they have degenerated into revilers and slanderers." Similarly, Nathaniel Beverley Tucker explained in his predictive novel *The Partisan Leader* that separation from the North and release from the burden of the protective tariff would greatly benefit the southern economy.[75] In other writings, Tucker specifically emphasized the policy of free trade, particularly with the South's natural ally Great Britain, as a crucial element in post-independence affluence.[76] So too did Robert Barnwell Rhett. With the policy of free trade, combined with the power of cotton, the South could look forward to both wealth and peaceful relations with the rest of the world. William Trescot thought that cotton would allow the new nation to become "the guardian of the world's commerce—the grave and impartial centre of that new balance of power."[77] More generally, as the radicals were fond of pointing out, the South enjoyed all the resources of population, territory, wealth, and nature to enjoy a prosperous independent existence. Such was the underlying argument of Edmund Ruffin, for one, in his fictional prediction of the South's future as an independent nation, *Anticipations of the Future.* Outside the Union, peace and affluence beckoned.

Independence promised liberation from territorial constriction as well as economic exploitation. Visions of expansion were another common feature of the radicals' imagined nation. In the minds of both Robert Barnwell Rhett and John C. Rutherfoord, for example, an independent South would be able to lay claim to certain North American territories—New Mexico, Utah, California—from which it was excluded in the present Union. But visions of territorial growth did not stop there. Rutherfoord, Rhett, and others also hoped for expansion further south. Southward expansion became an important goal for southern partisans in the 1850s, particularly in light of the South's failure to acquire new slaveholding territory within the Union. To the radicals, the prospect of a southern confederacy acquiring Cuba, Jamaica, Haiti, and other areas of the Caribbean and even Central America seemed rosy indeed. Even Lewis Ayer, who cautioned in 1855 against Cuban annexation as a distraction from the priority of southern independence, nonetheless looked favorably upon expansion *after* independence. "An Independent Confederacy of these Slave-holding States," he wrote, "might be enabled to shape the destinies of, not only Cuba, but the whole West India Archipelago; but not until we are masters of our own fortunes, can we do aught good for ourselves, or others."[78]

The dream of an independent South, then, promised to bring with it release from the oppressive constraints that the radicals felt within the Union. In addition to the straightforward protection of slavery, it promised an escape from the economic exploitation, the territorial constriction, the insulting degradation to which southern radicals objected so vehemently. It promised a return to the genuine spirit of the American Revolution, a spirit that had been fatally subverted by the North. It promised purification from the taint of association with an immoral and misguided North. Perhaps most important of all, it promised vindication for those prophets who had tried so long to convince the South that its interests and rightful destiny demanded national independence. "But indeed," Nathaniel Beverley Tucker confessed in 1850, "I do not know how to bear the thought of surrendering the hope of being remembered in future time as one of the founders of that glorious Southern Confederacy which I begin to see in prophetic vision."[79] Tucker and the other radicals had invested their lives, their selves, in the dream of southern nationalism. They had tried to bolster this dream with an array of assertions and arguments, drawing on American and transatlantic conceptions of nationalism, all designed to prove that the South deserved—needed—national independence. But would their dreams ever become reality?

3

The Pinch

AMERICAN NATIONALISM IN CRISIS

IN 1858 JAMES Henry Hammond, the South Carolina planter and politician, recognized an important truth: that the success of the secession movement would not depend primarily on the nationalist dreams of the radicals. Hammond took issue with the overly simplistic analysis of his fellow South Carolina politician William Porcher Miles, which "divides all Southern men into two classes . . . those who shape their course for Union at all hazard, and those who shape it for an independent Southern Republic." Such an analysis, Hammond contended, "omits 999/1000 voters & 49/50 men of substance. . . . This immense body goes for Union until it pinches them & then for dissolving it."[1]

As Hammond understood, the sectional crisis did not provide a neat referendum in which white southerners were asked to select between the clearly distinguished choices of "American nationalism" and "southern nationalism." For most, the options were not conceived of as unionism "at all hazard" versus southern independence at any cost. Rather, the majority of antebellum white southerners advocated a shifting and conditional unionism: continued loyalty to the current Union, but only so long as certain conditions were met. Southerners' ongoing allegiance would stand or fall depending on the extent to which the Union appeared to "pinch" them, more than on the idealized southern nationalism of Rhett, Ruffin, and others of their ilk.

Hammond's insight belies the assumption that, because the outcome was national independence, the process must have been driven by nationalism, a movement self-consciously designed to bring a nation and its governance unit into proper alignment, by any means necessary.[2] In fact, even many of the

people who participated in the movement that resulted in national independence do not appear to have been motivated by nationalism per se. Instead,
they participated for more localized and often personal reasons. For most
white southerners, the acceptance of secession did not result from a positive
embrace of the idea that the South possessed some naturally occurring national identity that mandated national independence. Rather, it resulted from
the conviction that the present Union with the North was so detrimental to
white southerners that it had to be terminated—with the nature of its replace-
ment mattering much less than the necessity that it be replaced.[3] Secession,
in short, was driven more by fear than by nationalist hope.[4]

Throughout the 1850s, and into the secession winter of 1860–61, the
majority of white southerners clung to the Union. They were proud American nationalists who regularly and easily enumerated the benefits of belonging to what they saw as the best country in the world. Yet maintaining
their attachment to the Union became increasingly difficult, beginning
with the sectional discord of 1846–51 and continuing through the Kansas
affair, John Brown's Raid, and finally the secession crisis of 1860–61. Nationalism became problematic for white southerners. It provoked increasing
debate and uncertainty, not only in the formal politics of Washington, D.C.,
and the various state capitals, but also within local communities, families,
and even individuals. Southerners actively engaged with these issues,
thinking carefully and arguing passionately about the underlying concepts
of nationalism, citizenship, union, and disunion.[5] They wove these concepts into the fabric of their lives and personal identities, employing the
language of affection and the metaphor of romance, for instance, to contemplate their shifting attachments to the Union, to their northern compatriots, to their region, and to their states. For many southerners, the bonds
of sympathy and affection that were supposed to join them to northerners
in a harmonious national community were disintegrating, jeopardizing the
value of American nationalism itself.

In the years preceding secession, white southerners felt the "pinch" of
the Union as membership in the United States came to seem more of a
liability than a benefit. This was not a straight road, and the final outcome
of an independent Southern Confederacy was by no means preordained.
Nor was it an easy journey: reevaluating their connections to northerners
and to the United States generated no small measure of sorrow, ambivalence, and friction among white southerners. Nationalism, citizenship,
allegiance—these were becoming ever more important, ever more complicated, ever more painful issues in the antebellum South.

The First Secession Crisis

White southerners confronted fundamental questions about their attachment to the Union during the crisis that began in 1846 and ended in 1851 with the failure of robust secession movements in several southern states. The crisis stemmed from the problem of what the United States ought to do with southwestern lands conquered during the Mexican War. Should the new territories be slave or free? In 1846, before the fighting was even over, the Pennsylvania congressman David Wilmot proposed that any lands gained as a result of the war should not permit slavery. The slaveholding South was appalled. Southern responses ranged across a broad spectrum, from those who favored immediate state-by-state secession, to "cooperationists" who advocated combined action by several southern states, to conditional unionists of varying hues, and, finally, at the end of the spectrum, firm unionists. Thanks to the eventual general acceptance of the Compromise of 1850, the crisis did not result in secession. But it did force secessionists, unionists, and the large majority in between to reflect deeply upon the meanings of nationalism and citizenship.

Midcentury separatists sometimes presented their crusade in terms of active southern nationalism, contending that southerners were so distinct from the North and the rest of the world that they deserved an independent political existence. Thus South Carolina secessionists invoked southern unity: the fact that "their language, tastes, sympathies, [were] the same," as one anonymous author put it, suggested that "they would almost seem to have been marked out by Providence as a people created for an union among themselves, and with no one else." If white southerners possessed a unique national identity, then they deserved, according to prevailing understandings of nationalism, the right to govern themselves as an independent nation-state. Such claims were heard particularly often in the cooperationist camp. The South Carolinian Langdon Cheves was probably the most prominent spokesman of this position, arguing for combined action in the language of romantic southern nationalism. "God and nature," he wrote in 1851, describing southerners as a whole, "have combined them by such social adhesion, such homogeneousness of interests, by such great and benign sympathies, of blood, of character and historical action, as to make their separation deplorable, dangerous and unwise." A unique and shared national identity mandated political independence for the whole South.[6]

Yet such pronouncements of natural, divinely ordained, and blood-based national identity were more often a side-dish to the entrée of secessionist rhetoric: the language of victimhood, humiliation, and oppression. Like the region's long-standing radicals, the "Southern Rights" associations and leaders that sprang up across the midcentury South stressed above all else their shared victimhood at the hands of a hostile North. Their protest comprised several main complaints: that the North threatened the white South's interest in slavery, and therefore the racial order it engendered; that the North exploited the slaveholding South with an unfair economic system; and that the North unjustly denied southerners' right of equal access to federal territory. All of this amounted to a general system of unreasonable oppression in the eyes of many white southerners. To them, the situation seemed serious, even life-threatening. Thus a constituent of South Carolina Governor Whitemarsh Seabrook wrote to him in 1850 of the need to resist the North now; otherwise, "they" would continue to exploit the South economically and raise African Americans up to equality with whites. The danger was so critical, he thought, "that the issues now submitted to the South, are life or death."[7] A resolution delivered at the same cooperationist meeting to which Langdon Cheves had written conveyed a similar sentiment:

> That in view of the humiliating condition of the Slaveholding States in this Confederacy—their rights violated—their Institutions proscribed—their character vilified—their offers of compromise rejected—and in view of the still greater dangers which are impending over them, we believe the time has come when this Union should be dissolved, and a new Government organized on the basis of a Southern Confederacy.

Humiliation, violation, proscription, vilification, rejection—these were the feelings which fuelled the secessionist cause.[8]

These feelings echoed around the midcentury South. "It is a high and sacred duty we owe to ourselves, our country and our children" to preserve southern rights and to resist northern encroachment upon them, a broadside printed by a Southern Rights association in South Carolina declared. If they did not resist, a terrible fate awaited them as "the vassals of the North." Much the same impulse prompted students at the University of Virginia to form their own Southern Rights Association. Despite the fact that the South had contributed disproportionately to the recent victory against Mexico, the students complained in a communication addressed to "the Young Men of the South," southerners were being unfairly excluded from the spoils. "And what has been our reward?" they asked. "To have our institutions branded as infamous, and ourselves treated as strangers and aliens in the land purchased by our treasure and our blood; to be debarred of all the benefits flowing from our rich and costly conquests, and to be cut off from their possession, both we and our heirs, forever." The slaveholding South was under attack, they warned; thanks to the growing northern hostility toward slavery, southerners were becoming "hemmed in."[9]

Even conditional unionists, who stopped short of advocating immediate secession, employed the language of vassalage and humiliation. The Central Southern Rights Association of Virginia was established in 1850 as a vehicle to advance southern interests inside—rather than outside—the Union. But its leaders were animated by the same sense of victimhood that was so central to the secessionist cause. In early 1851 they kicked into organizational high gear, holding meetings, issuing proclamations and resolutions, and so forth. The problem of dependence and inequality vis-à-vis the North was an especially trenchant theme. This was largely an economic problem that spilled into the realm of individual psychology. Southerners were not treated with proper respect, they complained: "We are dependent on the free states for the very necessities of life.—We have become a second Ireland." Perhaps even more cutting to white southerners were the personal ramifications of all of this. "We have ceased to be respected," read one report, "and are only the subjects of ridicule." "We are now tributary in every shape to the North," read another. "They are powerful and arrogant—we are weak and poor. Our rights are not respected. Every mail which reaches us brings fresh accounts of outrages upon Southern rights and Southern citizens." The message was that such a condition was simply unacceptable to southern men—especially Virginian men who could boast such noble revolutionary forebears.[10]

Leaders of the Central Southern Rights Association objected to the "disunionist" label, explaining that their purpose was not to break up the Union but only to seek redress for economic exploitation of the South at the hands of the North, through measures such as direct trade between southern ports and Europe, and the stimulation of southern manufacturing by nonimportation of northern goods. These measures could be carried on within the present Union and did not require secession. Clearly, challenges to American nationalism did not only take the form of outright separatism; allegiance assumed varying shades. In stopping short of active nationalism—the demand for political sovereignty for a clearly defined national community—white southerners were not exceptional in the nineteenth century transatlantic world. Nationalist movements were rarely clear-cut. Groups within multinational states such as the Habsburg Empire and the United Kingdom, for instance, advanced demands for greater autonomy, recognition, or "Home Rule"—solutions that contained strands of nationalism but that did not involve the final step of political independence.[11]

Southerners who opposed secession insisted that although the North had wronged the South, these wrongs had not yet become serious enough to warrant the ultimate reaction. According to the South Carolina moderate William Grayson, secession would produce instability rather than security, and although northern oppressions of the South did exist, they were not yet acute. In any case, being confined to the "social" rather than the "political" sphere, they would never warrant political separation, whatever their intensity. Grayson's critics retorted that he misapprehended both the character and the intensity of northern oppressions. "Have you not been identified with an institution, which has been interdicted?" asked one, making clear that the root of the problem lay in northern hostility to the institution of slavery. "Are not you classed with political lepers? [I]s not your republicanism denied, your equality scouted, your right, as a citizen of Carolina, to go to California, with all your rights as a citizen of Carolina, spurned?" "We desire disunion," wrote another critic,

> that we might be freed from the dominion of a majority, whose political creed is their interest, and whose religion is fanaticism. . . . We consent to our own degradation, when we remain in common bonds with those who regard us as their moral and religious inferiors, and who use the common halls of our government, to give constant expression to that feeling.

As Grayson's critics made clear, the umbrage at being considered inferiors in a relationship that ought to be one of equality helped drive secessionist sentiment during the crisis of midcentury. Grayson may or may not have been correct that northern oppression was more "social" than "political." Even if he was, his critics rejected his assumption that "social" oppressions did not warrant secession. Disrespect in any sphere of life was unacceptable.[12]

Opponents of secession also ventured more positive arguments in favor of the Union. These were sometimes presented in international context.

Grayson himself criticized secessionist attempts to dismantle such a powerful, prosperous Union of the very kind that "Italian and German Patriots" were even then striving to establish. Their federal Union had facilitated peace between the various states—"Nations as they are, with independent State Governments, with various interests"—which was far preferable to the divisive fragmentation of Europe, South America, or the Italian states. The Union gave its members strength and security on the world stage, benefits that would be lost in a new southern confederacy. Grayson's secessionist opponents disagreed, of course, arguing that the Union brought more harm than good to the southern states. One critic rebutted Grayson's international comparisons with one of his own: "Let us be careful, whilst we avoid the obscurity of petty States, that we do not subject ourselves to the tyranny of consolidation. Mexico has shared that fate. England, Scotland and Ireland, are now subject to one central power." Such was the danger that secessionists saw if the South stayed in the current Union.[13]

From his vantage in Paris, William C. Rives, a Virginia unionist serving as U.S. minister to France, saw considerable advantages in the Union's preservation. Rives was delighted to hear the news of the passage of the 1850 compromise measures, writing, "It enables us to hold up our heads here, more erect than ever, in the face of the [predictions] we have heard all around us for the last two months of the approaching dissolution of our glorious fabric of free government." The United States' position as global beacon had been salvaged. Furthermore, the compromise was to be celebrated for "the strong & unshaken attachment it has disclosed in the *body of the people* almost every where to the Union," especially in Virginia. For the people—as opposed to certain troublesome politicians—"loyalty to the Union is, both as a principle & sentiment, deeply rooted in their hearts." In an 1850 letter to a northern politician, Rives expressed gratitude for northern conservatives' commitment to the Union even amid the fanaticism of the abolitionists. He warmly appreciated northerners' "arousing themselves to the dangers of the Republic, & invoking the ancient spirit of brotherhood & the sacred obligations of plighted faith in the cause of the Union." Northerners would have to support such sentiment with adherence to the all-important fugitive slave law, according to Rives. This would help maintain "the invaluable blessings of the union to all its members & the vast issues of civil & political liberty, & social progress throughout the world which depend on its preservation." For Rives, then, the American crisis involved global stakes and called forth a renewal of historic ties of affection and sympathy between compatriots in the North and the South.[14]

As always, the Fourth of July brought alternative visions of nationalism and citizenship into sharp relief. One speaker at an 1851 Independence Day celebration in Mississippi raised the question of whether disunionists "should any longer be protected by the sanctity of the great Political Sabbath of our Freedom," and clearly believed that the answer should be no. Yet that was exactly what seemed to be happening in South Carolina, where celebrations of the holiday appeared to have been deviously hijacked by secessionists. Newspapers in other parts of the South complained about the disunionist tone of some Independence Day celebrations, and also of June 28, South Carolina's "Palmetto Day," which commemorated the Revolutionary Battle of Fort Moultrie. To editors outside of South Carolina, it seemed like sacrilege to use the memory of the American Revolution for "an orgie of Disunion." The Fourth, and the Revolution in general, ought to be used to strengthen the bonds of American nationhood, not to tear them apart.[15]

In this spirit, the majority of white southerners continued to use the holiday to express the hope that the Union could be preserved. In 1849 *Brownlow's Knoxville Whig and Independent Journal*, the mouthpiece of the fiery Tennessee unionist William "Parson" Brownlow, expressed approval of the fact that celebrations of the Fourth remained strong, and urged readers, "in these days of annexation and war, of Wilmot Provisos and threatened Disunion, [to] cling to the glorious arch by which our UNION is sustained, until all factions shall have crumbled under its weight!" The following year, the *Whig* again welcomed the holiday as an occasion when all Americans' patriotism could and should be renewed—a function that seemed ever more urgent as the specter of disunion loomed ever larger. North Carolina politician J. G. Ramsay agreed. On the Fourth of July, 1851, he delivered a speech to celebrate the opening of a new bridge connecting two adjacent counties. Ramsay believed the whole country should take inspiration from this physical demonstration of amity between the two counties; they were "bound together by a common bond of brotherhood, and as the improvements of the age are connecting us more closely together, so should it be with these United States." Casting his understanding of American nationalism in terms of affective bonds, he worried that "the fires of patriotism and affection are growing too faint and cold in the land of Washington," but he dearly hoped that the celebration of the Fourth would "rekindle those flames." The ties of friendship and brotherhood that united all Americans were under pressure, but unionists like Ramsay worked hard for their preservation.[16]

Most white southerners' unionism in the crisis of 1846–51 was not, however, without qualification. Many celebrations of the Fourth in those years were marked by an emphatically conditional unionism: the hope that the Union would survive, but only if southerners could feel assured that their rights were secure within it. This sentiment was evident at Independence Day celebrations across the South. A militia company in Richmond raised its glass collectively in 1851 to several typical toasts: one to the Union, which proclaimed, "We would join our hearts and hands for its preservation, so long as it is worth preserving"; and another to "Our Country," which went on to declare deep loyalty to the Unites States, and the willingness to sacrifice much on its behalf—but which ended with the qualification, "but it must be *without dishonor*."[17]

Such was the stance of those conditional unionists who, in James Hammond's estimation, continued to enjoy a majority even toward the end of the 1850s. This stance had existed at the beginning of the crisis, and it was cemented with southern responses to the Compromise of 1850. The compromise conceded to northerners the admission of California as a free state and the ending of the slave trade in Washington, DC; it gave southerners a strengthened Fugitive Slave Law to facilitate the reenslavement of escaped slaves who fled north; and to both sides it offered the compromise that the fate of slavery in the other southwestern territories would be determined by the will of the local electorate. Far from settling the underlying conflict, northerners and southerners simply agreed to accept partial fulfillment of their particular demands.[18] The compromise made nobody happy—its efficacy lay in the fact that all parties recognized that although they had not gotten what they wanted, nor had anybody else. From the perspective of the mainstream white South, the acceptance of the compromise was predicated upon an ultimatum to the North: southerners had generously agreed to give the Union another chance, but they would not tolerate further trespasses upon their rights. This was the line drawn in the sand by white southerners. If it were crossed, the Union would fall.

Challenges to Affective National Community

By the winter of 1860–61, the line did indeed appear to have been crossed. At the risk of oversimplifying events between 1851 and 1860, this section emphasizes southern anxieties about the disintegration of the affective bonds of sympathy that were seen as a crucial adhesive of national community. White southerners, whether politicians, newspaper editors, writers, or ordinary people, interpreted nationalism and citizenship in personal, everyday ways. Their affective national community seemed threatened by northern attacks on slavery, which southerners often interpreted as attacks on their everyday lives and identities. Southern unionists continued to work for the preservation of the affective bonds of American nationalism, but their task had become more difficult than ever by the beginning of the 1860s. By then, many white southerners were reevaluating their allegiance to the United States, and secession was becoming more widely palatable.

In reflecting upon this process themselves, white southerners often employed the language of affection, friendship, brotherhood, and even romance. From the beginning of the United States, some Americans—including prominent southern Republicans James Madison and Thomas Jefferson—had advanced a plan of Union based on affective bonds of sympathy or brotherhood, in contrast to what they saw as the more contractual, interest-driven union of the Federalists.[19] These affective bonds went on to inform antebellum conceptions of what held a large nation together. At the center of southern radicals' critique of American nationalism lay the contention that Americans were united only by politics or interest, and not by affection or kinship. Without the latter, it was believed, national community could hardly be said to exist at all. One of the clearest spokesmen for this position was William Gilmore Simms. Writing to a fellow southern novelist in 1851, Simms put a slightly different spin on his usual argument that Americans had never enjoyed true national bonds at all. In this particular letter, he wrote that Americans had once enjoyed such bonds but that they had subsequently been destroyed. The abolitionists, he explained, had "utterly subverted the only bond (that of sympathy) by which the people of our separate sections were ever truly held together. Common cause, common necessities, and the belief in a common feeling—these were the true articles of confederation." Feeling, sentiment, and affection were seen by many of Simms's contemporaries as the proper bonds of nationalism. Later in the decade, to provide just one example, a speaker at the University of North Carolina reminded his audience of an axiom attributed to an English statesman: "*The cement of reciprocal esteem and regard can alone bind together the parts of this great fabric.*" Such, according to this speaker and many others, was also true of the American nation in the 1850s. To the extent that these bonds of affection deteriorated, so too would the national community.[20]

Along with the language of affection came the metaphor of romance. When New Yorker William Peirce moved to Mississippi for several years in the 1850s, he could not escape the impingement of the sectional conflict upon his personal and romantic life. His father was against slavery and, therefore, the South. Peirce himself expressed derision for secessionists. None of that, though, stopped him from falling in love with a southern woman. Even so, their opposing regional origins ultimately doomed the relationship, with each being unwilling to leave permanently their own section and live in the other—"Her Scylla was Northern life," as Peirce put it; "my Charybdis was Southern life." In reporting the breakup to his sister, Peirce could not resist drawing parallels to deteriorating relations between North and South. "We have dissolved the union," he wrote—"this great and glorious republic consecrated by the blood of our fathers and the prayers of our mothers is dissolved—is seperated into a north and a south." Their personal problem had been caused by the same "question of north or south that has vexed Congress and the country for thirty years or more—and is still vexing it. But they can neither settle the question nor dissolve the Union. We have succeeded in doing the latter." As William Peirce told it, the sectional conflict both caused and was paralleled by his doomed intersectional romance.[21]

Peirce was not alone in drawing connections between personal love affairs and the conflict between North and South. Indeed, James M. Smythe wrote a lengthy novel on this very topic. Smythe's *Ethel Somers; or, The Fate of the Union* followed such works as *Uncle Tom's Cabin* in dramatizing the sectional conflict for its readers. In this case, though, the novel favored the South, not the North, and, rather than slavery, it took as its main theme relations across the Mason-Dixon line between white Americans. The story revolves around Edward Clinton, a well-heeled New Yorker who falls in love with an archetypal southern belle, Ethel Somers. Among other complications, their love is frustrated by the strained relations between their respective regions. Though Clinton is not at all an abolitionist, he does find slavery mildly distasteful. Unfortunately, due to the stormy sectional climate, even this is more than his beloved—the daughter of a southern-rights-supporting Mississippi planter—can accept.

At first, the connection between national politics and his love life seems odd to Clinton. When Somers responds ambivalently to his declaration of love, she explains her hesitation with the words "I was thinking of my country" (by "country" she means the South). Puzzled, Clinton asks, "What has your country to do with my love for you?" Before long, though, he becomes painfully aware that in this budding intersectional courtship, national affairs and personal relationships are inseparably intertwined. Updating his cousin on the situation, Clinton reveals that "love and politics are so intimately connected, that I am at a loss to know how to separate them." Herein lies the novel's major premise—that sectional relations depended upon personal affections—and that, as the subtitle of the novel suggests, "the fate of the Union" rested upon the ability of these fictional young lovers and their real-life counterparts to sustain their romances. As a northern friend tells Ethel Somers, "The difference between you and Edward is the difference between the South and the North. As it may be reconciled between you and him, so it may be between the two sections."

After almost four hundred pages, numerous plot twists, engagements, deaths, and several other intersectional pairings, Edward Clinton and Ethel Somers manage to overcome the sectional problem and (one presumes) go on to live happily ever after as husband and wife. Not a subtle novel, it concludes by reiterating the moral of the story: "And now, as the love of woman inspired one to search for truth, and removed the barriers to individual union and happiness, so let the love of our glorious Union produce results as happy for states and people." Affection, sentiment, and love, in other words, ought to replace animosity in North-South relations as in private romances. The conviction that affection was the surest bond of national unity, then, inspired this work of fiction just as it inspired the proclamations of southern intellectuals like Simms.[22]

Ethel Somers sharply contrasts the society of the slave South against the free-labor North—unfavorably, of course, to the North. Just as it personifies the sectional conflict in the figures of two young lovers, the novel also dramatizes the ostensibly personal issue of proper gender roles and imbues them with sectional meaning. Thus one of the book's more radical southern partisans, Judge Mortimer, draws a line between North and South in terms of appropriate gender roles:

> We have no women lecturers, no women's-rights conventions here. This usurpation of pantaloons in this country is confined to the free states. . . . Women were made to reign in private, and every departure from the modesty of this rule weakens the purity and sanctity of her power, and of course the bands of virtue, decency, and the good order of society. Nature made them women, and condemned them to petticoats.

And that, thought Mortimer, was precisely as it should be.[23]

For a range of nonfictional southern spokesmen as well, civilization itself rested on appropriate gender roles and relations. While the slave South was maintaining the proper order of things, the North, and sometimes the rest of the Western world, was not. In his 1856 graduation address to the Virginia Military Institute, George Rumbough explained that free society was foolish to question the natural, divinely ordained order of things. Listing the dangerous "isms" he saw to the north, Rumbough included women's rights, Bloomerism, and Free-Loveism, along with socialism, atheism, and abolitionism. The North's distorted ideas about slavery were not only tied up with its misguided ideas about religion, liberty, and government, but also with its foolish misconceptions of manhood and womanhood. Rumbough contrasted the South, "where woman, the most powerful, the purest, noblest element of society, is considered as an object of love," with the North, where woman "is viewed as an object of distrust, and far from beautifying, transcends the boundries of modesty and decency, and sighs for an MD suffix or the transcendant reputation of a philanthropic lecturer." One of many advantages of basing a society on slavery rather than free labor, according to Rumbough and others, was that the institution safeguarded hierarchies of gender as well as of race.[24]

Southern fears about gender proprieties illustrate how urgent the sectional conflict could become when it appeared to enter the realm of the home and family. One Virginia farmer, writing to a local newspaper in 1854, expressed just such fears. Responding to rumors that a female preacher had been plying her trade in the area, the farmer expressed first disbelief and then sharp anxiety. "Some hundreds are right uneasy about their wives," he wrote. "They are afraid that some of them womens rights folks, from the N., are traveling among us, and that some wives are encouraging them." Even an antislavery fanatic would be more acceptable than a feminist, thought the letter-writer. "One would spoil our negroes, but the other would spoil our wives and sweethearts, and either, would be made a bad piece of property." Perhaps intending that his readers should take the loaded word "insurrection" with a grain of salt (the word was strongly associated with slave revolts in the antebellum South) the farmer concluded: "It is feared that there will be an insurrection among the women, and that they will begin to chew tobacco and drink whiskey." Likewise, the North Carolina congressman David Outlaw recoiled at the apparent immorality of the society he encountered in Washington, DC. In Outlaw's eyes, it was the behavior of northern women there that caused moral deterioration. "There is a boldness," he wrote to his wife, "[a] brazenfacedness about

Northern city women, as well as a looseness of morals which I hope may never be introduced south." In this way those white southerners who worried about such matters sectionalized anxieties about moral decline, projecting those anxieties onto their image of the North.[25]

Seemingly divergent patterns of gender roles and relations indicated profound moral differences that seriously threatened the affective American national community. Though it might be possible to compromise on purely political matters, such a compromise was not feasible when it came to the sectional conflict's moral dimensions. In southern eyes, northerners were performing so badly in this regard that they were fatally threatening the bonds of sympathy that had formerly held the American nation together. Fundamental moral difference implied that North and South had developed different national identities. Once that conclusion was reached, the principle of nationality itself mandated separation.

As contemporaries recognized, this made the religious schisms of the 1840s even more disquieting. Long before the political secession of the southern states—even before the South's midcentury attempt at secession—the three major protestant denominations in the United States had each split into two. The Presbyterian schism, which took place in the late 1830s, involved sectional differences over slavery, and slavery was even more important to the Methodist and Baptist schisms in 1844 and 1845, respectively. As Benjamin Morgan Palmer explained in a sermon in November 1860, while he did not ordinarily address politics from the pulpit, the conflict over slavery was an appropriate topic, since it "was in its origin a question of morals and religion." The radical drift of northern religion came to symbolize fundamental social, cultural, and political difference. "The [northern] churches," one Alabama newspaper article warned, "are converted into Jacobin clubs, where sedition, violence and civil commotion are systematically and earnestly inculcated."[26]

Because antebellum Americans conceived of their nationalism in moral and religious terms, the splitting of the churches did not bode well for future national unity. Worrying about political disunion in the late 1850s, the Virginia lawyer and politician Robert F. Mercer could not help but think about the religious schisms. "A separation of the States, is among the events to be dreaded," he wrote, and explained that "it has been begun, in several of the largest religious sects." This did not augur well for the fate of political union, he thought, since "it was to the religious character of our people that we looked for the preservation of our Union: a Union that every days reflection tells me is the only safeguard of our liberty."[27] The survival of the nation depended upon each citizen living a moral and a pious life. But how could a national community—a sacred national community—be expected to endure if northerners and southerners could no longer worship within the same religious organizations? How could it endure if their very conceptions of morality and piety were diverging?

In the face of this worrying drift, southern unionist clergymen pushed back, pointing to the many advantages of membership in the United States and warning against the dangers of disunion. In Roswell, Georgia, N. A. Pratt's 1856 Thanksgiving sermon maintained that it would be madness to allow the Union to fall. Pratt blamed sectional extremists for inciting discord, but he believed that the underlying problem was divine disfavor. Americans had been "a rebellious nation, a sinful people, and God brings us under the discipline of the Rod." They ought to renew their religious commitment in order to save the Union. "I do most religiously believe," Pratt explained, invoking the common vision of America as a global beacon, "that nothing but the Union of these States, under God, has preserved us from similar evils; and our country, at the present moment, under all our causes of uneasiness and complaint, stands forth to the admiring and envying gaze of mankind, the freest, the happiest, and by far the most prosperous nation on the face of the globe." He asked his listeners to compare the security and prosperity afforded by the American Union with the fragmented state of South America. Such would be the fate, he cautioned, of a divided America.[28]

Unionist politicians were just as concerned as the clergy about the deterioration of affective American nationalism. The demise of the Whig Party in the early 1850s—the result of a number of causes, including slavery—was a political analog of the religious schisms. For almost two decades the Second Party System had helped unite Americans across sectional borders, promoting national links of sympathy and affection. But by the mid 1850s, only the Democratic Party remained as a stable national political party. Democratic politicians clung to it as a means of preserving the Union. Accepting the party's nomination for Georgia governor in 1855, Herschel V. Johnson celebrated southern Democrats' ties to their northern allies as the best way to safeguard the Union: "If we stand by them," he wrote, "we can sustain them; and with their co-operation, the South *may* maintain her rights *in* the Union." Without the friendship of northern Democrats, though, his dream of safeguarding both the Union and southern rights would become hopeless. In a speech in Baltimore the following year,

Johnson again pointed to the Democratic Party as a bond of Union and insisted to his countrymen that "the patriotism of this land, North, South, East, and West" must be exercised in order to preserve the Union. If northern Democrats did not continue to respect the rights of their southern friends, even if they were to "preserve the Union in name, still it will be destroyed in fact, the bond of brotherhood will have been severed." For Johnson, as for so many others, the "bond of brotherhood" was vital to the perpetuation of the Union.[29]

Other conservatives, north and south, also worked hard to maintain the affective bonds of American nationalism. William C. Rives continued to fight for the Union throughout the decade. Writing to a former northern Whig colleague in the summer of 1859, Rives agreed with him that the divisive issue of slavery had no place in national politics. Instead, politicians in all parts of the country should concentrate on more constructive issues, thus "binding together by the ties of interest & fraternal feeling the various parts & sections of our widely extended Republic."[30]

As Rives and his northern associate recognized, slavery lay at the heart of North-South difference and threats to American nationalism. This was often a simple case of economic interest: since the cotton boom that began in the post-Revolutionary decades, the South's economy had rested more than ever upon slavery, and therefore any challenge to its stability had to be resisted. Even those who did not actually own slaves themselves found compelling economic and political reasons to desire the maintenance of the slaveholding regime.[31] Even more pertinent here is white southerners' psychological investment in slavery and the race relations it supported—an investment so deep that the abolition of slavery became the white South's worst nightmare. Because African Americans were slaves—the lowest of the low—all southern whites could feel themselves equal members of the superior race. To many white southerners, abolition would entail the raising to equality of African Americans, the end of white supremacy, and, perhaps, violent race war. Even if things did not go quite that far, the specter of racial equality was bad enough. Racial fears were crucial to the unraveling of American nationalism. White southerners began to see a gulf between their commitment to white supremacy and white northerners' apparent challenges to it, or in some cases white northerners' preference for a different version of white supremacy, one that sought to exclude African Americans altogether. As this gulf appeared to expand, the sentiment of national community declined.[32]

White southerners' fears often encompassed not just interracial political equality but social equality and sometimes even interracial sex as well. Such was the concern of Benjamin Perry, an upcountry South Carolina politician who was a consistent unionist and defender of poorer voters against the planter elite. The North's stance in the conflict over the territories, he complained, sought to make the black slave "the equal of his master" and "to go with him to the polls and vote, to serve on juries . . . to meet the white man as an equal and visit his family, intermarry with his children and form one society and one family." Even for a man who remained committed to the Union, this merging of sexual and racial fears rendered northern hostility toward slavery a serious matter indeed.[33]

Fears of racial turmoil became especially acute following John Brown's October 1859 raid on the federal armory at Harper's Ferry, Virginia, with the intention of initiating a slave revolt. The raid failed, and Brown was executed, but his attempt sent shivers across the slaveholding South. The apparently widespread sympathy the raid attracted in the North galvanized white southerners, persuading them that northern aggressions had reached a crisis point. "The Harper's Ferry affair," Virginia politician John C. Rutherfoord noted in his diary, "has had the fortunate effect of revealing to the people of the white South, as if by one vivid flash of light, the true character of that danger" that John C. Calhoun had foreseen and cautioned against. But the most alarming aspect of this most alarming event, for Rutherfoord and for many others, was the broad northern support it seemed to have enjoyed. The raid was not the work of Brown alone, he thought, but rather was the logical consequence of Republican Party–style opposition to slavery, which was becoming increasingly popular across the northern states. Rutherfoord interpreted Brown's raid as being symptomatic of a broader and an increasingly dangerous northern hostility toward the slaveholding South.[34]

Another Virginian used different imagery to express a similar idea. In a letter to a northern friend, Nathaniel Cabell wrote, "It was as if an intrusive reptile should strike at the heel of a man who, suspecting nothing, was walking peacefully in his own garden," and the man subsequently discovered that the reptile had been placed there by a friend. Again, a relationship that should have been characterized by mutual affection was perceived instead as one marked by hostility and betrayal.[35] Another Virginian, the small-scale farmer, merchant, and teacher Elliott Story, reported in his diary that Brown's raid had generated considerable excitement in his community, and worried "that these events will have a weighty tendency to weaken the bonds of our Union."[36]

The same concerns prompted the Central Southern Rights Association of Virginia to reconvene, apparently for the first time in more than five years. Though they were undecided about how exactly to respond to Brown's raid, they agreed in late November that "calling a Convention of all the Southern States with the view of forming a Southern confederation" should, at the very least, be an option. By mid-December, the association was busy writing to the state legislature a letter that complained about northern aggressions and urged retaliatory action. The burning sense of resentment at perceived affronts was palpable. "Adding insult to theft and confiscation," read the memorial, "they have slandered the owners of the property they have stolen or destroyed, and by epithet and invective, by ridicule and vituperation, by caricature and falsehood and all the artillery of calumny and abuse, they have sought to traduce and degrade us in the eyes of the world." This was the language of honor and shame that historians have seen as being so central to antebellum southern culture.[37]

Reactions to Brown's raid were especially impassioned in Virginia, the state where Brown had made his attempt. But even for white southerners many miles away from Harper's Ferry, the incident set alarm bells ringing. In South Carolina, the state senate passed resolutions stating that "the assaults upon the institution of slavery, and upon the rights and equality of the Southern States," had only intensified in recent years.[38] In a private letter, D. H. Hamilton, a South Carolinian correspondent of William Porcher Miles, was equally worried. Even though Hamilton did not yet consider southern independence the best remedy, he was certainly not happy with the current state of affairs. It was becoming increasingly evident that the South must prepare to resist snowballing northern aggression. "John Brown was a type of his class," wrote Hamilton, "a sturdy fanatic, without humanity, without mercy." There would be more, Hamilton warned, where he had come from. "The South," he concluded, "is almost entirely hemmed in and nothing is left to us but desperate fighting."[39]

In addition to the approving wink the raid seemed to receive from such a broad sector of northern society, the Brown affair seemed so ominous because it threatened white southerners on a personal level. This is captured perfectly in a December 1859 letter written by northern-born Mississippi resident Stephen Duncan to his northern business agent. Abstract dangers to the South were one thing, he wrote. "But when our *real, tangible rights* are not only threatened in the worst shape, but *absolutely invaded,*" it made "every man owning slave property—a *true Southerner* in *feeling & action.*" The threat of northern abolitionists entering southern territory and whipping up an armed slave insurrection was, understandably, terrifying. Even though Duncan stressed the threat to slaveholders, it seems likely that nonslaveholding white southerners would also have been terrified by the prospect of a violent uprising. As Duncan indicated, this prospect represented a much more immediate threat to white southerners than the issue of whether slavery would be permitted in territories hundreds of miles to the west. It reinforced and personalized the sense of being under siege.[40]

Despite the gravity of this threat, southerners' attachment to the United States still endured. This was apparent in the Kentucky House of Representatives on December 19, 1859, just seventeen days after the execution of John Brown. The Reverend James Craik addressed the House that day, reminding state legislators of "the national character which, by a long course of Providential training, God had impressed upon the people of this country, as the meet preparation for a great and glorious mission." He also thanked God for the American system of federalism, which he thought should ensure harmony between the different component parts of the Union. Because of federalism, disunion was unnecessary; because of the divinely ordained mission of the American people, disunion would be a grave sin. Rehearsing the common unionist position that a minority of extremists on both sides were manipulating the moderate majority, Craik declared, "Take away the fanatical disunionists, North and South, and there is not a citizen of the United States whose patriotic feelings do not correspond to this historical fact. There is not a citizen who does not say and feel, THE UNITED STATES IS MY COUNTRY."[41]

Craik's brand of unequivocal unionism certainly persisted after Brown's raid, but it was becoming an increasingly difficult position to hold. A few weeks after the raid, a correspondent of Virginia unionist William C. Rives wrote, "I have never heretofore been at all apprehensive of the continued existence of our Federal Union—but I must confess, that the morbid sympathy manifested recently by many of the papers and individuals North of us in behalf of those engaged in the Harper's Ferry foray have cast a gloom over the future, more thundering and alarming, than ever before darkened the fate of our Republic." Rives shared these concerns. Writing to another political associate that December, he affirmed his ongoing commitment to the Union but agonized over the expressions of northern opposition to slavery that had followed Brown's raid. "I yet believe," he sadly concluded, "that neither the Constitution nor the Union can resist many such shocks."[42]

The uncertainty of even firm unionists like Rives indicates the gravity of these threats to Americans' affective national unity. In the face of mounting evidence that northerners were destroying the amity of American nationalism, white southerners reevaluated their commitment to the Union. They responded in a variety of ways—with changing political alliances, with the metaphor of personal romance, with anxieties about gender relations and the racial order. Through it all, the majority retained the conditional unionism that had crystallized during the first secession crisis. But with the threat to southern slavery, southern security, and southern honor that was revealed by Brown's raid, the advantages of American nationalism seemed ever more tenuous. As the Union continued to pinch, white southerners found it more and more difficult to cling on.

The Collapse of the Union

The ultimate pinches of the Union would come with the November 1860 election of Abraham Lincoln—which precipitated the secession of the seven southernmost states—and Lincoln's call for troops following the April 1861 bombardment of Fort Sumter—which in turn prompted the vacillating middle South states of North Carolina, Virginia, Tennessee, and Arkansas to secede as well. White southerners believed they were witnessing the culmination of an incremental disintegration of affective American nationalism. They viewed these events through the lens of personalized besiegement and with a sense of betrayal by former compatriots. Even though northern attacks upon slavery were still more prospective than actual, increasing numbers of white southerners believed that they constituted attacks upon themselves, and become so disillusioned with the Union that secession came to seem an attractive option.

The sense of impending upheaval was evident across the South as the fateful election approached. Sarah Lois Wadley, a Louisiana teenager, confided her interpretation of the developing situation to her diary. By late October, 1860, the sectional conflict had affected her in a number of ways. Her teacher, suspected of holding abolitionist sympathies, had left town. But most striking of all is her palpable personal investment in the burgeoning drama of secession. Wadley hoped that the Union would not fall, especially since she herself was of New England origin and southern residence. Even so, she could not help but worry that "the Union is but a name, there is no concord, no real heart Union any longer." "No real heart Union"—here in the words of a girl a month shy of her sixteenth birthday was precisely that break in the bonds of affection which, to Simms and other more formal theorists of nationalism, spelled the end of national unity. Behind Wadley's judgment was precisely that sense of personal peril that drove so many white southerners toward disunion. "The Abolitionists have sowed the seeds of dissension and insurrection among us," she wrote, referring to the rumors of slave arson and insurrection that swept the secessionist South; "those seeds are fast ripening and a bloody harvest seems impending; they have burnt our homesteads, killed our citizens, and incited our servants to poison us." In Wadley's repeated use of the word "our," in contrast to the "they" referring to the abolitionists, we can recognize a powerful sense of identification with a southern community that was being brought together by northern attacks. For Wadley, northerners and southerners were no longer united in national community. Despite her New England heritage, she concluded, "We can no longer claim them as brothers."[43]

Southern politicians capitalized on such feelings in promoting seces-sion. For the Alabama congressman Jabez L. M. Curry, the ascendancy of the Republican Party in the North signaled the end of affective union and should mean the end of political union too. "The bond of brotherhood between the North and the South," he told a Talladega audience in late November, "so far as political parties are concerned, is broken." The new party had sundered the regional friendship. Such was the inevitable out-come of a situation in which "Southern States and citizens of those States, because of the possession of slave property, are stigmatized and *pilloried* and reduced to inferiority." For Curry as for Wadley, as for countless white southerners in the winter of 1860–61, northern insults and attacks had simply gone too far. Curry even quoted a "northern writer" in describing the extent of the Republican Party's threat to southern life: "It threatens . . . with fire and sword every southern hearth, with death every southern man, and with dishonor every southern female, amid a saturnalia of blood." Curry's claim that northern attacks were not confined to the abstract polit-ical sphere—but instead directly threatened the home, the hearth, south-ern women, and every individual southern white man—reveals the emotional intensity that characterized much secessionist rhetoric. It was time to act, he insisted.[44]

Bombarded by such messages, many white southern men responded with martial bravado. In mid-December Waddy Butler wrote from Florida to his fiancée, Lucy Wood, who lived in Virginia. Butler was pleased to report on the general secession fever in Florida: "Every man, woman, and child in the State desire secession," he explained, "and are perfectly willing to fight in the 'cause.'" His words were energized by the heady combination of a widespread sense of being under assault from the North and the typical bluster of the affianced young male. "We are anxious for a bout with the North," he wrote, "and I believe we shall not be disappointed." Butler made clear that he felt personally invested in this conflict. "I shall rejoice beyond all measure," he boasted to his fiancée, "should there arise an opportunity of revenging some of the injustices and insults received by the South at the hands of the North. Should that opportunity ever come the Southern people will give their 'brethren' good cause to remember the day." Just like the teenaged Sarah Lois Wadley, Butler considered the former relationship of affection between "brethren" to be over. In his case, these feelings were compounded by his desire to prove his young manhood to his fiancée and the world.[45]

White men across the lower South perceived and pursued the same opportunity that winter. Associations of "minute men"—a term that deliberately recalled noble Revolutionary forebears—sprang up everywhere, vowing to defend the South against northern invaders. They convened regularly, complained of the slurs and injuries they were sustaining, and armed themselves, projecting a regimented, military image with their uniforms, their blue cockades, and other paraphernalia.[46] Advertisements for meetings of militia companies filled the pages of newspapers like the *Charleston Mercury*. The sentiment and the display of male bravado pervaded the whole region, involving men of all ages. William Gilmore Simms, in his mid-fifties by this time, was frustrated at not being in the proper physical condition to participate fully in the martial fervor. He likened himself to "a bear with a sore head, & chained to the stake. I chafe, and roar & rage, but can do nothing."[47] At the other end of the age spectrum were the boys, eager to join the fray. "How strange, how romantic life is now in Charleston! Almost every man is now dressed in some uniform," reported one of Caroline Howard Gilman's daughters in early 1861. She went on to convey the extent of the martial fervor with a haunting image of children playing at war: "Even the boys are arming," she wrote, "with little bodies, but with faces looking fixed and old like those of the men."[48]

The media as well as politicians fueled this mood of aggrieved bellicosity. Jingoistic poems filled the pages of newspapers and were reprinted
time and time again. Consider "The Southern Marseillaise," for instance,
which urged "sons of the South" to "awake to glory!" to protect their nearest and dearest ("Your children, wives, and grandsires hoary") against a
menacing enemy ("reckless fanatics . . . mongrel hosts . . . a thieving
band"). Also typical was "The Rally of the South," which appealed to "gallant men of Southern blood" to heed the warning signs of "fanatics insane
and ranging" and join together, "our country and our homes to save." The
message of this popular poetry was clear: the North represented an urgent
and immediate threat to white southern men's homes, families, wives,
and sense of personal honor. The time had come to stand up and fight.⁴⁹

Virginia politician and firebrand Henry A. Wise was particularly em-
phatic in connecting sectional politics to personal masculinity. Writing to
a political associate in January 1861, Wise worried about his state's lack of
active resistance. "I see how it all is," he wrote; "we are emasculated." This
was not the only time he cast white southern manhood as being at stake in
the sectional conflict. In one speech Wise vividly brought home to southern men the threat that northern aggressions posed to their individual and
group masculinities. Of everything they had to fear, he warned his fellow
Virginian men, by far the worst was "the peril *of not being found true to
ourselves.*" Invoking the language of "*shame and dishonor*"—which could
be applied to either individual southern men or to the South as a whole—
Wise went on to indict the Republican Party for a variety of crimes. The
most important charge was that they had fanned the flames of northern
hostility toward the South, encouraging northerners to, in Wise's words,
"malign our character, and so to contemn us as to pluck the very beard of
our manhood and self respect." If the language of shame and honor did
not make it clear enough, Wise's metaphorical "beard of our manhood"
made his point unmistakable. The northern menace was a direct threat to
southern masculinity.⁵⁰

In taking this tack, Wise was not alone. Playing up the personal,
domestic, and immediate nature of the northern threat was a common
technique, especially among politicians and newspaper editors. Readers of
the *Richmond Enquirer* that winter could scarcely avoid such appeals. In
addition to poetry, readers' letters, and editorials, there were reports of
public meetings held across the state to discuss the crisis. Throughout
these features ran a common thread: the conviction that northern aggression threatened Virginians' homes, families, and personal rights. An

announcement to "the Young Men of Lunenburg County" began with the following arresting statement: "Our homes are being invaded." "Our parents," it went on, "whose heads are blooming for the grave, are being foully insulted. . . . The virtue of our beloved sisters is being slandered." Casting the danger so close to home was surely intended to encourage readers to view the threat seriously indeed.[51]

Another *Enquirer* article reprinted the proceedings of a public meeting in Botetourt County. Virginia deserved equality within the Union, but did not, almost everyone present agreed, receive it. Echoing the common assumption that true national unity depended upon mutual affection, the Botetourt citizens complained that "in all the private relations of life instead of fraternal regard a 'consuming hate' which has but seldom characterized warring nations" existed. The sectional divide was created not just by politics in Washington, then, but also by the lack of affection in "all the private relations of life." Perhaps most important of all, this deterioration of affection literally threatened the lives of individual Virginians. The Botetourt meeting pointedly referred to Brown's raid as evidence. It was simply unacceptable that there had been not only a "hostile incursion upon [southern] soil" but also "an apotheosis of the murderers." John Brown, and the sympathy he had aroused at the North, reminded these Virginians that a Union without mutual affection, esteem, and respect was a Union that threatened their very survival.[52]

The fear of northern abolitionist-inspired slave uprisings haunted the South that winter, as it had done for much of the preceding year.[53] Back in Virginia, a group of Amelia County citizens were concerned that a local arsonist represented the arrival in their own vicinity of the deadly ramifications of the sectional conflict. A slave convicted of setting fires had been treated leniently by the county court. That decision was a worrying one, in the eyes of some locals—worrying enough for them to assemble on November 24 and issue formal resolutions protesting the acquittal. It set a bad example, they thought, and could only encourage further slave disobedience. They stood "ready to protect our fire-sides and property from the torch of the incendiary." What seems to have made the whole incident especially disturbing were its apparent connections to the broader sectional crisis. "The offence is in perfect keeping with Helper's notorious incendiary publication," one resolution read, referring to a southern-authored critique of slavery that had been enthusiastically received by the Republican Party—and roundly condemned by the slaveholding South. These concerned citizens interpreted the slave's actions as "bringing upon us the 'irrepressible conflict,' with all its consequent horrors." The malfeasant slave, in other words, brought the sectional conflict home to these citizens, connecting their personal, everyday existence with formerly abstract political events.[54]

Southern men responded with belligerent bluster. From across the South, they rushed in droves to newly forming volunteer companies. The motivations for these companies were often laid out at highly orchestrated sending-off ceremonies in which various sectors of the community would join together to express their commitment to the secessionist cause. A particularly rich example comes from Newberry, South Carolina, in January 1861. Like so many similar occasions, this one was full of potent connections between the broad issues of national allegiance and identity, on the one hand, and the personal lives and identities of the people responding to those issues, on the other. As the soldiers were leaving town for the army, local women presented them with a flag they had made. The flag and the ceremonies surrounding its presentation made clear why the men were doing what they were doing, and what part the women played. "Our Homes we Guard" was the motto on the flag. The women had written a speech to present along with it—but the speech was actually delivered by a male attendee, presumably to preserve appropriate gender roles. The speech set the image of men going off to fight to defend their women at home within a long historical pattern, one that stretched back to ancient Sparta. The women clearly viewed the men's task as a grave responsibility that had to be borne—not an opportunity that could be declined. At points their words challenged the men to fulfill their roles and live up to their side of the gender bargain: "Will you not prove *worthy* sons of a *noble* ancestry?" they asked, and went on to urge, "Be *brave then* and show yourselves *men*." As was happening all over the South, the white people of Newberry were navigating the changing claims of national identity and allegiance as a community, making sense of the new situation with reference to their personal lives, values, and relationships.[55]

Gender roles in this and other flag presentations were carefully circumscribed. Yet questions such as "Will you not prove *worthy* sons?" suggest that white women might, in the new circumstances, be prepared to challenge male authority. If men turned out to be incapable of discharging their duties—if they failed to uphold their end of the gender bargain— women gave notice that they would be held to account. Such moments revealed the possibility, at least, for new kinds of female interventions in politics during the secession crisis. Remembering the legendary contributions of their female forebears to the American Revolution, some women called for boycotts of northern goods, or suggested that southern women should use their domestic skills to economize during the crisis.[56] Other women submitted patriotic poems to southern newspapers, such as "C. B. J.," who introduced an ode entitled "Sons of the South!" with a challenge to the manhood of Virginia men. Like the women of Newberry, "C. B. J." goaded males on with a thinly veiled challenge to their manhood: "If any of the luke-warm *sons* of the 'Old Dominion,' find themselves wanting in the courage or resolution necessary to defend her rights," she wrote, "they may learn both from her *daughters*." From the very beginning, then, white southern women issued a warning: if their men wished to enjoy the privileges of manhood, they would have to live up to its responsibilities. The question of whether they would succeed would persist throughout the war, and beyond.

"Sons of the South!" exemplifies a body of popular poetry that flooded newspapers during the secession winter. The poem captures the major themes promoted by secessionists in both the upper and lower South. It began, "Sons of our glorious Southern land, / Home of the free and brave," and went on to urge those sons to rise up to confront what was portrayed as a direct threat to their domestic lives, "our hearths and homes to save" from the menace of former "Brethren" turned "traitors" who "crush our nearest, dearest rights, / Our household gods overthrow." The poem also reminded readers of the severity and immediacy of Brown's raid, emphasizing northern support for abolitionist "martyrs," and suggesting that further, even more serious invasions of the South were imminent.

The final stanza made another domestic appeal, one which also drew strength from its direct link to white southerners' personal identities. "Shall we thus tamely bide," the poet asked, "the loss of all the dearest rights, / For which our fathers died?" The memory of the American Revolution, as these lines suggest, could promote resistance to the North not just on an intellectual level but also on a more emotional, familial level that played on men's perceived responsibility to live up to their fathers— whether those fathers were literal or figurative. In a variety of ways, then, the rhetoric of secessionist propaganda was designed to appeal to white southerners' personal identities and everyday lives.[57]

To be sure, there were those in the upper and lower South who advocated secession on more rational, material grounds. This could either mean the simple protection of southerners' investment in slavery, or the expectation that manufacturing interests in the upper South could benefit more from union with the South than with the North: "Our customers are

in the South," observed one prosecession delegate at the Virginia secession convention, "our rivals in the North."[58]

There were those, too, who employed the rhetoric of a naturally occurring national identity that united the slaveholding states of the South into
a single community, a community that required national independence.
The same Virginia delegate contended,

> There are moral, as well as industrial and political considerations,
> which unmistakably point us to the South. There is to be found our
> own form of society; there are our nearest kindred; there are the
> habits and institutions of our own people; there we may wield the
> noblest form of power—a moral and intellectual dominion; there
> we may improve and perpetuate our own peculiar type of civiliza-
> tion; there we may build up a splendid Confederacy, homogenous
> in its feelings and its interests—a Confederacy that will change the
> moral sentiment of the world in reference to slavery.

Another delegate used the oft-repeated phrase "bone of our bone and flesh
of our flesh" to characterize what he saw as a united national identity that,
according to the principle of nationality, deserved expression in political
independence. This echoed the romantic, ethnic nationalism that had
become popular in Europe.[59]

In January 1861, Virginia politician R. M. T. Hunter analyzed the
upper South's situation in *De Bow's Review*. The secession of the lower
South was now a fact, he explained, and so the choice faced by the upper
South was not between union and disunion but whether to remain in
the old union with the North or to join the new one with the lower South.
In weighing those options, Hunter felt that economic imperatives, combined with the fact that the upper South shared more culturally with the
states to the south than those to the north, pulled the upper South toward
the new confederacy. But he was also careful to impress his audience
with the social dimension of the situation. In addition to the other advantages, the upper South would enter the new southern union as
equals. "We should enter into a government," as he put it, "whose constituents are bound together by common interests and sympathies, and
who treat each other with mutual respect." They ought also to belong to
a polity in which "our social system"—a common euphemism for slavery—was not "dwarfed and warred upon by the action of the government." If the upper South chose to remain in Union with the North, they

would do so in a minority, as inferiors. The ramifications would be dev-astating. "Who would voluntarily place a son in such a position?" asked Hunter.

> Humbled by the stamp of inferiority, placed upon him by his gov-ernment, conscious that he was attached to a political system from whose honor he was excluded by the circumstances of his position, and a member of a social system which was assailed and dwarfed by his own government, then it would not be long before he would lose, together with his sense of equality, that spirit of independence to which manhood owes its chief grace and its power.

Honor, equality, manhood—all were at stake in this decision, according to Hunter, and all had been endangered by union with the North.[60]

Even though the secession of the lower and upper South happened at different points in time and with different catalysts, they shared a common set of motivations. Southerners' material attachment to slavery should not be underestimated, nor secessionists' positive appeals to romantic south-ern nationalism. But key to the widespread acceptance of secession were fears about the breakdown of affective community and the apparent incur-sion of northern antislavery into the realm of the domestic and the per-sonal. As white southerners reevaluated American nationhood, they could not help connecting matters of citizenship and political allegiance with their personal fears and their identities as men and as women. The crisis of American nationalism had come home.

Clinging to the Union

The success of the secession movement obscured the significant opposi-tion it encountered. Many white southerners tried to resist secession, in one way or another, throughout that climactic winter. Even more, perhaps a majority, viewed secession with mixed feelings, torn between varying loyalties to the Union, their region, their states, and even their local com-munities.[61] Previously, most Americans had been able to keep these var-ious levels of loyalty in rough alignment, but in the secessionist South that became increasingly difficult and ultimately impossible. The result was countless moments of pain, ambivalence, and sometimes outright opposi-tion, as white southerners individually and collectively contemplated the shifting grounds of allegiance and nationhood.

In February 1861, just after the formation of the Confederate States but before the secession of the middle South states, the Arkansan W. M. Wilcox wrote to his brother, expressing regret that they disagreed on secession. "You are a Union man," he wrote; "I am a secessionist out and out." Even so, they shared core beliefs: "a love for the Union; that S.C. was too precipitate; that it is a bigoted little fool"; that the British government was a fine model; and in "the right of secession." Despite these shared beliefs, the brothers disagreed on the all-important question of whether secession was yet justified. W. M. believed that northerners' actions—particularly contraventions of the Fugitive Slave Law by individuals who assisted escaped slaves and by northern legislatures that passed "personal liberty" laws—warranted secession, whereas his brother thought the South should continue to strive to maintain the Union: "You think we have not tried to heal the wound, we have not worked for the Union as we should. I think we have. That's the rub." Even so, W. M. Wilcox could not turn his back completely on the affection for the Union that he and his brother shared. "As to a love for the Union," he explained, "I do not admit that anyone loves it better than I do. I feel a twinge in the region of the heart every time I think of a dissolution of this ever glorious Union." Still, he reached the conclusion, no matter how sorrowfully, that the Union's time was up. Of his brother's continuing unionism he commented, "Although the notes may to some sons sound as sweet as the dying Swan, to me sounds like some good old hard shell Baptist divine singing psalms to a dead horse." For the Wilcox brothers, secession hurt; even the brother who supported secession rued the downfall of a Union he had once loved.[62]

Southerners who remained committed to the Union viewed secession as a conspiracy engineered by an extremist minority. A Georgia man spoke for many in a January 1861 letter to Herschel V. Johnson, the National Democratic Party's vice-presidential candidate in 1860. "To think of it!" he wrote. "Our government the best on the face of the earth the last hope of freedom . . . is to be broken up civil war with all its horrors brought on us, we willing or not And for what! Why simply to appease the wrath of disappointed demagogues or cover the shame of unstinted corruption." Many others blamed South Carolina in particular for having cultivated a disunionist conspiracy ever since the days of nullification. These allegations ran through politicians' speeches and private correspondence alike, but they were nowhere advanced more passionately than in a January 1861 letter written by the Kentuckian R. M. Farleigh. Farleigh deeply regretted the hazards to his country, "once the pride of all the nations of the Earth," and placed the blame firmly at the door of South Carolina, a "pusillanimous state" that had endangered "the peace and harmony of the greatest nation that ever existed." "I would that I had a foot as big as half the Universe," he went on, "and the strength of ten thousand giants and I would kick her into a million fragments and scatter them through [eternity]." Many other unionists shared Farleigh's contempt for the extremists, especially those in South Carolina, who had engineered secession.[63]

In response, they fought to save the Union. Their efforts are normally given short shrift in histories of secession and the Civil War, but this is because the unionists lost their fight, not because they did not fight at all. The southern unionist campaign encompassed formal efforts to pass compromise measures in Washington, DC—efforts associated most visibly with the Kentucky unionist John J. Crittenden, architect of the failed Crittenden Compromise—as well as speech making, pamphlet writing, and letter sending across the South. For some, this became an all-consuming crusade. North Carolina politician James G. Ramsay wrote to his wife in January 1861, "I have but one idea. That is the preservation of the Union so far as North Carolina is concerned, and whatever I do or however I vote that will be the feeling that will guide me." Later that month he reported that he had "bought . . . a United States flag to day," and resolved that he would "speak for the Union under it all over Rowan county yet so help me God."[64]

The Unionist campaign was often framed in negative terms: it was a reaction against secession, a warning that things would get worse if secession took place. It was often motivated by localized concerns: existing political identities and conflicts, religious affiliations, or kinship.[65] But southern unionists also advanced more positive nationalistic arguments in favor of retaining the Union. For one thing, they pointed to the security and prosperity afforded by the Union and asked why the South would want to give them up. In the weeks leading to the presidential election, James L. Petigru privately predicted that Lincoln's election would not result in South Carolina's secession because "the country is too prosperous for a revolution." "If our planters were in debt," he explained, "or cotton was at 5 cents, as I have seen it, such a thing might be likely; but, our magnanimous countrymen are too comfortable for such exercise."[66] It is vital to recognize that the prosperity and security that caused unionists to value the Union included prosperity and security for the institution of slavery. Later in the war, southern unionists would face increasing tension between their commitment to slavery and their commitment to the Union, but in 1861 almost all of them championed a firmly proslavery vision of the United States.

FIGURE 3.1 John Crittenden; photograph by Julian Vannerson, 1859. (Library of Congress.)

The most visible unionists were political leaders, but there were count-less ordinary southerners who longed just as much for the Union to be preserved. Some of them wrote letters to unionist politicians like Kentucky's John J. Crittenden and Virginia's William C. Rives, allowing a bottom-up perspective on what was indubitably a broad-based movement. "I am in love with my beloved country," wrote one Georgia man to Crittenden in January 1861, "and am distressed about its present, and precarious situa-tion." He dearly valued the Union, purchased with "the blood of the revolu-tionary sires," rued his state's secession from it, and thought that this "once united and happy people of these united states ought to love one another, and I believe that they do, [out]side of fanatics and demagogs." Another man, who signed himself "A Southerner and Lover of His Country," wrote to both Crittenden and Rives, saying, "God knows I love my country & would make any sacrifice to save her," and asking, "Who is there so lost that would not love his country? Who so debased that would not sacrifice all to save her?" The best means of saving the Union, he believed, was for Americans "to love each other as brethren of one family." "The *People* love each other," he was sure, and "they *will* speak North South East & West before they will see the inheritance of their Fathers sealed in blood & the legacy of their children dashed . . . by the folly of demagogues & politicians."[67]

Similar ideas received more public expression just days before South Carolina's secession in a speech delivered by Georgia's Herschel V. Johnson. The speech contained strong arguments not only against secession but also in favor of the Union. "Our National flag is the symbol of power," Johnson told his audience, "and commands respect, upon land and sea; the emblem of liberty, wherever it floats, encouraging the hearts of the oppressed of all climes—the protector of commerce and civilization, it gives security to American rights and interests against foreign cupidity." As well as rehearsing the core American nationalist belief in the United States as a global beacon—a common theme of unionist speeches and writings—Johnson reminded listeners that the Union had been good for the South, including for its institution of slavery. "It is almost impossible," he said, "to over-estimate the value of this Union to slavery, as a security against its foreign foes." Though northerners had erred, he denied that their transgressions against the South warranted the hazardous step of secession: "The spirit which gave birth to the Federal Union was that of fraternity; its assiduous cultivation alone can preserve it." Southerners needed to work with errant northerners to restore the bonds of brotherhood and affection that had knit the Union together to begin with. Otherwise, Johnson argued, disunion would be disastrous for them all. Looking back to history, and voicing the same fears that had troubled American politicians in the decades following the Revolution, he saw no instances

> of the disintegration of a great Government, in which the fragments have been re-constructed into a wise and happy organization. But numerous instances are recorded, that such overturning ended in the loss of liberty and the long reign of anarchy and bloodshed. The probabilities are that we should have several small Republics, or it may be as many Republics as seceding States.[68]

Johnson's speech captured southern unionists' main arguments that winter: the fact that the Union had brought security and prosperity to the slaveholding South; the national mission to spread American ideals to those thirsting for freedom around the world; the need to reforge the affective bonds that had united northerners and southerners in national community; and the dangers, especially the perils of fragmentation, that disunion could bring.

Other would-be union savers added their own reasons for the preservation of the Union. One Virginia man, identifying himself as "Thos. H. Looker, U.S.A., *& a follower of Christ*," sent a circular to William Rives that urged clergymen in both the North and South to use their influence to restrain fanaticism and promote "feelings of common brotherhood" throughout the Union. Because "God still and ever controls the destiny of Nations," Looker thought that northerners and southerners alike ought to "acknowledge and bewail our National, our Ecclesiastical, and our personal sins, which have undoubtedly brought down upon our Country and People, these judgments and calamities."[69]

Robert J. Breckinridge, a prominent Kentucky minister, agreed that the fate of America and of all nations was in the hands of God and that "national judgments never come except by reason of national sins; nor are they ever turned aside except upon condition of repentance for the sins which produced them." In a sermon delivered on January 4, 1861, designated by President Buchanan as a "Day of National Humiliation," Breckinridge celebrated the usual "blessings" of membership in the Union—peace, prosperity, "the blessing of our glorious example to all nations and to all ages"—but also gave more explicit consideration to the basic concepts of nation and citizenship. He categorically denied the right of secession; if such a right did exist, he thought, "then we have no National Government, and never had any." The system of American federalism meant that the United States was a unitary nation *and* a collection of "sovereign States." And citizens' allegiance to both state and nation was inviolable. "The people, therefore, can no more legally throw off their national allegiance than they can legally throw off their State allegiance; nor can any State any more legally absolve the allegiance of its people to the nation, than the nation can legally absolve the allegiance due by the people to the State they live in." Contrary to secessionist opinion, Breckinridge firmly believed that the United States constituted a unitary—if federated—nation-state, and that citizens' allegiance to the national government was sacred.[70]

Even in the lower South, such views were not altogether vanquished in 1861. Mississippian Theodoric C. Lyon released a unionist pamphlet in 1861 in which he contended that "this Government is not merely a league of States, as was the old Confederation to which it succeeded and upon the ruins of which it was built, but a union, a consolidation—in so far as the derivation its powers is concerned—of States." Like Breckinridge, Lyon believed that each citizen owed allegiance to both nation and state, and that the former could not simply be overruled by the latter. Besides this legal dimension, southerners had a moral responsibility to their fellow Americans, the states of the Union being "held together, more or less, by a feeling of mutual reciprocity and dependency, founded upon a community of general interests." The stakes were high; America was "the only nation on earth whose foundations were laid in the appeal of faith . . . consecrated from its birth," and allowing its collapse would be almost sacrilegious. America's status as a beacon of liberty for the rest of the world meant that, "should this Government fall, the question of man's capacity for self government is forever settled." Here were strong reasons to work hard for the preservation of the Union.[71]

Even if the Union could not be saved, there were some in the middle and upper South who still did not wish to join the southernmost slaveholding states in the Confederacy. Reflecting their belief that the crisis had been whipped up by extremists on both sides—secessionists in the South and abolitionists in the North—some southerners preferred the option of a new "Middle Confederacy" consisting of the upper southern states and the lower northern states of the existing Union. "We must give the people of Ky, Tenn & Missouri something to fall back on," wrote one correspondent to John J. Crittenden, "& not leave them as the sole alternative a choice between a Northern & Southern Confederacy—That alternative— the only one is a Mississippi valley Confederacy." Another man wrote to William C. Rives, stating that his first preference would be that "not a star be erased from our Heavenly old flag, but that we hold together as the United States of North America." If that did not happen, though, he preferred anything to union with South Carolina, and suggested a "Middle Confederacy" that would include most of the existing American states outside of New England and the deep South. The secession crisis created a fluid geopolitical situation in which Americans could imagine, at least, the possibility of different kinds of federations to replace the old Union. A straightforward split into the United States and the Confederate States was not the only possible outcome of the secession winter.[72]

In April 1861, however, the fluidity of the winter gave way to the increasing likelihood of a clear divide between one nation-state in the North and another in the South. Following the South's bombardment of Fort Sumter on April 12–13, Abraham Lincoln's call for volunteers to put down the rebellion outraged even unionists in the middle and upper South. "Coercion" had become a line in the sand for conditional unionists, and once Lincoln crossed that line, the entry of at least the middle South states—and perhaps Kentucky, Missouri, and Maryland as well—became likely.

Not all southern unionists gave up easily. Virginia lawyer Robert Young Conrad, for example, who had acted as a self-described "orderly sergeant" of pro-unionists at Virginia's secession convention, was disgusted by the scenes he witnessed in Richmond after the Sumter incident. His letters home described "a great parade of mobocracy and military in the streets," with "one hundred guns fired, *in honour*, of the *disgrace* of our own National flag . . . and the flag of the Confederated Southern States hoisted on the roof of the Capitol, just over the Hall in which we sit." In the following days, Conrad recorded his sorrow at the demise of his beloved Union in what he saw as a rash and irresponsible movement. "My heart is very sad," he confessed to his wife, "viewing the now near prospect of civil—fratricidal war in our country—so young—so prosperous, the pride of our people, the hope of the world—which is not to lose all its *prestige*, become the object of contempt to the nations, and, we know not to what extent, the victim of our own folly and madness."[73] Conrad ended up retreating home as soon as he was able, and attempted—with some difficulty—to stay out of the war completely.

Conrad's fellow Virginia unionist William C. Rives also reacted to the news of Sumter with regret and sorrow. In the wake of the bombardment, Rives wrote to a friend in the state convention cautioning that now was no time for rash action. He knew there was a widespread feeling that the events at Sumter rendered it too late to hold together the North and South—including Virginia. Not so, he averred. The history of Switzerland—"not without some striking analogies to our own"—proved to Rives that there was still hope for the Union. "In 1847," he explained, "the ancient confederation of the swiss cantons was severed by the secession of seven of the cantons, who formed a separate confederacy under the name of the *Sonderbund*." This led to war, "and yet the parties finally agreed upon a reconstruction of their constitution, which has made their union firmer & closer than ever." According to Rives, "The border states, in our confederacy have a power, by their united action, to bring about the same result." Rives, like many southern unionists, opposed the rising tide of secession even after Sumter.[74]

Although some southerners continued their fight beyond April 1861—Tennessee's William Brownlow and Andrew Johnson, for instance—most, including Rives, reluctantly accepted their states' decisions to secede. In May, having been selected as a representative to the Confederate Congress, Rives explained that "as long as there was any hope of preserving the ancient union of the States on terms consistent with the rights & honor of the South, I adhered to it with the veneration & devotion which, from my earliest youth, I have ever cherished for the work of our fathers." But now that Virginia had seceded, he was obliged to respect his state's decision. "Where she goes, I will go; where she dies, I will die, and there I will be buried," he wrote, conveying a romantic-style attachment to his state that, in his eyes, simply had to outweigh his affiliation with the Union. The same was true of Herschel Johnson. Before their state's secession, Johnson wrote to fellow Georgia unionist Alexander Stephens, the future vice president of the Confederacy, expressing regret for the disunion that he feared was about to take place. He remained committed to the Union and resolved that "whatever I can do, I will do to avert impending calamities, to preserve our government & consequently, liberty—& its blessings." But even as he told Stephens that they should "maintain [their] conservative ground to the last," he conceded that their state was ultimately more important. "If beaten & Geo. cross the Rubicon, as loyal men, we will share her fate, feeling none the worse for having tried to prevent the deed of rashness." This is precisely what happened: Georgia crossed the Rubicon, and Stephens and Johnson leapt after her.[75]

Secession created particular problems for those southerners in active U.S. military service during the secession winter. Many followed the same principle as William Rives and Herschel Johnson. Once their states had seceded, they felt obliged to resign immediately from U.S. service. Robert E. Lee is often held up as a classic example of this. Yet the decision was rarely made without some distress. A young Virginian, Lunsford Lindsay Lomax, wrote to a friend in April 1861,

> I cannot stand it any longer and feel it my duty to resign. My state is out of the union and when she calls for my services I must go. I regret it very much and feel that it is almost suicidal. As long as I could conscientiously consider it a war upon the union and flag, I was willing to do my part, but it is a war between sections, the North against the South, and I must go with my relatives and sympathies.[76]

Charles Iverson Graves, a Georgian, was serving with the U.S. navy in Europe as news of Lincoln's election and the first wave of secession

FIGURE 3.2 *The First Flag of Independence Raised in the South, by the Citizens of Savannah, GA, November 8th, 1860.* Lithograph by R. H. Howell. (Library of Congress.)

reached him. These events caused him great anxiety. For one thing, he had seen war firsthand in Europe and had no wish to see its horrors in his own country. Even more problematic were the competing loyalties he felt to the United States on the one hand and to Georgia and the South on the other. "I feel almost broken hearted at the sad condition of our country," he confessed to his aunt. "I could never fight against the South, especially when I thought she was right. Yet I am now under a solemn oath to support the Constitution and to obey all orders of the President of the United States." The only solution was to resign from the U.S. navy, terminate his "solemn oath," and join the South instead. Months later, in January 1862, while in the Confederate service, he wrote to his cousin Maggie after a visit, "I had *so much* to think about the last day or two before I left that I forgot to ask Aunt Mary for my 'Union' letters:—please get them, and destroy them for me, together with the ones I wrote to you." With his allegiance to the Confederacy now more clear-cut, Graves presumably regretted earlier letters that had betrayed opposition or at least uncertainty toward secession. It seems that cousin Maggie did as she was asked: other than the missive about being "almost broken hearted," no "Union" letters remain in the Charles Iverson Graves Papers at the University of North Carolina at Chapel Hill.[77]

Graves's wish that evidence of his former unionism be destroyed raises the possibility that there was considerably more opposition or ambivalence toward secession in the South than the surviving evidence indicates. The popular euphoria that swept the secessionist South combined with long-standing slaveholder anxieties about slave loyalty to produce a climate in which open dissent could be dangerous. Allen Turner Davidson, a North Carolina businessman traveling in the Deep South during the spring of 1861, made no secret of his unionist proclivities in letters he wrote back home. He reacted with sorrow upon seeing the U.S. flag supplanted by the Confederate one in Georgia and Florida. "God save our glorious old state from the domination of such a lawless and desperate *Mob*," he wrote, but then stopped himself, in case "my letter should pass through the servilance of the 'vigilence' and then you would hear of me in the 'Tombs' for treason as *they* call it." Though Davidson was not so worried about secessionists' repression of dissent to mask his unionist feelings entirely, he observed a climate of conformity in the South that surely must have silenced unionist sentiment to some degree.[78]

As secession became an incontrovertible fact, it increasingly made sense for southerners to repress whatever unionist leanings they may have had and simply accept the inevitable. Swimming against the tide offered few advantages in an atmosphere of bellicose conformity. One Georgia woman wrote to her sister in February 1861 that her husband had "been much opposed to the secession movement but being in the ministry must submit, & can only hope now for the best." A similar message was contained in a letter written by a young Virginia woman in May 1861, following Virginia's secession vote. Anna Cadwallader reported to her brother, "Every body was for secession in Newton and I know you will drop this letter in amazement when I tell you that Papa voted the secession ticket." Their father had previously been "a strong union man" but had decided to vote secession because everyone else was doing so—even former unionists— and he had no wish to be the lone opponent of a measure that was sure to pass. Presumably their father shared Anna's sorrowful resignation that there was no longer any point resisting the inevitable:

> Oh it is an awful thing to think of. Our glorious old Union dissolved and I am afraid forever well for my part I cant help who is

for secession I am for Union always not that I advocate the Lin-
colns preceedings or Abolitionism either but I cant bear the
thought of our once Glorious Union the home of Our Washington
the land that the stars and stripes have floated over so long, to be
desolved and for the sake of a few wooly headed Negroes although
I suppose that as all the rest of the Southern States have seceded it
was as well for Virginia to seceed as not.[79]

One wonders how many other white southerners made the expedient
decision to hold their long-standing unionist feelings inside and accept secession as an irresistible force. Secessionists' successes masked the strength
and vitality of southern unionism throughout the secession winter. In addition to the many southerners who articulated positive arguments for the
Union—security, peace, national mission, religion, brotherhood—countless others felt some measure of ambivalence and regret as they witnessed
their beloved Union collapse around them.

THUS THE ROAD to secession for most white southerners was paved not
with the romantic dreams of a naturally occurring, ethnically grounded,
and divinely ordained nationalism, but with resentment at what James
Henry Hammond had termed the "pinch" of the Union. These pinches
forced white southerners to reassess the value of continued national unity
with their compatriots to the north, and their commitment to continued
membership in the United States consequently began to unravel. This
was a gradual, incremental process that many southerners resisted up to
the moment of secession and beyond. But by the early summer of 1861
it had resulted in the secession of eleven states. Once secession became
a reality, it was difficult to imagine a denouement that did not rest upon
concepts of the nation and nationalism. This was, after all, the golden age
of nationalism in the Western world.

The fact that the Confederacy did not result from a widespread, preex-
isting active nationalist movement should not lead to the dismissal of the
very concept of Confederate nationalism as somehow fraudulent. In this
regard it is by no means singular. Many nationalisms—American and Italian, among others—were born of comparable processes. While Italian
unification was achieved by moderate politicians animated by expediency
more than sentiment, long-term committed nationalists like Mazzini had
little influence on the achievement of independence and almost none on
the nation-state that resulted. The masses of Italians, meanwhile, like the

masses of white southerners, would rarely have thought of nationalism as an important objective.[80] Events in the 1850s in the United States were also comparable to those in the U.S.S.R. in the late 1980s, when an existing political arrangement became destabilized for reasons other than a nationalist movement, yet once the old arrangement began to disintegrate, nationalism became a convenient and appealing option. The Confederacy was neither the first nor the last example of a largely unplanned nationalism resulting from a complex, contested process in which few participants saw the creation of a new nation-state as the goal.[81]

Nor was it the only nationalism to be animated by perceptions of shared victimhood. The sense of being under assault from a hostile North, and to a lesser extent from a western world that was becoming increasingly opposed to slavery, had gained purchase during the sectional crisis of 1846–51. But for the majority of white southerners, northern aggression was still not sufficient to warrant the ultimate act of political separation. Instead, various forms of conditional unionism reigned. By the winter of 1860–61, though, conditional unionism was increasingly challenged by signs that the Union, rather than improving white southerners' lives, threatened them in urgent and personal ways. For the most part these were potential threats that had not yet materialized. Yet that did little to lessen their seriousness in southern eyes. At the core of these fears was the perception that the North's hostility to slavery threatened the South's economy and material well-being—based so firmly upon the peculiar institution. But around that core had sprung up a constellation of anxieties and resentments: the resentment of being considered inferior members of what should be a national community of equals; anxiety about the apparent loss of affection—both romantic and platonic—between North and South; the notion that the two regions had developed not just divergent economies or divergent ideas about race but divergent ideas about fundamental questions of morality, religion, and appropriate behavior. Southerners often cast the problems of nationalism in terms of affection, honor, morality, and gender identities. All of this came to a head during the secession winter, finding an outlet in the climate of secessionist conformity that swept the South. Even those southerners with serious misgivings about secession found it more and more futile to resist.

By the late spring of 1861 the existence of the Confederacy was an incontrovertible fact. Yet the problems of nationalism were by no means resolved. Some southerners would continue to cling to the Union, to one degree or another. And even for those who accepted the new nation-state, nationalism and citizenship continued to generate persistent questions of identity, belonging, and allegiance. What gave the Confederacy its own national identity? How would it differentiate itself from the United States? What did it mean to be a Confederate citizen? Why should Confederate nationalism matter at all?

4

Definitions

CONFEDERATE CITIZENSHIP AND
NATIONAL IDENTITY IN 1861

FEBRUARY 8, 1861, was no ordinary day in Montgomery, Alabama. Appending their signatures to the "Provisional Constitution of the Confederate States of America," forty-three men ushered into the world a new nation-state. No matter how many twists and turns there had been along the way, the Confederacy was now a fact. The secessionists' work was done. Or was it? In fact, signing the provisional constitution proved to be the easy part, the beginning rather than the end of Confederate nation making. For one thing, the document was signed by delegates from only six of the fifteen slaveholding states—the Texan contingent was several weeks late to Montgomery; the middle South states of North Carolina, Tennessee, Arkansas, and Virginia still remained committed to the Union; and the border South states, Delaware, Maryland, Kentucky, and Missouri, would never secede at all. The dream of a nation-state encompassing the entire slaveholding South was woefully incomplete. Furthermore, southern nation makers faced the difficult tasks of defining a new national identity, of achieving legitimate nation-state status in the eyes of the world, and of forging bonds between the new national government and those it claimed as its citizens.

These tasks required work abroad as well as at home, so the new government promptly sent three commissioners to Europe: William L. Yancey, the Alabama fire-eater; Pierre Rost, an aging Louisiana state supreme court justice; and A. Dudley Mann, a former U.S. diplomat from Virginia. Their mission was to approach Britain and other European countries and secure formal recognition for the Confederacy as an independent nation-state. By mid-August the three Confederates had become frustrated by Britain's cool reception. The British foreign secretary, Lord John Russell, had met with them informally but was now refusing to see them again. So they sent him a lengthy letter setting out case for Confederate recognition.

The commissioners insisted that secession was no revolution but an orderly, lawful response to oppression. Nor was it an infringement of sovereignty—which, they took care to explain, resided in the American people rather than in the government, as it was presumed to do in Europe. In fact, the sacred American tenet of popular self-government justified, even required, secession: "So far from the principle of American allegiance having been violated by the people of the seceding States, in those states alone is that principle upheld." Southerners were faithful to 1776, whereas northerners were "traitors." Because secession was a lawful response to oppression, the commissioners contended, international law mandated recognition. Aligning themselves with other successful independence movements, they expressed the hope that "the same sense of justice, the same views of duty under the law of nations" that had led the British government to recognize Texas, the Latin American republics, Greece, Belgium, and, most recently, Italy would lead it to recognize the Confederacy as well. They also cited other arguments for recognition: that it was in Britain's economic interests, due to the importance of southern cotton imports; that the Confederacy possessed the population, territory, and resources to function as a stable nation-state; that it had proven its ability to defend itself at Bull Run, the first—and, at that point, only—major battle of the war.

The commissioners were conscious of certain obstacles. They knew that Britain's relations with the United States made recognition difficult. But they insisted that it should take place nonetheless. They also realized that "the anti-slavery sentiment so universally prevalent in England, had shrunk from the idea of forming friendly public relations with a government recognizing the slavery of a part of the human race." But slavery was nonnegotiable. In any event, they maintained that this was not a war for or against slavery, pointing out that Lincoln himself had rejected abolition as a northern war goal.[1]

Confederate diplomats' efforts failed. But their statements are among the clearest expressions of the case for Confederate nationalism. As the references to Italy and other successful independence movements reveal, Confederates appealed to the nineteenth-century principle of nationality, just as secessionists had been doing for decades. They held up the Confederacy as a unique nation that deserved political status as an independent nation-state. Back home, too, political, cultural, and religious leaders, and ordinary southerners as well, advanced an array of arguments to substantiate this claim. These arguments took shape in the context of what southerners already knew about the concepts of nation, nationalism, and citizenship. Drawing on transatlantic thought as well as their long experience as American nationalists, Confederates advanced arguments that the Confederacy deserved political independence because southerners constituted a distinctive nation, a "people" with its own national identity, resting on singular characteristics and a unique cultural and intellectual life. They defined Confederate national identity in contrast to nefarious northerners and held that this distinctive nation had now found institutional expression in the Confederate nation-state, to which individual white southerners owed allegiance as citizens.

The Confederacy fits smoothly into interpretations of modern nationalism as the creation of nationalists who have "invented" or "imagined" ideas to justify the claims of a given group of people to national status.[2] Surely here more than anywhere nationalism was an artifact, the deliberate, self-conscious intellectual creation of cultural and political leaders, designed to rationalize political independence.[3] Yet while the modus operandi of nationalists is to present their ideas as being timeless, natural, and even providentially ordained, this is never actually the case. Awareness of this fact helps reveal variability and inconsistency where nationalists would claim unity and fixedness.

Confederate nationalists confronted a variety of problems in 1861. Among the more serious ones were those raised by the necessary recalibration of relations between white southerners and their northern former compatriots, and between the Confederacy and America. White southerners' ambivalence about which aspects of the old national identity to retain and which aspects to discard created acute dilemmas, especially since by seceding southerners had left the U.S. government in northern hands. The cultural borders between the North and the South remained unstable in 1861. So too did the territorial and population borders between the Union and the Confederacy. Because of contested areas in the border states and significant dissent in other parts of the Confederacy, particularly its low-slaveholding mountainous regions, the boundaries of the new nation-state were in flux throughout 1861 and indeed throughout the war. This uncertainty represented a serious challenge to the legitimacy of the Confederacy, which like all nation-states claimed supreme authority over the resources and the individuals within its territory. Then, too, there was the problem of slavery. This not only caused difficulties abroad, complicating relations with a predominantly antislavery Europe, but also at home, where it complicated Confederate leaders' efforts to secure the loyalty of nonslaveholding white southerners and of slaves themselves. For all these reasons, after secession nationalism and citizenship became increasingly problematic.

Attention to these problems as well as the confident assertions of nationalists illuminates white southerners' responses to three crucial questions in the first months of the Confederacy's existence: How could the Confederacy prove that it possessed a distinctive national identity? How was that national identity similar to and how was it different from the national identity of the United States? And, finally, what did Confederate citizenship mean for individual white southerners? Southerners' responses proved to be tentative, varied, and sometimes contradictory. The grounds of nationhood continued to shift even after the creation of the Confederate nation-state.

The Quest for National Legitimacy

In the wake of secession and the political formation of the Confederacy, white southerners faced the consuming challenge of proving to themselves and to the world that they constituted a legitimate nation, a "people" who deserved political independence. Confederate leaders recognized that national legitimacy was a prerequisite of successful existence in a world that was coming to be organized around the modern principle of nationalism.[4] As the radicals among them had been doing for years, white southerners ventured claims of a distinctive national identity that set them apart from the North and the rest of the world. In 1861, the stakes changed. Instead of arguing for an abstract right to exist as a nation, southern nationalists demanded international acceptance of an independence they claimed to have already achieved. Their assertions assumed a measure of institutional credibility and entered the realm of formal diplomacy.

Sometimes, simply asserting the existence of the new nation-state seemed sufficient. "A nation has been born in a day," one Virginia newspaper proclaimed in the wake of that state's secession, "and that bristling with arms!" "A Revolution has been consummated," declared *De Bow's Review*, "a people united, a Government established, a Constitution adopted, and a vigorous young power, forced upon the perilous career of independent empire, has vindicated its nationality and assumed its position among the powers of the earth." In Columbia, South Carolina, Grace Elmore marked the inauguration of the provisional president with the words, "The bells are ringing—we are now a nation with our own government, Jeff Davis, President." Everywhere across the South, the bells rang, the bands played, and white southerners reflected on the meanings of national independence.[5]

But how would southern leaders persuade the world that the Confederacy was, in fact, a nation-state? Grace Elmore's reference to "a nation with our own government" contains a hint. National legitimacy in the nineteenth century was understood in part in institutional terms. The project of southern nationalists, like that of their counterparts in Europe, was to bring the nation and the government into proper alignment. For this reason, as well as the obvious practicalities, the construction of a stable government was a vital foundation of the new nation-state. Thus one newspaper warned in late March, "We have a Government in existence here, able to maintain its nationality against the encroachments of any hostile power." Indeed, leading southerners had seen the urgency of forming a government, and an army, throughout the secession crisis. "What is advisable," wrote Florida's David Levy Yulee in early January, while still a sitting U.S. senator, "is the *earliest possible organization of a Southern Confederacy, and of a Southern Army.* . . . A strong Government, as eight states will make promptly organized, and a *strong army* with Jeff Davis for General-in-Chief, will bring them to a reasonable sense of the gravity of the crisis." South Carolina's William Henry Trescot, who had given a great deal of thought to nationalism before secession, agreed. In mid-January he wrote to Howell Cobb of the need to "organize a Southern government immediately. We must meet Lincoln with a President of our own." For Trescot, there were military and diplomatic considerations as well: "We want the military resources of the South concentrated at once; and above all, our foreign relations ought to be assured as quickly as possible. No attempt at foreign negotiations ought to be made by single States." The Confederacy would need institutional stability as quickly as possible if it were to be accepted as a nation-state. "The condition of weakness and confusion which will result from four or five States floating about is indescribable," Trescot explained. "Weld them together while they are hot."[6]

Trescot's words indicate the importance of creating not just a government but one that would be accepted formally by the rest of the world as the institutional embodiment of a nation: a genuine nation-state. The necessary foreign recognition would elude the Confederacy throughout its existence. Many commentators have assumed that recognition from one or more of the great powers of the day—particularly Britain or France— would have helped the South to achieve national independence even over northern resistance. White southerners understood that the litmus test of national status was administered by world opinion. Thus in his well-known poem "Ethnogenesis," originally entitled "Ode on the Meeting of the Southern Congress," Henry Timrod rejoiced:

> At last, we are
> A nation among nations; and the world
> Shall soon behold in many a distant port
> Another flag unfurled!

For the next four years, Confederate diplomacy would be designed to achieve this very goal—and would be frustrated every step of the way.[7]

In those first few months, the Confederate State Department and its agents crafted an array of diplomatic arguments. These were directed particularly toward Britain, to a lesser degree toward France, and ultimately to the rest of Europe and the world. Recognizing Confederate independence, diplomats claimed, was in the economic interests of Britain, France, and other countries, because of the importance of southern cotton to their manufacturing sectors. Self-interest aside, they also held up recognizing the Confederacy as the right thing to do. Southerners not only had ample reason to desire national independence—northern oppression—they also had the resources to make it work. Diplomats often cited statistics from the U.S. census of 1850 as proof that the new Confederacy possessed sufficient territory, population, and natural resources to take its place among the powers of the world. Just as importantly, the argument went, southerners had every legal right to break away from the old Union and form a new one. This was no revolution but a conservative resumption of power that properly belonged to the people of the states, not the United States as a whole.[8]

Confederate diplomats also appealed to the principle of nationality. The initial instructions from Secretary of State Robert Toombs to Commissioners Yancey, Rost, and Mann informed them that recent British policy toward "the recognition of the right of the Italian people to change their form of government and choose their own rulers encourages this Government to hope that they will pursue a similar policy in regard to the

Confederate States." When John Slidell was appointed Confederate minister to France in September 1861, the State Department instructed him to
inform the French government that

> it is in the name of the sacred right of self-government that the
> Confederate States appear before the tribunal of the nations of the
> earth and submit their claims for a recognized place among them.
> They approach His Imperial Majesty of France with the more confi-
> dence as he has lately championed this great cause in the recent
> Italian question so much to the glory of himself and the great people
> over whom he rules.[9]

Confederates claimed that they were true to the principle of nationality
while northerners were not. When Robert Toombs sent commissioners to
Washington, DC, to demand U.S. recognition of the Confederacy, he suggested that they instruct their hosts in American diplomatic history, particularly what he described as the policy the United States had "invariably
adopted in its intercourse with foreign nations—that of recognizing de
facto Governments and the right of every people to create and reform their
political institutions as they may will and determine." Following this
policy would mean recognizing Confederate independence. The U.S. government disagreed, of course, and the apparent inconsistency continued
to rankle southerners. Later in 1861 an editorial in a Richmond newspaper
complained that northerners' opposition to the South's right of "self-government" was incompatible with their former support for national self-de-
termination. "They were all agog at the notion of freedom for Ireland,"
protested the editorial. "They exulted at the movement for Hungarian liberty, and rushed forward to flatter and fawn upon KOSSUTH. . . . They raised
a shout of gratulation at the overthrow of Austrian rule in Italy. They
hooted at the idea of union between Ireland and Great Britain." All of this
made the North's current opposition to southern self-government—to the
principle of nationality—hypocritical.[10]

Southerners themselves were hardly impartial in their own implemen-
tation of the principle of nationality. Their enthusiasm for it had always
been tempered by skepticism about certain peoples' suitability for self-
government. Even when they themselves were frustrated by the world's
reluctance to grant them national legitimacy, they were not always willing
to grant it to others. Thus when Santiago Vidaurri, leader of the breakaway
Mexican state of Nuevo León, contacted Confederate agents proposing

some form of alliance between the two aspiring new governments, the Confederacy politely demurred. Though it reciprocated Vidaurri's friendliness, the Confederate State Department informed its man on the ground that such an alliance would be "impolitic" at present. The Confederate agent was instructed to explain that "the Government of the Confederate States feels a deep sympathy with all people struggling to secure for themselves the blessings of self-government, and is therefore much interested in the cause [and] progress of these provinces"—but that the Confederacy found it inexpedient to convert that sympathy into action.[11]

Hence Confederates adopted a similar stance toward Nuevo León as Europeans adopted toward the Confederacy, and for similar reasons. It was simply not in the self-interest of more established governments to support independence movements prematurely. Self-interest was the overriding force in international politics, as friends of the South recognized. An English friend of Charleston's Henry Gourdin wrote in June 1861 expressing sympathy for the Confederate cause and the right of self-government: "As a People you have a right to choose your own Government." However, he continued, "whether in the estimation of foreign nations you exercise your right wisely is another question," and he correctly warned that "revolutions are generally at first received with [distrust] by settled foreign Governments." Likewise, another English friend of the South, the member of Parliament William Gregory, wrote to James M. Mason in July 1861 that although he himself supported the Confederacy's bid for independence, he did not anticipate swift recognition. "There is an impression," he explained, "that the superior numbers, and greater wealth of the North will ultimately prevail, and our Government is very naturally unwilling to acknowledge as an independent nation, that which after all may be only a temporarily dissociated number of States." This "wait and see" stance proved to be a major obstacle to recognition of the Confederacy.[12]

Gregory also highlighted another obstacle to British recognition of the Confederacy: slavery. "The Commissioners have a very difficult card to play," he informed Mason; "there is, as you are well aware, a strong anti-slavery feeling in the Country," which greatly impeded Confederate diplomacy. Some southerners were aware that their peculiar institution was viewed with some distaste by most Europeans. Writing during a sojourn in Paris in the secession winter, one Tennessee woman informed her family back home, "Mrs Stowe & the abolitionists have done their work so thoroughly that it is doubtful either England or France would dare to take the part of slaveholders however much they might desire it as I believe L. Napoleon does." Confederate diplomats certainly recognized the problem. In their first dispatch from London, William L. Yancey and A. Dudley Mann reported that "the public mind here is entirely opposed to the Government of the Confederate States of America on the question of slavery, and that the sincerity and universality of this feeling embarrasses the Government in dealing with the question of our recognition." Yet they always insisted that the slavery problem would not be fatal to the prospects of Confederate recognition. They were more right than wrong. European self-interest would determine responses to Confederate diplomacy more than antislavery sentiment.[13]

Confederates pursued their quest for legitimacy not only in the field of formal diplomacy but in other, more diffuse ways as well. As they did so, they continued to conceptualize nationalism—whether American, southern, or a blend of the two—in the context of transatlantic thought. No matter how important the swift creation of a national government and diplomatic corps, those alone did not make a nation in the eyes of the world. Cultural and racial distinctiveness were also important criteria of a genuine national identity. White southerners knew this well by 1861. If their bid for national independence were to be sustained, they recognized that they had to make a case for their distinctiveness as a "people."

Literature and the arts offered one important testing ground. The year 1861 saw an outpouring of popular poetry and songs crafted to celebrate and to substantiate the new nation. These were published widely as broadsides and pamphlets, and reprinted in newspapers across the South. As literature, they tended to have little merit. As reflections of popular understandings of secession and the creation of the Confederacy, however, they are revealing. The composition and distribution of these songs and poems embodied the assumption that literature and the arts ought to be deployed in the service of the nation, not merely as descriptions of Confederate nationality but also as means by which dispersed members of the nation could communicate their common national identity.[14]

Consider, for example, the way the *Richmond Enquirer* introduced the lyrics to "Southern Song of Freedom" in May 1861. The newspaper printed the song, submitted by a reader, as a possible "national anthem." The themes of the lyrics were typical, celebrating the South's noble volunteers, national symbols such as the flag, and the defense of southern freedom and homes against perfidious northern attack. Under the heading "A National Song," the *Enquirer* explained that "an appropriate national song for the Southern Confederacy" was being much deliberated upon that summer. "Plenty of patriotic poetry can be obtained," it observed, "but a purely American melody, one that will take with the masses, is hard to be found." Setting aside the *Examiner*'s use of the word "American" rather than "southern" or "Confederate," note the assumptions contained in these words about the nature of nationalism and its expression. First, there is the basic assumption that any nation worth its salt required a national anthem. Second, there is the implied belief that that anthem ought to be born of, and satisfy the tastes of, "the masses." This same assumption was reiterated in the *Enquirer*'s assertion that, "should the people adopt it, it will become our national anthem." Here was a crucial statement not just of the importance of culture to national identity but also of the importance of that culture's rootedness in "the people" of the nation themselves.[15]

Cultural definitions of national identity encompassed the higher branches of literature as well as popular songs and poems. Long-standing calls for the southern reading public to support southern periodicals, and southern literature more generally, multiplied in the new circumstances. "I have never before taken interest enough in our periodicals or papers," wrote one Texan to *De Bow's Review*, "but it is now a patriotic duty, as I consider, to use our efforts in getting our people to read our Southern writers." Newspaper editors across the South agreed, printing notices of southern publications and urging that they be supported as never before. Praising the May 1861 issue of another long-running southern periodical, the *Southern Literary Messenger*, the editors of the *Charleston Mercury* declared that literary independence was as important a goal as political independence: "Let our writers write, as our soldiers fight, and our people cheer both parties, whether wielding sword or pen."[16]

Many commentators saw 1861 as a year of great possibility for southern literature. "We have been as servilely dependent on the North," claimed one *Charleston Courier* editorial, "for cheap reading, as for machinery and notions." For precisely this reason, the present crisis offered the promise of "honey in the jaws of the lion." The southern people were at last asserting their autonomy, learning to act independently of the North. But, the *Courier* cautioned, they should not "neglect the cultivation of that grand and important element of national strength and independence, our mental power." If they were to make the most of this opportunity—if they were to create a strong nation—southerners would have to achieve intellectual and literary as well as political independence.[17]

Would they succeed? In 1861, opinions were mixed. Running through the debate were old insecurities and anxieties as well as some evidence of a new confidence. The sectional crisis had been stoked by an inferiority complex in the white South, and not even secession and the assertion of political independence quashed this underlying insecurity. Beneath many of the hortatory calls for southern literary enterprise ran the nagging doubt that encouragement alone could not give the South a high-quality national literature. One article on the "Disenthralment of Southern Literature" worried that, even with political independence, southerners might fall back into the old rut of intellectual dependence on the North. Though the anonymous author tried to be upbeat about the chances of that happening, he or she could not hide the anxiety that southern literature might never get off its feet: "The old taunt of 'Who reads an American book?' may be revived, with the change, 'Who reads a Southern book?' But, if so, Southerners will only have themselves to blame." As these words reveal, even in those heady first few months, the new nationalism was by no means free from the provincial anxiety that had characterized not just prewar southern nationalism but American nationalism as well. Along with many other features of American national identity, Confederate national identity inherited a sort of postcolonial insecurity.[18]

Other commentators seemed more optimistic about the potential of southern literature in an independent Confederacy. In closing his review of a foreign work that had been translated by a southerner, for instance, George Fitzhugh took the occasion to express the hopeful belief that "the literature of the South is about to be encouraged by the Southern people. No books written in the North, except those on physical science, can safely be read at the South." He thought that, so long as southerners gave their own authors the attention they deserved, "we shall soon have a literature much superior to any in the English language, because it will be more original, profound and comprehensive." In accounting for this prediction, Fitzhugh emphasized the factor that for him, as for so many others, underpinned the South's claim to distinctiveness and nationality: slavery. Because of their unique institution, Fitzhugh thought, an independent South could look forward to developing a unique literature.[19] Even for an optimist like Fitzhugh, though, in 1861 a distinctive southern literary culture was only a potential substantiation of the South's national identity. No serious commentator claimed that it already existed in mature form. When it came to culture more broadly—the general system of beliefs, values, and practices that define a group of people—many white southerners in 1861 felt that they stood on safer ground.

During the first months of the Confederacy's existence, white south-erners at home and abroad advanced a range of arguments to substantiate Confederate nationalism. While diplomats in Europe invoked the prin-ciple of nationality, as well as more interest-based arguments, in order to secure a place for the new nation-state in the international community, cultural and political leaders at home maintained that southerners repre-sented a unique nation according to the precepts of nineteenth-century nationalism: a people with its own cultural and intellectual identity that warranted political independence. These arguments were often tentative, and from the perspective of the twenty-first century, their claims seem hollow. But nationalists in the early Confederacy were simply doing what nationalists everywhere do best: glossing over disagreements and weak-nesses to assert a strong, unified national identity. To prove the existence of a Confederate national identity would be to prove the legitimacy of the Confederate nation-state.

The South and the North

Sooner or later the claim of a distinctive Confederate nationality ran up against the intractable question of what differentiated southerners from their former compatriots to the north. The two groups had lived together as Americans for decades, and they shared many of the characteristics that typically define a nation: language, ethnic makeup, history, political values, religious culture. Proving that southerners were truly different from northerners—so different as to mandate political separation—formed a central problem in the Confederacy's quest for national legitimacy at home and abroad. Many white southerners took on this challenge with alacrity, positing southern distinctiveness against the North in newspaper articles, speeches, and private communications. Following a common pat-tern, they defined their own identity in part by contrasting themselves against another group.

Their argument sometimes employed the vocabulary of race. "No civil strife is this," ran one especially florid iteration in the July issue of *De Bow's Review;* "no struggle of Guelph and Ghibelline; no contest between York and Lancaster; but a war of alien races, distinct nationalities, and opposite, hostile and eternally antagonistic governments." As was often the case, this author looked back to the English Civil War, reflecting a common ar-gument that descendents of one side had settled America's northern states and descendants of the other the South. "Cavalier and Roundhead," in this interpretation, "no longer designate parties, but *nations*, whose separate foundations were laid on Plymouth Rock and the banks of the James River." An article in the same publication later that year traced the roots of the North-South divide even further back in English history—all the way to 1066, when the French invasion had brought into contact but had not completely fused the Norman and Anglo-Saxon peoples. Centuries later, when the English settled in America, the two peoples had still not merged together, and each tended to settle in different parts of the country. Whereas the Anglo-Saxons flocked to New England, "the Norman—chivalrous, impetuous, and ever noble and brave—attained its full development in the Cavaliers of Virginia, and the Huguenots of South Carolina and Florida." From there it was but a small step to 1861 and the undeniable separation into one nation in the North and another in the South. Though such arguments were only ever peripheral to the development of Confederate nationalism, they were made, and they represent the attempt of some white southerners to fit their new national identity into the model of ethnicity- or race-based national identity that they saw in other parts of the world.[20]

Similar ways of thinking—albeit less formally expressed than in the articles that appeared in *De Bow's Review*—characterized ordinary white southerners' understandings of secession and the creation of the Confederacy. A revealing example appeared in a letter written by Louisianan Roland Jones to his brother in late February. Much had happened since their last communication, he wrote: "A new republic has sprung into being like Minerva from the hair of Jove." He went on to describe vividly the differences between northerners and southerners, highly unfavorably to the former. Jones did not talk specifically about Cavaliers and Puritans, but he did racialize the North-South difference by reading it back into the past. In his brief history of the "Northern scoundrels," Jones claimed, "Their ancestors fled from Europe and settled in the wilderness of America because, in the old country, they could not have their own way about everything." If anyone dared hold a different opinion than them, according to Jones, they would persecute the dissenter. And "to this day that same spirit animates [the] bosoms of their descendants." Like the articles in *De Bow's Review*, Jones's letter codified the North-South divide as racial—and therefore irreversible.

Along with Jones's historical-racial interpretation of the conflict came a sweeping indictment of northern society and character. Typical of northern society in general, he believed, were Republican party leaders, "who look upon nothing as sacred or holy; who scoff at the religion of the Bible, denounce the Constitution, the noble work of our great & good ances-tors. . . . How can we live with these people any longer?" Furthermore, these enemies desired the abolition of southern slavery, which struck Jones as being most disagreeable. In the face of this onslaught, he asked, "would we not ourselves be slaves, if we submitted, would we not be *cow-ards* if we did not resist"? Evidently, Jones carried such enmity toward the North and its people that he felt the same personal stake in the crisis that had driven so many white southerners away from the Union. Vividly cap-turing the personal, domestic valence of the North-South conflict, Jones declared, "I will not live in the same house, sit at the same table & sleep in the same bed with my mortal enemy." As was the case for so many south-erners, national bonds that had been cast in terms of domestic affection appeared to have been rent by irreligious, antislavery, and generally nefar-ious northern actions. Since their northern former compatriots were so disagreeable, white southerners must deserve national independence.[21]

As is often the case with national identities, Jones and many of his peers defined the Confederacy not only in positive but also in negative ways—against the North. It would have been difficult to spend a day in most parts of the South in 1861 without hearing examples of antinorthern invective. With every negative characterization of the North and its people, white southerners asserted their own national distinctiveness and made that distinctiveness appear more positive.[22] Antinorthern rhetoric was not entirely new. Yankees had long been the butt of southern insults. But such attacks became more common, and more malicious, in the wake of seces-sion and the formation of the Confederacy. Yankees were cheats and liars, it was claimed; they were fickle, faddish, corrupt, hypocritical, intolerant, greedy, and materialistic. They were overrun by dangerous foreign immi-grants. They held distorted religious beliefs, having turned their backs on the Bible as the true word of God. Their political practices were stained by corruption, ambition, partisanship, and a tendency toward centralization that belied the proper states-rights heritage of the founding generation and their Constitution. In short, the North was a misguided society headed for disaster.

Those educated in history saw ancient parallels. The *Charleston Mer-cury* was reminded when it looked northward of ancient Greece and Rome on the precipice of decline. "Gorged with ill-gotten wealth, run riot in lavish prosperity, with God behind and Mammon before them, respecters of nothing, believers in nothing," northerners were falling into precisely the same cycle of decay that had destroyed the ancient republics—the same republics that had always been such an important model for Americans. The present-day North called to mind Greece at the height of luxury, corruption, and decay—a country that was "drunk with prosperity. Effeminate in habits, emasculate in mind, all manhood was sunk in levity and licentious imaginings." The message was clear: northerners were headed for ruin, and it was good that southerners had gone their own way.[23]

The language of effeminacy and emasculation was not uncommon. In differentiating their own society from that of the North, white southerners in 1861 continued to invoke gender as they had done prior to secession. Southern men contrasted their own manliness with that of their northern counterparts. Naturally, the southerners came out on top. "The hardy sons of the South," an Alabama paper declared in the days after Sumter, "are not men worn down by servile toil, but men trained from childhood to the use of arms, to habits of self reliance and self command." The "[starving] hirelings of the North" would be no match for such fine specimens. Although the newspaper editorialist did not come right out and say so, his comparison of northern and southern masculinities turned on the crucial difference of slavery: surely it was slavery that permitted southern men to avoid "servile toil," to develop "self reliance and self command" rather than becoming like the "hirelings" of the free-labor North. This was precisely the kind of problem that ideologues of the slaveholding South tended to gloss over in their bombastic assertions of southern unity. One is left to wonder how nonslaveholding readers might have responded.[24]

North-South comparisons went beyond manhood to comprise the entire complex of gender roles and responsibilities. For instance, the conventional wisdom among white southerners who thought and wrote about such things was that their society had a much better notion of the rightful place of women. Articles in De Bow's Review, for example, argued that whereas white southern women adhered to appropriate gender roles, their northern counterparts did not. Southern women, according to one author, "confine themselves exclusively to the pursuits and associations becoming their sex, and abhor the female lecturers and abolition and free love oratrixes, and Bloomers, and strong-minded women of the North." On the subject of the "'Woman's Rights' doctrine," another proclaimed: "For that pestilent doctrine, springing latest-born and ugliest from the foul embrace of Yankeeism and infidelity, we have no sympathy." Echoing and building upon prewar commentary, southern writers continued to contrast the orderly gender relations in the South with apparent gender chaos in the North.[25]

To Georgian Susan Cornwall, northern women's abandonment of proper gender roles constituted one way, at least, in which they had sunk even below the depths of African Americans. "We hear of [white northern] women," she complained to her diary, "who have forgotten their sex and in their immodest love of publicity, have mounted the rostrum and poured forth incendiary harangues teeming with falsehood and disgusting revelations of their own depravity." Cornwall's opinion of African Americans' capabilities was emphatically negative. Yet she did note one glimmer of hope for the race, stemming from the fact that "no black woman has so far belied her sex or forgotten her proper sphere." As white southerners reflected on what distinguished them from northerners, Cornwall and others saw divergent gender regimes as a significant part of the divide.

Sooner or later, though, everything came back to the sine qua non of Confederate national identity: racial slavery. Cornwall's detour into gender conventions was set within a much lengthier harangue about the racial inferiority of African Americans, a condition which meant that slavery was the best circumstance for them. "While the Northerners profess to see nothing in a state of slavery but degradation for the slave & sin in the slaveholder," she wrote, "we consider it a condition highly honorable to both parties, when viewed in a proper light."[26] Cornwall's words remind us that behind this whole complex of comparisons between South and North—the gender conventions, the political philosophies, the apparent differences in character, religion, and morality—lay the fundamental difference between slavery and free labor. Every characteristic that white southerners pointed to when defining their peculiarity as a nation ultimately stemmed from their peculiar institution. If pressed, few would have denied that slavery lay at the foundation of the arguments they made to support their bid for national status.

Although Jefferson Davis famously minimized the importance of slavery to Confederate national identity—presumably because to do otherwise would have been so problematic for nonslaveholders at home and for the predominantly antislavery Western world—other leaders were more candid.[27] In his well-known "cornerstone" speech of March 1861, Confederate vice president Alexander Stephens pointed to "African slavery" as the "immediate cause" of secession. Unlike the United States, which held a misguided belief in "the equality of the races," the Confederacy recognized the divine truth of racial *in*equality. Indeed, Stephens said, the Confederacy's "foundations were laid, its cornerstone rests, upon the great truth that the negro is not equal to the white man; that slavery, subordination to the superior race, is his natural and moral condition." Herein, for Stephens, lay the essence of the Confederacy's claim to a distinct national identity. "Our new Government," he explained, "is the first, in the history of the world, based upon this great physical, philosophical, and moral truth."[28]

In 1861, there were both Stephenses and Davises: those who unequivocally acknowledged the basis of the new nation in slavery, and those who sought to minimize it. Often, though, the difference between the two groups was one of emphasis more than substance. Particularly revealing in this respect was an editorial that appeared in the *Richmond Examiner*. "Those who suppose the present difficulties of the United States," it began, "to be the result of an agitation against negro slavery, see only the surface." "The true cause of the approaching separation of this country into two parts," it went on, appealing directly to the great principle of nationality, "is the fact that it is inhabited by two peoples, two utterly distinct nations." Even though those two nations shared much in common, the editorial asserted, they were "now divided as far as the North Pole is distinct from the Equator, and as hostile as the feline to the canine species of animal." Thus far, the *Examiner* seemed to be minimizing the importance of slavery to secession and emphasizing the importance of national differences. When it went on to further analyze those national differences, though, the editorial was led inexorably back to slavery. Apparently contradicting its opening contention that slavery was the mere "surface" of the split, the editorial subsequently referred to slavery as

> the basis of our lives in the South. It has developed our peculiar qualities and peculiar faults, all of them the exact reverses of those created by the system of leveling materialism and of numerical majorities which has attained in the North a logical perfection of application hitherto unknown and unheard of in any part of the whole world. Under the operation of these causes, we repeat the North and the South have come to be inhabited by two nations. They are different in everything that can constitute difference in national character; in their persons, in their pronunciation, in their dress, in their port, in their religious ideas, in their sentiments toward women, in their manners to each other, in their favourite foods, in their houses and domestic arrangements, in their method of doing business, in their national aspirations, in all their tastes, all their principles, in all their pride and in all their shame. The French are not more unlike the English than the Yankees are unlike the Southerners.

This was quite a laundry list of national differences between North and South. As the *Examiner* made clear, all were thought to stem, in one way or another, from the distinguishing feature of slavery.[29]

The Confederacy and America

Differentiating the South from the North was the easy part. Far more difficult was the task of explaining how the Confederacy differed from the United States of America. It was one thing to vilify one's enemy; it was another entirely to leave behind the nation to which southerners had belonged for almost a century—the nation to which they had contributed so much; the nation for which, as recently as the Mexican War, they had bled and died; the nation, most importantly of all, associated with the revolutionary legacy that they valued so highly. Few white southerners would have said that the creation of the Confederate States equaled a wholesale rejection of America. Yet none could deny that it was the southern states that had voluntarily left the old Union to create a new one. These facts led to a profound ambivalence about the extent to which Confederate national identity should and could replicate American national identity. How would white southerners reconcile the new with the old? How would they balance continuity and change? What would be the relationship between American and Confederate nationalisms?

Foundations indicating the answers to these questions were laid with the drafting of the provisional Confederate constitution. For ideological reasons, as well as for obvious practical ones, the delegates in Montgomery basically replicated the United States constitution, with only a few alterations. To be sure, the changes were not insignificant: the protection of slavery, explicit mention of God, extra limitations on the authority of the central government, and safeguards against the corruptions of partisan patronage. But these were seen as refinements and perfections rather than new departures. In presenting the new constitution to his constituents, Alabama politician Robert H. Smith explained that it was essentially the same as the old, with a few necessary additions, which in his estimation had "greatly purified our Government." Purification was a common way of understanding the relationship between the old and the new. As the long-standing secessionist Louis T. Wigfall told a Charleston crowd, the actions of the delegates at Montgomery had merely restored that government to the form it should have taken all along. Restoration, purification, perfection—these were the terms southerners used to signify that the new government was based very much on the old. Employing a construction metaphor, one commentator declared: "We have builded a new temple out of the materials that composed the old one, and the glory of the latter house is greater than that of the former."[30]

If seceding southerners represented the real America, why should errant northerners retain the trappings of American national identity? Some white southerners argued that they should not—that the South, not the North, deserved to inherit the symbols and heroes of American national identity. As the new government deliberated on the need for a national flag—a crucial component in establishing its nationality in the eyes of the world—there were calls for the South to retain the stars and stripes, or something very close to it. Writing to William Porcher Miles, the chair of the Confederate Congress's Committee on Flag and Seal, M. E. Huger remarked that he was "much interested in the Flag, that is to represent to the world our Southern country." Even though neither he nor Miles cared much for the old stars and stripes, he knew that many of their fellow southerners did. The flag selection committee ought to give it, or some very similar design, careful consideration. It was already "well known and respected, . . . simple, easily distinguished, easily made & understood, for nearly a century has signified our country to the world, & to which we have a right." With the words "our" and "right," Huger signaled sympathy with the widespread feeling that the stars and stripes belonged as much to the South as it did to the North.[31]

Alabamian John Pelham agreed. "Although I am a most ultra secessionist," he wrote to his family, "I am still proud of the American flag. It does not belong to the North any more than to us, and has never had anything to do with our wrongs." Because he recognized that both sides had a claim on it, Pelham thought the best solution would be for each to set it aside, "as a memento of our past greatness and of our Revolutionary renown." Whatever happened, he rejected the idea that the North should continue to use it as a national standard. "They have no right to use it," he insisted, "and we should not permit them. It should be stored away with [our] other household gods, cherished and preserved spotless and unstained, 'not a single stripe erased or poluted, not a single star obscured.'"[32]

Along with the U.S. flag, southerners also advanced claims to ownership of American heroes and history. George Washington loomed particularly large, just as he had before secession. Many saw echoes of Washington's military and political leadership in Jefferson Davis. As the teenaged Louisianan Sarah Lois Wadley remarked in the summer of 1861, "Truly we have in him a second Washington." Later that year, looking north, Wadley perceived there a drift toward despotism that mocked Washington's legacy. Northerners "are unworthy of the heritage of this name," she wrote; "henceforth Washington the Father of our country, his memory, his virtue, his valor, they remain the heritage alone of his native state, and the fair sisters that with her form our youthful Confederacy."[33]

Georgian Susan Cornwall also believed that Confederates ought to retain some aspects of American national identity, including Washington. Reacting to the news of the formation of the Confederate government in early February 1861, Cornwall rejoiced at this historic event, hoping that God would go on to "make of us a great people." Even though she welcomed independence and separation from the North, she still thought southerners ought to maintain ties to their old national identity. "There is much of poetry," she wrote, "in the hitherto national attachment to the Union. It is like uprooting some of our holiest sentiments to feel that to love it longer is to be treacherous to ourselves and our country." This supplanting of long-held allegiances clearly brought regret as well as joy. The transition from the United to the Confederate States was by no means unproblematic. But for Susan Cornwall the Confederate future would benefit from maintaining its links to the American past. "We can love the past of our glorious country still," she wrote, "and remember her as a maiden does her dead mother. We can forget her faults and remember her virtues."[34]

Later that month, Cornwall was inspired by the occasion of Washington's birthday to reflect on his place in Confederate national identity. "To day is the anniversary," she wrote, "of the birth of one of the greatest of men. Washington the pure patriot, the sincere Christian." Cornwall echoed Sarah Lois Wadley's stress on the hero's southern origin: "We of the South rejoice that he was 'one of us,' trained amid the same surroundings as the Southerner of to day." But Cornwall was even more specific about why Washington's memory rightly belonged to the South in the present conflict. "May we not believe," she asked, "that the development of his character was aided by the very institutions so repugnant to the Northern devotee of Liberty"? Washington, that is, had been a slaveholder (Cornwall made no mention of the fact that he had freed his slaves upon his death), and therefore his memory sustained the slaveholding South rather than the antislavery North. The same point was made that May at a public meeting in Virginia. Washington had been a slaveholder, a speaker there proclaimed, "fighting for the freedom of the white, and the slavery

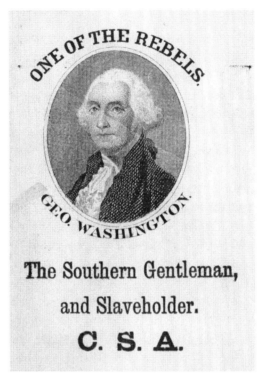

FIGURE 4.1 One of the Rebels. (Civil War Pictorial Envelope Collection, Southern Historical Collection, Wilson Library, the University of North Carolina at Chapel Hill.)

of the black race," and present-day southerners were doing the same thing. The legacy of Washington was claimed for slavery, secession, and the South.[35]

With Washington came the whole Revolutionary generation—indeed the whole American Revolution. Affirmations of the continuity between 1861 and 1776 were legion. They filled speeches, poems and songs, newspaper editorials, and private writings alike. To give just one representative example: in the summer of 1861 a letter to the *Richmond Examiner* reminded readers that southerners were at that time "standing where our forefathers stood in the great struggle for colonial independence." Lincoln and his followers in the North "hypocritically" claimed to be doing the same thing, but southerners were the real heirs of the American Revolution. "They stand alone now," "Virginius" wrote, "in asserting the great principle of the Declaration of Independence, that 'Governments divine their legitimate force only from the consent of the governed.' This great principle their 'brethren' of the North have abandoned." This letter writer

NEW YORK UNION ENVELOPE DEPOT, 144 BROADWAY

A Southern Man with Union principles.

FIGURE 4.2 A Southern Man with Union Principles. (Civil War Pictorial Envelope Collection, Southern Historical Collection, Wilson Library, the University of North Carolina at Chapel Hill.)

said what countless other southerners were saying or thinking: the South was faithful to the revolutionary legacy, which it was even then reenacting; the North, in contrast, had betrayed it.[36]

The changed political situation mandated serious reflection on the meaning of American Independence Day below the Mason-Dixon Line. In the wake of secession and the creation of the Confederacy, there were some who felt that Independence Day should expire along with the United States. One soldier noted in his diary on July 4, 1861, "Once the Sons of the South hailed its coming with joy, but now we heed it not for the United States are no more." In Charleston, Alfred Dunkin, who had been invited to deliver a Fourth of July oration, declined to deliver a speech, observing that "times have changed." The present was such a volatile time that he felt it inappropriate to hold forth on "a past Independence." Instead, he suggested that they ought instead to have a public speech on December 20, the anniversary of South Carolina's secession, the day "on which was asserted and vindicated the principles of the 4th July, 1776." Even though they fought for the principles of the original American Revolution, Dunkin felt that they ought to be publicly celebrating declarations of southern, rather than American, independence. Dunkin's letter raises an intriguing question: why did southerners not celebrate a new, specifically Confederate independence day? Surprisingly, there is little evidence of significant support for this idea, perhaps because different states seceded from the Union on different dates, perhaps because the demands of war proved too distracting, or perhaps because so many white southerners saw the Confederacy as a continuance of the United States rather than a departure from it.[37]

The majority verdict, though, was that Confederates had every right—and even a duty—to continue to celebrate the Fourth. As the editor of the *Mobile Register* put it, the anniversary "belongs to the South as fully as to the North, . . . it cannot be dropped from the National calendar of the Confederate States." A few days later the *Register's* editor reprinted an excerpt from a Louisiana newspaper that contained a similar sentiment: "The Yankees have robbed us of too much already. We have no idea of giving up the national anniversary—not a bit of it. The Fourth of July is ours." In one of the few formal Fourth of July orations held below the Mason-Dixon Line in 1861, Alexander Terrell told his Texas audience that in separating from those northerners, southerners had clearly acted in alignment with the principles of '76. The earlier revolutionaries had provided an invaluable example of courageously standing up for their rights and refusing to allow a dominant power to exercise control over them. The principle for which that generation fought was not, Terrell took care to point out, universal liberty but rather the very limited conception that the right of self-government was appropriate in their particular situation. In fighting for the same ideals, Terrell declared, Confederates were actually fighting "the second war for independence."[38] Many others, in newspapers, speeches, diaries, and letters, agreed that the Confederacy had a strong claim to ownership of the holiday, based on the apparent similarities between 1776 and 1861.[39]

In claiming ownership of the holiday, some white southerners thought that northerners' failure to live up to the legacy of the Revolution meant that they had forfeited their claim to the Fourth. One Confederate soldier complained to his aunt how hypocritical he felt northern celebrations were when he heard salutes being fired at Washington, DC, from his camp on the morning of July 4, 1861. "What mocking," he thought, that northerners were "celebrating their independence and at the same time striving to deprive their assistants in the strife of the very boon which they estimate so highly." The North, in his judgment, had no right to continue to commemorate a movement whose principles they had discarded.[40]

Whereas many commentators stressed the absolute similarity of 1776 and 1861, others began to concede that there were inconsistencies between the Confederacy's principles—particularly its commitment to racial slavery—and some aspects of the American Revolution.[41] The editor of the *Richmond Examiner* urged his readers in 1861 that they should always remember the Revolution and the Fourth of July. But he also informed them that it was time to consign one element of the Revolution—the Declaration's second paragraph—to the dustbin. Why on earth, he wondered, had a group of slaveholders tacked a radical statement of universal equality onto the beginning of the document? The Declaration was based on faulty logic, he concluded; it had functioned as a Trojan horse, and abolitionists had used it to destroy the Union. Instead of being hypocritical now, southerners should jettison the Declaration and distinguish between the revolutionaries' actions, which were noble, and their own explanation of those actions, which ought to be ignored. Likewise, the *Charleston Courier* aligned southern secession with carefully selected features of the Declaration of Independence, and compared the despotism of Abraham Lincoln with that of George the Third. "While we reject utterly the barefaced and transparent fallacies with which the production of MR. JEFFERSON opens," the *Courier* asserted, in seceding the southern states had faithfully acted out another passage of the Declaration: the passage concerning the right of a people to resist oppression and to govern themselves. Discerning commentators selected those aspects of the Revolutionary heritage that seemed to fit and jettisoned those that did not.[42]

Other white southerners similarly felt that while the Fourth should continue to be marked below the Mason-Dixon Line, it should not be marked in exactly the same way. Charleston's '76 Association, which had been organizing Independence Day celebrations for almost thirty years, decided to hold a scaled-back celebration in 1861, in recognition of the changed circumstances. Louisianan Sarah Lois Wadley was also uncertain about what to make of the holiday. In 1861 she recorded in her diary that the Fourth had passed very quietly, her mind having been "so much occupied by other things that I had almost forgotten the day." She read in the papers that the anniversary had been marked by the closing of businesses and stores, by the firing of salutes, and so forth, but nothing too raucous. She was glad about that: "I think that the day should have been observed with unusual strictness, but it is natural and right that the feeling should have been more of sober thankfulness and religious prayer than of noisy joy." Across the South that July, the question of how the Fourth ought to be celebrated—if at all—remained unresolved.[43]

For Sarah Lois Wadley as for many southerners, uncertainty about the Fourth reflected broader anguish about the transition from the United States to the Confederate States. With disunion and the Confederacy now established facts, her regret lingered. Reporting in her diary that Jefferson Davis and Alexander Stephens had been chosen to lead the Confederate States, she realized that she "had almost written the United States." The slip provoked sorrowful reflection. "How sad to think," she observed, "that we are united no longer, that we are no more natives of one common country, necessary as is the separation how can we think of it without grief." A Union that had been based in no small part on the mutual affection of its members—what she had earlier termed a "real heart Union"—could not be dismantled without some heartache. Wadley and many others did not experience the separation with unalloyed joy.[44]

Like Wadley, Alabama planter William Proctor Gould expressed approval of Confederate independence that was tinged with regret. In a scrapbook containing newspaper clippings on the crisis, Gould included one story, "What the Yankee Nation Has Come To," which detailed the extreme depths to which northern society had sunk. He felt compelled to add some notes of his own, explaining his personal response to the public issues of national identity and allegiance. "Although for many years," he wrote, "indeed, for the greater part of my life, the South has been the home of my choice, and in all human probability, in the South my bones will find their last resting place, yet, I cannot, if I would, forget that Yankee blood courses in my veins." The current state of the North depressed him. It was, after all, his "native land." Even so, northerners' behavior had been so egregious that reunion was unthinkable. "Devoted as I once was to the Union of the whole United States," he explained, "if the settlement of the question at this moment depended on my single voice, it would not be given in favor of reconstruction." In considering how white southerners navigated their changing national allegiances, it is crucial to bear in mind the sorrowful backward glances cast by Gould and like-minded southerners.[45]

For William Proctor Gould and Sarah Lois Wadley, leaving the United States was especially problematic because they had been born in the North. For many others, family ties stretching across what was now a de facto international border complicated their feelings about allegiance and identity. Helen Swift, a young North Carolina woman, confronted just such complications in the letters she wrote to her aunt in Pennsylvania during 1861. In March, attending boarding school in Alabama, Swift discussed secession with sorrow and resignation, writing, "I regret very much that the Union is dissolved yet I had much rather for it to be so than be under the jurisdiction of such a bitter enemy of the South as that stanch abolitionist Lincoln is." In June, back home in Wilmington, North Carolina, she told her aunt about a letter she had received from another northern correspondent, who, she wrote, "hopes we are not infected by the poisonous serpent Secession. But it is useless, I feel, to cry 'Union,' where there is and can be none—tho' it was almost a death blow to many Southerners to give it up." Southerners had clung to the Union as long and as hard as they could, she believed. But antislavery had driven them against their will over the precipice of secession. Even as she explained that southerners had had to prioritize "liberty" over the Union, she obviously remained attached to the United States. Writing about another aunt, this one a fervent secessionist, Swift expressed surprise that "she glories in it—the Separation I mean by it. I do not understand how any one can do that. It is at best a painful tearing asunder of old ties, painful because of the necessity."[46]

Balancing competing ties to the United and the Confederate States was nowhere more difficult than in the border region. The slaveholding states of Kentucky, Missouri, Maryland, and Delaware would ultimately remain in the Union, but in 1861 their residents felt painfully torn between North and South. At the end of April, 1861, a leading unionist politician, John J. Crittenden of Kentucky, wrote to his son, then in the U.S. armed forces, urging him not to follow the many southern soldiers and sailors who were resigning to join the Confederate military. Crittenden rejected the excuse that because Americans' primary loyalty was to their state, once their states seceded there was no choice but to leave the Union and join the Confederacy. "This supposes they have *No Nation*," he complained, "no National Flag &c." And in any case, he hoped that Kentucky's strong unionism meant that his son would never be faced with this difficult choice: "[Kentucky] loves the Union & will cling to it as long as possible. And so, I hope, will you. Be true to the government that has trusted in you. And stand fast to your Nation's flag, the Stars and Stripes." Another Kentuckian, Susan Fishback, maintained a similarly firm commitment to American nationalism in the summer of 1861. In July she wrote to a friend about her attendance at "a real, old fashioned, fourth of July," with "patriotic speeches, and flag presentations, and national songs sung by little girls in white," all of which she heartily approved of. By September, Fish-back was feeling concerned about the developing military conflict, but she found solace in her patriotism, writing, "Love of country has always been more of a religious sentiment with me than any thing else, and I have felt that if this blessed government was to be broken up, all that makes life desirable would be gone." Border-state unionism clearly remained pow-erful throughout 1861 and beyond.[47]

Other border-state southerners made the decision to side with the Confed-eracy, even as their states formally remained in the Union. This was always a more difficult decision to make because it required them to reject existing allegiances—to the United States and to their own state—and embrace a new allegiance to the Confederacy. Pro-Confederates in majority-Union areas of the border South found the new circumstances especially trying. Samuella Hart Curd, originally from Richmond, Virginia, moved with her new hus-band to Missouri in 1860. Perhaps because of her Virginia background, she sympathized greatly with the Confederate cause. On the Fourth of July, 1861, she rued the conflict that was tearing apart the once happy country, and described a sort of civil war in microcosm as local celebrators fought "quite a conflict as to whether Dixie, or Star Spangled banner should be sung." She was delighted that "Dixie gained the day, hurrah!" As 1861 progressed it became increasingly difficult to be a Confederate sympathizer among union-ists. Curd found herself having to hold her tongue when politics came up in conversation ("I kept perfectly silent . . . for if once started I become excited & can do no good"). She bemoaned the frequent presence of Union troops ("Oh! it is humiliating to me to have them here"). And more than once she declared in her diary, "Oh! don't I wish I was in Dixie." Although Curd did not record any overt conflict with members of her family, she did observe such conflicts within other Missouri families. After a busy day of visiting in Octo-ber 1861, she wrote, "The times were generally discussed, I found union and Secession in the same family. This question is dividing more families than any other that has ever stirred the public mind."[48]

If the Civil War was a "brothers' war," it was most visibly so in the bor-der states. Confronting so difficult a choice between the Confederacy and the United States, different members of border-state families made dif-ferent choices. The inevitable result was pain. In many cases, the conflict, and the pain, was overt. In some cases, such as that of the young Kentuck-ian L. P. Yandell, even the possibility of family differences generated anx-iety. Yandell, a physician, was working in Memphis, Tennessee, as the secession crisis gathered steam. He applauded South Carolina's secession and hoped both Tennessee, his temporary home, and Kentucky, his native state, would follow the Palmetto State out of the Union. The proposal that Kentucky and other border states maintain neutrality between the two sides was, for him, untenable. Yet he believed his father supported this policy, which caused him palpable anxiety. "It is painful to differ so totally with my dear Father, who has so much wisdom and experience," he lamented, but he took solace in the hope that "he will soon think as I do." His letters, however, continued to express worry that his father would not in fact convert to the Confederate cause. "I was disappointed," he wrote to his father in late April, "in not getting a letter from you yesterday informing me of a change of sentiment in yourself and Kentucky." And a couple of days later, "I hope my course meets with your approbation." Fortunately for Yandell, his father did come to support secession and his son. But for many other border southerners, family divisions deepened, festered, and rivaled the war itself as a source of anguish.[49]

The competing pulls of the Confederate and the United States not only tore families apart but also generated overwhelming internal conflicts within individual southerners. Consider the case of John C. Pegram, a young Kentuckian in the U.S. navy. Pegram opted to support the Union and remain in the navy. He did not much sympathize with secession, viewing it like most unionists as the work of corrupt, self-serving demagogues. But even so, he felt the pull of both southern and American identities and allegiances. "Although Dear Pa," he wrote in July 1861, "I am a Southerner and love the South, yet I am an American." The situation was complicated by the fact that Virginia members of the Pegram clan fought for the Confederacy. This "war between brothers," with "families even divided and hostile to each other," upset him greatly. "Just to think," he wrote to his father,

> some of my dearest relations in arms against their Govt but Thank God dear Father there are some Pegrams left who still love their country and are willing to sacrifice *all* to its interests and its service. While my heart bleeds for my dear relations in Va *my* patriotism burns more the brighter though it be the sadder and I have no higher ambition than to live with the stars & stripes waving over me and to die with the same glorious bunting for my winding sheet.

This was effusive, heartfelt American nationalism. But Pegram then made the surprising admission that his own decision to side with the Union had not been easy. "I pray that God will forgive me," he continued, "for any ideas I ever had of deserting the ever-to-be honored flag of our Liberty." In a subsequent letter he again referred to his shame that at the beginning of the crisis he had been "pretty nearly rank secession."[50]

Pegram also expressed concern about his father's loyalty, worrying in August 1861 that he had come to question unionism. "If you my dear Father are hostile to the government which I am serving," he wrote, "I cannot agree with you in your opinions." When his father's loyalty later became clear, Pegram was greatly relieved. Still, Pegram's unionism was conditional. He would give his all for the Union, he explained, so long as he believed that the conflict was one of "loyal Americans against discontented and rebellious subjects of an easy government of their own choice." But if it ever became clear that in fighting for the Union he was, he wrote, "aiding 'Northern Abolitionists' against my Southern kin then and not 'til then will I leave the service I have adopted and curse myself for a fool at being so badly disposed."[51]

Pegram's ambivalence continued as the war progressed. At the beginning of 1862 he wrote to his mother about the current state of affairs. He was tired of the U.S. Congress devoting so much attention to "the eternal nigger," he complained; it was "enough to make a southerner sick." Even so, he pledged continued allegiance to the United States, so long as the war effort truly fought for Union and not the nefarious designs of the abolitionists. "As much as I love the South," he explained, in a passage deeply evocative of the tension between southern and American identities, "and I boast of my Virginia and Kentucky and Louisiana kin, even up here among the Northerners, I love my country as well, and deplore the separation, deplore the causes that make my love for the South and my love for my country, two different things."[52]

As a border-state southerner who fought for the Union, John Pegram experienced these competing pulls in different ways than most men and women in states further south, men and women who were forced to balance time-honored affiliations with the Union against contending loyalty to their states, to their region, to the new Confederacy. Yet the underlying issues were the same. In 1861, there was no resolution to the problem of how Confederate national identity related to American national identity. White southerners did not wish to yield American national identity to northerners. On the contrary, many in the South believed that northerners had perverted that national identity and had less of a claim to it than did southerners themselves. But the fact that the governmental institutions of

American nationalism remained in northern hands rendered this argument problematic. It had been the South, and not the North, that had taken its leave of the Union. Furthermore, the importance of the strikingly unequal institution of slavery to the Confederacy generated inconsistencies with a revolutionary tradition that was coming to be associated more closely with the principle of equality. And so, despite frequent claims that Confederate national identity was a purified instantiation of American national identity, and despite attempts to claim selected aspects of revolutionary memory for the South alone, the precise relationship between the Confederacy and America was for the moment left undetermined.

Creating Confederate Citizens

Not only did Confederates have to define their collective national identity and position themselves in relation to America, the North, and the wider world, they also had to define Confederate citizenship. As they well knew, being a legitimate nation-state in the modern world involved classifying certain individuals as "citizens" and others as "aliens," and delineating the rights and responsibilities that bound citizens and the nation-state together. To some extent, these definitions were determined by central government officials. But in a broader sense, Confederate citizenship took shape in a diffuse, collaborative, and sometimes contentious process involving not only political leaders but also writers, newspaper editors, soldiers, and indeed men and women from all walks of life.

The Confederacy's central government never formally codified a system of national citizenship. As was the case in the United States until the Fourteenth Amendment to the Constitution in 1868, the terms of citizenship for those born in the states that formed the Confederacy were left to the individual state governments. However, as in the antebellum United States, the Confederate government moved toward defining national citizenship by establishing a line between citizens and noncitizens on an incremental, piecemeal basis. This line was complicated by the presence of slaves, who were denied citizenship status, and who were subject to the authority of their owners rather than the direct authority of the government. In the logic of Confederate citizenship, as with U.S. citizenship, African Americans functioned as internal "others" against which the white citizenry was defined.

There were external "others," too, who fell into the categories of "alien enemy" or simply "alien." From the very beginning, Confederate officials recognized the importance of identifying foreign nationals within their borders—particularly citizens of the United States—and treating them accordingly. The line between citizens of the Confederate States and citizens of the United States had to be clear. In May 1861 the central government began in earnest to draw firm boundaries around its own citizenry, initiating procedures for the confiscation of property owned by U.S. citizens within its borders and requiring all debts owed by Confederates to northerners to be paid instead to the Confederate treasury. In August the Confederacy went a step further with a new law that defined all citizens of the United States within Confederate territory as "alien enemies." It proclaimed that all men (the duties and responsibilities of formal citizenship were understood in gender-exclusive terms) "adhering to the United States and acknowledging the authority of the same" should leave the bounds of the Confederacy "within forty days"—unless they swore an oath to the Confederacy. Finally, the Confederacy followed up with the Sequestration Act, which enabled the authorities to confiscate property—both actual property and outstanding debt—owned by U.S. citizens.[53]

Just as differentiating Confederate and American identities generated intractable problems, particularly in the border regions, so too did the attempt to distinguish citizens from aliens. The line between the two was difficult to pin down with any precision. In theory the Confederate government drew this line using two principal criteria: location and loyalty. Yet the physical borders between the Confederacy and the Union shifted constantly during the Civil War, with the numerous contested areas complicating the problem of exactly which territory the Confederacy could legitimately claim to control—and, therefore, which people it controlled.[54] Throughout the war white southerners' allegiances and cultural identities shifted, too. Both variables rendered it impossible in practice for the Confederate government to draw a rigid line between U.S. and Confederate citizens.

The large numbers of persons within Confederate borders who remained loyal to the Union, to one degree or another, challenged the legitimacy and the security of the fledgling Confederate nation-state. Any genuine nation-state had to be in control of those residing in its territory. Accordingly, among the many arguments that Confederate diplomats made in their attempt to win foreign recognition was the claim that the Confederacy's population was internally united.[55] But control over the relevant territory and population was even more crucial in domestic terms. Thus as early as 1861, with its national borders already in flux, the

Confederacy reacted strongly to dissenters who resisted secession and the authority of the Confederate States. Dissent was particularly strong in mountainous areas of the Confederacy, areas where slaveholding was limited and where southerners of all classes, but especially poorer southerners, resented the Confederacy's presumption of authority. In northwestern Virginia, such dissent resulted in the carving off of the new, loyalist state of West Virginia. In other parts of the South—areas such as northern Alabama, northern Georgia, and western North Carolina—opposition to secession persisted long after the summer of 1861, growing later in the war into organized peace movements. Dissent was especially acute in eastern Tennessee. Tennessee's governor Isham Harris was faced in the later months of 1861 with major challenges to his authority—and, by extension, the Confederacy's. In conjunction with the Confederate military and political authorities, Harris was perfectly willing to use force to quash unionist dissent. Already there were signs of the brutal, guerilla-style warfare between unionists and Confederates that would continue in contested territories throughout the Civil War.

In addition to opposing unionists with force, Harris and other southern officials used their authority to arrest, punish, and imprison—in short, to stifle dissent within the territory over which they claimed authority. A document submitted to Harris in late 1861 provides a revealing window into the basic ideas about loyalty that underpinned the Confederacy's response to dissent. The "List of Political and State Prisoners, for Governor Harris" catalogued dissenters who had been imprisoned in the fall of 1861. In addition to their names and the dates and locations of their arrests, the list also contained a column labeled "charges." These charges included "aiding the enemy," "piloting the Yankees," and "tampering with slaves," but there were also references to loyalty and identity. One man had been arrested for being a "very violent Union man," while another was identified as an "Obnoxious Union Dutchman of Nashville," with no further details. What seems clear is that opinions and affiliations, not only actions, could be considered crimes. The descriptions of the charges brought against these political prisoners reveals an important aspect of the Confederacy's distinction between citizens and noncitizens.[56]

Government officials were not the only ones who used beliefs and apparent loyalties to the Union as a means of classifying individuals during 1861. In the climate of conformity engendered by secession and war, labeling somebody a "unionist" could be a powerful weapon against them. For instance, in May 1861 a group of Virginia citizens sent a petition to their state's governor urging him to reconsider the appointment of one Dr. George Hammil to the post of assistant surgeon in Virginia's First Infantry. In informing the governor that Hammil was the wrong man for the job, the petitioners did not cite any lack of medical competency but rather attacked his character and his beliefs. Hammil should be replaced, they urged, because he was "a man who holds the strongest union sentiments, and [is] even regarded where known as a abolitionist [and] is a native of Pensylvania." Because of his northern background, his Union loyalties, and his questionable stance on slavery, they wrote, Hammil did not deserve the position. In one sense, these petitioners were simply exerting their influence to deny a job to an enemy, but in a broader sense they were claiming the right to help determine the line between loyal Confederate and unionist, between citizen and alien. Throughout the war, in countless everyday acts such as this one, ordinary southerners joined political leaders in establishing and policing the boundaries of Confederate citizenship.[57]

For some southerners, the Confederacy brought with it opportunities for self-reinvention. Especially in the context of the beginning of military operations, the shifting of allegiances offered the promise of a new start, the chance of proving themselves in the world, to men across the South. The young Georgian H. C. Kendrick, for instance, wrote home from his camp in Virginia about the personal ramifications of his position as a Confederate soldier. His youthful, sometimes naive gusto was typical of many. "I want to be in all the fights . . . in the war," he wrote to his brother. "I think Thom., that I shall kill a yankee before I get back yet." H. C. Kendrick was clearly enjoying his first months in the army. He was in good health. He had learned to cook for himself. To his brother he wrote, "I enjoy my time the best in the world. patriotism glows within my heart rapidly as the sun runs." And to his father, "I am well & fat as a fig and a little saucy." This was clearly a young man for whom military service offered personal enrichment. With his glowing patriotism and his new found personal independence, H. C. Kendrick was happy.[58]

He was also aware of the responsibilities being a citizen-soldier entailed. Later in 1861, he reported to his sister that he had been reflecting during a military maneuver on his role in the war and the new nation-state. "I was struck," he told her, "with the importance of the post which we hold [,] then the most dangerous of all others. I felt under strong responsibilities knowing that the very destination of our country depended upon the care we took in holding that line." Here was a clear connection between the action of the individual citizen and the fate of the nation. For H. C.

Kendrick, his daily duties as a soldier directly affected the safety of the nation.[59] Perhaps Kendrick had read some of the articles regarding soldierly duty that permeated the southern press in 1861. Under the headline "The Duty Which the Soldier Owes to his Country," the *Richmond Enquirer* urged that during wartime every citizen ought to subordinate his own needs to the interests of the country. A letter printed in another Virginia paper conveyed a similar opinion. The letter was written to a young soldier by his father, who cautioned the new recruit that "when a soldier shoulders his rifle under the flag of his country, he must surrender to that country his will, his whims, tastes, fancies & prejudices." Above all, the father admonished, soldiers must obey orders.[60]

Men in uniform perceived direct, consequential connections between themselves and the nation. As the testimony of H. C. Kendrick illustrates so well, ordinary soldiers in the ranks were keenly aware that Confederate nationhood was not the concern of intellectuals and leaders alone. Moreover, if the making of national identity and citizenship took place in the lowliest ranks of the army as well as the halls of formal power, it also involved ordinary southerners who never donned a uniform at all.

Such was the message of "Our Cause," a newspaper article that was reprinted across the South. "It is quite natural," observed the *Montgomery Advertiser* in introducing its printing of the article, "that brilliant deeds should attract attention, and plainer but not less substantial proofs of patriotism pass unheeded." But emphasizing the "brilliant" at the expense of "plainer" acts should be avoided: "'An army with banners' excites enthusiasm, but the poor widow who gives her son shows patriotism as lofty as the soldier 'in the imminent deadly breech.'" Southerners should, in other words, recognize that nationalism—its making and its sustenance—was an everyday affair, by no means confined to the more visible efforts of the few. The *Advertiser* made this point by way of introduction to a private letter sent from Charleston, a letter containing several examples of everyday nationalist commitment. The letter praised "the quiet patience" of those who performed the "most onerous of the soldiers' duties," along with "the steady perseverance of our women, young and old, in making up knapsacks, haversacks, and cartridges," and the "generous indulgence of employers who do the clerk's work in his absence, and continue his salary all the while." Citizenship, in other words, was an everyday phenomenon—those nameless people, performing the most quotidian of tasks, were instrumental in the making of Confederate citizenship.[61]

White southerners knew that their everyday acts as individuals carried national meaning whether the nation in question was the United States or the new Confederacy. In many respects, the concepts of nationalism and citizenship remained constant even as the object of national allegiance changed. White southerners continued to conceptualize their individual responsibility to the nation's well-being in strongly moral and often religious terms. This continuity was evident, for example, in an article entitled "National Morality" that appeared in both the religious and the secular press in the summer of 1861. Beginning with the assertion that "nations have their moral character," it went on to contend that the fate of any given nation depended to a large degree upon that character. Asking, "What shall the moral character of our nation be?" the article insisted that "every citizen must bear his part in answering that question." This article specifically pointed to Sabbatarianism as a way for the Confederacy to demonstrate its worthiness. Pointing out that the federal government of United States had "been a great a Sabbath breaker," delivering the mail on Sunday, the author fervently hoped that the Confederacy might initiate a new religious as well as a new political departure. "If we really acknowledge God, as a nation," it concluded, "let us keep our cause clear with him by honoring his law." It was plain that the responsibility for this rested with each individual.[62]

White southerners imagined and enacted the responsibilities of citizenship in other ways, too. The Confederacy's fate rested on their wallets, for one thing, as well as their proper behavior. The new nation-state could not operate without finances, and one of the Confederate government's initial revenue-raising ventures was to float a national loan. On February 28, 1861, the Confederate Congress authorized the Treasury Department to borrow money from members of the public by issuing ten-year bonds up to a total value of fifteen million dollars. Buying into the loan offered a way of making a voluntary contribution to the upkeep of the nation-state— a contribution, importantly, which would accrue benefits to the purchaser as well as the country. As the *Montgomery Advertiser* put it, "The loan is a matter in which patriotism and pocket are most happily blended," and official notices from Treasury Secretary Christopher G. Memminger made much the same point. Significantly, the loan was made available in small denominations, to encourage less wealthy southerners to participate. The opportunity to enact one's citizenship financially was meant to be accessible to all. "Each man," as one proloan group put it, "must feel as though the success of the whole Republic was suspended upon his individual action." Here, then, was a pecuniary analog to the religious precept of individual behavior determining the fate of the nation.[63]

Confederate citizenship was defined in a variety of ways: recognition of the duties of the citizen-soldier, the perception that the fate of the nation depended upon one's morally upright behavior, and the more straightforward financial contributions that linked ones wallet to the health of the national government. In the first months of the Confederacy's existence, white southerners explored other connections between the individual and the nation as well. Drawing on prior understandings of nations and nationalism, as well as on the feeling of personal embattlement that had paved the road to secession, white southerners crafted Confederate citizenship with reference to existing personal identities and experiences.

Gender was crucial. Even an apparently straightforward convention, such as referring to the nation as "she," signaled the importance of ideas about gender to the conceptualization of nationalism. As has been the case with many nationalisms, especially during times of war, southern men often imagined their nation as a female who deserved the same protection from southern men as did individual southern women. Writing to his fiancée in the days after Sumter, Waddy Butler warned that his plans to fight would likely disrupt their relationship for a while. Until the conflict was over, Butler pledged complete devotion to his country: "She shall be my sole mistress, and at her feet I am content to cast everything." Having imagined the new nation in this way, male citizens felt keenly—and personally—the duty to protect her from northern enemies.[64]

William Gilmore Simms's long-standing commitment to southern independence also merged nationalism with gender. In 1861, "Oh, the Sweet South!," his poem that envisioned the region as both lover and mother, was republished. Whichever feminine role the South took on, the duty of male citizens was clear: to protect the female nation from the northern threat, just as they were determined to protect their real-life wives, sweethearts, and mothers. Both images defined men's responsibilities to the new nation by merging the masculine imperatives of individual men's everyday lives with the cause of national defense.[65] Later in 1861, when his son Gilmore was preparing to depart for the war, Simms himself made the connection clear. "You are to remember," he advised, "that you are to defend your mother country, & your natural mother, from a hoard of mercenaries & plunderers, and you will make your teeth meet in the flesh." "Be a man, my son, faithful & firm," he went on, "and put yourself in God's keeping." Simms thus cast the individual male's national responsibility in heavily gendered terms: in order to perform the duties of manhood, his son's duty was to protect both his literal mother and his figurative mother, the Confederate nation.[66]

This message was reinforced by politicians and the media. In May 1861 a Richmond newspaper published a poem entitled "The Southern War Song." In urging southern men to fight, the poem invoked two closely related phenomena: attachment to the soil they lived on and attachment to their families. Southern men ought to fight "for the land our mothers liv'd on"; they ought to fight so that

> The invader's foot must never
> Be pressed upon our soil
> . . . .
> In which our fathers sleep,
> Their blessed graves our care, boys,
> Most sacredly must keep.

In its final stanza, the poem referred to the

> Sweet tears of love and pride,
> As our wives and sweethearts bid us
> Go meet whate'er betide.

This was typical of many popular poems and songs that played on southern men's personal identities and familial relationships in urging them to fight. Consider the broadside poem "North Carolina: A Call to Arms." Addressing the "sons of Carolina," the poem urged them on by reminding them of their personal obligation to protect their homes and families:

> Oh! think of the maidens, the wives, and the mothers,
> Fly ye to the rescue, sons, husbands and brothers,
> And sink in oblivion all party and section
> Your hearthstones are looking to you for protection!

As North Carolinians, as "sons, husbands and brothers," and as fathers, these men must fight in order to prove their manhood by defending home and family. Despite the state-specific nature of this exhortation, it seemed clear that all these layers of identity merged into a national one, as they rallied "round the flag of the South."[67]

Our Homes, Our Wives, Our Children.

FIGURE 4.3 Our Homes, Our Wives, Our Children. (Civil War Pictorial Envelope Collection, Southern Historical Collection, Wilson Library, the University of North Carolina at Chapel Hill.)

Southern women as well as men used ideas about gender as a bridge between the individual and the nation. In formal terms national citizenship was an exclusively male affair, but women played crucial roles—both symbolic and active—in Confederate national identity and citizenship. It is emblematic that in the very first sentence of the first speech he made upon his arrival in Montgomery (the first capital of the Confederacy) as provisional Confederate president, Jefferson Davis delivered a ringing declaration of national community that was clearly gender specific: "*Fellow Citizens and Brethren of the Confederate States of America,*" he began, "now we are brethren, not in name merely, but in fact—men of one flesh, one bone, one interest, one purpose."[68] White southern women forged their own relationships to the nation, their own notions of Confederate citizenship, with reference to ideas about gender roles and responsibilities. Questions of what it meant to be a woman, what it meant to be a southerner—what it meant to be a southern woman—were answered together, not separately.[69]

The implications of 1861's tumultuous political events for women were uncertain. A couple of weeks before the delegates assembled at Montgomery to create the new nation-state, Virginian Lucy Wood wrote a letter to her fiancé, Waddy Butler, in Florida. "Though we are foreigners to each other now," she wrote, she was certain "that yours will soon be the common cause with us." Personally, she found it difficult to commit herself fully to the Confederate cause: she thought the new nation would reopen the African slave trade, a policy which she could not countenance. "But," she went on—clearly worried that she had crossed a gender divide in expressing this political opinion—"I have no political opinion, and have a peculiar dislike to all females who discuss such matters." Though the convention had always been flouted, American women—perhaps especially in the slaveholding South—were in theory excluded from the political arena.[70] But in the upheaval of the secession winter, Lucy Wood was obviously uncertain of what role she *should* strive to fulfill, and ended up adopting a wait-and-see attitude. When the time came, she pledged that she would be, in her words, "willing to do everything in my power consistent with my character of a southern lady for the sake of my Country; to deprive myself of every comfort of life and to give life itself; and when that time comes I shall learn what part I ought to play, and I shall perform it, let the dangers be what they may." At the moment of the Confederacy's creation, the precise nature of the relationship between the Confederate nation and individual women like Lucy Wood was undecided.[71]

Wood and countless other white southern women tentatively began to define Confederate citizenship in a variety of ways. Some of these were fairly predictable. Like many others, Wood demonstrated support for departing southern soldiers by waving them off as they left home for army camps and the front. As the purportedly weak maidens whom true southern men were obliged to protect, women provided a powerful sense of purpose for male citizenship. Alabamian James G. Hudson was doubtless not the only soldier who found in female well-wishers a valuable stimulant. Traveling through Georgia between Alabama and the Virginia front, Hudson cherished the capacity of such well-wishers "to inspire the Soldier with patriotism and nerve his arm for the contest."[72]

But it was obvious from the beginning that simply waving would not be enough. For one thing, in such a large-scale mobilization, outfitting troops with the supplies they needed was a formidable task. Women across the South formed sewing organizations to produce socks, shirts, and the like for their men. These groups provided both material and moral support for men in the armies. When the Ladies Volunteer Aid Society of the Pine Hills was formed in Louisiana in the summer of 1861, the woman they chose as their president made it clear that their animating purpose was to help "our brave volunteers," who had ventured forth to defend "our country and our homes." Women could supply the soldiers with the necessaries of life: sewing and knitting items of clothing, and making foodstuffs such as pickles. "Above all," she went on, "we can pray," and she resolved that each meeting should open and close with prayer.[73]

Lucy Wood was typical in concentrating on sewing and praying. During May 1861, she frequently noted the amount of time she and others were spending sewing for the troops. Toward the end of the month, she wrote that amid all that work the only real exercise she took was, "sometimes to walk up to a prayer meeting in the afternoon where we meet together to offer up prayers in behalf of our country, and those who have left this place for our defense." This routine, she acknowledged, could be onerous. But she was determined to continue working. "But what if we do grow weary, must we therefore stop?" she asked. "No, our needles are now our weapons, and we have a part to play as well as the rest." In sewing for the troops, in other words, women such as Lucy Wood believed that they were contributing just as much to the cause as their men. Wood had been uncertain earlier that year about precisely what the shift in national allegiances would require from southern women. Now, she was becoming surer: "Yes, yes, we women have mighty work to perform for which we will be responsible."[74]

Waving, sewing, and praying—these were the staple activities with which white southern women demonstrated their support for their men, their country, and their cause. But this was not all. Like many other southern women, especially the young, Lucy Wood defined citizenship in other ways, too—some of which fit less comfortably with conventional gender roles. A couple of days after the Confederate victory at Fort Sumter, when Virginia's secession appeared imminent but was not yet official, Wood reported to her fiancé, Waddy Butler, "Yesterday I levelled Louis's Union flag to the ground with my own hands, though it was right hard work." Here was an act with unequivocal nationalist implications: the physical destruction of the symbol of the former Union. And here was an act with equally visible gender implications. Did the leveling of a flag fall within the accepted range of female activities before the secession crisis? Did it now? In the collisions of citizenship and womanhood, Lucy Wood tested the meanings and boundaries of both. Earlier that year, of course, she had resolved to be, she wrote, "willing to do everything in my power consistent with my character of a southern lady for the sake of my Country." In the months following—in acts that came also to include shooting practice and volunteering at a local hospital—Wood actively remade those key words, "southern" and "lady," and what the two meant in combination.[75]

There were many Lucy Woods in the South that summer, all of them navigating the meanings of citizenship and femininity in their own ways. Margaret Josephine Gillis, a young Lowndes County, Alabama, woman, recorded in her diary of 1861 many of the same activities with which Lucy Wood and so many others forged their own relationships with the emergent Confederate nation. Gillis attended barbecues and other send-offs for departing troops. In mid-June she reported that Jefferson Davis had called a national fast day "for the benefit of our beloved 'Sunny South,'" an occasion that she observed "sacredly." She was involved with other local women in sewing shirts for the troops. And in common with other young white southern women, Margaret Gillis felt a measure of that same martial bellicosity that drove their young male counterparts into uniform. Traveling through a local town with the intention of viewing the Confederate flag that was waving there, Gillis experienced a powerful feeling of national commitment. Though she had seen some flag designs which she would have preferred over the one ultimately selected, Gillis nonetheless proclaimed, "But I love that one because it was chosen by a *Southern* Congress, and as I looked at it floating in the breeze, and heard the roll of the drums from the camp outside town I felt very like taking up arms myself." The categories of femininity and citizenship clearly collided in sentiments such as this one.[76]

Gillis fashioned her citizenship in other ways, too. In late February, Gillis reported news of Jefferson Davis's inauguration and expressed the hope that more southern states would have seceded by the time Abraham Lincoln was inaugurated in early March. The mention of the northern president-elect reminded her of something she had done earlier in the month. "I sent Lincoln a right impudent Valentine," she wrote, "but I hope no one will ever find out." Other southern women used their gender-specific power to police national allegiance within the South in other ways, sending hoopskirts and underwear, for instance, to southern men who were slow to join the Confederate armies.[77]

Such gendered demonstrations of allegiance were not always in the service of the Confederacy. Another young Alabama woman, Elizay Bell, connected romance and loyalty in similar ways, but to different ends. Bell, a unionist, had asked her brother, a Confederate sympathizer, to "pick out me a sooter." But in the context of shifting allegiances in April 1861, she changed her mind, worried about the kind of man he might select. "If thare is none but disunion men thare," she wrote, "for god sake let them alone for I would disdain to keep company with a disunionist for if he will cecede from the government that has always sustained his Rights he would cecede from his family." For unionists as well as Confederates, connections between romance and politics ran deep, in both directions. More generally, the loyalties of wartime unionists often took shape in similar processes as those of Confederates. For both groups, public allegiances were intertwined with private lives, family relationships, and personal identities.[78]

Whether unionist or Confederate—or, even more likely, a shifting combination of the two—southern men and women defined citizenship in 1861 by looking to the materials of their everyday lives and individual identities. To be sure, political leaders played an important role in defining the constituency and the meaning of Confederate citizenship, attempting to draw lines between citizens and noncitizens and delineating the rights and responsibilities that citizenship entailed. But politicians never fully controlled these definitions. In important ways, Confederates' definitions replicated those that had been dominant in the antebellum United States. Religion and the imperatives of democratic citizenship combined to create strong individual obligations to the Confederate nation, just as they had created individual obligations to the United States. Other aspects of Confederate citizenship, however, developed in response to the new circumstances of 1861. The necessity of forming new national institutions, together with the prospect and then the commencement of war, compelled white southerners to forge new connections between the individual and the nation. In so doing, both men and women grounded citizenship in evolving conceptions of masculinity and femininity.

AS WHITE SOUTHERNERS began to define Confederate national identity and citizenship, they drew on what they already knew about those concepts, derived from European thought as well as their long, first-hand experience with American nationalism. They understood that to be accepted as a legitimate nation-state, the Confederacy would need strong institutions—a government, military forces, and diplomatic missions. But according to mid-nineteenth-century transatlantic conventions, the "nation" part of "nation-state" mattered too: nationality required a distinct national identity, vested in a unique "people" with its own cultural identity and ideally its own racial or ethnic makeup as well. In large part, white southerners sought to establish their distinctive national identity by emphasizing their differences from northerners. The worse the Yankees could be made to look, the better—and the more deserving of national status—the southerners themselves would appear.

Even as they went to such great lengths to differentiate themselves from northerners, however, southerners did not wish to desert completely the country that the two groups had once shared. American ideals and symbols, and the heritage of the American Revolution in particular, continued to exert a powerful draw even after white southerners declared their political independence from the Union. This generated considerable pain and uncertainty. Many white southerners rejected, to one degree or another, the authority of the Confederate government and endeavored to remain in the United States. Even for those with firm commitments to the Confederacy, the problem of how to reconcile the new with the old remained difficult. In general, though, it was to existing components of American national identity and citizenship that southerners were most likely to look as they reflected on their new circumstances. The Revolutionary ideal of self-government remained a central element of their political practice and their claim to national legitimacy. Religion and democratic thought still combined to bind individual citizens to the nation's well-being, and to remind those individuals that their moral comportment would determine the fate of the nation. American nationalism would be a guiding influence throughout the Confederacy's existence.

White southerners also embedded their ideas about nationalism and citizenship within their personal identities, especially gender identities. For men, national identity shaped and was shaped by their traditional roles as protectors of women, children, and homes. And for women, traditional "female" tasks such as sewing, praying, and supporting their men took on national meaning, even as nationalism held out the possibility of the expansion of those traditional roles. These connections were fluid rather than fixed, and they differed over time, across space, and between individuals. But amid the countless permutations that they assumed, one common characteristic held true: after secession the problems of citizenship and nationalism demanded unprecedented quantities of creative energy. This was true for supporters of the Confederacy, dissenters, and those in between. By the end of 1861, nationalism was an inescapable and an increasingly consequential feature of life in the South.

5

War

SUFFERING, SACRIFICE, AND THE TRIALS
OF NATIONALISM

THE POLITICAL AND cultural creativity of the spring and summer of
1861 quickly gave way to the sober recognition that the ultimate test of
Confederate legitimacy would be the ability to maintain territorial integrity by force of arms. It was upon that ability that the Confederacy's status
as a nation-state would stand or fall. The outcome was not preordained,
and along the way not only the territorial but the intellectual and cultural
grounds of nationhood were transformed. War wove the problems of nationalism more deeply than ever before into the fabric of white southerners' lives, particularly in the form of newly powerful sacred bonds of
suffering. Some white southerners embraced these bonds, finding transcendent meaning in nationalist sacrifice, while others recoiled, rejecting
the Confederate government's authority and renewing their allegiance to
the old Union. Regardless of one's position, in the crucible of war, nationalism came to matter more than ever.

William Henry Trescot, the South Carolina planter, diplomat, and historian, understood something of this. In an 1863 public letter to a former
friend from the North, Trescot observed that war had altered the prewar
intellectual strands of southern nationalism. The Civil War, as he saw it,
was merely the most recent response to a problem that had brought many
changes to "the political map of the world for the last two centuries": the
problem of "how for the peace of the world and the welfare of mankind to
make each government the actual representative of the living interests of
the people it controls." "The answer," evident in the southern case and in
many others, including Greece, Italy, and parts of Latin America, "has

been by the restraint or destruction of overgrown empires, and the creation or recognition of new governments or nationalities." Nationalism was a historical force, in other words, and to resist the proper alignment of a "people" with its "government" was to stand in the way of history itself. Furthermore, in claiming nationality for the South, Trescot made the well-worn comparison with the American Revolution. That event, in his eyes, had proved "that a colony—a part of an existing nationality—might by the development of its resources, become large enough and complete enough for an independent national existence." This process had caused the revolution of 1861 just as surely as that of 1776.

However, by 1863, when Trescot penned his public letter, circumstances had fundamentally changed. The experience of war had served, in his estimation, to further divide South from North and, therefore, to further substantiate the South's national independence: "If an earthquake had cleft this continent in twain, we could not be further separated than we are by that great, red river of blood, which, swollen by the dismal streams from Manassas and Murfreesboro, Antietam and Fredericksburg, now rolls its fearful barrier between two hostile nations." It is difficult to imagine a more powerful dividing line than the "great, red river of blood" produced by two years of war. The fighting had also, according to Trescot, united the white South across social class divisions. "No man," he wrote, "anticipated the spontaneous, energetic, passionate unanimity of this whole southern people in the cause of southern independence, which this war has developed." The experience of war had fused white southerners into a community that had not previously existed. In concluding his letter, Trescot further distinguished between prewar and wartime nationalism, asserting that "the cause to which [the South] devoted herself on conviction" before the war "is now sacred by the blood of her martyrs, and glorious by the deeds of her heroes." The experience of war, in other words, had transformed the political and intellectual "conviction" of the few into a "sacred" and "glorious" crusade sustained by the tangible "deeds" and emotional commitment of the many.[1]

Of course, William Henry Trescot cannot be taken completely at his word. As an advocate of southern independence before and during the war, he had obvious reasons for emphasizing the positive in his evaluation of Confederate nationhood. And as a wealthy slaveholder, he had obvious reasons for portraying the war's impact on white class relations as a story of increasing harmony rather than one of growing disaffection and discord. Contrary to Trescot's assertions, war did not affect white southerners' nationalism in one consistent and unambiguous pattern. Rather, the Civil War fostered a climate of shifting and ambiguous loyalties.

When modified by this major caveat, Trescot's observations about war's transformative impact point the way toward a new approach to Confederate nationalism. Rather than intervening in the old debate about how strong or weak Confederate nationalism was, the persistence and transformation of southern conceptions of nationalism and citizenship can be evaluated. Rather than assuming that because the South lost the Civil War, its nationalism must have been somehow inadequate, attention can instead be paid to how white southerners drew on their long-standing engagement with these concepts to manage the stresses—practical, intellectual, and cultural—of modern war.[2] To a considerable degree the problems of 1861 persisted. White southerners continued to navigate between old ties to the Union and new ties to the Confederacy; they continued to contemplate differences between themselves and their erstwhile compatriots to the north; and they continued to ponder the meanings of national independence. Yet the brutality of war and changing fortunes on the battlefield ushered in important changes as well.

Looming over all of this was the power of the Confederate government, which fundamentally altered the landscape of nationalism in the South. The national government in Richmond was the institutional expression of the idea of a separate southern nation; it was the "state" in the Confederate nation-state. In the course of the war it claimed increasingly far-reaching authority over citizens and other individuals within its borders, and over the economy and society as well as the politics of its territory. Antebellum suspicions of centralized political power were overcome by the practical exigencies of war, which necessitated the centralization of political power in Richmond. Conscription, taxation, and other policies altered the terms of citizenship and tightened the nexus between individuals and the national government.[3]

Throughout the modern world, war has been instrumental in sharpening borders between nation-states and validating nation-states' claims to international authority, as well as in transforming internal relations between nation-states and their citizens. The pressures of mobilization have caused national governments to demand ever greater commitment from their citizens—in the form of money, loyalty, and life. War has helped create new expectations about the role of the state in the national economy and the responsibility of the state to guarantee citizens certain rights in exchange for their loyalty. Finally, war has stimulated the formation and hardening of national identity.⁴ In the Confederate South war forged new connections between nationalism, suffering, morality, gender obligations, redemptive religion, and blood sacrifice. In some cases these changes drove southerners into increasingly fervent commitment to the Confederacy; in other cases they pushed them back toward the Union. In the crucible of war, ideas about nationalism and citizenship would come to matter to white southerners in more immediate ways than they ever had before.

Enduring Bonds of Union

Throughout the Civil War, white southerners continued to navigate between the competing claims of Confederate and American national identities. Even firmly committed Confederates who wished to leave the United States behind forever debated the extent to which the Confederacy represented a purification of the existing American nationalism, and the extent to which it was a new entity. Throughout the war this problem continued to trouble those who gave serious thought to the character of Confederate national identity. For the many southerners who were uncertain about whether they wanted the Confederacy to exist at all, sacred ties to the United States afforded some measure of stability amid the changing landscape of nationalism and citizenship. For everyone, balancing an array of loyalties— to the United States, the Confederacy, the slaveholding South, and the individual states—became more difficult after 1861.

For some, it was the essential Americanness of the Confederacy that stood out. As they had been doing for years, some white southerners continued to claim the mantle of American nationalism by claiming its heroes and its history. "Rebels! Tis a holy name! / The name our fathers bore" went one poem, which Lucy Butler took the trouble to copy down in her journal.

> "Our Father, Washington,
> Was the Arch Rebel in the fight
> And gave the name to us:—a right
> Of father to the son."⁵

It was no accident that Washington's image appeared on Confederate currency and stamps as well as on the national seal. It was no accident, either, that Jefferson Davis was inaugurated as elected president of the Confederate States on February 22, 1862—the 130th anniversary

FIGURE 5.1 Statue of George Washington in Richmond; photograph by Andrew J. Russell, 1865. (Library of Congress.)

of Washington's birth. Standing beneath a statue of Washington in Richmond, Davis took the opportunity to portray Confederates as the true heirs of the American Revolution, fighting for the same rights the earlier generation had won.[6]

If it was clear that the South owned the memory of Washington, it was equally clear that the errant North did not. "To-day is Washington's birth day," wrote one Alabama soldier, "& the Yank-guns fired in celebrat. of it could plainly be heard. What a farce that those fanatical wretches should be celebrating the birth day & pretending to have admiration for the grt. & good Wash'g." Likewise, Sarah Lois Wadley, the Louisiana teenager, continued to claim the memory of Washington for the Confederacy, just as she had done in 1861. On "the birthday of Washington" in 1864, she wrote in her diary, "An anniversary sacred to the memory of freedom. Alas, how it is now polluted" by the Yankee occupiers' election that was being held that day.[7]

Claims on the American heritage were sometimes made even more explicit. Just over a year into the war, the *Richmond Examiner* took issue with Jefferson Davis's continued use of the name "United States" to describe the country they were at war with. "In using that term," the *Examiner* complained, "the President virtually acknowledges the North as the United States, and places us before Europe as rebels or revolutionists." In addition to the implications for European countries' possible recognition of the Confederacy, it was also a matter of justice. The North did not deserve to retain the name, since it had trampled upon the spirit of the Constitution which had created the United States. If anything, the South had "more right" to the name because it had done a better job of preserving the Constitution.[8]

Most Confederates, of course, were too preoccupied with the war to spend much time debating ownership of the American heritage. But one day each year prompted many white southerners to reflect on the former United States and the anniversary of its birth. Independence Day celebrations were, as one would expect during wartime, muted. But in spite of the lack of public festivities, some commentators continued to assert the continuity between the American and the Confederate revolutions, as well as the South's ownership of the Fourth, and they continued to insist that the principles of the revolution commemorated by the anniversary lay at the heart of the Confederacy's bid for independence. The Fourth even kept its place in at least one Confederate composition textbook. Among subjects such as "Roses," "A Picnic," and "A Sleigh Ride" appeared "Fourth of July." The textbook asked students to answer questions about the origins and nature of the Fourth, what typically happened on the day, and finally inquired: "Ought not its observance to be perpetuated?"[9]

Kentuckian Confederate officer Edward Guerrant would have replied to that question with a resounding yes. On the Fourth of July, 1862, he wrote at some length in his diary about what he called this "once glorious and happy day." Though the Fourth awakened sorrow as well as pride, he resolved to restore its glory: "This day 86 years ago our fathers declared we *would* be free & today we'll prove it or baptize it in our lifeblood." Guerrant's pledge of blood in the cause of Confederate independence is a perfect example of how the fact of war infused existing strands of nationalism with a new intensity. One year later, in 1863, Guerrant again noted the occurrence of what he now termed "Freedom's Birth Day." Again, he stressed the continuity between the American and southern independence movements, identifying the Confederacy as the only "heir" of the Revolution. For the new nation, today was "the anniversary of her mothers birth . . . its memories disgraced by a degenerate offspring"—that is, the North. Guerrant promised to "cling with grateful veneration to its hallowed recollections, and revive its spirit in our patriotic actions!"[10]

Others believed that northerners had proved themselves unworthy of the holiday and no longer had any claim to it at all. Edmund Ruffin, for whom acerbic criticism of the North was an old habit, was horrified by northerners' flying of flags and firing of salutes on July 4, 1862. "What striking inconsistency—what a farce," he wrote in his diary, that northerners should celebrate the Declaration of Independence, which had established "the *right* of every oppressed people to assert their independence & separate nationality," while they were engaged in attempting to deny with force the South's right to do that very thing. Northerners had diverged so much from the principles of the Fourth—and, for that matter, from the principle of nationality—that they had no right to celebrate it at all.[11]

For some southerners the holiday became an odd, unsettling occurrence. As the war progressed, when southerners noted the Fourth at all, it was often to remark on how much the day had changed, or to reflect with sadness on its occurrence in such calamitous circumstances. The *Charleston Mercury* captured this when it reported in 1862 that the Fourth "happens strangely at this momentous juncture." One Virginia woman wrote in an 1862 diary entry, "The fourth was not celebrated I don't expect by either side." That same year, soldier James Kilpatrick similarly observed, "Everything quiet. . . . No one seems to think that today was once an observed anniversary." Writing to her mother in 1864, one woman wondered how the anniversary would be marked this year. She reported, "Ernest & Charlie have got each a gun and are going to get some powder & shot, but it seem melancoly to me[.] I am afraid our independance is gone[.]"[12] Throughout the war, many white southerners encountered the Fourth—and American nationalism in general—with ambivalence and uncertainty.

August 4, 1866.]   HARPER'S WEEKLY.   485

SECRET MEETING OF SOUTHERN UNIONISTS.—[SKETCHED BY OUR SPECIAL ARTIST, A. R. WAUD.]

PICTURES OF THE SOUTH.

FIGURE 5.2 Secret Meeting of Southern Unionists; sketch by A. R. Waud, *Harper's Weekly*, August 4, 1866. (Library of Congress.)

For southern unionists the problem was, in this respect at least, more straightforward. For them it was the Confederacy and not the North that had distorted the genuine spirit of American nationalism and the true legacy of the American Revolution. In one wartime pamphlet, for example, the Mississippi unionist John W. Wood rejected efforts to align 1861 with 1776. His opposition to the Confederacy resulted in part from the conviction, widespread among southern unionists, that secession had been the result of the deceitful conspiracy of an elite ruling class that ran counter to the interests of the large majority of white southerners. Wood was also inspired by a strong patriotic affection for the United States. It had been a wonderful country, he insisted, and Americans in the North and the South ought to repair "the mystic ties of brotherhood" that they had previously enjoyed. In marked contrast to Confederate nationalists, he felt that the symbols and holidays of American nationalism ought to inspire a reunification of the United States. "A love for the Union should be cherished," he wrote, "and renewed upon all suitable occasions. The fourth of July, and the twenty-second of February, should again be celebrated throughout the length and breadth of the country."[13]

Margaret Nourse, a Virginia woman who remained firmly devoted to the United States, attempted to do just that on July 4, 1862. "It has always been one of my festivals," she wrote in her diary; "I have often shed tears of joy upon it; for two years they have been tears of deep sorrow. I carried my flag up stairs & hung it up for one day at least." Although Nourse would become frustrated with the Lincoln administration later in the war, in 1862 she was Union through and through. "I was so enthusiastically proud of my country," she exclaimed, "& I cannot think calmly of the destruction of it; I cannot contemplate such a state of things, I must turn away." Blaming the South for sundering the Union, Nourse wished that Virginia had never seceded, viewing it as a forced and unjust "expatriation" of unionist southerners like herself.[14]

Southern unionists remained committed to the Union for a wide variety of reasons. Local community dynamics, family relationships, political ideology, and much else besides helped determine loyalties in the American Civil War. Unionists included the northern-born; former Whigs who identified secession with their long-standing Democratic enemies; nonslaveholding farmers who resented what they saw as a "rich man's war and a poor man's fight"; conservatives who thought their property, human and otherwise, would be safer within the Union than outside it—and even the simply cantankerous who refused to go along with the crowd. By definition all southern unionists viewed the relationship between the South and the United States in starkly different terms than those who supported the Confederacy. Kentucky minister Robert J. Breckinridge spoke for many unionists in arguing that the United States, North and South, represented a genuine national community that ought to stay together. He indicated that this was so partly for reasons of shared self-interest—southerners and northerners had all prospered under the Union and could do so into the future—but also because of the inexorable force of nationality itself. Interpreting this force in a very different way from Confederate nationalists, he urged, "Let mankind, at length, receive the sublime truth, that great nations do not die. . . . That nationalities once established are, according to any measure of time known to history, really immortal. . . . That this is, in truth, a great nation, and that the nationality shared by the American people, is not only thoroughly established, but one of the most distinct and powerful that ever existed." The United States was a single nation and the white South ought to return to its place as part of it.[15]

Herschel V. Johnson, the Georgia Democrat who had resisted secession but accepted his state's decision to leave the Union, reflected on these issues in a revealing letter of October 1862. With the war now more than a year old, Johnson was not optimistic about the Confederacy's chances. Even if the Confederacy did win, he held out hope that victory would result in the reunion of the old United States rather than a permanent separation, reflecting his belief "that this great territory between the two oceans, can never have permanent peace except under one flag." His understanding of U.S. nationalism was changing rather than fixed: "This was not formerly my opinion. But observation & reflection have brought me to this conclusion." Later in the war, in response to an invitation to take part in an organized peace movement, Johnson demurred, explaining that it could not at present succeed because of the Lincoln administration's inflexible terms, and because of northern misunderstandings about the very nature of the Union. Northerners "attach an undue importance to the mere fact or form of the Union," Johnson wrote, "ignoring the principle or objects of the Union, and forgetting that it ceases to be valuable when it fails to secure that object and maintain those principles." This is exactly what had happened, Johnson believed: northerners had neglected the core principle of the Union, self-government, and southerners had been forced to leave. But they had not done so "in contempt of that Union; in a wanton disposition to insult its flag and to destroy the government of which it is the emblem." No, "secession was not resorted to merely to throw off the Union. Our people loved the Union, and honored its once glorious flag, for the rich memories that clustered around it. They left it with a reluctance and a regret to which history will scarcely do justice. They were, as they are now, wedded to the principles on which the Union was founded; they separated from it, but to vindicate and maintain them." Johnson was clearly torn between his allegiance to the state of Georgia—which necessitated allegiance to the Confederacy—and his continuing affection for the United States.[16]

Whereas Johnson and many others confined their unionism to private reflections and the occasional letter, some white southerners struggled more actively for a return to the United States. Dissent was especially pronounced in the predominantly mountainous areas of the South with low rates of slaveholding, areas that had tended to oppose secession in the first place. As the war progressed, the demands of armed service and the deteriorating economic situation combined with heartfelt loyalties to the Union to produce a significant movement for peace. Not all dissent should be interpreted as evidence of unionism: desertion and other forms of dissent were often driven by other factors; frustration at the Confederate government did not automatically mean rejection of the whole idea of the Confederacy. But in many cases the peace movement was clearly inspired by a nationalistic belief that the southern states ought properly to belong to the United States and not the Confederacy.

Unionists, then, were troubled by the practical problem of how to restore the former relationship between the South and the United States. But for those who supported the Confederacy, the problem was how to recalibrate southernness and Americanness now that the national borders had been redrawn. The problem had been present in 1861. Confederates had seceded from the Union, but wished to claim aspects of its nationalism for themselves. They had separated from the nation-state formed by America's Revolutionary generation, but they mostly wished to claim the heritage of that generation, and indeed of Americanism itself, for themselves. This was no easy task, and the problem of continuity versus novelty persisted throughout the war. Too little continuity, and white southerners' enduring attachment to the American past might strain to breaking point their new ties to the Confederacy. Too much, and the claim of a distinctive Confederate national identity became vulnerable.[17]

The Barbaric Northern Foe

War itself went some way toward settling such problems. Escalating violence intensified the existing tendency to assert a distinctive Confederate national identity by contrasting southerners against northerners. In creating what William Henry Trescot called a "great, red river of blood," war differentiated South from North to a degree that would not have been possible in peacetime. This substantiated national difference inside and outside the Confederacy's borders: in Europe the image of a barbaric northern foe featured in Confederate diplomacy, while at home it often reinforced the nationalistic commitment of southerners themselves.

As the war progressed, assertions of fundamental national disparity between North and South multiplied. The *Richmond Examiner* and its contributors were particularly vocal in this regard. In the weeks after the Battle of Manassas, one correspondent ardently opposed the very suggestion of reconstruction with the North. Instead, he urged that southerners ought to institute national distinctiveness from the North in every way possible, from a different system of revenue to different weights, measures, and currency. "Would to God that our language was different from theirs," he concluded, invoking what was seen as a principal marker of national identity by nineteenth-century thinkers as well as by modern scholars. As the war progressed, the *Examiner* continued to assert national difference. In April 1862, the paper approvingly excerpted a passage from the *New Orleans Bee* that detailed racial distinctions between Yankees and southerners. Whereas northerners were intolerant, abusive of power, and inclined toward fads and "isms," southerners were a more honest, moral people who distrusted "new-fangled theories." To the *Examiner*, this confirmed that the war was not only about the protection of slavery against northern assaults but also about "certain radical and irreconcilable differences of nationable character" between North and South. The theme persisted. In December 1862, for instance, the *Examiner* printed an editorial criticizing Lincoln's claim that the United States was one nation indivisible—a natural fact, in the opinion of the U.S. president, proved by the lack of any distinct geographical barrier between North and South. Conceding that no such barrier existed, the *Examiner* shifted the terms of the debate with the argument that "moral differences of race, and political differences of institutions, constitute means of separation as effective and insurmountable as any physical barrier interposed by nature." Jews and Gypsies were adduced as proof that racial distinctiveness could equate to national distinctiveness even in the absence of a clearly demarcated territory.[18]

Assertions of difference between northerners and southerners had never been equanimous. They frequently placed North and South in a sort of moral ranking, with the North and its people, of course, at the negative end of the scale. War heightened this tendency: now Yankees became even greedier, more intolerant, more self-righteous, more crass, more prone to wild "isms," more likely to lie and steal and cheat than ever before. Just as it had for years, the image of the Yankee served as a dustbin into which white southerners dumped all distasteful human characteristics, and, furthermore, as a negative reference point against which they defined their own character. The worse the Yankees could be made to look, the more admirable and virtuous—the more distinctive—southerners themselves became.

Once war was underway, negative depictions of Yankees became more widespread and more extreme. Such depictions permeated popular culture as well as public and private writings of all kinds. One poem described northerners as a race of tyrants and liars, "like savage Hun and merciless Dane." Lucy Johnston Ambler recorded a similar impression of the northern cavalry who ransacked her northern Virginia home. Leaving no doubt as to her opinion of the depths to which they had sunk, she asked "Is there a man among them? They seem like demons from the lower regions." The immediate impact of war, in Ambler's case, rendered northern soldiers not just different, not just strangers, but almost subhuman. A little more lightheartedly, one North Carolinian informed his mother that he had recently seen a group of Yankee prisoners, "of all colors, ages, sizes, and sexes, and from all nations." The soldier viewed this motley crew as a strange bunch, wondering if his younger brother "wants a young Yankee," presumably as some sort of exotic pet. War thus intensified the time-honored technique of substantiating southern national identity with the contrasting image of the alien Yankee.[19]

Such images were particularly potent symbols of Confederate national identity's distinctiveness when they highlighted the barbarity of the invading Yankee soldier. Earlier criticism of northerners had been strong enough, but it paled in comparison to wartime portrayals of Yankee soldiers' inhumanity. From the earliest days of the war, Yankee soldiers' callous barbarity became an article of faith in the Confederacy. Newspapers were filled with stories of Yankee soldiers contravening the conventions of "civilized" warfare. They had little respect for private property and stole, pillaged, and burned with abandon. They respected neither the injured—firing on hospitals—nor the dead—mutilating Confederate soldiers even after they had been killed. "From every side," wrote one Confederate bureaucrat in his diary, "evidence of the barbarity, savageness, and insolent assumption of the Yankee government in the policy on which they have resolved in the conduct of war, thicken." Northern warfare, with its deportation of families, threats against civilians, and attempts to promote slave insurrection, was despicable. "The Earth," he concluded, "contains no race so lost to every sentiment of manliness, honor, faith, or humanity."[20]

Some northern atrocity stories seem unbelievable. In July 1862, one southern newspaper printed an intercepted letter that had purportedly been written by a Philadelphia woman. The woman wanted her correspondent to ask a northern soldier "to cut off the head of a rebel and boil it five hours, so that all the flesh may come off readily, and then saw the skull in two from the front, and he will find the unevenness of the thickness to be mostly inside." Whether genuine or not, the fact that this letter was printed in a respectable southern newspaper indicates the degree to which Confederate culture sought to dehumanize the northern enemy. When intensified by the passions of war, such tendencies can become even more extreme—making our head-boiling story more understand-able, if no more palatable.[21]

White southerners recognized the connection between atrocity stories and their ongoing quest to differentiate themselves from northerners. In June 1861, before war had properly commenced, Lucy Wood noted in her diary, "We hear every day of the most atrocious acts that our northern friends (who are so earnestly striving for a reunion with their sister States) are committing." As Wood's ironic references to "our northern friends" and their desire for reunion intimated, news of northern barbarity bol-stered the claim of a separate national identity for the Confederacy, insofar as it further hardened the line between South and North. Jefferson Davis certainly appreciated this function. In his inaugural address in February 1862, Davis declared that all hope of reunion "must have been dispelled by the malignity and barbarity of the Northern States in the prosecution of the existing war." Davis would repeat this same point throughout the war, never missing an opportunity to protest and to publicize northern methods of waging war. Every time he did so, he broadened the gulf between South and North that much more. Like Trescot's "river of blood," the line sepa-rating barbarity and civilization promised to strengthen and intensify the Confederacy's claims to distinctiveness and independence.[22]

These atrocity stories made the sometimes abstract issues of national difference and national defense much more immediate and much more urgent. They helped bring not just the war but also the problems of na-tionalism home to white southerners. When Jefferson Davis, for instance, railed against an enemy who had "laid waste our fields, polluted our altars, and violated the sanctity of our homes," he not only honed the image of northerners as brutal enemies but also cast the idea of national difference and the imperative of national defense in very tangible and very urgent domestic forms. The Yankee soldier's threat to the southern home ren-dered him more alien than ever and meant that it was more important for southern men to defend their homes and their country at the same time.[23]

Such rhetoric of defending the home was frequently laden with over-tones of gender and sexuality. A story of "Yankee Outrages" that ran in newspapers across the South, for instance, described northern soldiers "thrusting themselves into people's homes" as well as stealing private property. Even worse, "several rapes were committed, in one case a gen-tleman being compelled to witness an outrage perpetrated on his daugh-ter in his house right before his own eyes." Sexualized atrocity stories took the demonization of the North to new heights. According to the

Montgomery Advertiser in October 1864, a "Yankee Blackguard" had made a speech in which he had threatened southern womanhood. With southern men off fighting and southern women at home, he was reported to have remarked, northerners had an opportunity to "show them that we can *raise a better breed* than the generation of Southerners that we are now killing off."[24]

Sometimes the North's sexual threat to the southern gender order blended with its threat to the southern racial order. Northern invasions of southern homes imperiled not just southern women but also the purportedly stable race relations which the South had built around the institution of slavery. Thus Jefferson Davis and other leaders warned of the Yankee threat to southern homes, women, families, and slave discipline—all elements of the same menace. And reporting on "Outrages by the Yankees in Mississippi," the *Richmond Examiner* told of women being whipped and hanged by barbaric northern soldiers, and even of women being "ravished by negroes, incited to the deed by Federal soldiery, who stood by and witnessed the revolting scene." Intensified by the racial component, stories of northern atrocities against southern white women further deepened the line between North and South.[25]

Allegations of northern barbarity also offered valuable evidence for southern spokesmen and spokeswomen making the case for independence on the international stage. One group of South Carolina women, for instance, solicited help from around the world in an 1864 fundraising initiative. In requesting sympathy and aid for their cause, the women employed the rhetoric of civilization and of classic nineteenth-century nationalism, depicting Confederates as a people bravely struggling for their freedom against a brutal and oppressive foe. Such a people would not— could not—yield to an oppressor who had "disgraced the civilization of the 19th century." Similarly, an 1863 pamphlet entitled *Address to Christians throughout the World* solicited international sympathy in response to the barbarism of the northern war effort. The ministers who were signatories to this appeal cited the North's emancipation policy as one example of its barbarism. The policy was intended to spark race war, the ministers implied: "This measure is in no proper sense an act of mercy to the slave, but of malice toward the master." Earlier in the war, the editor of the *Richmond Examiner* had drawn attention to the fact that the North was "doing all it can to envenom the war": using inhumane fighting methods, laying waste to the southern land, stealing private property, arming slaves to fight against their masters, and practically transforming southern whites into slaves themselves. "These spittings of venom in the North," the *Examiner* thought, "do us good. The mask of civilization is taken from the Yankee war; in the eyes of the world it is degenerated into unbridled butchery." Like the South Carolina women's circular, this editorial recognized that portrayals of a barbaric North could help the South's cause on the international stage.[26]

Such portrayals became a component of formal Confederacy diplomacy as well. In January 1864 Secretary of State Judah Benjamin wrote to John Slidell, the Confederate commissioner in France, "No crime is too revolting for this vile race, which disgraces civilization and causes one to blush for our common humanity," and he went on to list Yankee outrages, including the incitement of slave resistance. That same month Benjamin wrote to a Confederate agent in Britain to complain about the British government's failure to end the mass suffering of the American Civil War. He berated "the conduct of a cabinet which has betrayed the cause of humanity wherever power has sought to repress right," using Poland as another example of Britain's callous disregard for unjust oppression. However, the humanitarian argument that Europe should help stop the American war—to the Confederacy's advantage, of course—had little influence on European governments. As the French emperor Napoleon III explained to John Slidell, "The policy of nations is controlled by their interests and not by their sentiments."[27]

Judah Benjamin's 1864 comparison with Poland echoed prewar secessionist arguments, but also referred to more recent events. In 1863, Polish nationalists again rose against their Russian occupiers, not only creating a political problem for European governments but also affecting Confederate diplomacy. The *Richmond Enquirer* interpreted this as the revolt of "an ancient and glorious nation, against that crushing, killing union with another nationality and form of society. . . . At bottom, the cause of Poland is the same cause for which the Confederates are now fighting." The United States expressed a measure of sympathy for Russia, causing Confederates to accuse northerners of opposing self-government across the world. Thus Henry St. Paul castigated northerners for "licking the boots of the Russian Autocrat, still reeking with Polish blood," and "fawning before the Russian Tzar and humbly begging for an alliance to crush at the same time and bury in the same grave, Southern and Polish Liberty!" Meanwhile, Confederates on the ground in Britain and France were more worried that events in Poland were distracting the European powers from helping to end the American Civil War.[28]

In addition to pleading for European support on humanitarian grounds, Confederate diplomats continued to make the same arguments they had posited in 1861: they appealed to European economic interest, invoked the principle of nationality, and with increasing validity argued that the Confederacy had proved its nationhood by surviving as an independent nation-state over the long term. None of these arguments, however, counteracted Napoleon's candid admission that above all else European countries' calculations of their own interest would determine their actions on the international stage. Furthermore, slavery became even more of an obstacle to Confederate recognition once the Union's emancipation policy went into proper effect.[29]

Even though they did not secure recognition of the Confederacy as a legitimate nation-state, Confederate portrayals of Yankee barbarity do seem to have garnered a measure of sympathy in Europe. In 1864, British sympathizers formed a Society for the Promotion of the Cessation of Hostilities in America, an organization that showed the effectiveness of the new strategy of requesting European help to end the American war for primarily humanitarian reasons.[30] At home, too, negative images of the Yankee strengthened Confederate resolve and reinforced the Confederacy's claim to national distinctiveness, imbuing the war against the North with larger meaning. It became not just a war between nations but a war between barbarity and civilization itself.

Centralization, Conscription, and Confederate Citizenship

Between 1861 and 1865 the Confederate government in Richmond supervised a massive expansion of governmental authority that would have been unthinkable before the Civil War. The Davis administration exercised its new political power in a number of ways, instituting new taxation policies, occasionally suspending habeas corpus, and regulating salt and niter production and the railroad infrastructure. But the centerpiece of government power was conscription. In the early months of the war there was no shortage of volunteers, but by the winter of 1861–62 it had become apparent that the war would be a long one, and that the Confederacy would struggle to field sufficient armies. In a March 1862 message to Congress, Jefferson Davis observed that current methods of raising troops for the Confederate armies were impracticable and were generating harmful conflicts between national and state authorities. He therefore called for a national system of conscription. When this system was passed into law the following month, it required three years of military service from white men between 18 and 35 years old. (In September 1862 the upper age limit was raised to 45.) Congress exempted those who could provide a substitute or who fell into certain occupational categories, such as politicians, teachers, and railroad workers.[31]

Confederate conscription represented a revolutionary new development in governmental authority. It would be another year before the Union implemented national conscription. There had been no national draft during the Revolution or in any U.S. war since then, and there surely would have been public outrage had one been attempted. As in other countries, beginning with revolutionary France, conscription policies forged a new kind of nationalism, a new kind of citizenship, by demanding an equal, uniform commitment on the part of all male citizens to the preservation of the nation-state.[32] Although the direct reach of conscription only extended to men, the enforced absence of their male relatives obviously had considerable impact upon women too, altering their own obligations to the nation-state and its war effort. Claiming the authority to compel adult male citizens to risk their lives for the national war effort constituted a massive expansion of central power.

The draft was certainly seen in this light by its critics. Georgia governor Joseph Brown, for example, kept up a long, angry correspondence with Jefferson Davis in protest of what he saw as a criminal abridgement of states' rights. State-centered criticisms of national government policies showed that federalism was a problem for Confederate nationalism just as it had been in the prewar United States. A fairly typical dissent came from George Gordon, a state senator from Georgia. In a speech to the Georgia senate Gordon argued that conscription was an unconstitutional abrogation of states' rights that never would have been condoned by the constitutional framers. (That Gordon spent far more time talking about the U.S. framers than their Confederate counterparts exemplified the degree to which Confederate constitutionalism remained rooted in U.S. precedent.) However, Gordon made clear that he would only oppose conscription in principle, on the grounds of constitutionality. He would do nothing to resist it in practice, because he recognized that to do so would harm the Confederate war effort appreciably—perhaps fatally. "Do I seek to induce Georgia to assert her own separate sovereignty by reason of this infringement of it?" he asked. "God forbid. That is not my object. As a citizen I am willing to submit to much more than this to bring this war to a successful close." Gordon's stance—principled reservations combined with practical support of Confederate conscription—represented a typical form of opposition. With the phrase "as a citizen" he signaled that acceptance of measures like conscription, so long as they were militarily necessary, was part of the obligation of Confederate citizenship.[33]

Conscription was at the forefront of a general trend toward central state intervention in the Confederate economy. The potential for more extensive intervention was evident from the policy's inception. The Confederacy's "class" (occupational) exemptions system empowered government officials to classify certain types of economic activity as being more important to the war effort than soldiering—and therefore empowered them to promote certain types of economic activity over others. The extent of the central government's economic reach became even more apparent with a major overhaul of the Confederate draft in February 1864. In addition to expanding the lower and upper age limits of the draft to 17 and 50, respectively, the new law also decreased the number of automatic exemptions but provided the administration with the ability to detail any soldier to perform any civilian task. If, in other words, the Confederate government wished one of its male citizens to work in an iron foundry or on a hog farm, it could compel him to do so just as easily as it could compel him to fight on the Virginia front. The implications were far reaching: as one historian has concluded, "In theory at least the law gave the administration the power to manage totally the Southern economy as it related to labor."[34]

With conscription and other policies the Confederate government continued its efforts to draw a sharp line between citizens and aliens. This was an ongoing task that was complicated by a number of problems: constant fluctuations in the Confederacy's territorial borders and therefore its population boundaries; dissent from a range of southerners white and black, male and female; and the difficulties presented by groups such as women, slaves, and foreign immigrants who did not fit into the "citizen" versus "alien" binary. Although in theory government officials defined the constituency and the meaning of Confederate citizenship, in practice those definitions were shaped in a more diffuse, collaborative process.

Changing and often disputed borders between the United States and Confederate States meant that the national conscription policies of both countries were difficult to enforce at the margins.[35] So too were other government functions such as the collection of customs revenue. When the unionist North Carolinian John Hedrick was appointed U.S. customs collector in occupied Beaufort, North Carolina, in the summer of 1862, his job was hampered by the confusion of boundaries between the U.S. and the Confederacy. Hedrick was uncertain about the scope of U.S. authority as far as revenue laws were concerned. Should he be collecting payments in North Carolina state currency or should he insist on U.S. notes? Which vessels were permitted to dock and which were not? Which goods, exactly, counted as contraband? These and similar questions, all generated by the instability of national boundaries, hindered the ability of both national governments to exercise authority over the relevant territories and populations.[36]

Hedrick also commented revealingly on the uncertain loyalties of the residents of the occupied North Carolina coast. "Some are Secessionists," he observed, "but the greater number are Union men now and I think always have been." Theirs was a complicated, volatile unionism. Many local men had fought in the Confederate armies, whether by choice or coercion. Hedrick hired one man who "took the oath of allegiance to the United States the second day after he was released and [had] always been a Union man." "Many men," Hedrick explained, "have been forced into the Rebel Army by circumstances. It was either join the army or be counted and treated as a traitor." Clearly, outward acts did not always mirror inner loyalties. But the same could also be true of southern sympathizers who affected unionism; later that summer Hedrick realized that in many cases "the oath of allegiance does not amount to much. A man, who is mean enough to be a rebel, will do most anything to save his property." As Hedrick was witnessing first hand, loyalty was difficult to pin down during the Civil War, especially in areas that were contested, reoccupied, or close to the hazy borders between the warring nation-states. "The people about here are so so," he concluded. "They profess to be Union, but are not fighting Union men. Some have taken the oath of Allegiance, others the oath of Neutrality, and others still, have refused to take any oath."[37]

Another example of ambiguous loyalty can be found in a letter written by Confederate general Jubal Early to the well-known Virginia unionist Robert Young Conrad. A certain Dr. Boyd had been arrested as an active Union spy, Early claimed, not merely for holding unionist opinions, as had been alleged. To be sure, Early insisted, the Confederate government possessed the authority to arrest for treason anyone with unionist loyalties. But in practice, the Confederacy normally turned a blind eye to southern unionism so long as it was passive; "It has not been a part of the policy of the Confederate authorities to arrest persons who take no active part in the war, & who do not give information to the enemy."[38] Even government policy makers recognized the impossibility of enforcing absolute inner fealty.

The Confederate government did adopt a more coercive stance, however, when its citizens either actively aided the enemy or when they refused to fulfill the government-mandated responsibilities of citizenship. The most serious such responsibility was military service. Struggles over the everyday enactment of conscription became the most frequent expression of a two-way negotiation between individuals and the government over the terms of citizenship. At their most extreme, individual contributions to this process took the form of desertion. In countless acts of desertion from Confederate military service, white southern men rejected the authority of the national government. Their motivations were not always explicitly antinational—far more frequent was the simple desire to return home to normal life and to provide for their families amid worsening economic conditions—but regardless of intent, desertion invariably functioned on some level as a challenge to the government's definition of citizenship.[39] The Confederacy responded with coercive force, expending valuable manpower to hunt down and sometimes to execute deserters. Thomas Haughton, a local enrolling officer in eastern North Carolina, wrote to his superiors with mounting desperation in the summer of 1864, asking for assistance in these tasks. "Conscription will be a dead letter until I can get some such assistance," he wrote, pleading for men, guns, and ammunition to round up the almost "two hundred Deserters & recusant Conscripts lying in the woods." Reporting that "two thirds of the county are Lincoln men," he warned that without help he would be physically overwhelmed.[40] It is difficult to imagine a starker manifestation of contentious negotiations between the government and individuals over the rights and responsibilities of citizenship.

Ordinary southerners participated in the forging of Confederate citizenship in more positive ways, too. The ideal of the brave citizen soldier defending home, family, and country, for example, reverberated widely in Confederate culture, providing broad cultural validation for the governmental policy of conscription. In the context of war, a widely held sense of masculine duty to protect one's home and the honor of female relatives fused with a burgeoning national Confederate duty to protect southern white women and the South as a whole from the northern threat.[41] This connection had been established in the spring and summer of 1861, as the white South was mobilizing for war. Thereafter, the realities of war served as an ever more powerful cement between individual and national masculinities. Soldiers continued to identify protection of home, family, and country as a primary motivation for fighting—reflecting antebellum ideas about patriotism stemming from affection of one's family and local community—only now the danger was that much more immediate, and the responsibility that much more serious. When in the fall of 1862 the Confederate Congress turned its attention to the design of a national seal, the House and the Senate versions featured the motif of a male soldier defending both a house and a frail female figure.[42] Though both designs were eventually rejected in favor of a very cavalier-like George Washington, the iconography of the male protector continued to pervade Confederate culture. Everyday ideas about gender became more important than ever to conceptions of citizenship.

Thus one patriotic ode steeled soldiers' masculine resolve with reference to home, ancestry, and women. "Our loved ones' graves are at our feet, / Their homesteads at our back," the poet wrote, "No belted Southron can retreat / With woman on his track." As they had done since the earliest days of the Confederacy, popular songs and poems continued to portray the romantic and sexual benefits of manhood as being contingent upon the fulfillment of nationalist male responsibilities. Two of the South's most accomplished poets took up this very theme. Paul Hamilton Hayne's "My Mother-Land" listed, among the motivations for fighting the war, the masculine duty

> to preserve for noble wives
> The virtuous pride of unpolluted lives,
> To shield our daughters from the ruffian's hand.

Writing from the perspective of a woman, Alexander B. Meek posed the question "Wouldst Thou Have Me Love Thee?" He went on to explain that if men wanted women's love, they had to deserve it. And in order to deserve it, they had to commit themselves to their country's call. "Dost thou pause?" asked Meek—"Let dastards dally— / Do thou for thy country fight!" Moreover, Meek's female narrator insisted that even death would be preferable to cowardice. "Rather would I view thee lying," she affirmed,

> On the last red field of strife,
> 'Mid thy country's heroes dying,
> Than become a dastard's wife![43]

Similar themes of male duty appeared, somewhat less dramatically, in the everyday writings of ordinary southerners. In September 1861, Elizabeth Collier, a North Carolinian, urged her state's men along: "Sleep not, rest not, men of North Carolina, til each armed foe expires." But along with encouragement to fulfill the duties of citizenship came a clear warning of the consequences of shirking. "If there is one coward among you," she wrote, "shoot him down." Four years later, with the war over and the Confederacy defeated, Collier believed that her anxieties about male cowardice had been well founded. "Men of the South," she wrote in 1865, "are you dead to all shame?" She berated southern men for having themselves chosen the option of surrender: "You have no *country*—no *honor*— *you are a disgraced and ruined people.*"[44]

During the war, most southern soldiers appear to have accepted, in theory if not always in practice, their masculine responsibility to women, home, nation, and government. Mississippian soldier Harry Lewis, for example, interspersed a record of daily activities in letters home to his mother with some reflections on the purpose of it all. Responding to her fears that he was unhappy in the army, he acknowledged that the prospect of battle did produce anxiety. "But every sensible and patriotic man," he explained, "knows that on the morrow he must battle for his rights, and on his deeds and bearing hangs the honor and existence of the Confederacy and the sanctity and preservation of home and family." For Lewis, as for so many other southern soldiers, the individual responsibility to protect home and family merged with the national responsibility to protect the nation.[45] Of course, responsibility to nation did not always align so neatly with male responsibility to women, family, and home—particularly under the burden of economic hardship. In those instances when southern men saw duty to country and duty to family as being irreconcilable, they often prioritized the needs of their families. One North Carolina soldier, facing hard times in the spring of 1863, went so far as to write to the state governor, Zebulon Baird Vance. "Please pardon the liberty which a poor soldier takes in thus addressing you," he began, "as when *volunteering* he left a wife with four children to go to fight for his country." With life becoming harder and harder for their families at home, he warned, many poorer soldiers like himself could not continue to put country above family: "As a mans first duty is to provide for his own household the soldiers wont be imposed upon much longer." Clearly, different aspects of masculine responsibility sometimes came into conflict. Yet throughout the war most Confederate men found some way to maintain the balance, perhaps hoping that in the long term fulfilling the duties of citizenship would ultimately help their families as well.[46]

This frustrated soldier's letter to the governor was part of a much larger trend. Just as the central government demanded more from its citizens, with measures such as conscription, so too did those citizens demand more of their government. They wrote letters and petitions to government officials, at both state and national levels, insisting that the government had a responsibility to help its people meet the hardships of war. For example, the records of one Confederate Bureau of Conscription office in North Carolina are filled with citizens' petitions requesting that certain individuals be exempted from the draft. The reasons given were varied: a crucial occupation, slave security, family dependents, crops to bring in, a wife on her death bed, even a man with one leg shorter than the other. It is important to note that similar letters and petitions were received by officials at the state as well as the Confederate level, indicating modifications of political power at the state as well as the national level. Individual southerners, challenged by the pressures of war, actively renegotiated their relations with both state and national governments.[47]

Many of the letters to government officials were written by women. Such letters clearly represented a claim on some degree of citizenship rights by southern women. Indeed, the exigencies of war created possibilities for white southern women as well as men to reconstitute their relationship with the central government (and with state governments too), arguing that because government made greater demands upon them, they were entitled to make greater demands on government. Along with the responsibilities of contributing to the Confederate war effort, in other words, came certain rights of citizenship.[48] As the war progressed, material hardships and the near-total mobilization of manpower further increased the importance of female support for the Confederate war effort. Although the supporting roles for which women were most often praised hardly liberated them from the constraints of conventional gender roles, war could provide some new opportunities. The simple absence of a large proportion of working-age white men meant that southern white women had to shoulder new responsibilities, in the household as well as the farm and other workplaces. In many ways, white southern women continued to be connected to the national government largely through their male relatives. But in other ways the context of war enabled women to forge new, potentially empowering national roles for themselves.

To be sure, the old prewar idea—that women were particularly important to nationalism because nationalism grew out of the domestic realm—persisted. One orator, addressing an audience of young women late in the war, reminded them that throughout history women had been crucial to nationalism, since "being by nature more tender and sensitive than man, more imbued with pity and enthusiasm," they were more inclined than were men to cherish the "delightful idealities of home and country."[49] In the context of war, the importance of women's moral authority increased. Such was the belief of educator Edward Joynes, a staunch advocate for the training of female teachers in the Confederate South. Because a whole generation of southern men was so occupied with war, Joynes believed, "the responsibilities of the women of the South will be greater in the next times than ever heretofore, or ever perhaps hereafter. They will occupy a larger space not only in relative numbers, but in relative influence, in society, and their intellectual and moral culture will exert a profounder influence upon the character and destiny of the country." Not only would women's influence be greater, according to Joynes; it would also be more critical than ever. After all, the South stood "on the threshold of a new civilization." It was in the process of fighting for its national independence, and the education that female teachers would provide was absolutely vital to the long-term success of that effort. Education, he explained, "embraces the very sources of the national life, and, conceived in its moral as well as intellectual aspects, it may almost be said to be omnipotent in its influence upon national character." If the South's bid for national independence were to succeed, it would need more female teachers with the capacity to generate suitably moral strands of national responsibility.[50]

War opened up other possibilities for the expansion of women's national roles. Women's charitable relief activities, for instance, became so important to the Confederate war effort that the government formed partnerships with women as a necessary means of fighting the war.[51] In late 1862, Jefferson Davis received a letter from a group of women who proposed the formation of a "Confederate Soldiers Aid Society." The women revealingly described themselves as "Mississippi and Alabama Citizens"—conveying in no uncertain terms their conception of their relationship to the Confederate government. They offered to gather clothing and other supplies, which they expected the government to then distribute in a public-private collaboration. In 1863 Caroline Howard Gilman reported that she and other women had been specifically requested by the staff of Confederate hospitals and by "the Confederate authorities" to contribute necessary items such as sheets to the war effort. And in 1864 the Confederate secretary of the navy wrote to thank a group of "noble women" from South Carolina for the $30,000 they had raised for the "construction of iron clad gun boats." These examples of partnerships between government and female aid organizations went beyond private charity work into the realm of semiofficial national service. They redefined women's connections to the Confederate government and opened up the possibility for women to claim some of the rights—as well as the responsibilities—of citizenship.[52]

At least one (and in all likelihood most) of the South Carolina women who raised the $30,000 had a strong record of public activity even before secession and the formation of the Confederacy. Mary Amarinthia Snowden, who helped organize the Ladies Relief Association of Charleston and other pro-Confederate enterprises during the war, drew on a long personal history of patriotic endeavor which in the 1850s had involved her in the Ladies' Calhoun Monument Association and the Ladies' Mount Vernon Association.[53] Women's activities during the war built on a firm foundation of prewar participation in a range of public, political, and patriotic activities.[54] To be sure, the circumstances of war altered the possibilities. But still, the development of a quasi-citizenship for Confederate women had been foreshadowed to some degree by women's involvement in public life in the United States before 1861.

This wartime acceleration and modification of prewar tendencies helps explain the remarkable reactions of two Confederate women to Union victory in 1865. That May, the young Louisiana woman Sarah Lois Wadley recorded in her diary an angry reaction to the defeat of the South. "Oh it is all gone, I am compelled to see it; we are subjugated," she wrote. "I am too sorrowful to weep." Wadley went on to cast her frustration in the explicit terms of citizenship: "I cannot bear to stay here, I will never call myself a citizen of the United States, let it be where it will, only away from here." A similar sentiment was voiced by a woman in the South Carolina upcountry. "Amelia," she wrote in 1865, with Confederate defeat imminent, "I would rather be a subject [of] England, of France—even of Russia, than a *free* citizen of *their* vile government!"[55] These statements are deeply ironic. Both women protested against a condition—national citizenship—from which they were formally excluded in both the United States and the Confederate States. But in the context of the new relationship between southern women and the Confederate state that had emerged over the previous four years, it is hardly surprising that southern women saw themselves as national citizens. Their wartime experiences, building on prewar foundations, enabled them to claim a type of citizenship that was not recognized in the law but that nonetheless reflected a robust, reciprocal dependence between women and the Confederate nation-state.

The transformations of war were so far-reaching that they even raised the possibility of a different place for African Americans within the Confederate national community. At various stages of the war, the idea was occasionally floated that the Confederacy might solve its manpower problem by enlisting male slaves to fight in the army. By the winter of 1864–65, the Confederacy's prospects looked so bleak that a critical mass of the southern leadership, including both Jefferson Davis and Robert E. Lee, lent their support. And so, in the final months of its existence, the Confederacy invited slave owners to donate their slaves' labor to the Confederate army, with many advocates expecting that any such slaves would be emancipated by their owners. Male slaves were offered freedom in exchange for fighting for the Confederacy. The plan came too late to be properly implemented. And the outcome for black Confederate soldiers was not precisely enumerated. Would their wives and children have remained slaves? Would they have been granted any rights other than notional freedom? It seems likely that the best they could look forward to would be some quasi-enslaved status not dissimilar to the "free person of color" status of the antebellum years, more traditional "subjects" than modern "citizens." Still, given the significance of military service to white men's citizenship status, the plan to arm and free male slaves is an intriguing illustration of the extent of the ongoing transformations of Confederate citizenship. Presumably the extensive use of slaves as soldiers would have forced some kind of reassessment of the place of African Americans in the national community, perhaps even some form of gradual emancipation.[56]

In the Confederate crucible of war, definitions of citizen, state, and nation—and understandings of the relationships between the three—were complex and constantly in motion. These transformations were driven to no small degree by the Davis administration. The Confederate government implemented an extraordinary expansion of central authority, intervening in the national economy, creating a massive military and civilian bureaucracy, and controlling the day-to-day economic activities, even the lives and deaths, of its citizens. Yet Richmond's control was never absolute. The ongoing fashioning of Confederate citizenship was a collaborative process. Ordinary Confederates—both men and women—responded to government's accelerating claims upon them with demands of their own: for help with the economic consequences of war, for protection from the enemy, for a way to rationalize the sacrifices they made on behalf of the Confederacy. Thus was Confederate citizenship made.

The Sacred Bonds of Suffering

Increasingly, the duties of Confederate citizenship comprised suffering and loss. While the losses war inflicted and the hardships it demanded served to alienate some white southerners from the Confederacy, suffering brought others closer together in national community. When viewed in a religious light, wartime sacrifices—particularly the ultimate sacrifice of death—promised to strengthen Confederate nationalism and to provide the legitimacy that was otherwise so elusive. God seemed to be testing his chosen people in a fiery crucible, through which beckoned redemption for the individual and the nation alike.

White southerners frequently conceived of sacrifice in nationalistic terms. One soldier, John Thurman, writing in 1862 from an army camp to his wife at home, consoled her, saying, "It is the lot of many to make the same sacrifice and . . . it becomes the duty of every Patriot to make any sacrifice that our country demands." In another letter he said that even though he missed her terribly, he believed he was fighting in a noble cause, "and if needs be must sacrifice every other consideration [.] And for my God, my Country, my wife & my children all—to give even my life as a ransom to [save?] our country from disgrace and insult." He truly sympathized with the hardships his wife Sallie had to face. But even so, she must not become "dispondant" over her suffering, but should rather "bear them my dear wife like a Christian and Patriotic wife and mother." John Thurman's words make clear his understanding of how war defined gender-specific obligations of national responsibility: while he as a man should leave home to fight in the army and possibly sacrifice his life, Sallie's duties as a woman—as a "Christian and Patriotic wife and mother"— were to stay at home and endure suffering, possibly including the loss of her husband.[57]

Sacrifice thus lay at the core of Thurman's concept of citizenship for women as well as men. But these conceptions were fluid rather than fixed. By 1865, after three long years of service, John Thurman himself was reconsidering his earlier sentiments due to the deficiencies he saw in the loyalty of others. "As long as all were true to themselves & their country," he wrote to his wife, "none had more hope than I. none more willing to bear their part." But now he questioned the integrity of the government and of some among his fellow white southerners. In a letter of March 1865, Thurman questioned the synergy of duty to country and to family that had earlier sustained him, finding it tempting, he wrote, to "take you and my dear little ones and relinquish all else of interest to my once dear country. & turne my back on it for ever, swearing never to cast an other vote but know no country farther than my own happiness & intrest lead." For John Thurman the course of the war—not suffering per se but its uneven distribution—stretched almost to breaking point the bonds he had earlier forged between himself and the Confederacy. But, importantly, the bonds did not break. Thurman fought on until April 1865. Although he did experience a crisis of loyalty, his frustration was directed at government policies and the infidelity of certain of his countrymen—not at the nation itself.[58]

In the Civil War South, the suffering of war generated an assortment of reactions, ranging from increased commitment to outright rejection—and, as the example of John Thurman illustrates, many shades of ambivalence in between. For an unconditional unionist such as Tennessee's William "Parson" Brownlow, the hardships of war only served to reinforce deeply held loyalties to the Union. For others, loyalties shifted. Edward W. Gantt of Arkansas began in 1861 as a staunch secessionist and fought for the Confederate armies first as a colonel and later as a brigadier general. But by 1863, disillusioned with the course of the war and the policies of the Confederate leadership, Gantt left the army, renounced the Confederacy, and advocated a return to the Union.[59] More common than a complete switch of allegiance, however, was the wavering experienced by John Thurman. For many white southerners, the hardships of war produced not a wholesale rejection of the Confederate cause but rather targeted protests against deserters, ineffective leaders, or the "speculators" who appeared to be profiting from the sacrifices of others.[60] Perhaps most common of all were what the historian Dan Sutherland has termed "anti-government Confederates," southerners who supported the overall cause but opposed specific policies undertaken by their leaders.[61]

In many cases, suffering generated renewed devotion. Anticipating this, in one public speech Jefferson Davis tried to steel Confederates' resolve by linking an acknowledgment of suffering with remembrance of the revolutionary generation. "To show ourselves worthy of the inheritance bequeathed to us by the patriots of the Revolution," he urged, "we must emulate that heroic devotion which made reverse to them but the crucible in which their patriotism was refined." The suffering of war helped define Confederates' conceptions of national responsibility.[62] This was, in part, the old story of a South united in shared victimhood. Recall Ernest Renan's observation that "suffering in common unifies more than joy does. Where national memories are concerned, griefs are of more value than triumphs, for they impose duties, and require a common effort."[63] Recall too the prewar radicals' oft-repeated litanies of complaints about northern oppression, and the role that perceptions of northern attacks had played in the unraveling of American nationalism. Southern nationalists had long portrayed the South as a victim and an underdog, and whipping up resentment of apparent northern oppression had long fuelled southern nationalism. They realized that when it comes to justifying claims to national independence, victimhood confers power.[64] In the nineteenth-century Western world, the principle of nationality privileged those claims to national independence that were based on allegations of oppression at the hands of a stronger power. The narrative of northern oppression mandating southern national independence was well established.

Because of the realities of war, this old narrative was infused with a new element, one more potent and with more capacity to unite the white South in national community than could ever have been possible in peacetime. The new element was, of course, blood. In addition to filling William Trescot's "great, red river" of national separation, the blood of the Civil War functioned as a sort of sacred adhesive of Confederate nationalism, binding individuals to each other and to the nation in the potent and sanctified bond of human sacrifice. One of the defining characteristics of modern nationalism in general is the notion that individuals ought to be prepared to give their own lives in order to protect the nation. Preeminent nationalism scholar Anthony Smith has summarized it this way:

> The self-sacrificing citizen, the fallen patriot . . . the mass sacrifice of the people, the glory of patriotic valour, the everlasting youth of the fallen, the overcoming of death through fame—these are the stock in trade of nationalist values, myth, and imagery. They have become standard actors and motifs in the national salvation drama, the agents and vehicles of the nation's deliverance and subsequent triumph.[65]

This was also true of the Confederacy; thus William Trescot's observation, in the letter with which this chapter began, that the southern cause had been made "sacred by the blood of her martyrs."

Even before the war had properly begun, the trope of nationalist death sacrifice was already widespread. The idea loomed large not only in the European concepts of nationalism from which southerners learned so much but in antebellum American concepts as well. One of the most vital strands of American nationalism had always been the celebration of the revolutionary generation's wartime sacrifices, especially that of life. So even in the first months of the Confederacy's existence, white southerners instinctively conceived of their national responsibility in terms of death sacrifice.[66]

The glory of serving one's nation through death was frequently iterated. In a speech to departing troops early in the war, the well-known clergyman Benjamin Palmer sought to steel their resolve. If they should fall in battle, he reassured them, "it is little to say that you will be remembered. . . . You shall find your graves in thousands of hearts, and the pen of history shall write the story of your martyrdom." Similarly, and even more poetically, one contributor to *De Bow's Review* described the many southern men who were ready to fight and, if necessary, to make the ultimate sacrifice of death,

> who, now, with united hands and hearts, and garlands of cypress encircling their brows, cheerfully take their seats around the banquet table of death, and prepare to make the patriot's last, sad sacrifice. And they are cheered by the beautiful and inspiring thought that, though they may perish, yet their country will still survive, and be great among the nations, long after centuries shall have swept over their honored dust; while the soft South winds will come to whisper fond requiems over their manes, and bring the wild flowers of their own native clime to keep sweet vigils over the warrior's long rest!

The "patriot's last, sad sacrifice" would earn him national immortality.[67]

That death sacrifice would bring immortality seemed obvious to white southerners, who had come of age celebrating the immortality of the Revolutionary generation. Indeed, across the modern world, nationalism has appealed to individuals with its offer of what only religion could previously provide: life after death. Confederate nationalism, in promising white southerners immortality and the chance to connect their life and death with something larger than themselves, was, in this regard, typical. Like citizenship more generally, this was often conceived in contractual terms: in exchange for death came the assurance of subsequent commemoration. "Another ray of light hath fled," read one poem about a dead Confederate soldier,

> another Southern brave
> Hath fallen in his country's cause and found a laurelled grave—
> Hath fallen but his deathless name shall live when stars shall set.

In April 1862, wondering about the results of a recent battle, Sarah Wadley resolved that, if Confederate soldiers did "die in body, their names shall live in our memory, and when in after days the stains of blood have been obliterated . . . , we shall remember and generations after us shall bless those who died for their country." Similarly, a newspaper obituary celebrated the life and death of a young patriot who had died for his country, but remarked that at least there was some consolation in the knowledge that "his country will write upon its records his name, as one who freely offered his life to secure that independence." In the present and the future, the sacrifice of one's life to the nation would not go unremembered.[68]

Of course, wartime deaths were not always interpreted in positive, nationalistic terms. Death caused dreadful pain even for the staunchest Confederate partisans. For those who were less certain about the probity of the Confederate cause, the deaths of loved ones could be even more distressing because they had been incurred in a worthless cause. Writing about the death of a friend in 1862, the South Carolina unionist James L. Petigru sadly reported that "he died a martyr to a cause that was not his own." The dead soldier had apparently not believed in the Confederate cause but had, like many others, followed it "from a sentiment of State pride, and met his end like a gallant man." For Petigru, then, his friend's death was explicable in terms of masculinity and state identity—but not Confederate nationalism.[69]

Even so, the promise of national immortality surely helped ease the pain felt by many other grieving friends and relatives. This promise was a staple component of informal reports of soldier's deaths as well as printed obituaries. Recording in her diary the results of one battle, Lucy Wood mournfully wrote, "There fell one of the truest bravest patriots that all the land contained." She took considerable solace, though, in the knowledge that he had fallen "with heart burning to serve his country, and mark out his nation's freedom." Relatively late in the war, Mississippian Harry Lewis fell in battle. His brother John, writing to their mother with news of Harry's death, echoed Harry's own nationalistic idealism. Along with the fact that Harry had died reasonably free of pain, John wrote, "the remembrance of the cause he sacrificed his young manhood for, fills up to me much of his loss." And even if all his mother's sons were lost in battle, John believed it would be worthwhile, since "a man cannot be too good to die for his home—his country."[70]

John Lewis was by no means the only southern man to face the difficult task of relaying the news of a brother's death back home. Nor was he the only one who invoked nationalism to ease the pain. "It is a source of great consolation," wrote Thomas Davis, reporting the 1863 death of his brother to their mother, "to know that he died an honorable death, a sacrifice upon the alter [sic] of his country." Indeed, the only thing more important than that was that the dead soldier had "lived a life of such immaculate purity."[71] When Thomas himself was killed the following year, a newspaper obituary carried a similar message: the soldier's death was rendered easier to bear by the fact that he had lived a Christian life, and by the fact that he had taken his place on "the long list of martyrs who have fallen by the hands of our cruel and relentless foe, offering their lives a free sacrifice on the altar of their country." His spirit remained, the obituary went on, "infusing the glow of patriotism in our breasts."[72]

The sacrifice of loved ones, as these last words suggest, could serve to strengthen the commitment of the living to the nationalist cause for which their loved ones had died. Nationalism offered an appealing way to imbue the death of friends and family with sacred meaning. Margaret Preston, for instance, the sister-in-law of Thomas "Stonewall" Jackson, had committed her pen to the southern cause by writing patriotic poetry, just as her husband had committed himself by fighting in the war. When he died, rather than becoming alienated, she instead rededicated herself to the cause in which he had died. She dramatized her own experience in a long poem, *Beechenbrook: A Rhyme of the War*, which portrayed a woman who gladly sends her husband off to fight for home and country, even urging him to die rather than to submit. War's hardships become greater for our heroine, and her husband dies. But she does not despair, and, if anything, her devotion to Confederate independence is strengthened by her loss.[73]

Even the deaths of soldiers one had never even met could reinvigorate national responsibility. Although he was glad about the Confederacy's recent victory in the summer of 1864, soldier Richard E. Jaques reminded his fiancée that they ought to spare a thought for the bereaved—those who "must shed the scalding tear for some loved one who has offered his life as a sacrifice upon ~~his~~ our country's altar." The fact that Jaques initially wrote "his," then crossed it out and replaced it with "our," is revealing. The act of sympathizing with the dead and their families prompted Jaques to affirm shared membership in a national community—a community united by death sacrifice. He remained hopeful that things would work out in the end. "Youthful confederacy," he wrote, "baptized in the blood of her [martyred] sons may she soon emerge from her trials and proudly hold her [place] among the nations of the Earth."[74]

In addition to uniting them in a community of grief, death sacrifice also placed a heavy responsibility on survivors to ensure that the fallen had not died in vain. A printed broadside and postcard commemorated the life and nationalist death of the Virginian William Tysinger in precisely these terms. "Give my sword to my mother," read the caption on the postcard, below a picture of the fallen soldier. "Tell her I died in defense of my country." Such a message, imparted from beyond the grave, must have placed a powerful burden on survivors to continue to fight for the Confederacy. This was precisely the idea that Benjamin Palmer intended his eulogy of a fallen soldier to convey. "*Our country,*" he proclaimed, "*is endeared to us by every bereavement we sustain.* This death binds with a new sanction to our heart the cause to which he fell so cheerfully as a martyr." Everyone should be inspired by such deaths, said Palmer, to "rally around the tombs of our dead, and fight the last battle of freedom over their honored dust." The Confederate dead, by the time Palmer delivered this message in late 1862, were beginning to replace—or at least take their place alongside—the Revolutionary dead as sacrifices to a sacred trust which must be defended to the last.[75]

The idea of rallying around the graves of the dead was not unique to Palmer. The same thought suggested itself to Kate Foster, a planter's daughter, while she was attending church in occupied Mississippi in 1863. The sight of Union soldiers in the same church as her sickened her. Later, at home, she comforted herself by resolving in her diary, "When they take *all* from us, we will rally around the sacred tombs of our honored dead & fight the last battle for freedom on their consecrated graves." Surely they would be successful, she thought. Indeed, they had to be. "Ask our 'honored dead,'" she fumed, "if souls such as theirs could rest, and know the insolent invader had a Southern home, rendered holy by their loving presence in days gone by. No!" Again, the sacrifice of those who

FIGURE 5.3 Captain W. E. Tysinger broadside. (Virginia Historical Society.)

FIGURE 5.4 "Our National Confederate Anthem," sheet music cover, 1862. (Library of Congress.)

had already died placed an inescapable burden on the shoulders of those who survived, compelling them to keep up the fight. And it would be worth it, according to Foster: "We will come out of the furnace doubly purified for the good work and fight that God has given us to do. For to the people of this Confederacy is given the sublime mission of maintaining the supremacy of our Father in Heaven."[76]

As Foster's words make clear, the memory of national martyrs derived much of its potency from its religious dimension. Nationalism's promise of immortality did not replace existing religious beliefs; rather, it drew upon and extended them. The bonds of blood and sacrifice with which white southerners connected themselves to the nation were, emphatically, sacred bonds. Confederates considered themselves to be God's chosen people in much the same way as the majority of antebellum Americans, in both the North and South, had. This religious faith continued to condition Confederates conceptions of citizenship and national identity.[77]

God, for one thing, could be looked to as a sort of director of the Civil War. In the early stages of the war, Grace Elmore fully believed that God was watching over and protecting his people. "The days of the Israelites are returning," she thought, "so visibly has the power of God been shown in keeping a weaker nation from the hands of the lawless robber." Chosenness, in Elmore's judgment, was rooted in the very underdog, oppressed status that had always been so central to southern nationalism. Many others agreed that the events of the Civil War were ultimately controlled by God rather than by man. Thus a small printed pamphlet, entitled *Patriotic Prayer for the Southern Cause*, appealed for the favor of "Our Heavenly Father high and mighty King of kings and Lord of Lords— who dost from thy throne behold all the dwellers on earth, and reignest with power supreme . . . over all kingdoms, empires, and governments." God was the God of nations, and to him Confederates appealed for national legitimacy. Such was the premise behind the many national fast days called for by Jefferson Davis. Such was the message of the countless sermons that rang forth across the country on those occasions. Henry H. Tucker's November 1861 effort, "God in the War," was typical in its admonition that God, not man, controlled the outcome of the war and the destiny of the Confederate nation.[78]

As had been the case with American nationalism before the war, though, Confederates' continued status as God's chosen people was not necessarily guaranteed. With tremendous advantage came tremendous responsibility. Confederates reminded each other that in order to be good citizens, they must be good Christians—and vice versa. In a sermon reflecting on the fate of a group of deserters who had recently been executed, for example, John Paris told a group of soldiers that to abandon one's duty to the army and nation was to abandon one's duty to God. "The true christian is always a true patriot," he advised. "Patriotism and Christianity walk hand in hand."[79]

Throughout the war, the fate of the nation was frequently and closely linked to the piety and morality of Confederates—both as a community and as individuals. Under the title "The Word of God a Nation's Life," George F. Pierce cautioned that, because "government is an institution of heaven," the Confederacy ought to take care to be a pious nation, with laws and rulers that were guided by the principles of Christianity. Pierce was glad to report that the Confederate Constitution and its frequent fast days proved its adherence to this necessity. But Confederates were far from perfect, particularly in their love of money, and had to keep improving themselves. "O my countrymen," he said, "let us reverence the Lord of Sabaoth, and let us remember that our country is to be preserved and perpetuated, not by science, wealth, patriotism, population, armies or navies, but by every word that proceedeth out of the mouth of the Lord." In part, Pierce was contending that the Confederacy's leaders ought to be devout, moral men, if the new nation were to earn God's favor. However, tapping into one of the long-standing assumptions of American nationalism, Pierce noted that in relatively democratic countries such as theirs, "nations have a sort of collective unity, and between rulers and people there is a reciprocal responsibility[:] if there be connivance in evil, each is amenable for the guilt of the other." Every individual in the Confederacy—not just national leaders—had a direct responsibility for the moral character of the whole nation, and, therefore, for its very survival.[80]

Many Confederates, soldiers and civilians alike, took the sacred responsibilities of citizenship seriously indeed. Writing home in 1863, for instance, H. C. Kendrick expressed gratitude that he was in his family's prayers. Indeed, he felt that more piety was needed across the land. The situation was not likely to improve, he felt, "until the hearts of the citizens and soldiers, get right and become humble before God." Reporting that his own regiment had been spending a great deal of time attending to their religious lives, he insisted, "We must be soldiers of the cross, as well as of the confederate fields." Countless messages of religious renewal made their way from camp to home front and back again. North Carolinian Thomas Davis, writing home late in 1864, echoed Kendrick in his approval of the strength of religious activity on the home front. "Many think that the war is sent upon us as a punishment for our sins and that it will last until we grow better," he reported. Although he did not agree with such a judgment, he was certainly glad to see moral improvement. "Certainly, if all our people were Christians, the war would soon end, for then every man would do his duty, and that is all we need to whip the Yankees." For a variety of reasons, then, Confederate soldiers believed that the surest way to achieve national victory was for each individual to act as a Christian.[81]

Whereas Thomas Davis gave little credence to the idea that the war and its hardships were imposed on his nation as divine punishment, many of his compatriots felt sure that such was in fact the case. After all, if one believed that God was directing the course of the war, and that each individual bore some responsibility for the moral character of the nation, what other conclusion could be reached? Surely, military defeats were evidence of moral and religious failings among the Confederate people. This was precisely how many Confederates interpreted military defeats and their continued failure to establish their national independence by winning the war. From hellish conditions in the trenches near Petersburg in 1864, John Hendricks Kinyoun wrote home, "The Horros and Suffering no mortal tounge or pen can describe." Like many of his contemporaries Kinyoun viewed suffering in religious terms. "I would that our chastisement both north and South was complete," he explained, "so we could stop this blood shed and carnage but it will not stop untill our just punishment has been meuesured out to us in it[s] full portion." Earlier in the war, within the same few days in the spring of 1862, Jefferson Davis had received two letters from two different citizens suggesting that military reverses had been caused by lack of proper attention to religion and morality. One writer suggested that God was refusing victory to the Confederacy because of the drunkenness and bad behavior of its officer corps, while another thought it must be due to the fact that the Confederate post office delivered the mail even on Sunday. Indeed, stopping the official delivery of mail on the Sabbath became something of a crusade. Documents circulated around the country reminding Confederates of the connection between national piety and national victory, urging readers to campaign for an end to the Sunday mails. "God will not be mocked," cautioned one. "We must serve Him as a nation, in sincerity and truth, if we wish His blessing." Other commentators warned southerners that the war might represent divine punishment for slaveholders' failure to reform their peculiar institution into a more humane version of bondage. Whatever specific sins were highlighted, the common theme was that only individual and collective rectitude could secure the survival of the nation. Whereas this belief had deep roots in prewar American nationalism, the national import of individual morality was greatly heightened during wartime.[82]

Viewed in light of the logic that defeats were punishments for sinful or immoral behavior, the steadily decreasing success of the Confederate

forces in the latter stages of the war naturally produced despair and disil-
lusionment.[83] In some cases, this led to the loss of hope. In other cases, it
led to the angry apportionment of blame on others. Many were the
harangues against the "traitors" and "croakers" who jeopardized the Confederate cause. The Confederate government was another frequent target
of angry recriminations, as were profiteering "speculators."[84]

Sometimes less obvious targets came under attack. One Alabama soldier, clearly losing hope by 1864, wrote to his sister complaining about the
"demoralization of female virtue" on the home front. "What will the country come to?" he asked. It appeared as though "the people at home has lost
all virtue and lost all religion and respect for Christianity. We will never
succeed," he went on, "unless there is a change in people at home who call
themselves Christians." Virginia soldier Charles Fenton James made a
similar point, chastising his sister for attending dances, and warning her
that the fate of the nation depended upon the everyday moral comportment of its members. Morality, piety—even the rhythm of one's feet—
were national affairs.[85]

The logic connecting individual morality with national survival, by
way of an omnipotent God, presented serious challenges to Confederate
morale. However, in emphasizing these challenges other historians
have largely overlooked the capacity of this logic to strengthen ties
between the individual and the new nation-state. Conditioned by their
Christianity to expect divine trials and tribulations, the majority of mid-
nineteenth-century southerners, and Americans more generally, viewed
reprimands from on high as challenging opportunities rather than as
reasons to capitulate. Their Christianity, one might put it, was not supposed to make them feel good. Accordingly, the hardships of war, viewed
through the lens of Christianity, could be seen as being not so much
destructive as constructive of good character. War was not so terrible, in
the grand scheme of things, wrote North Carolinian Walter Lenoir, and
there was reason for optimism even if things did become difficult.
"When I remember that adversity only serves to develop the better qualities both of men and nations," he concluded, "I can not but believe that
your manly and loyal nature will be aroused by the calamities of our
country, and that your despondency will give place to a firmness which
will even border on cheerfulness."[86]

Lenoir's cousin William Bingham elaborated at length on a similar
theme in a letter he wrote to Walter the following year. Advocacy for peace
with the North, a formidable force by the time Bingham wrote in late

1863, had caused him to rethink his initial certainty that the Confederacy would easily establish a great slaveholding republic. Such a prize demanded sacrifice, he thought, and a people who could not endure considerable hardship might not deserve it at all. "If when dangers begin to thicken our people should forget how the hand of Jehovah was outstretched for their deliverance, and should say 'Let us go back into Egypt that we perish not in this wilderness,'" they might not merit their privileged status as God's chosen people. The Confederacy could *only* successfully establish its nationality, he judged, in return for suffering: "If we reach the promised land of independence, it will be after a long and painful journey through the desert." The hardships of war were not meaningless obstacles, in Bingham's understanding. They were the very point. They were the true test of nationality, and the means by which it was to be forged.[87]

Similarly, amid her complaints about the "miserable croakers" and "traitors" who were unwilling to undergo hardships for the national cause, Elizabeth Collier vowed to sacrifice as much as was necessary, in the belief that victory could not otherwise be obtained. If southerners refused to make sacrifices, she thought, "we do not deserve to be *free* & rest assured God will not suffer us to be free, for He only helps those who help themselves—unless we are willing to make great personal sacrifices." The war, for Collier, was a divine test of Confederate nationality—and in order to survive it, real Confederates had to learn to sacrifice. "Oh God," she exclaimed in another diary entry, "Thou art purifying us through much suffering." A similar assumption informed a *Richmond Examiner* editorial in the spring of 1862. Though the war might prove to be long and hard, the editorial urged readers to endure. "Jehovah," after all, "kept Moses and the people of His love wandering forty years in the desert ere He gave them a country and independence." The religious lens through which many Confederates viewed the world suggested that shared suffering and sacrifices were the only means of achieving national independence.[88]

Other white southerners reached similar conclusions. Suffering and sacrifice simply had to result in victory, thought Kate Foster. "Can any one for a moment think," she asked,

> that God will allow so many of His people to fall in what they thought and think a good cause and then for their deaths to be as naught in the balance of peace. Because God has it seems to us withdrawn his all-protecting hand are we to lose faith in his power?

No, we need chastisement. . . . If we put our trust in Him he will guide us through darkness into light.

Soldier H. C. Kendrick saw good reason for optimism, too. "I havn't a doubt," he assured his parents, "but that we (the people of the South), are destined to freedom, as the Christian is to inherit eternal bliss in a future state." Kendrick clearly viewed the necessary divine trial of a nation in much the same light as Christianity's prescription of necessary trial for depraved humans. Granted, eternal bliss may cost many lives. But, Kendrick concluded, that was precisely the point: "The harder the trial, the sweeter the liberty."[89]

Such was the lesson not only of Christian salvation but also of the very concept of nineteenth-century nationalism. As white southerners looked over the Atlantic and across the globe, it was clear to them that the establishment of national independence frequently entailed suffering through the hardships of war. "All nations which come into existence at this late period of the world," the Episcopal Bishop Stephen Elliott explained, "must be born amid the storm of revolution and must win their way to a place in history through the baptism of blood." Presumably Elliott was thinking of examples such as the Kingdom of Italy, established in 1861 after several years of military conflict and many more years of attempts at violent revolution by nationalists such as Mazzini and Garibaldi. Perhaps he was even thinking of mid-nineteenth-century exercises in nation making through military conflict in places as diverse as Paraguay and China.[90] Even more likely, Elliott was thinking of the most important example of all, the founding of the United States in the War of American Independence. Another southern clergyman, John Paris, had precisely this parallel in mind when he told an audience of Confederate soldiers, "War is the scourge of nations." Yet it was, he believed, a necessary trial. "God is no doubt chastising us for our good," he said—and it would be worth it in the end: "We are only drinking now from a cup, from which every nation upon the face of the earth have drank before us. We have walked the bloody road of revolution for three years; and still we face the foe. Our fathers trod it for seven, and in the end were successful." National independence, it seemed, could only be achieved by first suffering through the trials of war.[91]

PARIS'S COMPARISON WITH the American Revolution echoes Jefferson Davis's exhortation that Confederates ought to "emulate that heroic devotion" of the revolutionary generation "which made reverse to them but the crucible in which their patriotism was refined." The old intellectual arguments for southern independence—including the likening of 1861 to 1776—continued to feature in Confederate definitions of national identity and citizenship. But four years of war, and the spilling of more blood than anyone in 1861 could have imagined, shifted the nature of that remembrance. An independent South was still held up as a purified version of the original America. But now it seemed as though genuine American purity was more of a process than a state. Like their forefathers before them, white southerners believed that they too would have to undergo severe trials under the eye of a watchful God if they were to deserve national independence.

The experience of war tested and refined southern notions of nationalism and citizenship. It filled William Henry Trescot's "great, red river" with the blood of hundreds of thousands, marking the line between South and North in the starkest way imaginable. It brought nationalism home to white southerners: in the literal and symbolic fear of barbaric Yankee invaders; in the national meaning it gave to the everyday ideas and practices of gender; in the ideal of national sacrifice it inflicted upon just about every aspect of daily life. War reinvigorated and elevated to a new plane the existing narrative of a suffering South, a community united by external attack, a community blessed by virtue of its suffering. The injection of blood into the old narrative sanctified the South's claim to national independence. Interpreting the hardships of war through this narrative of undeserved oppression, through the logic of Christian suffering, and through the models of nationalism they observed in other parts of the world, Confederates persuaded themselves that their long-standing victimhood was the surest sign of all that they truly deserved national independence.

All of this, generated by the unprecedented demands of war, brought the individual and the nation into closer and more violent contact than ever before. To be sure, such collisions could and often did result in hesitation, disaffection, and even rejection. But they could also form the basis for more emotionally intense conceptions of citizenship than had previously existed. Of course, Confederates' bid for independence was defeated on the battlefield. But the bonds of blood and sacrifice, forged in the crucible of war, would form the foundations of Lost Cause mythology and an enduring white southern identity that continued to see righteousness in oppression, redemption in suffering.

Conclusion

DURING THE LONG years of intense North-South conflict over slavery, nationalism and citizenship were embedded more and more deeply within white southerners' lives. Navigating a shifting landscape of political allegiances and cultural loyalties—to their states and their region, to the United States and the Confederate States—they had been forced to address fundamental questions. What made a nation a nation? Could an individual or a group change nationality at will? How should one balance different layers of identity and loyalty when they came into conflict? How did nation-states secure and maintain legitimacy at home and abroad? What were the rights and responsibilities of citizenship?

Most white southerners had begun this period as enthusiastic American nationalists. Proud to be part of the United States, they had celebrated their states' and their region's central contributions to what they held up as a great nation, a pioneer of democratic citizenship and a model for the rest of the world to follow. Like all nationalisms, however, antebellum American nationalism was an artificial construct, not a naturally occurring organism. It was tentative and unfinished. Though robust in many respects, American nationalism was troubled by federalism, which divided sovereignty and compromised the supposedly supreme authority of the nation-state; by the fluidity and incompleteness of various strands of nationhood—civic, cultural, and racial; and, of course, by slavery, which caused two groups of American to disagree so fundamentally on the political economy and cultural identity of the United States that they broke the nation-state in two. Slavery was the issue that tore the United States apart. But because the disagreement over slavery assumed territorial form, the way the country collapsed—and the way its inhabitants understood this collapse—was shaped by ideas about nationalism and citizenship.

In the years leading to 1861, a small number of radical southerners, mostly from South Carolina, campaigned for withdrawal from the Union. Their principal motivation was the defense of slavery against apparently increasing northern hostility, a motivation that was exacerbated by a long-term shift in the balance of political power from South to North. But their desire to preserve slavery did not lead to southern nationalism automatically. They were also galvanized by a personalized sense of being under siege, and they went on to rationalize their proslavery crusade using the ideas and the language of oppositional nationalism. Arguing that southerners' distinctive economic and social interest in slavery had produced a distinctive nation, secessionists utilized the globally ascendant concept of nationalism in order to promote political independence for the South.

The radicals were few in number and extreme in their views. But with the political conflict over slavery that was catalyzed by the Mexican War and which subsequently intensified, even the firm American nationalism of the moderate southern majority experienced serious strain. White southerners were by and large committed to the preservation of the Union, but only the Union as they defined it: a proslavery Union that maintained southern rights, including the right to own slaves and to have access to new western territories; a Union of mutual respect and sympathy in which compatriots North and South were united by bonds of genuine affection. That Union seemed to be disintegrating as the 1850s rolled on, due to northerners' increasing hostility towards slavery and their decreasing respect and sympathy for white southerners. Resentment at this disintegration pushed the South toward secession. Even so, right up to the moment of secession—and beyond—countless white southerners retained affection for the Union, giving rise to active unionism and lingering attachments to American identity, American ideals, and American history. Eleven southern states seceded, but not without considerable ambivalence, uncertainty, and outright opposition.

Enduring connections to the United States complicated but did not derail southern efforts between 1861 and 1865 to construct a new nation-state, the Confederate States of America. In the mid-nineteenth-century Western world, claims of supreme political authority were invariably advanced within the framework of modern nationalism. Confederates accordingly set about building the institutions of a modern nation-state—a government, an army, a diplomatic corps—as well as establishing those institutions' legitimacy in the eyes of the world and of the Confederacy's own citizens. Drawing on emerging conventions of transatlantic nationalism, as well as their long experience as American nationalists, Confederates endeavored to define a distinctive national identity and a set of expectations about the roles of individual Confederate citizens. Their efforts were beset by serious problems. Slavery represented a weak basis for national distinctiveness in a transatlantic world that was increasingly opposed to the peculiar institution, and in an American South where the nonslaveholding majority's fealty to the regime could not be taken for granted. Furthermore, the substance of Confederate national identity and the loyalty of its citizens were also complicated by persistent political ties to the United States and cultural ties to American national identity. Withdrawing from one nation-state and creating another were not straightforward undertakings.

Throughout the Civil War, similar problems continued to vex Confederate nationalism. White southerners still faced the difficult task of navigating competing allegiances to the United States and the Confederate States, not to mention more local loyalties to state, county, community, and even family. Their uncertainty gave rise to out-and-out unionism—the peace movements that gained strength later in the war, particularly in low-slaveholding, mountainous regions—as well as more widespread and ongoing ambiguity about the role of American national ideals and American history in the new nation-state. Even so, the Confederate nation-state became more robust during the war years, both politically and culturally. The Confederacy underwent dramatic central-state formation, with the Richmond government taking unprecedented control over the national economy and over the lives of individual citizens. Combined with this process of state formation, Confederates also continued to define and redefine national identity and citizenship. Amid the pressures of war, a wide range of white southerners participated in the formation of ever-tighter connections between citizen, nation, and government, connections embodied most dramatically in the Confederacy's culture of death sacrifice. Inspired by Christianity, the examples of nationalist movements elsewhere, and their own memories of the American Revolution, Confederates persuaded themselves that shared suffering and sacrifice proved their national legitimacy more powerfully than anything else.

The Confederate nation-state perished on the battlefields of the Civil War. Yet white southerners' varied experiences with nationalism between 1848 and 1865—their proud American nationalism, their proslavery separatism, their nation-state-breaking and nation-state-making, their ambivalence towards southern and American identities, and their construction of national identity through hallowed sacrifice—would all go on to shape their post-1865 future. As the southern states gradually reintegrated into the Union, the landscape of American nationalism kept on shifting. White southerners continued to participate in this process. Long after defeat, they still struggled with the challenges of reconciling southernness with Americanness, their region's racial practices with their nation's ideals. By the early twentieth century, white reconciliation on the national stage had enabled the inauguration of a new racial regime that closed off the revolutionary possibilities that Union victory and emancipation had held out to African Americans: the promise of a racially inclusive American national identity and full entry into national citizenship for African Americans, or at least African American men. Instead, the white supremacist character of American national identity and citizenship were reaffirmed. Meanwhile, white southerners used highly selective memories of slavery and images of the Confederate war effort as a romantic "Lost Cause" to fashion a new kind of regional identity. Because it did not seriously involve the political claim of independence, this postwar white southern identity should not be called nationalism. But it drew deeply on central strands of the Confederate nationalism that had developed during the war itself, particularly the belief that shared victimhood and suffering united white southerners in a sacred community of sacrifice.[1]

The persistence of tensions between regional and national loyalties in the United States, complicated as ever by the political framework of federalism, remind us that, despite what nationalists say, nationalism is not a unitary or a total phenomenon. Nations are not self-evident. Nor is the political project of nationalism. If nations really were naturally occurring—if the boundaries between nations were obvious; if there were absolute and measurable differences between each one; if the authority of each national government really was uncontestable and supreme—our world would be a much simpler place. Instead, the modern world has been burdened with the intractable problems of nationalism: What ultimately justifies the nation-state's claim to absolute authority? How are the borders of the nation (and the nation-state) to be determined? Who adjudicates rival claims to nationhood? These problems have structured many of the destructive, transformative wars that have shaped the world over the last two centuries. One hundred and fifty years ago they helped convert a conflict over the place of slavery in America's future into a brutal war fought between two self-styled nation-states, fighting for rival visions of national borders and national identities, each one using the ideas of

nationalism and citizenship to claim authority for their actions and to rationalize the extraordinary demands they made on their citizens. Thus did
a peculiar society based on a peculiar system of racial and economic oppression play its own part in what is perhaps the least peculiar story of the
modern world: the ascendancy of citizenship and the nation-state.

Abbreviations

ADAH Alabama Department of Archives and History,
          Montgomery, Alabama

  DU Rare Book, Manuscript, and Special Collections Library, Perkins Library,
          Duke University, Durham, North Carolina

  FHS Filson Historical Society, Louisville, Kentucky

  LOC Library of Congress, Washington, DC

  SHC Southern Historical Collection, Wilson Library,
          University of North Carolina, Chapel Hill,
          North Carolina

SCHS South Carolina Historical Society, Charleston,
          South Carolina

  USC South Caroliniana Library, University of South Carolina,
          Columbia, South Carolina

  VHS Virginia Historical Society, Richmond, Virginia

Notes

INTRODUCTION

1. Charles Fenton James to Emma James, February 13, 1865, Charles Fenton James Letters, VHS.

2. Key statements of the "weak" argument include Paul D. Escott, *After Secession: Jefferson Davis and the Failure of Confederate Nationalism* (Baton Rouge: Louisiana State University Press, 1978), and Richard E. Beringer et al., *Why the South Lost the Civil War* (Athens, GA: University of Georgia Press, 1986). On the "strong" side, see especially Gary W. Gallagher, *The Confederate War: How Popular Will, Nationalism, and Military Strategy Could Not Stave Off Defeat* (Cambridge, MA: Harvard University Press, 1997); Gallagher. "Disaffection, Persistence, and Nation: Some Directions in Recent Scholarship on the Confederacy," *Civil War History* 55.3 (2009): 329–353; William Blair, *Virginia's Private War: Feeding Body and Soul in the Confederacy, 1861–1865* (New York: Oxford University Press, 1998).

3. This trend began with Drew Gilpin Faust's *The Creation of Confederate Nationalism: Ideology and Identity in the Civil War South* (Baton Rouge: Louisiana State University Press, 1988), some of the conceptual insights of which were foreshadowed by David M. Potter, "The Historian's Use of Nationalism and Vice Versa," *American Historical Review* 67 (1962): 924–950, reprinted in Potter's *The South and the Sectional Conflict* (Baton Rouge: Louisiana State University Press, 1968), 34–83. The most comprehensive work on Confederate nationalism is Anne Sarah Rubin's *A Shattered Nation: The Rise and Fall of the Confederacy, 1861–1868* (Chapel Hill: University of North Carolina Press, 2005), which provides a valuable overview of nationalist culture in the Confederate and postwar South. Robert E. Bonner has revealed the powerful emotional dimensions of Confederate nationalism in his *Colors and Blood: Flag Passions of the Confederate South* (Princeton, NJ: Princeton University Press, 2002), and has placed

southerners' emphatically proslavery nationalism into long-term American as well as Confederate perspectives in his *Mastering America: Southern Slaveholders and the Crisis of American Nationhood* (Cambridge, UK: Cambridge University Press, 2009). Other important works are George C. Rable, *The Confederate Republic: A Revolution against Politics* (Chapel Hill: University of North Carolina Press, 1994); Ian Binnington, "'They Have Made a Nation': Confederates and the Creation of Confederate Nationalism" (PhD diss., University of Illinois, 2004); Peter Onuf and Nicholas Greenwood Onuf, *Nations, Markets, and War: Modern History and the American Civil War* (Charlottesville: University of Virginia Press, 2006); and Michael Bernath, *Confederate Minds: The Struggle for Intellectual Independence in the Civil War South* (Chapel Hill: University of North Carolina Press, 2010).

4. As David Potter incisively observed, many people have been reluctant to see Confederate nationalism as genuine because of the tendency to approach nationalism in "valuative" terms; nobody wants to be seen to sanction the legitimacy of a failed movement that was based on slavery. Potter also cautioned against "too simple an equation between nationality and culture." The conventional model of nationalism centers on a distinctive ethnocultural identity, and so the fact that Confederate nationalism was based more on political and economic interests in slavery, and that its claims to ethnocultural distinctiveness were relatively weak, has also been seen as proof of the lack of nationalism. (Potter, "The Historian's Use of Nationalism," 51.)

5. As David Potter explained, although historians on some level know that "nationalism is a relative thing, existing in partial form," they often "treat it as an absolute thing, existing in full or not at all." (Potter, "The Historian's Use of Nationalism," 39.)

6. On unionism, see John C. Inscoe and Robert C. Kenzer, eds., *Enemies of the Country: New Perspectives on Unionists in the Civil War South* (Athens, GA: University of Georgia Press, 2001); Margaret M. Storey, *Loyalty and Loss: Alabama's Unionists in the Civil War and Reconstruction* (Baton Rouge: Louisiana State University Press, 2004); Daniel E. Sutherland, ed., *Guerrillas, Unionists, and Violence on the Confederate Home Front* (Fayetteville: University of Arkansas Press, 1999); Robert Tracy McKenzie, "Contesting Secession: Parson Brownlow and the Rhetoric of Proslavery Unionism, 1860–1861," *Civil War History* 48 (2002): 294–312. One exception to the general tendency of most studies of Confederate nationalism is a collection of essays honoring the career of Emory Thomas, which emphasizes variety as a major theme: Lesley J. Gordon and John C. Inscoe, eds., *Inside the Confederate Nation: Essays in Honor of Emory M. Thomas* (Baton Rouge: Louisiana State University Press, 2005). The essays in this collection by Brian Wills ("Shades of Nation: Confederate Loyalties in Southeastern Virginia," 59–77), Frank J. Byrne ("The Literary Shaping of Confederate Identity: Daniel R. Hundley and John Beachamp Jones in Peace and War," 79–98),

Rod Andrew, Jr. ("The Essential Nationalism of the People: Georgia's Confederate Congressional Election of 1863," 128–146), and Christopher Phillips ("'The Chrysalis State': Slavery, Confederate Identity, and the Creation of the Border South," 147–164) are especially insightful on diversity and change over time.

7. The most helpful work on the changing landscape of nationalism in nineteenth-century Europe is Joep Leerssen, *National Thought in Europe: A Cultural History* (Amsterdam: Amsterdam University Press, 2006), but see also Geoff Eley, "Culture, Nation, and Gender," in *Gendered Nations: Nationalisms and Gender Order in the Long Nineteenth Century*, ed. Ida Blom, Catherine Hall, and Karen Hagemann (Oxford: Berg, 2000), 27–40; Elie Kedourie, *Nationalism*, 4th ed. (Oxford: Blackwell, 1993); Stefan Berger, "National Movements," in *A Companion to Nineteenth Century Europe, 1789–1914*, ed. Stefan Berger (Malden, MA: Blackwell, 2006), 178–192; Alexander Maxwell, "Multiple Nationalism: National Concepts in Nineteenth-Century Hungary and Benedict Anderson's Imagined Communities," *Nationalism and Ethnic Politics* 11 (2005): 385–414; Graeme Morton, *Unionist-Nationalism: Governing Urban Scotland, 1830–1860* (East Linton, UK: Tuckwell, 1999); and Timothy Baycroft and Mark Hewitson, eds., *What Is a Nation? Europe 1789–1914* (Oxford: Oxford University Press, 2006), which contains the Eötvös quotation (quoted in Mark Cornwall, "The Habsburg Monarchy: 'National Trinity' and the Elasticity of National Allegiance," 172).

8. Rollin G. Osterweis, *Romanticism and Nationalism in the Old South* (New Haven, CT: Yale University Press, 1949) contains suggestive, though often overly speculative, arguments about the influence of European nationalisms upon the American South, while Onuf and Onuf, *Nations, Markets, and War*, sets the nineteenth-century United States within the context of liberalism, political economy, and modern nationalism. The most insightful comparative study is Don H. Doyle's *Nations Divided: America, Italy, and the Southern Question* (Athens, GA: University of Georgia Press, 2002), which compares nationalism and regionalism in the United States and Italy. See also Frank Towers, "The Origins of the Antimodern South: Romantic Nationalism and the Secession Movement in the American South," in *Secession as an International Phenomenon*, ed. Don H. Doyle (Athens, GA: University of Georgia Press, 2010), 174–190; Bruce Cauthen, "Confederate and Afrikaner Nationalism: Myth, Identity, and Gender in Comparative Perspective" (PhD diss., University of London, 1999); Enrico Dal Lago, *Agrarian Elites: American Slaveholders and Southern Italian Landowners, 1815–1861* (Baton Rouge: Louisiana State University Press, 2005); and Bryan P. McGovern, *John Mitchel: Irish Nationalist, Southern Secessionist* (Knoxville: University of Tennessee Press, 2009). Other efforts to view Civil War–era nationalism in comparative perspective have focused on the American North: Susan-Mary Grant, *North over South: Northern Nationalism and American Identity in the Antebellum Era* (Lawrence: University Press of Kansas, 2000); Grant, "Americans Forging a New Nation, 1860–1916," in *Nationalism in the New World*,

ed. Don H. Doyle and Marco Antonio Pamplona (Athens, GA: University of Georgia Press, 2006), 80–98; Grant "'The Charter of its Birthright': The Civil War and American Nationalism," *Nations and Nationalism* 4, no. 2 (1998): 163–185; Thomas Bender, *A Nation among Nations: America's Place in World History* (New York: Hill & Wang, 2006), 116–181; C. A. Bayly, *The Birth of the Modern World, 1780–1914: Global Connections and Comparisons* (Malden, MA: Blackwell, 2004), 161–165; Carl Degler, "One among Many: The United States and National Unification," in *Lincoln, the War President*, ed. Gabor S. Boritt (New York: Oxford University Press, 1992), 91–119; David M. Potter, "The Civil War," in *The Comparative Approach to American History*, ed. C. Vann Woodward (New York: Oxford University Press, 1968). On the broad importance of transatlantic exchange to antebellum southern intellectual life, see Michael O'Brien, *Conjectures of Order: Intellectual Life and the American South, 1810–1860*, 2 vols. (Chapel Hill: University of North Carolina Press, 2004).

9. See Paul Quigley, "Secessionists in an Age of Secession: The Slave South in Transatlantic Perspective," in Doyle, *Secession as an International Phenomenon*, 151–173. The adjectives "imagined" and "invented" refer, of course, to Benedict Anderson, *Imagined Communities: Reflections on the Origin and Spread of Nationalism*, 2nd ed. (London: Verso, 1991); and Eric Hobsbawm and Terence Ranger, eds. *The Invention of Tradition* (Cambridge, UK: Cambridge University Press, 1983). The premise that nations are artificially created artifacts has underpinned many of the most influential recent works on nationalism. In addition to these books and Homi K. Bhabha, ed., *Nation and Narration* (New York: Routledge, 1990), which emphasize the process of cultural creation, see also Ernest Gellner, *Nations and Nationalism* (Oxford: Blackwell, 1983), who stresses the socioeconomic transformations that generated nationalism, and John Breuilly, *Nationalism and the State*, 2nd ed. (Manchester: Manchester University Press, 1993), who sees nationalism primarily as the product of politics. Although I have learned a great deal from all of these key works, constructionist interpretations can go too far in portraying nationalism as an instrument used willfully by leaders to guide the masses. Nationalisms typically take shape in relation to patterns of thought and layers of identity that already exist; they develop within the context of what Anthony Smith has referred to as "sacred foundations." See Anthony D. Smith, *The Nation in History: Historiographical Debates about Ethnicity and Nationalism* (Hanover, NH: University Press of New England, 2000); Smith, *Chosen Peoples: Sacred Sources of National Identity* (New York: Oxford University Press, 2004); C. A. Bayly, *Origins of Nationality in South Asia: Patriotism and Ethical Government in the Making of Modern India* (New Delhi: Oxford University Press, 1998); Bayly, *Birth of the Modern World*, esp. 204, 280; John Armstrong, *Nations before Nationalism* (Chapel Hill: University of North Carolina Press, 1982).

10. See, for example, Rubin, *Shattered Nation*, 250n4. The notable exceptions are Onuf and Onuf, *Nations, Markets, and War*, and Bonner, *Mastering America*.

11. This premise informs John McCardell, *The Idea of a Southern Nation: Southern Nationalists and Southern Nationalism, 1830–1860* (New York: Norton, 1979); Manisha Sinha, *The Counterrevolution of Secession: Politics and Ideology in Antebellum South Carolina* (Chapel Hill: University of North Carolina Press, 2000).

12. On American nationalism before and during the Civil War, see Peter J. Parish, "An Exception to Most of the Rules: What Made American Nationalism Different in the Mid-Nineteenth Century?" *Prologue: Quarterly of the National Archives*, 27, no. 3 (Fall 1995): 219–229; Paul C. Nagel, *This Sacred Trust: American Nationality, 1798–1898* (New York: Oxford University Press, 1971); Hans Kohn, *American Nationalism: An Interpretive Essay* (New York: Macmillan, 1957); Clinton Rossiter, *The American Quest, 1790–1860: An Emerging Nation in Search of Identity, Unity, and Modernity* (New York: Harcourt Brace Jovanovich, 1971); Wilbur Zelinsky, *Nation into State: The Shifting Symbolic Foundations of American Nationalism* (Chapel Hill: University of North Carolina Press, 1988), and relevant sections of Lloyd Kramer, *Nationalism: Political Cultures in Europe and America, 1775–1865* (New York: Twayne, 1998). Older studies focused mostly on the northern states even though they claimed to cover "American" nationalism. The northern focus is more explicitly analyzed in Melinda Lawson, *Patriot Fires: Forging a New American Nationalism in the Civil War North* (Lawrence: University Press of Kansas, 2002), and Grant, *North over South*.

13. For instructive comparisons see Linda Colley, *Britons: Forging the Nation, 1707–1837* (New Haven, CT: Yale University Press, 1992), and especially Grant, *North over South*. Opposing positions in the longstanding debate over North-South difference can be found in Edward Pessen, "How Different from Each Other Were the Antebellum North and South?" *American Historical Review* 85 (1980), 1119–1149; and James M. McPherson, "Antebellum Southern Exceptionalism: A New Look at an Old Question" *Civil War History* 29 (1983): 230–244, reprinted in *Civil War History* 50 (2004): 418–433.

14. Ernest Renan, "What is a Nation?" in Bhabha, *Nation and Narration*, 19.

15. Michael Hechter, *Internal Colonialism: The Celtic Fringe in British National Development, 1536–1966* (Berkeley: University of California Press, 1975); Wendy Bracewell, "Rape in Kosovo: Masculinity and Serbian Nationalism," *Nations and Nationalism* 6, no. 4 (October 2000): 563–590; Colin Williams, ed., *National Separatism* (Cardiff: University of Wales Press, 1982); Bayly, *Birth of the Modern World*, esp. 119, 217. David Potter also compared postcolonial nationalisms to a prewar southern identity that he saw as being produced by resentment against the North: Potter, *The Impending Crisis, 1848–1861* (New York: Harper & Row, 1976); Potter, "Historian's Use of Nationalism." See also Kohn, *American Nationalism*, 114.

16. Joshua Searle-White, *The Psychology of Nationalism* (New York: Palgrave, 2001), esp. 91–94.

17. Historians of the American South have used gender to critically analyze, reevaluate, and even collapse the categories of public and private. See especially Stephanie McCurry, *Masters of Small Worlds: Yeoman Households, Gender Relations, and the Political Culture of the Antebellum South Carolina Low Country* (New York: Oxford University Press, 1995); Laura Edwards, *Gendered Strife and Confusion: The Political Culture of Reconstruction* (Urbana: University of Illinois Press, 1997); Amy Murrell Taylor, *The Divided Family in Civil War America* (Chapel Hill: University of North Carolina Press, 2005); Stephen W. Berry II, *All That Makes a Man: Love and Ambition in the Civil War South* (New York: Oxford University Press, 2003).

18. Kramer, *Nationalism*.

19. As the historian Scott Reynolds Nelson has observed, "War is wonderful for historians, folks who love to rummage in the lives of others, because the hazy line between public and private becomes nearly invisible." The later chapters of this book draw on evidence from a broader array of white southerners—including women and non-elite white men—who ordinarily left little trace of their ideas about nationalism, but who were forced by the pressures of war to engage more directly with it. Nelson, "Red Strings and Half Brothers: Civil Wars in Alamance County, North Carolina, 1861–1871," in Inscoe and Kenzer, *Enemies of the Country*, 38. See also Storey, *Loyalty and Loss*.

20. The pioneering work here was George L. Mosse, *Nationalism and Sexuality: Respectability and Abnormal Sexuality in Modern Europe* (New York: Fertig, 1985), but the following have also been very helpful: Andrew Parker, Mary Russo, Doris Sommer, and Patricia Yaeger, eds., *Nationalisms and Sexualities* (New York: Routledge, 1992); Catherine Hall et al, eds., "Special Issue on Gender, Nationalisms and National Identities," Special issue, *Gender and History* 5, no. 2 (Summer 1993); Annie Whitehead et al, eds., "Nationalisms and National Identities," Special issue, *Feminist Review* 44 (Summer 1993]; Joane Nagel, "Masculinity and Nationalism: Gender and Sexuality in the Making of Nations," *Ethnic and Racial Studies* 21, no. 2 (March 1998), 242–269; Sonya O. Rose, "Sex, Citizenship, and the Nation in World War II Britain," *American Historical Review* 103, no. 4 (1998): 1147–1176; Blom, Hall, and Hagemann, *Gendered Nations*.

21. Carlton Hayes, "Nationalism as a Religion," in *Essays on Nationalism* (1926; New York: Russell & Russell, 1966), 93–125; Anthony D. Smith, *Chosen Peoples*; Kramer, *Nationalism*, 62–83. See also George L. Mosse, *Fallen Soldiers: Reshaping the Memory of the World Wars* (New York: Oxford University Press, 1990); Anderson, *Imagined Communities*, 9–11.

22. See E. J. Hobsbawm, *Nations and Nationalism since 1780: Programme, Myth, Reality*, 2nd ed. (Cambridge, UK: Cambridge University Press, 1992), 9–10; Michael Hechter, *Containing Nationalism* (New York: Oxford University Press, 2000), 4–6. Hechter and Hobsbawm both point out that this definition is also

shared by other major nationalism scholars, such as Ernest Gellner and John Brueilly. It was also widely accepted in the nineteenth century, by both European and American thinkers.

23. Joane Nagel, "Masculinity and Nationalism," 247.

24. Paul Lawrence's reflections have been especially helpful in thinking through the different aspects of nationalism: Lawrence, *Nationalism: History and Theory* (Harlow, UK: Pearson Longman, 2005), 3–6.

25. Hobsbawm, *Nations and Nationalism*, 14–45. Similarly, Joep Leerssen has defined "national thought" as "a way of seeing human society primarily as consisting of discrete, different nations, each with an obvious right to exist and to command loyalty, each characterized and set apart unambiguously by its own separate identity and culture." (Leerssen, *National Thought in Europe*, 15.)

26. On the everyday dissemination and perpetuation of national identities, see Michael Billig, *Banal Nationalism* (London: Sage, 1995).

27. The term could feasibly incorporate black southerners as well, but this study is limited to white southerners, because African Americans had such different connections to nationalism and citizenship in the Civil War–era South. Stephanie McCurry has suggested ways to incorporate African Americans and ordinary women into the study of Confederate citizenship and state formation in *Confederate Reckoning: Power and Politics in the Civil War South* (Cambridge, MA: Harvard University Press, 2010). On black southerners' politics and citizenship, see Steven Hahn, *A Nation under Our Feet: Black Political Struggles in the Rural South from Slavery to the Great Migration* (Cambridge, MA: Harvard University Press, 2003).

28. This statement is inspired by the general thrust of postmodern scholarship on nationalism, but see in particular Maxwell, "Multiple Nationalism," and Eve Kosofsky Sedgwick, "Nationalism and Sexualities in the Age of Wilde," in Parker et al., *Nationalisms and Sexualities*, 241.

CHAPTER 1

1. E. W. Caruthers, *A Discourse Delivered at the Alamance Academy, July 4th, 1848* (Greensborough, NC: Printed by Swaim and Sherwood, 1848), 6, 25, 27.

2. Robert E. Bonner, *Mastering America: Southern Slaveholders and the Crisis of American Nationhood* (Cambridge, UK: Cambridge University Press, 2009); David M. Potter, "The Historian's Use of Nationalism and Vice-Versa," in *The South and the Sectional Conflict* (Baton Rouge: Louisiana State University Press, 1968), 34–83.

3. W. W. Holden, *Oration: Delivered in the City of Raleigh, North Carolina, July 4th, 1856* (Raleigh, NC: Holden & Wilson, "Standard" Office, 1856), 7; E. J. Hobsbawm, *Nations and Nationalism since 1780: Programme, Myth, Reality,* 2nd ed. (Cambridge, UK: Cambridge University Press, 1992), 14–45; Lloyd Kramer,

Nationalism: Political Cultures in Europe and America, 1775–1865 (New York: Twayne, 1998); Timothy Baycroft and Mark Hewitson, eds., *What Is a Nation? Europe 1789–1914* (Oxford: Oxford University Press, 2006); Elie Kedourie, *Nationalism*, 4th ed. (Oxford: Blackwell, 1993); Joep Leerssen, *National Thought in Europe: A Cultural History* (Amsterdam: Amsterdam University Press, 2006).

4. D. Barton Ross, *The Southern Speaker, or Sixth Reader: Containing, in Great Variety, the Masterpieces of Oratory in Prose, Poetry, and Dialogue* (New Orleans: J. B. Steel, 1856), 61–62.

5. J. G. Ramsay, *Love of Country: An Address Delivered Before the Ciceronian and Platonic Societies of the United Baptist Institute, Taylorsville, N.C., May 31, 1860* (Salisbury, NC: J. J. Bruner, Printer, 1860), 3–5. See also Paul C. Nagel, *This Sacred Trust: American Nationality, 1798–1898* (New York: Oxford University Press, 1971), 132.

6. William Sparrow, *The Nation's Privileges, and Their Preservation: A Sermon Preached on the Day of Our National Anniversary, 1852, in Christ Church, Alexandria, Va* (Philadelphia: T. K. and P. G. Collins, 1852), 38.

7. David H. Porter, *Religion and the State: A Discourse Delivered in the First Presbyterian Church, Savannah, Georgia, July 4th, 1858* (Savannah, GA: Power Press of John M. Cooper & Co., 1858), 5–6, 10–11, 12. The "state" in Porter's title referred not to the states that united to form the United States of America but rather the institution of secular government. For the importance of religion to American nationalism in the antebellum South, see also Eugenius Aristides Nisbet, *Address on the Seventy-third Anniversary of American Independence (July 4th, 1849): Delivered at the Request of a Committee on Behalf of the Citizens of Macon* (Macon, GA: Rose, 1849); Coleman Yellott, *Oration Delivered by Coleman Yellott, Esq., of Baltimore, at the Celebration at St. Timothy's Hall, Baltimore County, Maryland, July 5th, 1852* (Baltimore: Jos. Robinson, 1852); J. C. Coit, *A Discourse upon Governments, Divine and Human: Prepared by Appointment of the Presbytery of Harmony, and Delivered before That Body During Its Sessions in Indiantown Church, Williamsburg District, S.C., April, 1853* (Columbia, SC: Printed by T. F. Greneker, 1853); Benjamin M. Palmer, *Influence of Religious Belief Upon National Character: An Oration Delivered before the Demosthenian and Phi Kappa Societies of the University of Georgia, August 7, 1845* (Athens, GA: Printed at the Banner Office, 1845). On American conceptions of a divine national mission, see Ernest Lee Tuveson, *Redeemer Nation: The Idea of America's Millennial Role* (Chicago: University of Chicago Press, 1968); Conrad Cherry, ed., *God's New Israel: Religious Interpretations of American Destiny*, rev. ed. (Chapel Hill: University of North Carolina Press, 1998); and Nicholas Guyatt, *Providence and the Invention of the United States, 1607–1876* (New York: Cambridge University Press, 2007).

8. Virtue was central to the ideology of republicanism. Because power inevitably corrupts, the ideology held, citizens of a republic had to be constantly on their guard against threats to their liberty—in other words, they had to cultivate

virtue in themselves and others. Republicanism was underpinned by historical thought. See J. G. A. Pocock, *The Machiavellian Moment: Florentine Political Thought and the Atlantic Republican Tradition* (Princeton, NJ: Princeton University Press, 1975); Bernard Bailyn, *The Ideological Origins of the American Revolution*, rev. ed. (Cambridge, MA: Belknap Press of Harvard University Press, 1992), esp. 144–159; Trevor Colbourn, *The Lamp of Experience: Whig History and the Intellectual Origins of the American Revolution* (1965; repr., Indianapolis: Liberty Fund, 1998); Lester H. Cohen, *The Revolutionary Histories: Contemporary Narratives of the American Revolution* (Ithaca, NY: Cornell University Press, 1980); Stow Persons, "The Cyclical Theory of History in Eighteenth Century America," *American Quarterly* 6 (1954): 147–163; Harry L. Watson, *Liberty and Power: The Politics of Jacksonian America* (New York: Hill & Wang, 1990); Dorothy Ross, "Historical Consciousness in Nineteenth-Century America," *American Historical Review* 89 (1984): 909–928. While the sweeping concept of republicanism has come under fire—see especially Daniel T. Rodgers, "Republicanism: The Career of a Concept," *Journal of American History* 79, no. 1 (June 1992): 11–38—it remains useful for understanding Americans' conceptions of the relationship between individual morality, citizenship, and the health of the nation.

9. Letter from a student [name illegible] to William Porcher Miles, March 25, 1848, William Porcher Miles Papers, SHC; William Gilmore Simms, *Self-Development: An Oration, Delivered before the Literary Societies of Oglethorpe University, Georgia; November 10, 1847.* (Milledgeville, GA: Published by the Thalian Society, 1847), 23; Charles M. Taggart, *The Moral Mission of Our Country: Two Discourses Delivered Before the Unitarian Christians, of Charleston, S.C. on Sunday, July 3d* (Charleston, SC: Steam Power-Press of Walker and James, 1853), 8.

10. William L. Clark, Jr., *Importance of Integrity of National Character: An Oration, Delivered by Invitation of the Citizens of Winchester, Virginia, in the Old Lutheran Church, July 4, 1853* (Winchester, VA: Printed by Senseney & Coffroth, 1853), 10, 15.

11. Linda K. Kerber, *Women of the Republic: Intellect and Ideology in Revolutionary America* (Chapel Hill: University of North Carolina Press, 1980). Subsequent historians have reassessed the reality of women's roles in the United States between the Revolution and the Civil War, but republican motherhood was undoubtedly powerful as an ideal in postrevolutionary and antebellum American nationalism.

12. Thomas M. Hanckel, *Government, and the Right of Revolution: An Oration, Delivered before the '76 Association, and Cincinnati Society, on Monday, July 4th, 1859, by Thos. M. Hanckel, Esq., a Member of the '76 Association* (Charleston, SC: Printed by A. J. Burke, 1859), 22; James C. Britton, "The Decline and Fall of Nations in Antebellum Southern Thought: A Study of Southern Historical

Consciousness," (PhD diss., University of North Carolina, 1988); Ross, *Southern Speaker*, 231–232.

13. Liah Greenfeld, *Nationalism: Five Roads to Modernity* (Cambridge, MA: Harvard University Press, 1992); Kramer, *Nationalism*, esp. 18–41; Hobsbawm, *Nations and Nationalism*; Benedict Anderson, *Imagined Communities: Reflections on the Origin and Spread of Nationalism*, 2nd ed. (London: Verso, 1991), 7; Kedourie, *Nationalism*, 1–11; Otto Pflanze, "Nationalism in Europe, 1848–1871," *Review of Politics* 28 (April 1966): 129–143.

14. Peter Onuf and Peter Thompson, eds., *State and Citizen: British America and the Early United States* (University of Virginia Press, forthcoming); Rogers M. Smith, *Civic Ideals: Conflicting Visions of Citizenship in U.S. History* (New Haven, CT: Yale University Press, 1997); James H. Kettner, *The Development of American Citizenship, 1608–1870* (Chapel Hill: University of North Carolina Press, 1978); Linda K. Kerber, "The Meanings of Citizenship," *Journal of American History* 84, no. 3 (December 1997): 833–854; Douglas Bradburn, *The Citizenship Revolution: Politics and the Creation of the American Union, 1774–1804* (Charlottesville: University of Virginia Press, 2009). For the international context, including a clear description of the citizenship ideals of the French Revolution, see Rogers Brubaker, *Citizenship and Nationhood in France and Germany* (Cambridge, MA: Harvard University Press, 1992).

15. Bradburn, *Citizenship Revolution*; Rogers M. Smith, "The 'American Creed' and American Identity: The Limits of Liberal Citizenship in the United States," *Western Political Quarterly* 41 (1988): 225–251.

16. Madison quoted in Rogan Kersh, *Dreams of a More Perfect Union* (Ithaca, NY: Cornell University Press, 2001), 78; Frederick A. Porcher, *An Oration Delivered Before the Inhabitants of Pineville, So. Ca., on Monday, July 4, 1831, the 56th Anniversary of the Declaration of American Independence* (Charleston, SC: Printed by J. S. Burges, 1831), 13; Herschel V. Johnson, "An Address delivered before the Alumni Society of the University of Georgia, in the College Chapel at Athens, on the 2nd of August, 1842, by Herschel V. Johnson," Herschel V. Johnson Papers, DU.

17. See Hans Kohn, *American Nationalism: An Interpretive Essay* (New York: Macmillan, 1957), chap. 5; Clinton Rossiter, *The American Quest, 1790–1860: An Emerging Nation in Search of Identity, Unity, and Modernity* (New York: Harcourt Brace Jovanovich, 1971), 131–134; Paul C. Nagel, *One Nation Indivisible: The Union in American Thought, 1776–1861* (New York: Oxford University Press, 1964), ch. 5; Thomas Bender, *A Nation among Nations: America's Place in World History* (New York: Hill & Wang, 2006), 116–181; and Peter Onuf and Nicholas Greenwood Onuf, *Nations, Markets, and War: Modern History and the American Civil War* (Charlottesville: University of Virginia Press, 2006), 221–223.

18. John Taylor Wood to Lola, September 30, 1858, John Taylor Wood Papers, SHC.

19. "The Foreign News," *Columbus (GA) Enquirer*, May 2, 1848; "Remarks of Hon H V Johnson of Georgia on the Resolutions of Congratulations to the French People," April 6, 1848, newspaper clipping in the Herschel V. Johnson Papers, DU. For American sympathy with European revolutions, see also A. B. Meek, "Ireland. A Fragment.—1848," in *Songs and Poems of the South* (Mobile, AL: S. H. Goetzel & Co., 1857), 198; Bartholomew Carroll and B. F. Porter, *Speeches of Hon. B. F. Porter, and B. R. Carroll, Esq., Delivered Before the Association of the Friends of Irish Independence, in Charleston, So. Ca., on Wednesday Evening, May 31st, 1848* (Charleston, SC: Burges, James & Paxton, Printers, 1848); David T. Gleeson, *The Irish in the South, 1815–1877* (Chapel Hill, NC: University of North Carolina Press, 2001), 68–70.

20. Nelson Mitchell, *Oration, Delivered before the Fourth of July Association, by Nelson Mitchell, Esq., on the Fourth of July, 1848* (Charleston, SC: James S. Burges, 1849), 16; "Anniversary Celebration," *Richmond Enquirer*, July 11, 1848; "Fourth of July Celebration at Cedar Grove, Amelia County," *Richmond Enquirer*, July 18, 1848.

21. "Remarks of Hon H V Johnson"; Timothy M. Roberts, *Distant Revolutions: 1848 and the Challenge to American Exceptionalism* (Charlottesville: University of Virginia Press, 2009); Elizabeth Fox-Genovese and Eugene Genovese, *The Mind of the Master Class: History and Faith in the Southern Slaveholders' Worldview* (Cambridge, UK: Cambridge University Press, 2005), 41–68; Michael A. Morrison, "American Reaction to European Revolutions, 1848–1852: Sectionalism, Memory, and the Revolutionary Heritage," *Civil War History* 49, no. 2 (2003): 111–132; Charles M. Wiltse, "A Critical Southerner: John C. Calhoun on the Revolutions of 1848," *Journal of Southern History* 15 (1949): 299–310.

22. "The Fourth of July," *Brownlow's Knoxville Whig*, July 6, 1850; "Meeting for the Benefit of the Hungarian Refugees," *New Orleans Bee*, January 15, 1850; O. A. Lochrane, *An Oration, Delivered before the Hibernian and Irish Union Societies of Savannah, on the 18th March, 1850* (Savannah, GA: G. N. Nichols, 1850), 22–24. See also "PHH" [Paul Hamilton Hayne], "A Song of Ireland," *Southern Literary Messenger* 17, no. 6 (June 1851): 386; "Celebration of the Fourth of July at Goddin's Spring," *Richmond Enquirer*, July 16, 1850. American abolitionists such as William Lloyd Garrison believed that both Unions—the British and the American—were unjust: W. Caleb McDaniel, "Repealing Unions: American Abolitionists, Irish Repeal, and the Origins of Garrisonian Disunionism," *Journal of the Early Republic* 28 (2008): 243–269.

23. "Oration Delivered at the request of the City Council, Louisville Ky, July 5th 1852. By R. J. Durrett Esq. Member of the Louisville Bar," copy in the Reuben Durrett Papers, FHS. More recent (and more discerning) analysis of the international significance of the Declaration can be found in David Armitage, *The Declaration of Independence: A Global History* (Cambridge, MA: Harvard University Press, 2007).

24. Michael H. Hunt, *Ideology and U.S. Foreign Policy* (New Haven, CT: Yale University Press, 1987), 92–124, esp. 102–106; Timothy M. Roberts, *Distant Revolutions*.

25. Timothy M. Roberts, *Distant Revolutions*; Donald S. Spencer, *Louis Kossuth and Young America: A Study of Sectionalism and Foreign Policy, 1848–1852* (Columbia: University of Missouri Press, 1977); Bender, *A Nation among Nations*, 129.

26. "Austrian Politics," *Southern Literary Messenger* 18, no. 9 (September 1852): 535; [William Gilmore Simms], "Kossuth and Intervention," *Southern Quarterly Review* 6, no. 11 (July 1852): 234.

27. Entry for January 21, 1852, Cox Family Journal, 1851–1868, FHS.

28. James Johnston Pettigrew, *Notes on Spain and the Spaniards, in the Summer of 1859, With a Glance at Sardinia: By a Carolinian* (Charleston, SC: Steam-Power Presses of Evans & Cogswell, 1861), 1. See also William Preston to sister, August 7, 1859, Preston Family Papers, FHS; John Taylor Wood to wife, July 21, 1859, John Taylor Wood Papers; "Martyrdom of the Patriots: Italy 1830," *Southern Literary Messenger* 26, no. 3 (March 1858): 184–187; *Carrier's Address, to the patrons of the Louisville Courier, January 1, 1860* (broadside, FHS); Howard Rosario Marraro, *American Opinion on the Unification of Italy, 1846–1861* (New York: Columbia University Press, 1932); Francis P. Porcher, "A Plea for Italy," *Russell's Magazine*, June 1858, 214–221. Of course, southern support for Italian unification was not universal. For the argument that the Italians did not really constitute a unified nation, and that they were neither "desirous" nor "capable" of self-government, see James A. Corcoran, "Prospects of Italy—Italian Liberalism," *Russell's Magazine*, August 1858, 452–462.

29. See for example Kohn, *American Nationalism*; Greenfeld, *Nationalism*.

30. Susan-Mary Grant, *North over South: Northern Nationalism and American Identity in the Antebellum Era* (Lawrence: University Press of Kansas, 2000), esp. 19–36; Kurt Mueller-Vollmer, "The Discourse of a National Literature in the Early Republic, 1785–1846," in *Negotiations of America's National Identity*, ed. Roland Hagenbuchle and Josef Raab in cooperation with Marietta Messmer (Tübingen, Germany: Stauffenburg Verlag, 2000), 1:280–295. Most commentators would agree that neither the ethnic nor the civic model is found in pure form; any given nationalism contains strands of each. See Anthony D. Smith, *The Nation in History: Historiographical Debates about Ethnicity and Nationalism* (Hanover, NH: University Press of New England, 2000), 5–26; Baycroft and Hewitson, *What Is a Nation*. As Dorothy Ross has argued with reference to a small group of northern intellectuals, Americans tended to adapt European ideas even as they imported them. Dorothy Ross, "'Are We a Nation?' The Conjuncture of Nationhood and Race in the United States, 1850–1876," *Modern Intellectual History* 2 (2005): 327–360.

31. Switzerland was in a similar position: a multiethnic state that did not fit into the ethnocultural norm of nineteenth-century nationalism but whose leaders

attempted to claim legitimate national status on the international stage. Like Americans, the Swiss often described their national distinctiveness in terms of their multiethnic character. (Oliver Zimmer, "Switzerland," in Baycroft and Hewitson, *What Is a Nation*, 102.)

32. "Character of the American People," *Southern Quarterly Review* 2, no. 2 (February 1857): 393–405; Pettigrew, *Notes on Spain*, 59; Kersh, *Dreams of a More Perfect Union*, 115; George Fredrickson, *The Black Image in the White Mind: The Debate on Afro-American Character and Destiny, 1817–1914* (New York: Harper & Row, 1971), 97–102.

33. John Charles Chasteen, *Americanos: Latin America's Struggle for Independence* (New York: Oxford University Press, 2008).

34. George M. Fredrickson, "The Historical Construction of Race and Citizenship in the United States," in *Diverse Nations: Explorations in the History of Racial and Ethnic Pluralism* (Boulder, CO: Paradigm, 2008), 21–38. As Fredrickson observes, "What is distinctive" about American nationalism and citizenship "is the coexistence of a universalistic affirmation of human rights and a seemingly contradictory set of exclusions based on race or color" (35). Robert Wiebe similarly highlights democracy and racism as the key components of American nationalism in his book *Who We Are: A History of Popular Nationalism* (Princeton, NJ: Princeton University Press, 2002). On Native Americans' "liminal" status between the categories of citizen and alien, see Susan Scheckel, *The Insistence of the Indian: Race and Nationalism in Nineteenth-Century American Culture* (Princeton: Princeton University Press, 1998), esp. 9.

35. Bradburn, *Citizenship Revolution* ("denization" is a theme of chap. 7); Rogers M. Smith, *Civic Ideals*; Kettner, *Development of American Citizenship*; Reginald Horsman, *Race and Manifest Destiny: The Origins of American Racial Anglo-Saxonism* (Cambridge, MA: Harvard University Press, 1981); Michael O'Brien, *Conjectures of Order: Intellectual Life and the American South, 1810–1860* (Chapel Hill: University of North Carolina Press, 2004), 1:215–252 (quotation at 1:248); Fredrickson, *Black Image*, 71–164; Dorothy Ross, "Are We a Nation"; Kramer, *Nationalism*, chap. 5; Leerssen, *National Thought in Europe*.

36. Rogers M. Smith, *Civic Ideals*; Kettner, *Development of American Citizenship*; Elizabeth R. Varon, *Disunion! The Coming of the American Civil War, 1789–1859* (Chapel Hill: University of North Carolina Press, 2008), 303 (*New York Times* quotation).

37. Rogers Brubaker points out that ethnic and cultural notions of nationhood are not one and the same, but that cultural forms of nationalism tend to be more ethnicized than political forms, partly due to the assumption that culture is transmitted through the family. Brubaker, *Citizenship and Nationhood*, 99.

38. Alexander Beaufort Meek, *Americanism in Literature: An Oration before the Phi Kappa and Demosthenian Societies of the University of Georgia, at Athens, August 8, 1844* (Charleston, SC: Burges and James, Printers, 1844), quotation at 30;

"National Ballads," *Southern Literary Messenger* 15, no. 1 (January 1849): 10–15; Matt W. Ransom, *Address Delivered before the Dialectic and Philanthropic Societies of the University of North Carolina, June 4, 1856* (Raleigh, NC: "Carolina Cultivator" Office, 1856), 7–8, 21–22; Kohn, *American Nationalism,* 51–70. For prominent New England examples, see Ralph Waldo Emerson, "The American Scholar," and Margaret Fuller, "American Literature," both available in *The Heath Anthology of American Literature,* ed. Paul Lauter, Richard Yarborough, and Juan Bruce-Novoa, 2nd ed. (Lexington, MA: Heath, 1994), 1:1529–1541, 1:1655–1662.

39. William Gilmore Simms, "Americanism in Literature" (1845), in *The Simms Reader: Selections from the Writings of William Gilmore Simms,* ed. John Caldwell Guilds (Charlottesville: University Press of Virginia, 2001), 272, 277.

40. D. Barton Ross, *Southern Speaker,* 161.

41. Pettigrew, *Notes on Spain,* 55–56.

42. John E. Ward, *Address Delivered before the Georgia Historical Society, on its Nineteenth Anniversary, February 12, 1858, by John E. Ward.* (Savannah, GA: George N. Nichols, Printer, 1858), 5; Strong quoted in Michael Kammen, *A Season of Youth: The American Revolution and the Historical Imagination* (Ithaca, NY: Cornell University Press, 1978), 12; H. G. Jones, ed., *Historical Consciousness in the Early Republic: The Origins of State Historical Societies, Museums, and Collections, 1791–1861,* (Chapel Hill, NC: North Caroliniana Society and North Carolina Collection, 1995); Joyce Appleby, Lynn Hunt, and Margaret Jacob, *Telling the Truth about History* (New York: Norton, 1994), chap. 3; Cohen, *Revolutionary Histories;* James P. Holcombe, *Sketches of the Political Issues and Controversies of the Revolution: A Discourse, Delivered before the Virginia Historical Society, at their Ninth Annual Meeting, January 17, 1856* (Richmond, VA: Published by the Society, 1856), 4. For instructive comparisons, see Stefan Berger, Mark Donovan, and Kevin Passmore, eds., *Writing National Histories: Western Europe since 1800,* (London: Routledge, 1999); Thomas N. Baker, "National History in the Age of Michelet, Macaulay, and Bancroft," in *A Companion to Western Historical Thought,* ed. Lloyd Kramer and Sarah Maza (Malden, MA: Blackwell, 2002), 185–204.

43. Bartholomew R. Carroll, *"The Claims of Historical Studies upon the Youth of Our Country": An Oration Delivered before the Polytechnic and Calliopean Societies, of the Citadel Academy, at their Annual Commencement, April 8th, 1859* (Charleston, SC: Walker, Evans & Co., 1859), 5, 11.

44. See Anthony D. Smith, *Chosen Peoples,* esp. 190, Grant, *North over South,* 19–36.

45. Anderson, *Imagined Communities,* 22–36. On the Fourth of July see Paul Quigley, "Independence Day Dilemmas in the American South, 1848–1865," *Journal of Southern History* 75, no. 2 (May 2009): 235–266; Diana Karter Appelbaum, *The Glorious Fourth: An American Holiday, an American History* (New York: Facts on File, 1989); Robert Pettus Hay, "Freedom's Jubilee: One Hundred Years of the Fourth of July, 1776–1876" (PhD diss., University of Kentucky, 1967); Matthew

Dennis, *Red, White, and Blue Letter Days: An American Calendar* (Ithaca, NY: Cornell University Press, 2002); David Waldstreicher, *In the Midst of Perpetual Fetes: The Making of American Nationalism, 1776–1820* (Chapel Hill: University of North Carolina Press, 1997); Len Travers, *Celebrating the Fourth: Independence Day and the Rites of Nationalism in the Early Republic* (Amherst: University of Massachusetts Press, 1997); Wilbur Zelinsky, *Nation into State: The Shifting Symbolic Foundations of American Nationalism* (Chapel Hill: University of North Carolina Press, 1988), 69–73; Fletcher M. Green, "Listen to the Eagle Scream: One Hundred Years of the Fourth of July in North Carolina (1776–1876)," *North Carolina Historical Review* 31 (1954): 295–320, 529–549.

46. Contention and political struggle are major themes of Waldstreicher, *Perpetual Fetes*, and Travers, *Celebrating the Fourth*.

47. "Fourth of July in Richmond," reprinted from the *Richmond Whig*, *Richmond Enquirer*, July 8, 1851; "Anniversary Celebration," *Richmond Enquirer*, July 11, 1848; D. Barton Ross, *Southern Speaker*, 351. For several poetic celebrations of the soldiers who went to fight the Mexican War, see William Gilmore Simms, *Areytos, or Songs and Ballads of the South, with other Poems* (Charleston, SC: Russell & Jones, 1860). On the emotional power of the commemoration of blood sacrifice, see Kramer, *Nationalism*; Anthony D. Smith, *Chosen Peoples*, chap. 9; George L. Mosse, *Fallen Soldiers: Reshaping the Memory of the World Wars* (New York: Oxford University Press, 1990).

48. Carlton Hayes, "Nationalism as a Religion," in *Essays on Nationalism* (New York: Russell & Russell, 1966), esp. 107–109 on the sacred rituals of American nationalism; Anderson, *Imagined Communities*; Anthony D. Smith, *Chosen Peoples*; Kramer, *Nationalism*, 62–83. On American nationalism as a "civil religion," see Robert N. Bellah, "Civil Religion in America," *Daedalus* 96 (1967): 1–21; Zelinsky, *Nation into State*, 232–245.

49. Robert W. Landis, *The Duty and Obligations of American Citizens in Relation to the Union: An Oration Pronounced in Somerset, Kentucky, on February 22, 1860* (Somerset, KY: White & Barron, 1860).

50. "The Fourth of July," *Brownlow's Knoxville Whig*, July 6, 1850.

51. "The Declaration of Independence," *Vicksburg Weekly Whig*, July 5, 1854.

52. "Bishop Hughes's Discourse," *Columbus (GA) Enquirer*, January 11, 1848; Andrew H. H. Dawson, *An Oration on the Origin, Purposes and Claims of the Ladies' Mt. Vernon Association* (Savannah, GA: E. J. Purse, Printer, 1858), 9. For the significance of Washington to early American nationalism, see Zelinsky, *Nation into State*, 31–35. On heroes and modern nationalism, see Anthony D. Smith, *Chosen Peoples*, 41–42.

53. *Charleston Courier* clipping, August 27, 1856, in William Gilmore Simms Scrapbook E, Part 2, Charles Carroll Simms Collection, USC; John R Thompson, "Patriotism: A Poem," *Southern Literary Messenger* 22, no. 5 (May 1856): 342; Elizabeth R. Varon, *We Mean to Be Counted: White Women and Politics in Antebellum*

Virginia (Chapel Hill: University of North Carolina Press, 1998), 124–136 ("Woman's patriotism" quote at 132); Bonner, *Mastering America*, 196–205.

54. On women and nationalism see Andrew Parker et al., eds., *Nationalisms and Sexualities* (New York: Routledge, 1992); Catherine Hall et al., eds., "Special Issue on Gender, Nationalisms and National Identities," Special issue, *Gender and History* 5, no. 2 (Summer 1993); Annie Whitehead et al., eds., "Nationalisms and National Identities," Special issue, *Feminist Review* 44 (Summer, 1993); Sonya O. Rose, "Sex, Citizenship, and the Nation in World War II Britain," *American Historical Review* 103, no. 4 (1998): 1147–1176.

55. "Our Fourth of July Celebration," *Mobile Daily Register*, July 2, 1857. See also J. Lansing Burrows, "Address before the Mount Vernon Association, July 4th, 1855," *Southern Literary Messenger* 21, no. 8 (August 1855): 514–518. On Giuseppe Garibaldi's similar status as "a Christ-like cult figure," see Don H. Doyle, *Nations Divided: America, Italy, and the Southern Question* (Athens, GA: University of Georgia Press, 2002), 38, 61–62; Lucy Riall, *Garibaldi: Invention of a Hero* (New Haven, CT: Yale University Press, 2007).

56. Compare Giuseppe Mazzini's vision of nationalism as a "political religion," as explored by Simon Levis Sullam, "The Moses of Italian Unity: Mazzini and Nationalism as Political Religion," in *Giuseppe Mazzini and the Globalisation of Democratic Nationalism, 1830–1920*, ed. C. A. Bayly and Eugenio F. Biagini (Oxford: Oxford University Press for the British Academy, 2008), 107–124.

57. Maiken Umbach, "Nation and Region: Regionalism in Modern European States," in Baycroft and Hewitson, *What Is a Nation*, 79.

58. Potter, "Historian's Use of Nationalism."

59. Ibid., 15; Mitchell, *Oration*, 24; Meek, *Americanism in Literature*, 25–30; Henry W. Hilliard, *The Spirit of Liberty: An Oration, Delivered before the Literary Societies of the University of Virginia on the 27th July, 1859* (Montgomery, AL: Barrett & Wimbish, 1860); Henry W. Miller, *Address Delivered before the Philanthropic and Dialectic Societies of the University of North Carolina, June 3, 1857* (Raleigh, NC: Holden & Wilson, 1857), 12; Peter S. Onuf, *Jefferson's Empire: The Language of American Nationhood* (Charlottesville: University Press of Virginia, 2000).

60. B. Johnson Barbour, *An Address Delivered Before the Literary Societies of the Virginia Military Institute, at Lexington, on the 4th of July, 1854* (Richmond, VA: Macfarlane & Fergusson, 1854), 19; William Gilmore Simms, dedication to *Wigwam and the Cabin* (1856), in *The Simms Reader*, 9.

61. "Mr. Rives' Address," *Virginia Historical Register* 1 (January 1848), quoted in O'Brien, *Conjectures of Order*, 1:336.

62. William Waightstill Avery, *Address Delivered before the Two Literary Societies of the University of North Carolina, June 4, 1851* (Raleigh, NC: William W. Holden, 1851), 7–8.

63. O'Brien, *Conjectures of Order*, 1:333–363.

64. Choate's 1858 Fourth of July address, quoted in Greenfeld, *Nationalism*, 472–473.

65. On the political and intellectual problems of American federalism see Forrest McDonald, *States' Rights and the Union: Imperium in Imperio* (Lawrence: University Press of Kansas, 2000).

66. The standard work on nullification remains William W. Freehling, *Prelude to Civil War: The Nullification Controversy in South Carolina, 1816–1836* (New York: Harper & Row, 1966).

67. James L. Petigru to William Elliott, September 28, 1832, James L. Petigru Papers, LOC.

68. Alfred Huger to William Porcher Miles, June 1, 1860, William Porcher Miles Papers, SHC. In nineteenth-century central and eastern Europe, there were many examples of the opposite: civic-style allegiances at the local or regional level, and cultural-style identities at the national level. Perhaps there were examples of this in the United States too. My point is not that Huger's specific ordering of loyalties was common to all but rather that he illustrates the presence of multiple forms of national (or potentially national) identity within the same individual. See Umbach, "Nation and Region," 66.

69. "The French Republic," *Southern Quarterly Review* 14, no. 27 (July 1848): 197–241; Pettigrew, *Notes on Spain*, 33, 376; Timothy M. Roberts, *Distant Revolutions*, 130–131.

70. Stephen Jacobson, "Spain: The Iberian Mosaic," in Baycroft and Hewitson, *What Is a Nation*, 211; Brubaker, *Citizenship and Nationhood*, 50; Zimmer, "Switzerland," 100–119; Constantin Iordachi, "The Ottoman Empire: Syncretic Nationalism and Citizenship in the Balkans," in Baycroft and Hewitson, *What Is a Nation*, 135; Abigail Green, *Fatherlands: State-Building and Nationhood in Nineteenth-Century Germany* (Cambridge, UK: Cambridge University Press, 2001).

71. Bender, *A Nation among Nations*, 133–150; Chasteen, *Americanos*, 160–161; Terry Rugeley, "The Brief, Glorious History of the Yucatecan Republic: Secession and Violence in Southeast Mexico, 1836–1848," in *Secession as an International Phenomenon*, ed. Don H. Doyle (Athens, GA: University of Georgia Press, 2010), 214–234; Graeme Morton, *Unionist-Nationalism: Governing Urban Scotland, 1830–1860* (East Linton, UK: Tuckwell, 1999). Bender's approach built on Kohn, *American Nationalism*, 100, and Robert C. Binkley, *Realism and Nationalism, 1852–1871* (New York: Harper & Brothers, 1935).

CHAPTER 2

1. Lewis M. Ayer, *Southern Rights and the Cuban Question: An Address, Delivered at Whippy Swamp, on the Fourth of July, 1855* (Charleston, SC: A. J. Burke, 1855), 19, 8–9.

2. In emphasizing this sense of personal victimhood, I draw upon existing psychological interpretations of the radicals: William L. Barney, *The Road to*

Secession: A New Perspective on the Old South (New York: Praeger, 1972), 85–100; Bertram Wyatt-Brown, *Hearts of Darkness: Wellsprings of a Southern Literary Tradition* (Baton Rouge: Louisiana State University Press, 2003), esp. 33–91; Eric H. Walther, *William Lowndes Yancey and the Coming of the American Civil War* (Chapel Hill: University of North Carolina Press, 2006). The most important general works are John McCardell, *The Idea of a Southern Nation: Southern Nationalists and Southern Nationalism, 1830–1860* (New York: Norton, 1979), and Eric Walther's group biography *The Fire-Eaters* (Baton Rouge: Louisiana State University Press, 1992).

3.   Here I draw inspiration from Rollin G. Osterweis, *Romanticism and Nationalism in the Old South* (New Haven, CT: Yale University Press, 1949) and, more generally, from the international emphasis of several recent studies of antebellum southerners: Michael O'Brien, *Conjectures of Order: Intellectual Life and the American South, 1810–1860* (Chapel Hill: University of North Carolina Press, 2004); Brian Schoen, *The Fragile Fabric of Union: Cotton, Federal Politics, and the Global Origins of the Civil War* (Baltimore: Johns Hopkins University Press, 2009); Edward Bartlett Rugemer, *The Problem of Emancipation: The Caribbean Roots of the American Civil War* (Baton Rouge: Louisiana State University Press, 2008); Peter Kolchin, *Unfree Labor: American Slavery and Russian Serfdom* (Cambridge, MA: Belknap Press of the Harvard University Press, 1987); Kolchin, "The South and the World," *Journal of Southern History* 75, no. 3 (August 2009): 565–581.

4.   [Frederick A. Porcher], "Southern and Northern Civilization Contrasted." *Russell's Magazine,* May 1857, 98–103; James Chesnut, Jr., "The Destinies of the South," *Southern Quarterly Review* 7 (January 1853): 187; William H. Trescot, *Position and Course of the South* (Charleston, SC: Walker & James, 1850), 6. For a forceful reminder of the centrality of proslavery to secessionism in South Carolina, see Manisha Sinha, *The Counterrevolution of Slavery: Politics and Ideology in Antebellum South Carolina* (Chapel Hill: University of North Carolina Press, 2000). Eugene Genovese has been influential in demonstrating the extent to which prewar southern slaveholders believed that their peculiar institution underpinned a unique "civilization" and "worldview." See especially Genovese, *The Political Economy of Slavery: Studies in the Economy and Society of the Slave South* (New York: Random House, 1965); Genovese, *The World the Slaveholders Made: Two Essays in Interpretation* (New York: Random House, 1969); Elizabeth Fox-Genovese and Eugene D. Genovese, *The Mind of the Master Class: History and Faith in the Southern Slaveholders' Worldview* (Cambridge, UK: Cambridge University Press, 2005).

5.   William J. Grayson, *The Hireling and the Slave, Chicora, and Other Poems* (Charleston, SC: McCarter & Co., 1856), 44. See also William J. Grayson, "The Late Financial Difficulty—Southern and Northern Labor," *Russell's Magazine,* December 1857, 260–263.

6. James Henry Hammond, "Speech on the Admission of Kansas, under the Lecompton Constitution, Delivered in the Senate of the United States, March 4, 1858," in *Selections from the Letters and Speeches of the Hon. James H. Hammond*, ed. Clyde N. Wilson (1866; Spartanburg, SC: Reprint Company, 1978), 318–320. The classic study of how earlier generations of slaveholders based their own freedom upon slaves' unfreedom is Edmund Morgan, *American Slavery, American Freedom: The Ordeal of Colonial Virginia* (New York: Norton, 1975). On the efforts of Hammond and his generation to ground freedom and republicanism in racial slavery, see Drew Gilpin Faust, *James Henry Hammond and the Old South: A Design for Mastery* (Baton Rouge: Louisiana State University Press, 1982).

7. "Report of the Slave Trade Committee," reprinted in the *Newberry (SC) Rising Sun*, May 26, 1858. For more on Spratt and other South Carolinians who stressed the dangers of democracy in defending slavery and advocating secession, see Sinha, *Counterrevolution of Slavery*.

8. Trescot, *Position and Course of the South*, 11–13; "Address, 1851, of the Southern Rights Association of the University of Virginia to the Young Men of the South," William Henry Gist Papers, USC. Brian Schoen has recently reinterpreted Trescot and others as rational economic thinkers who pushed their region toward secession based on reasonable calculations about the southern cotton economy's place in the international economy. Schoen, *Fragile Fabric of Union*. See also Peter Onuf and Nicholas Greenwood Onuf, *Nations, Markets, and War: Modern History and the American Civil War* (Charlottesville: University of Virginia Press, 2006); John Majewski, *Modernizing a Slave Economy: The Economic Vision of the Confederate Nation* (Chapel Hill: University of North Carolina Press, 2009). On nullification, see William W. Freehling, *Prelude to Civil War: The Nullification Controversy in South Carolina, 1816–1836* (New York: Harper & Row, 1966).

9. Trescot, *Position and Course of the South*, 11–13.

10. Ibid., 12–13; Chesnut, "Destinies of the South," 200; Nathaniel Beverley Tucker to James Henry Hammond, March 16, 1848, in Nathaniel Beverley Tucker Papers, DU.

11. "Morals in Free States," undated newspaper clipping, William Gilmore Simms Scrapbook A, Charles Carroll Simms Collection, USC; Benjamin Evans to William Porcher Miles, March 4, 1858, William Porcher Miles Papers, SHC. On nationalism and "respectability" in Europe, see George L. Mosse, *Nationalism and Sexuality: Respectability and Abnormal Sexuality in Modern Europe* (New York: Fertig, 1985), 1–22.

12. Nathaniel Beverly Tucker, *Prescience: A Speech, Delivered by Hon, Beverly Tucker, of Virginia, in the Southern Convention, Held at Nashville, Tenn., April 13th, 1850* (Richmond, VA: West & Johnson, 1862), 36; Rhett quoted in Paul C. Nagel, *One Nation Indivisible: The Union in American Thought, 1776–1861* (New York: Oxford

University Press, 1964), 248; John C. Calhoun, "A Discourse on the Constitution and Government of the United States," in *The Papers of John C. Calhoun*, ed. Clyde N. Wilson, vol. 28 (Columbia: University of South Carolina Press, 2003), 233; "Thomas Cooper's 'Value of the Union' Speech, July 2, 1827, reprinted in *The Nullification Era: A Documentary Record*, ed. William Freehling (New York: Harper & Row, 1967), 25.

13. Jesse T. Carpenter, *The South as a Conscious Minority, 1789–1861*, ed. John McCardell (1930; Columbia: University of South Carolina Press, 1990); William Porcher Miles to Christopher Gustavus Memminger, January 10, 1860, Christopher G. Memminger Papers, SHC; Edmund Ruffin, *The Diary of Edmund Ruffin*, ed. William Kauffman Scarborough (Baton Rouge: Louisiana State University Press, 1972–1989), entries for January 30, 1858, August 8, 1860. In this sense, southern nationalism fits into the "internal colonialism" thesis that Michael Hechter has developed in reference to separatist nationalisms in Britain. Hechter, *Internal Colonialism: The Celtic Fringe in British National Development, 1536–1966* (Berkeley: University of California Press, 1975).

14. Walther, *Fire-Eaters*, 17; Ayer, *Southern Rights*, 8–9. For revealing examples of this attitude, see William Lowndes Yancey's letter to the *New York News*, January 25, 1845, in William Lowndes Yancey Papers, ADAH; and D. H. Hamilton to William Porcher Miles, January 23, 1860, William Porcher Miles Papers, SHC. Some of this frustration found an outlet in the movement for expansion into the tropics: Robert E. May, *The Southern Dream of a Caribbean Empire, 1854–1861*, rev. ed. (Gainesville: University Press of Florida, 2002).

15. William Porcher Miles, *Oration Delivered before the Fourth of July Association* (Charleston, SC: James S. Burges, 1849), 16–17; William Gilmore Simms to James Henry Hammond, June 10, 1858, in *The Letters of William Gilmore Simms*, vol. 4, ed. Mary C. Simms Oliphant, Alfred Taylor Odell, and T. C. Duncan Eaves (Columbia: University of South Carolina Press, 1955), 63. See also Porcher, "Southern and Northern Civilization Contrasted," 106; William Gilmore Simms, "Antagonisms of the Social Moral, North and South," Charles Carroll Simms Collection, USC; Langdon Cheves, *Speech of Hon. Langdon Cheves, in the Southern Convention, at Nashville, Tennessee, November 14, 1850* (n.p.: Southern Rights Association, 1850), 29. Of course, the radicals minimized the considerable political power that the South had always exercised in the Union: see Don E. Fehrenbacher, *The Slaveholding Republic: An Account of the United States Government's Relations to Slavery* (New York: Oxford University Press, 2001).

16. Miles, *Oration*, 17.

17. William Gilmore Simms, "Southern Convention—Second Session," Charles Carroll Simms Collection, USC; Wigfall quoted in Walther, *Fire-Eaters*, 179. See also Benjamin C. Pressley, *Reasons for the Dissolution of the Union, Being a Reply to the Letter of the Hon. W. J. Grayson, and to his Answer to one of the People* (Charleston: A. J. Burke, 1850), 8.

18. Wyatt-Brown, *Hearts of Darkness*, esp. 42, 74; Nathaniel Beverley Tucker to James Henry Hammond, March 13, 1847, in Nathaniel Beverley Tucker Papers, DU. On psychological connections between individuals and nationalism, see also Joshua Searle-White, *The Psychology of Nationalism* (New York: Palgrave, 2001); Michael Hechter, *Containing Nationalism* (New York: Oxford University Press, 2000), 30, 99; Barney, *The Road to Secession*, 85–100; Robert E. May, "Psychobiography and Secession: The Southern Radical as Maladjusted 'Outsider,'" *Civil War History* 34 (1988): 46–69.

19. William Gilmore Simms to John Esten Cooke, April 14, 1860, in Simms, *Letters*, 4:216; Simms, *Areytos, or Songs and Ballads of the South, with other Poems* (Charleston, SC: Russell & Jones, 1860), 9. The poem was reprinted during the secession crisis: *Southern Literary Messenger* 32, no. 1 (January 1861): 5

20. O'Brien, *Conjectures of Order*, 471; Walther, *Fire-Eaters*, 49–50; William Lowndes Yancey to Benjamin C. Yancey, September 8, 1838, William Lowndes Yancey Papers, ADAH. In his recent biography, Eric Walther emphasizes the psychological reasons for Yancey's radicalism, including his "dysfunctional" childhood: Walther, *William Lowndes Yancey*.

21. Perry quoted in John Barnwell, *Love of Order: South Carolina's First Secession Crisis* (Chapel Hill: University of North Carolina Press, 1982), 150. The classic work on honor in the antebellum South remains Bertram Wyatt-Brown, *Southern Honor: Ethics and Behavior in the Old South* (New York: Oxford University Press, 1982). More recently, Stephen W. Berry II has linked the personal and public ambitions of white southern men in *All That Makes a Man: Love and Ambition in the Civil War South* (New York: Oxford University Press, 2003), and Christopher J. Olsen has made a strong case for "the language of honor masculinity as the lingua franca of sectionalism" in *Political Culture and Secession in Mississippi: Masculinity, Honor, and the Antiparty Tradition, 1830–1860* (New York: Oxford University Press, 2000); quotation at 53.

22. Newspaper tributes to Brooks, both after his caning of Sumner and after his death a year later, fill a scrapbook in the Preston Brooks Papers at the Caroliniana Library, University of South Carolina. The "Southern men" quote is from an unidentified editorial therein entitled "Mr. Brooks' Castigation of Mr. Sumner." J. H. Adams to Preston Brooks, May 26, 1856, Preston Brooks Papers, USC. See also Emory M. Thomas, *Confederate Nation: 1861–1865* (New York: Harper & Row, 1979), 20. Brooks was not the only martyr to this cause; John C. Calhoun was similarly remembered as a martyr to the southern cause: see Rhett, *The Political Life and Services of the Hon. R. Barnwell Rhett, of South Carolina, by "A Cotemporary" (the Late Hon. Daniel Wallace); Also, His Speech at Grahamville, South Carolina, July 4th, 1859* (n.p.; microfilmed by SCHS), 29.

23. Louisa Cunningham to Sarah Yancey, March 8, 1850, Benjamin C. Yancey Papers, SHC.

24. Elizabeth W. Rhett to Robert B. Rhett, October 17, 1851, Robert Barnwell Rhett Papers, SCHS.

25. Unification has been more visible precisely because it was so much more successful in the short term than separatism. Moreover, success or failure often determines whether we label a given movement "separatism" or "nationalism." See Don H. Doyle, *Nations Divided: America, Italy, and the Southern Question* (Athens, GA: University of Georgia Press, 2002), 86; Potter, "The Historian's Use of Nationalism and Vice Versa," in *The South and the Sectional Conflict* (Baton Rouge: Louisiana State University Press, 1968), 34–83.

26. See Paul Quigley, "Secessionists in an Age of Secession: The Slave South in Transatlantic Perspective," in *Secession as an International Phenomenon*, ed. Don H. Doyle (Athens, GA: University of Georgia Press, 2010), 151–173. Frank Towers has argued that secessionists' use of romanticism also contained strands of antimodernism and a desire to follow a different path than the northern United States and western Europe: Towers, "The Origins of the Antimodern South: Romantic Nationalism and the Secession Movement in the American South," in Doyle, *Secession as an International Phenomenon*, 174–190.

27. Yancey quoted in Walther, *Fire-Eaters*, 62.

28. Rhett, *Political Life and Services*, 42.

29. Henry L. Pinckney, Jr., *An Oration Delivered on the Fourth of July 1851, before the '76 and Cincinnati Societies* (Charleston, SC: Printed by A. E. Miller, 1851), 14; Herman Belz, ed., *The Webster-Hayne Debate on the Nature of the Union: Selected Documents* (Indianapolis: Liberty Fund, 2000), 8, 46; J. Mills Thornton, *Politics and Power in a Slave Society: Alabama, 1800–1860* (Baton Rouge: Louisiana State University Press, 1978), 214. I am grateful to Frank Towers for drawing the Hayne quotation to my attention.

30. John Mitchel, *The Last Conquest of Ireland (Perhaps)*, ed. Patrick Maume (Dublin: University College Dublin Press, 2005), xviii; Bryan P. McGovern, *John Mitchel: Irish Nationalist, Southern Secessionist* (Knoxville: University of Tennessee Press, 2009), 122–123; D. George Boyce, *Nationalism in Ireland*, 2nd ed. (London: Routledge, 1991), 20.

31. Joan S. Skurnowicz, *Romantic Nationalism and Liberalism: Joachim Lelewel and the Polish National Idea* (Boulder, CO: East European Monographs, 1981), 133, 77–78; István Deák, *Lawful Revolution: Louis Kossuth and the Hungarians, 1848–1849* (London: Phoenix, 2001), 261–264; John Breuilly, *Nationalism and the State*, 2nd ed. (Manchester: Manchester University Press, 1993), 59; Joseph Frederick Zacek, *Palacký: The Historian as Scholar and Nationalist* (The Hague: Mouton, 1970), 84; David Armitage, *The Declaration of Independence: A Global History* (Cambridge, MA: Harvard University Press, 2007), 124; Onuf and Onuf, *Nations, Markets, and War*, 309, 314, 317; Lucy Riall, *Risorgimento: The History of Italy from Napoleon to Nation-State* (New York: Palgrave Macmillan, 2009), 124; C. A. Bayly and Eugenio F. Biagini, eds., *Giuseppe Mazzini and the Globalisation*

of Democratic Nationalism, 1830–1920 (Oxford: Oxford University Press for the British Academy, 2008); Ernest Renan, "What is a Nation?" in *Nation and Narration*, ed. Homi K. Bhabha (New York: Routledge, 1990), 8–22; Searle-White, *Psychology of Nationalism*, 91–94. For a different interpretation, see Enrico Dal Lago, *Agrarian Elites: American Slaveholders and Southern Italian Landowners, 1815–1861* (Baton Rouge: Louisiana State University Press, 2005), 183–184, which contrasts conservative, negative nationalists in the southern United States and southern Italy with more positive, active nationalisms in other parts of Europe.

32. E. J. Hobsbawm, *Nations and Nationalism since 1780: Programme, Myth, Reality*, 2nd ed. (Cambridge, UK: Cambridge University Press, 1992), 101 (Mazzini quotation), passim; Elie Kedourie, *Nationalism*, 4th ed. (Oxford: Blackwell, 1993), 51–52; Rogers Brubaker, *Citizenship and Nationhood in France and Germany* (Cambridge, MA: Harvard University Press, 1992), 99; Hechter, *Containing Nationalism*, 4–6. The British historian Lord Acton, commenting on the Hungarian nationalist movement, phrased it even more concisely: "The state and nation must be co-extensive." Thomas Bender, *A Nation among Nations: America's Place in World History* (New York: Hill & Wang, 2006), 126–127. Europeans tended to use the term "state"; I use the term "government" to avoid confusion with the individual states of the United States.

33. Mayer quoted in O'Brien, *Conjectures of Order*, 206; Benjamin M. Palmer, *Influence of Religious Belief upon National Character: An Oration Delivered before the Demosthenian and Phi Kappa Societies of the University of Georgia, August 7, 1845* (Athens, GA: Printed at the Banner Office, 1845), 16. Even Webster's dictionary assumed that nations did not always match up to governments. A nation was defined as "a body of people inhabiting the same country, or united under the same sovereign or government," although "it often happens that many nations are united under the same government, in which case, the word *nation* usually denotes a body of people speaking the same language, or a body that has formerly been under a distinct government, but has been conquered, or incorporated with a larger nation." Noah Webster, *An American Dictionary of the English Language*, Unabridged, Pictorial Edition (Philadelphia, Pa.: J. B. Lippincott & Co., 1859), s.v. "Nation."

34. Lewis M. Ayer, *Patriotism and State Sovereignty: An Oration, Delivered before the Two Societies of the South-Carolina College, on the Fourth of December, 1858* (Charleston, SC: Printed by A. J. Burke, 1859), 7, 9–11.

35. William D. Porter, *State Pride: An Oration Delivered before the Calliopean and Polytechnic Societies of the State Military School, at Charleston, on the 5th April, 1860* (Charleston, SC: Walker, Evans, & Co., 1860), 11–12, 16, 20.

36. Walther, *Fire-Eaters*, 36.

37. William H. Trescot, "Oration Delivered before the South-Carolina Historical Society, Thursday, May 19, 1859," in *Collections of the South Carolina Historical*

Society (Charleston, SC: South Carolina Historical Society, 1859), 3:9–10. See also Charles A. Dunwody, *Address of Charles A. Dunwody, before the Citizens of Roswell and the Roswell Guards, July 4, A.D. 1860* (Marietta, GA: Statesman Book and Job Office Print, 1860), 12.

38. Markus Kornprobst has argued that "epistemes"—templates of normative nationality—"delineate those constructions of national identity that are conceivable for and intelligible to elites." "Episteme, Nation-Builders and National Identity: The Re-construction of Irishness," *Nations and Nationalism* 11, no. 3 (July 2005): 404. See also David M. Potter, *The Impending Crisis, 1848–1861,* completed and edited by Don E. Fehrenbacher (New York: Harper & Row, 1976), 461.

39. Lloyd Kramer, *Nationalism: Political Cultures in Europe and America, 1775–1865* (New York: Twayne, 1998), 42–61. Ethnicity has been the most common, though not the only, justification for separatist movements across the modern world: see Colin Williams, ed., *National Separatism* (Cardiff: University of Wales Press, 1982).

40. John Hutchinson, *The Dynamics of Cultural Nationalism: The Gaelic Revival and the Creation of the Irish Nation State* (London: Allen & Unwin, 1987), 22.

41. Zacek, *Palacký*; Skurnowicz, *Romantic Nationalism and Liberalism,* quotation at 120. On the importance of history and historians to nationalism in western Europe, see Stefan Berger, Mark Donavan, and Kevin Passmore, eds., *Writing National Histories: Western Europe since 1800* (London: Routledge, 1999).

42. Osterweis, *Romanticism and Nationalism*; Ritchie Devon Watson, Jr., *Normans and Saxons: Southern Race Mythology and the Intellectual History of the American Civil War* (Baton Rouge: Louisiana State University Press, 2008).

43. Chesnut, "Destinies of the South," 181–182; John McCrady, *"Home Education a Necessity of the South": An Oration Delivered before the Chrestomathic Society of the College of Charleston, on Friday March 2d, 1860* (Charleston, SC: Steam Power Presses of Walker, Evans, & Co., 1860), 26–27.

44. McCrady, *Home Education a Necessity,* 27; John S. Ezell, "A Southern Education for Southrons," *Journal of Southern History* 17, no. 3 (August 1951): 303–327.

45. Thomas N. Baker, "National History in the Age of Michelet, Macaulay, and Bancroft," in *A Companion to Western Historical Thought,* ed. Lloyd Kramer and Sarah Maza (Malden, MA: Blackwell, 2002), 190; Hans Kohn, *Prophets and Peoples: Studies in Nineteenth Century Nationalism* (1946; repr., New York: Collier Books, 1961), 100–121. See also Skurnowicz, *Romantic Nationalism and Liberalism,* 133, 77–78; Zacek, *Palacký,* 84; Berger, Donavan, and Passmore, *Writing National Histories.*

46. McCardell, *Idea of a Southern Nation,* 200–226 (Polk quote at 217); Nathaniel Beverley Tucker to James Henry Hammond, March 13, 1847, May 29, 1849 in Nathaniel Beverley Tucker Papers, DU.

47. Southern Education Society, *To the People of the Slaveholding States*, undated circular, Rare Book Collection, Wilson Library, University of North Carolina at Chapel Hill, 4, 8.

48. William Gilmore Simms to James Chesnut, Jr., February 5, 1852, and Simms to James Henry Hammond, March 27, 1858, in Simms, *Letters*, 3:158, 4:45; Meek quoted in O'Brien, *Conjectures of Order*, 701. On the role of literature in southern nationalism, see John Budd, "Henry Timrod: Poetic Voice of Southern Nationalism," *Southern Studies* 20 (1981): 437–446; Eugene Current-Garcia, "Southern Literary Criticism and the Sectional Dilemma," *Journal of Southern History* 15 (1949): 325–341; McCardell, *Idea of a Southern Nation*, 141–176.

49. A. B. Meek, *Songs and Poems of the South* (Mobile, AL: S. H. Goetzel & Co., 1857), v.

50. William G. Simms, "Pickett's History of Alabama," *Southern Quarterly Review* 5 (January 1852): 182–209; [Simms], "Ramsay's Annals of Tennessee," *Southern Quarterly Review* 8 (October 1853): 337–368; William H. Trescot, *Position and Course of the South*, 19; [Porcher], "Southern and Northern Civilization Contrasted," *Russell's Magazine*, May 1857, 98–100; Paul Quigley, "'That History is Truly the Life of Nations': History and Southern Nationalism in Antebellum South Carolina," *South Carolina Historical Magazine* 106, no. 1 (January 2005): 7–33; Jon L. Wakelyn, *The Politics of a Literary Man: William Gilmore Simms* (Westport, CT: Greenwood, 1973), 115–136; Osterweis, *Romanticism and Nationalism*, 137–138. According to Stuart Jones, in late-nineteenth-century Europe "'nation-building' entailed not just an 'objective' process of national integration, but also telling the nation stories about itself; persuading the nation that it had not just come into being." This was perhaps even more true of southern nationalism before the Civil War, which rested almost entirely on "stories" with few "objective" features at all. Jones, "Taine and the Nation-State," in Berger, Donovan, and Passmore, *Writing National Histories*, 85.

51. E. Merton Coulter, "What the South Has Done about Its History," *Journal of Southern History* 2 (1936): 3–28. As Carl Degler has rightly pointed out, the lack of a shared, distinctive national history fundamentally distinguished southern nationalists from their counterparts in places like Hungary and Poland: Degler, "One among Many: The United States and National Unification," in *Lincoln, the War President*, ed. Gabor S. Boritt (New York: Oxford University Press, 1992), 93.

52. Ruffin, *Diary*, June 22, 1859, May 23, 1860.

53. McGovern, *John Mitchel*.

54. See Lucy Riall's approach to "the politics of national identity" (*Risorgimento*, esp. 131), and more generally Breuilly, *Nationalism and the State*, chaps. 4–5; Kedourie, *Nationalism*, 94. As the theorist Etienne Balibar has contended, the ethnic basis of any nation is a "fictive ethnicity." "No nation," Balibar explains, "possesses an ethnic base naturally, but as social formations are nationalized,"

groups of people become "ethnicized—that is, represented in the past or in the future *as if* they formed a national community." Etienne Balibar and Immanuel Maurice Wallerstein, *Race, Nation, Class: Ambiguous Identities* (London: Verso, 1991), 96.

55. In addition to Breuilly, *Nationalism and the State,* see Otto Pflanze, "Nationalism in Europe, 1848–1871," *Review of Politics* 28 (April 1966): 136–137; Hechter, *Containing Nationalism;* Timothy Baycroft and Mark Hewitson, eds., *What Is a Nation? Europe 1789–1914* (Oxford: Oxford University Press, 2006), 11, 331–332; Mark Cornwall, "The Habsburg Monarchy," in ibid., 171–191.

56. Riall, *Garibaldi;* Riall, *Risorgimento;* Denis Mack Smith, *Mazzini* (New Haven, CT: Yale University Press, 1994).

57. William L. Yancey to James Slaughter, June 15, 1858, FHS.

58. John Peter Richardson, *Oration, Delivered in Clarendon, on the Fourth of July, 1851* (Columbia, SC: Printed at the South Carolinian Office, 1851); David F. Jamison, "The National Anniversary," *Southern Quarterly Review* 2, no. 3 (September 1850): 190–191; William H. Trescot, *Oration Delivered before the Beaufort Volunteer Artillery, on July 4th, 1850* (Charleston, SC: Press of Walker & James, 1850); Thomas M. Hanckel, *Government, and the Right of Revolution: An Oration, Delivered before the '76 Association, and Cincinnati Society, on Monday, July 4th, 1859, by Thos. M. Hanckel, Esq., a Member of the '76 Association* (Charleston, SC: Printed by A. J. Burke, 1859); A. V. Huff, Jr., "The Eagle and the Vulture: Changing Attitudes Toward Nationalism in Fourth of July Orations Delivered in Charleston, 1778–1860," *South Atlantic Quarterly* 73 (1974): 10–22; Joseph Ralph James, Jr., "The Transformation of the Fourth of July in South Carolina, 1850 to 1919" (MA thesis, Louisiana State University, 1987), esp. 26–43.

59. Manisha Sinha, for example, has portrayed South Carolina secessionists as American counterrevolutionaries: Sinha, *Counterrevolution of Slavery.*

60. See Morgan, *American Slavery, American Freedom.*

61. W. W. Holden, *Oration Delivered in the City of Raleigh, North Carolina, July 4th, 1856* (Raleigh, NC: Holden & Wilson, "Standard" Office, 1856), 8–9. As Don Fehrenbacher argues, the authors of the Constitution may have attempted to maintain neutrality on the question of slavery, but subsequent generations transformed it into a mostly proslavery document. (Fehrenbacher, *Slaveholding Republic.*)

62. Ruffin, *Diary,* July 20, 1857, and October 20, 1858; George Fitzhugh, *Cannibals All! Or, Slaves without Masters,* ed. C. Vann Woodward (1857; Cambridge, MA: Belknap Press of Harvard University Press, 1960), quotation at 69; George Fitzhugh, "The Declaration of Independence and the Republican Party," *De Bow's Review* 29, no. 2 (August 1860): 175–187. On the changing meanings of the Declaration in American culture, and selective deployment of it by both northerners and southerners, see Pauline Maier, *American Scripture: Making the Declaration of Independence* (New York: Random House, 1997), esp. 175–202;

Armitage, *Declaration of Independence*, 63–102; Garry Wills, *Inventing America: Jefferson's Declaration of Independence* (Garden City, NY: Doubleday, 1978); Merrill D. Peterson, *The Jefferson Image in the American Mind* (New York: Oxford University Press, 1960), 162–189.

63. Ayer, *Southern Rights*, 3–7.

64. Nathaniel Beverley Tucker to James Henry Hammond, February 18, 1836, April 27, 1847, and March 13, 1850, Nathaniel Beverley Tucker Papers, DU; William Gilmore Simms, *The Sources of American Independence: An Oration, on the Sixty-Ninth Anniversary of American Independence, Delivered at Aiken, South-Carolina, before the Town Council and Citizens Thereof* (Aiken, SC: Published by Council, 1844), 31; William H. Trescot, *Oration Delivered before the Washington Light Infantry on the 22d February 1847* (Charleston, SC: Printed by Walter & Burke, 1847), 10–11. See also Trescot, *Beaufort Volunteer Artillery*, 11–12; Willoughby Newton to Edmund Ruffin, September 15, 1860, Edmund Ruffin Papers, VHS; Cheves, *Speech of Hon. Langdon Cheves*, 4; William C. Davis, *Rhett: The Turbulent Life and Times of a Fire-Eater* (Columbia: University of South Carolina Press, 2001), 72. Modern scholars have tended to agree that the founding generation may have created a government but not a nation. See, for example, Peter J. Parish, "An Exception to Most of the Rules: What Made American Nationalism Different in the Mid-Nineteenth Century?" *Prologue: Quarterly of the National Archives*, 27, no. 3 (Fall 1995): 220; John M. Murrin, "A Roof without Walls: The Dilemma of American National Identity," in *Beyond Confederation: Origins of the Constitution and American National Identity*, ed. Richard R. Beeman, Stephen Botein, and Edward C. Carter III (Chapel Hill: University of North Carolina Press, 1987), 333–348. According to David Armitage, the Declaration was far more influential as a model of state formation than nation formation in the decades after 1776. Armitage, *Declaration of Independence*.

65. Ayer, *Southern Rights*, 8; Michael Kammen, *A Season of Youth: The American Revolution and the Historical Imagination* (Ithaca, NY: Cornell University Press, 1978), 46–47, 51; Benedikt Stuchtey, " Literature, Liberty, and Life of the Nation: British Historiography from Macaulay to Trevelyan," and Ceri Crossley, "History as a Principle of Legitimation in France (1820–1848)," both in Berger, Donovan, and Passmore, *Writing National Histories*, 31, 49; Hanckel, *Government, and the Right of Revolution*, 25; William Henry Trescot, *The Diplomacy of the Revolution: An Historical Study* (New York: D. Appleton & Co., 1852), 144–154.

66. [William Gilmore Simms], "South Carolina in the Revolution," *Southern Quarterly Review* 14 (July 1848): 37–77 (quotations at 44, 76); [Simms], "The Siege of Charleston in the American Revolution," *Southern Quarterly Review* 14 (October 1848): 261–337. The review was expanded and published as *South Carolina in the Revolutionary War: Being a Reply to Certain Misrepresentations and*

Mistakes of Recent Writers, in Relation to the Cause and Conduct of this State (Charleston, SC: Walker & James, 1853). See also Simms, *Sources of American Independence*, 20–23.

67. Simms to Hammond, December 15, 1848, in Simms, *Letters*, 2: 465; Andrew P. Butler, "The South's Sacrifices in the Revolution," *De Bow's Review* 21 (August 1856), 199; Lawrence M. Keitt, "Patriotic Services of the North and the South," *De Bow's Review* 21 (November 1856): 491–508 (quotation at 492); John Hope Franklin, "The North, the South, and the American Revolution," *Journal of American History* 62 (1975): 5–23; Eileen Ka-May Cheng, *The Plain and Noble Garb of Truth: Nationalism and Impartiality in American Historical Writing, 1784–1860* (Athens, GA: University of Georgia Press, 2008), 228–231 ("cudgeling" quotation at 228).

68. William E. Mikell, *Oration Delivered before the Washington Light Infantry on their Fifty-Second Anniversary, at the Institute Hall, February 22, 1859* (Charleston, SC: Steam Power Press of Walker, Evans & Co., 1859), 6. Calhoun quoted in Robert E. Bonner, *Mastering America: Southern Slaveholders and the Crisis of American Nationhood* (Cambridge, UK: Cambridge University Press, 2009), 163. See also Samuel Gilman and William D. Porter, *Proceedings of the Semi-Centennial Celebration of the Washington Light Infantry, 22d and 23d February, 1857* (Charleston, SC: Walker and Evans, 1857), 39.

69. Louisa Cunningham to Mary Araminthia Snowden, January 3, 1854, Mary Amarinthia Snowden Papers, USC. As Elizabeth Varon has shown, many participants viewed the association as an embodiment of women's roles as mediators in the sectional conflict, and in 1858 the name was in fact changed to Mount Vernon Ladies' Association of the Union. Varon, *We Mean to Be Counted: White Women and Politics in Antebellum Virginia* (Chapel Hill: University of North Carolina Press, 1998), 124–136.

70. Drew Gilpin Faust, *The Creation of Confederate Nationalism: Ideology and Identity in the Civil War South* (Baton Rouge: Louisiana State University Press, 1988), 14, 27; Fleetwood Lanneau, quoted in Huff, "The Eagle and the Vulture," 21; Trescot, *Position and Course of the South*, 19. Compare the Catalans and Basques in Spain—even before the development of serious separatist movements in the late nineteenth century, both groups positioned themselves as the original Spaniards. See Stephen Jacobson, "Spain: The Iberian Mosaic," in Baycroft and Hewitson, *What is a Nation*, 219.

71. Frederick A. Porcher, "Characteristics of Civilization," *Russell's Magazine*, November 1857, 109.

72. In addition to the sources specifically cited below, the following paragraphs draw upon Edmund Ruffin, *Anticipations of the Future, to Serve as Lessons for the Present Time, in the Form of Extracts from Letters from an English Resident in the United States, to the London Times, from 1864 to 1870* (Richmond, VA: J. W. Randolph, 1860); Tucker, *Prescience*; Cheves, *Speech of Hon. Langdon Cheves*; Simms,

"Antagonisms of the Social Moral"; Edward E. Baptist, "Dreams so Real: Seces-sion and Fantasy Fiction," paper delivered to the Southern Historical Associa-tion, Memphis, Tennessee, November 5, 2004. On the language of disunion as a prophecy and a threat, see Elizabeth R. Varon, *Disunion! The Coming of the American Civil War, 1789–1859* (Chapel Hill: University of North Carolina Press, 2008).

73. The problem of southern disunity is a central theme of William Freehling's *The Road to Disunion*, 2 vols. (New York: Oxford University Press, 1990–2007).

74. "To the Hon W. J. Grayson," signed "One of the People," n.p., bound at USC with [W. J. Grayson], "Letter to His Excellency Whitemarsh B. Seabrook, Gover-nor of the State of South-Carolina, on the Dissolution of the Union (Charleston, SC: A. E. Miller, 1850), 12; "A Century Hence," handwritten notes in Rutherfoord Family Papers, VHS.

75. Rutherfoord, "A Century Hence"; Daniel H. London, *Speech of Daniel H. London on the Commercial, Agricultural & Intellectual Independence of Virginia and the South, Delivered in the Hall of the House of Delegates on the Night of the 5th January 1860; and his Letter to Joseph Segar, Esq, Respecting the Pilot Laws* (Richmond, VA: Printed at Enquirer Book and Job Office, 1860), 37; Nathaniel Beverley Tucker, *The Partisan Leader: A Tale of the Future*, ed. C. Hugh Holman (1836; Chapel Hill: University of North Carolina Press, 1971), esp. 65–66, 249.

76. Tucker to James H. Hammond, February 17, 1836 and December 27, 1849, Nathaniel Beverley Tucker Papers, DU.

77. Trescot, *Position and Course of the South*, 24. Southerners' optimistic economic vi-sions, based on the power of cotton and the advantages of free trade, are analyzed in Schoen, *Fragile Fabric of Union*, and Onuf and Onuf, *Nations, Markets, and War*.

78. Walther, *Fire-Eaters*, 144–150; Rhett, *Political Life and Services*, 39–40; Ruther-foord, "A Century Hence"; Ruffin, *Diary*, April 20, 1858; Robert E. May, *Southern Dream of a Caribbean Empire, 1854–1861* (Gainesville: University Press of Florida, 2002); Ayer, *Southern Rights*, 22; Nathaniel Beverley Tucker to James Henry Hammond, April 18, 1850, Nathaniel Beverley Tucker Papers, DU. Curiously, Tucker not only envisioned that Cuba and Jamaica would function as outlets for the South's surplus slave population; he also imagined that "a colony [of] our best and most intelligent free negroes" could be established "in the tropical parts of South America where none but Negroes and monkeys can live," and perhaps lay the foundation for eventual emancipation in the very distant future.

79. Nathaniel Beverley Tucker to James Henry Hammond, February 2, 1850, Nathaniel Beverley Tucker Papers, DU.

CHAPTER 3

1. James Henry Hammond to William Porcher Miles, October 23, 1858, William Porcher Miles Papers, SHC.

2. The title of the relevant volume in the authoritative History of the South series speaks for itself: Avery Craven, *The Growth of Southern Nationalism, 1848–1861* (Baton Rouge: Louisiana State University Press, 1953). See also John McCardell, *The Idea of a Southern Nation: Southern Nationalists and Southern Nationalism, 1830–1860* (New York: Norton, 1979); Manisha Sinha, *The Counterrevolution of Secession: Politics and Ideology in Antebellum South Carolina* (Chapel Hill: University of North Carolina Press, 2000). This interpretation is similar to what Eric Van Young has termed "outcomism" in his analysis of the road to Mexican independence: Van Young, "Revolution and Imagined Communities in Mexico, 1810–1821" in *Nationalism in the New World*, ed. Don H. Doyle and Marco Antonio Pamplona (Athens, GA: University of Georgia Press, 2006), 184–207. For similar points regarding Italy and Germany, see John Breuilly, *Nationalism and the State* (Manchester: Manchester University Press, 1993), 96–122.

3. This argument, and several of the points I make to support it, build upon the insights of David M. Potter, *The Impending Crisis, 1848–1861* (New York: Harper & Row, 1976), 469–478, passim; and Potter, "The Historian's Use of Nationalism and Vice Versa," in *The South and the Sectional Conflict* (Baton Rouge: Louisiana State University Press, 1968), 34–83; and more generally by the "contingency" approach of William Freehling and Edward Ayers: Freehling, *The Road to Disunion* (New York: Oxford University Press, 1990–2007); Ayers, *What Caused The Civil War?: Reflections on the South and Southern History* (New York: Norton, 2005).

4. Many historians have emphasized fear of northern antislavery in explaining secession: Eugene D. Genovese, *The Political Economy of Slavery: Studies in the Economy and Society of the Slave South* (New York: Random House, 1965), esp. 243–270; William L. Barney, *The Road to Secession: A New Perspective on the Old South* (New York: Praeger, 1972), esp. 3–48; Barney, *The Secessionist Impulse: Alabama and Mississippi in 1860* (1974; Tuscaloosa: University of Alabama Press, 2004); Steven A. Channing, *Crisis of Fear: Secession in South Carolina* (1970; New York: Norton, 1974); Charles B. Dew, *Apostles of Disunion: Southern Secession Commissioners and the Causes of the Civil War* (Charlottesville: University of Virginia Press, 2001). Others have seen secessionism as being driven more by perceived threats to white liberty than to black slavery: Lacy K. Ford, Jr., *Origins of Southern Radicalism: The South Carolina Upcountry, 1800–1860* (New York: Oxford University Press, 1988); J. Mills Thornton, *Politics and Power in a Slave Society: Alabama, 1800–1860* (Baton Rouge: Louisiana State University Press, 1978); Michael F. Holt, *The Political Crisis of the 1850s* (1978; New York: Norton, 1983).

5. On the importance of the concepts and language of union and disunion, see Paul C. Nagel, *One Nation Indivisible: The Union in American Thought, 1776–1861* (New York: Oxford University Press, 1964); Elizabeth R. Varon, *Disunion!*

The Coming of the American Civil War, 1789–1859 (Chapel Hill: University of North Carolina Press, 2008).

6. "To the Hon W. J. Grayson," signed "One of the People," at USC, bound with [W. J. Grayson], "Letter to His Excellency Whitemarsh B. Seabrook, Governor of the State of South-Carolina, on the Dissolution of the Union (Charleston, SC: A. E. Miller, 1850), 12; Benjamin C. Pressley, *Reasons for the Dissolution of the Union, Being a Reply to the Letter of the Hon. W. J. Grayson, and to his Answer to One of the People* (Charleston, SC: A. J. Burke, 1850), 15; "Co-operation Meeting, Held in Charleston, SC, July 29th, 1851" (n.p., n.d., USC), 11.

7. Thomas [Lekie?] to Whitemarsh Seabrook, September 9, 1850, Whitemarsh Seabrook Papers, SHC.

8. "Co-operation Meeting," 14.

9. "Association of Claremont Election County for the Defence of Southern Rights," Broadside, October 22, 1850, USC; "Address, 1851, of the Southern Rights Association of the University of Virginia to the Young Men of the South," typescript in William Henry Gist Papers, USC, 2.

10. "Record of the Organization and Transactions of the Central Southern Rights Association of Virginia," handwritten volume, VHS, quotations at 46; *The Proceedings and Address of the Central Southern Rights Association of Virginia, to the Citizens of Virginia, Adopted January 10, 1851* (Richmond, VA: Printed by Ritchies and Dunnavant, 1851), 11.

11. Chris Williams, "The United Kingdom: British Nationalisms during the Long Nineteenth Century," in *What Is a Nation? Europe 1789–1914*, ed. Timothy Baycroft and Mark Hewitson (Oxford: Oxford University Press, 2006), esp. 275. Graeme Morton's interpretation of "Unionist-Nationalism" in Scotland is to a certain degree comparable to the "southern rights" agenda in the United States. Morton, *Unionist-Nationalism: Governing Urban Scotland, 1830–1860* (East Linton, UK: Tuckwell, 1999).

12. Grayson, *Letter to his Excellency*, 16; "To the Hon W. J. Grayson," 5; Pressley, *Reasons for the Dissolution*, 8.

13. Grayson, *Letter to his Excellency*, 3–7; Pressley, *Reasons for the Dissolution*, 7.

14. William C. Rives to [Los?] Gales, September 30, 1850; William C. Rives to C. R. Ingersoll, November 25, 1850 (draft), both in William C. Rives Papers, LOC.

15. "Fourth of July," *Vicksburg Whig*, July 16, 1851; "Fort Moultrie and the Secessionists," *Richmond Whig*, July 4, 1851 ("orgie" quote); "Independence Day in South Carolina," *Richmond Whig*, July 15, 1851; "More Madness" and "The Day!" *Richmond Enquirer*, July 4, 1851; "Independence Day," *Richmond Enquirer*, July 8, 1851; "The Fourth of July in South Carolina," *Richmond Enquirer*, July 15, 1851.

16. "Fourth of July Celebration," *Brownlow's Knoxville Whig and Independent Journal*, July 7, 1849; "The Fourth of July," *Brownlow's Knoxville Whig and Independent Journal*, July 6, 1850; "The Union of our Fathers," and "The Day," *Richmond Whig*, July 4, 1851; "To-day," *Richmond Enquirer*, July 4, 1850; J. G. Ramsay,

"Friends and fellow citizens of the county of Davie," speech delivered July 4, 1851, J. G. Ramsay Papers, SHC.

17. "Celebration of the Fourth of July, 1850," *Richmond Enquirer*, July 9, 1850. See also Joshua G. Wright, *An Oration: Delivered in the Methodist Episcopal Church, Wilmington, N. C. on the Fourth of July, A.D. 1851* (Wilmington, NC: Printed at the "Herald" Book and Job Office, 1851), 21.

18. David Potter has astutely observed that "armistice" is a more accurate description than "compromise": Potter, *Impending Crisis*, 90–120.

19. Rogan Kersh, *Dreams of a More Perfect Union* (Ithaca, NY: Cornell University Press, 2001); Paul C. Nagel, *One Nation Indivisible*, 71–87; Peter S. Onuf, *Jefferson's Empire: The Language of American Nationhood* (Charlottesville: University Press of Virginia, 2000). This model of union calls to mind Benedict Anderson's interpretation of nationalism as a "deep, horizontal comradeship." Anderson, *Imagined Communities: Reflections on the Origin and Spread of Nationalism*, 2nd ed. (London: Verso, 1991).

20. William Gilmore Simms to John Pendleton Kennedy, May 12, 1851, in Simms, *Letters of William Gilmore Simms*, vol. 3, ed. Mary C. Simms Oliphant, Alfred Taylor Odell, and T. C. Duncan Eaves (Columbia: University of South Carolina Press, 1954), 123; Henry W. Miller, *Address Delivered Before the Philanthropic and Dialectic Societies of the University of North Carolina, June 3, 1857* (Raleigh, NC: Holden & Wilson, 1857), 24. Somewhat ironically, the quotation referred to North American colonists' attempts to leave the British Empire. See also *Proceedings and Address of the Central Southern Rights Association of Virginia*; Ferdinand Jacobs, *The Committing of Our Cause to God: A Sermon Preached in the Second Presbyterian Church, Charleston, S.C., on Friday, the 6th of December; A Day of Fasting, Humiliation, and Prayer, Appointed by the Legislature of South Carolina, in View of the State of Our Federal Relations* (Charleston, SC: A. J. Burke, 1850), 3.

21. William Peirce to Ellen Peirce, October 18, 1855, Ellen E. Peirce Papers, DU. The next month (in a letter dated November 30, 1855), Peirce was preparing to leave the South for good, and was predicting civil war because sectional hostility was so intense.

22. James M. Smythe, *Ethel Somers; or, The Fate of the Union* (Augusta, GA: H. D. Norrell, 1857), 55, 61, 288, 381. The novel was published anonymously; Smythe is identified as the author by the online database Wright American Fiction (http://www.letrs.indiana.edu/w/wright2/). Southern writers continued to use gender and romance to make sense of North-South relations, both during the Civil War and after it. See Amy Murrell Taylor, *The Divided Family in Civil War America* (Chapel Hill: University of North Carolina Press, 2005), 63–89; Nina Silber, *The Romance of Reunion: Northerners and the South, 1865–1900* (Chapel Hill: University of North Carolina Press, 1993).

23. Smythe, *Ethel Somers*, 355.

24. George P. C. Rumbough, handwritten speech, July 4, 1856, VHS. See also Frederick A. Porcher, "Characteristics of Civilization," *Russell's Magazine*, November 1857, 97–110; George Fitzhugh, "The Declaration of Independence and the Republican Party," *De Bow's Review* 29, no. 2 (August 1860): 175–187; Fitzhugh, *Cannibals All! Or, Slaves without Masters*, ed. C. Vann Woodward (Cambridge, MA: Belknap Press of Harvard University Press, 1960); "Education of Southern Women," *De Bow's Review* 31, no. 4–5 (October 1861): 281–390; Michael O'Brien, *Conjectures of Order: Intellectual Life and the American South, 1810–1860* (Chapel Hill: University of North Carolina Press, 2004), 1:39.

25. Letter quoted in Frederick F. Siegel, *The Roots of Southern Distinctiveness: Tobacco and Society in Danville, Virginia, 1780–1865* (Chapel Hill: University of North Carolina Press, 1987), 113–114; Outlaw quoted in Stephen W. Berry II, *All That Makes a Man: Love and Ambition in the Civil War South* (New York: Oxford University Press, 2003), 134. See also Victoria Bynum, *Unruly Women: The Politics of Social and Sexual Control in the Old South* (Chapel Hill: University of North Carolina Press, 1992), 35–58; Elizabeth Fox-Genovese and Eugene D. Genovese, *The Mind of the Master Class: History and Faith in the Southern Slaveholders' Worldview* (Cambridge, UK: Cambridge University Press, 2005), 551; George L. Mosse, *Nationalism and Sexuality: Reshaping the Memory of the World Wars* (New York: Oxford University Press, 1990); Linda Colley, *Britons: Forging the Nation: 1707–1837* (New Haven, CT: Yale University Press, 1992), 237–282; Brian Steele, "Thomas Jefferson's Gender Frontier," *Journal of American History* 95, no. 1 (June 2008): 17–42.

26. Benjamin Morgan Palmer, *The South: Her Peril and Duty* (1860), in *Southern Pamphlets on Secession, November 1860–April 1861*, ed. Jon L. Wakelyn (Chapel Hill: University of North Carolina Press, 1996), 66; *Mobile Daily Register*, July 10, 1856; Mitchell Snay, *The Gospel of Disunion: Religion and Separatism in the Antebellum South* (1993; Chapel Hill: University of North Carolina Press, 1997); Fox-Genovese and Genovese, *Mind of the Master Class*, 613–635.

27. Charles F. Mercer to Muscoe R. H. Garnett, November 28, 1857, Hunter Family Papers, VHS.

28. N. A. Pratt, *Perils of a Dissolution of the Union: A Discourse, Delivered in the Presbyterian Church, of Roswell, on the Day of Public Thanksgiving, November 20, 1856* (Atlanta: C. R. Hanleiter, & Co., Printers, 1856).

29. Herschel V. Johnson to "Gentlemen," June 8, 1855, Herschel V. Johnson Papers, DU; newspaper clipping, report of Johnson's speech at the Democratic Mass Meeting in Baltimore, September 12, 1856, Johnson Papers.

30. William C. Rives to Hiram Ketchum, June 29, 1859, William C. Rives Papers, LOC.

31. See Thornton, *Politics and Power*; Ford, *Origins of Southern Radicalism*; Stephanie McCurry, *Masters of Small Worlds: Yeoman Households, Gender Relations, and*

the *Political Culture of the Antebellum South Carolina Low Country* (New York: Oxford University Press, 1995), Steven Hahn, *The Roots of Southern Populism: Yeoman Farmers and the Transformation of the Georgia Upcountry, 1850–1890* (New York: Oxford University Press, 1983); Harry L. Watson, "Conflict and Collaboration: Yeomen, Slaveholders, and Politics in the Antebellum South," *Social History* 10 (1985): 273–298.

32. George M. Fredrickson has explored the concept of *"herrenvolk* equality" in the American South in *The Black Image in the White Mind: The Debate on Afro-American Character and Destiny, 1817–1914* (New York: Harper & Row, 1971), and *White Supremacy: A Comparative Study in American and South African History* (New York: Oxford University Press, 1981), 115–244.

33. Ford, *Origins of Southern Radicalism*, 185–186.

34. Entries for November 1859 and December 12, 1859, Diary of John Coles Rutherfoord, Section 12, Rutherfoord Family Papers, VHS. For a valuable account of the raid and its repercussions, including the "emotional" repercussions, see Potter, *Impending Crisis*, 356–384.

35. Quoted in Merrill D. Peterson, *John Brown: The Legend Revisited* (Charlottesville: University of Virginia Press, 2002), 18–19.

36. Elliott L. Storey Diary, November 21, 1859, VHS.

37. "Record of the Organization and Transactions of the Central Southern Rights Association of Virginia," December 16, 1859. On honor see Bertram Wyatt-Brown, *Southern Honor: Ethics and Behavior in the Old South* (New York: Oxford University Press, 1982); Wyatt-Brown, *The Shaping of Southern Culture: Honor, Grace, and War, 1760s–1880s* (Chapel Hill: University of North Carolina Press, 2001); Kenneth Greenberg, *Masters and Statesman: The Political Culture of American Slavery,* (Baltimore: Johns Hopkins University Press, 1985); Christopher J. Olsen, *Political Culture and Secession in Mississippi: Masculinity, Honor, and the Antiparty Tradition, 1830–1860* (New York: Oxford University Press, 2000).

38. "Resolutions of South Carolina," December 27, 1859, Christopher G. Memminger Papers, SHC.

39. D. H. Hamilton to William Porcher Miles, January 23, 1860, William Porcher Miles Papers, SHC.

40. Quoted in William Kauffman Scarborough, *Masters of the Big House: Elite Slaveholders of the Mid-Nineteenth-Century South* (Baton Rouge: Louisiana State University Press, 2003), 282. For southern women's perceptions of Brown's raid as a domestic threat, see George C. Rable, *Civil Wars: Women and the Crisis of Southern Nationalism* (Urbana: University of Illinois Press, 1989), 42–43.

41. James Craik, *The Union: National and State Sovereignty Alike Essential to American Liberty: A Discourse Delivered in the Hall of the House of Representatives at the Capitol in Frankfort, Ky., December 19, 1859* (Louisville, KY: Morton & Griswold, 1860).

42. B. H. Magruder to William C. Rives, November 13, 1859, William C. Rives to G [Gonett?], December 27, 1859, both in William C. Rives Papers, LOC.

43. Sarah Lois Wadley Diary, October 26, 1860, SHC. As Charles Dew has demonstrated, the commissioners dispatched between southern states during the secession winter similarly emphasized racial fears in promoting secession (Dew, *Apostles of Disunion*). See also Channing, *Crisis of Fear*.

44. Jabez L. M. Curry, *Perils and Duty of the South: Substance of a Speech Delivered by Jabez L. M. Curry, in Talladega, Alabama, November 26, 1860* (Printed by Lemuel Towers, 1860), 3, 4, 6.

45. Waddy Butler to Lucy Wood, December 14, 1860, Lucy Wood Butler Papers, SHC.

46. "Minute Men, Saluda Association," handwritten minutes, 1860, USC; *Constitution of Minute Men, For the Defence of Southern Rights, Adopted at Laurens C. H., Oct 31, 1860*, broadside, USC.

47. William Gilmore Simms to William Porcher Miles, December 31, 1860, in Simms, *Letters*, 4:315. For similar sentiments, see Simms's letters to James Lawson in December 1860, ibid.

48. Caroline Glover to sisters, January 11, 1861, Caroline Howard Gilman Papers, SCHS.

49. "The Southern Marseillaise," *Charleston Mercury*, January 1, 1861; "The Rally of the South," *Charleston Mercury*, January 15, 1861.

50. Henry A. Wise to George Booker, January 20, 1861, George Booker Papers, DU; "Letter from Ex-Governor Wise," *Richmond Enquirer*, January 8, 1861.

51. "To the Young Men of Lunenberg County," *Richmond Enquirer*, December 18, 1860.

52. "A Valuable Document," *Richmond Enquirer*, December 18, 1860.

53. See Channing, *Crisis of Fear*; Barney, *Road to Secession*, 146–152; and Barney, *Secessionist Impulse*, chap. 4.

54. "Public Meeting in Amelia County," *Richmond Enquirer*, December 4, 1860.

55. "Newberry," *Charleston Mercury*, January 22, 1861. For a different interpretation of flag presentation ceremonies, see Wayne K. Durrill, "Ritual, Community and War: Local Flag Presentation Ceremonies and Disunity in the Early Confederacy," *Journal of Social History* 39 (2006): 1105–1122.

56. "To the Women of Virginia," *Richmond Enquirer*, November 27, 1860; Lucy Wood to Waddy Butler, January 21, 1861, Lucy Wood Butler Papers, SHC. On Virginia women's shifts between unionism and secessionism, see Elizabeth R. Varon, *We Mean to Be Counted: White Women and Politics in Antebellum Virginia* (Chapel Hill: University of North Carolina Press, 1998), 137–168.

57. "Sons of the South," *Richmond Enquirer*, November 27, 1860.

58. George Reese, ed., *Proceedings of the Virginia State Convention of 1861, February 13–May 1* (Richmond: Virginia State Library, 1965), 2:104.

59. Ibid., 2:104, 1:333.

60. R. M. T. Hunter, "The Border States—Their Position after Disunion," *De Bow's Review* 30, no. 1 (January 1861): 116.

61. William Freehling has emphasized the moderate stance of the majority in *Road to Disunion*, arguing that the manipulations of a small number of radical extremists—and no small amount of chance—pushed the moderates towards secession.

62. W. M. Wilcox to G. Wilcox, February 26, 1861, typescript, W. M. Wilcox Papers, DU.

63. George Alsall to Herschel V. Johnson, January 7, 1861, Herschel V. Johnson Papers, DU; R. M. Farleigh to "Galt," January 14, 1861, Beall-Booth Family Letters, FHS. For secession as an extremist conspiracy, see also "Hon Herschel V Johnson's Speech in Philadelphia," newspaper clipping, September 17, 1860, Herschel V. Johnson Papers; James Ramsay, speech on the Union, ca. 1860, James G. Ramsay Papers, SHC; W. S. Bodley to A. Burwell, November 22, 1860, Bodley Family Papers, FHS; S. S. Nicholas, *South Carolina, Disunion, and a Mississippi Valley Confederacy* (Louisville, KY, 1860).

64. James G. Ramsay to wife, January 13, 1861, January 24, 1861, J. G. Ramsay Papers, SHC. On the politics of unionism in the upper South, see Daniel Crofts, *Reluctant Confederates: Upper South Unionists in the Secession Crisis* (Chapel Hill: University of North Carolina Press, 1989).

65. Robert Tracy McKenzie, "Contesting Secession: Parson Brownlow and the Rhetoric of Proslavery Unionism, 1860–1861," *Civil War History* 48 (2002): 294–312, esp. 308–309.

66. James L. Petigru to Edward Everett, October 28, 1860; James L. Petigru to Alfred Huger, September 5, 1860, both in James L. Petigru Papers, LOC.

67. Edmund Dumas to John J. Crittenden, January 23, 1861, "A Southerner and Lover of his Country" to Crittenden, December 19, 1860, both in John J. Crittenden Papers, LOC; "A Southerner and Lover of his Country" to William C. Rives, February 5, 1861, William C. Rives Papers, LOC. Both the Crittenden and the Rives papers contain many further examples.

68. Speech at Louisville, Georgia, December 15, 1860, newspaper clipping, Herschel V. Johnson Papers, DU.

69. Thomas H. Looker to John J. Crittenden, December 24, 1860, John J. Crittenden Papers, LOC.

70. Robert J. Breckinridge, *Discourse of Dr. R. J. Breckinridge, Delivered on the Day of National Humiliation, January 4, 1861* (Lexington, KY, 1861), 2, 3, 8, 10.

71. Theodoric C. Lyon, *Do the Times Demand a Southern Confederacy?: The Constitutionality, Rightfulnesss & Expediency of Secession* (Columbus, MS: privately printed, 1861).

72. S. S. Nicholas to John J. Crittenden, December 27, 1860, John J. Crittenden Papers, LOC; William Massie to William C. Rives, February 8, 1860, William C. Rives Papers, LOC. See also N. M. Ludlow to John J. Crittenden, January 1, 1861,

and Thomas Brewer to John J. Crittenden, January 7, 1861, both in Crittenden Papers; William C. Rives to Alexander Ritchie, December 8, 1860, Thomas B. Latrobe to William C. Rives, December 15, 1860, both in Rives Papers.

73. Robert Young Conrad to wife, April 14 and April 15, 1861, Robert Young Conrad Papers, VHS.

74. William C. Rives to G. W. Summers, April 15, 1861, William C. Rives Papers, LOC.

75. William C. Rives to John Janney, May 1, 1861, William C. Rives Papers, LOC; Herschel V. Johnson to Alexander H. Stephens, November 20, 1860, Herschel V. Johnson Papers, DU. See also Herschel V. Johnson to A. E. Cochran, October 25, 1862, Johnson Papers. For another example, see the description of Benjamin Humphreys in Olsen, *Political Culture and Secession*, 170.

76. Lunsford Lindsay Lomax Letter, April 21, 1861, VHS.

77. Charles Iverson Graves to Aunt Mary, January 17, 1861 and March 16, 1861; Charles Iverson Graves to cousin Maggie, January 7, 1862 (this letter is misdated 1861, but has been corrected by an archivist to read 1862); all in Charles Iverson Graves Papers, SHC. For an example of a unionist (and in this case an abolitionist) destroying his papers later in the war, see J. W. Calvert to E. M. Davis, February 20, 1863, FHS.

78. Allen Turner Davidson to wife, April 4, 1861, Allen Turner Davidson Papers, SHC.

79. C. A. Swift to Anna Mercur, February 2, 1861, Anna Mercur Papers, SHC; Anna Bell Cadwallader to brother John, May 24, 1861, John N. Cadwallader Papers, VHS. On community coercion and diminishing unionism in the wake of Fort Sumter, see Crofts, *Reluctant Confederates*, 345–346.

80. Lucy Riall examines these "ironies of Italian unification" in *Risorgimento: The History of Italy from Napoleon to Nation-State* (New York: Palgrave Macmillan, 2009); see also Dennis Mack Smith, *Mazzini* (New Haven, CT: Yale University Press, 1994). On the early United States, see John M. Murrin, "A Roof without Walls: The Dilemma of American National Identity," in *Beyond Confederation: Origins of the Constitution and American National Identity*, ed. Richard R. Beeman, Stephen Botein, and Edward C. Carter III (Chapel Hill: University of North Carolina Press, 1987), 333–348; and on Germany see John Breuilly, *The Formation of the First German Nation-State, 1800–1871* (Basingstoke, UK: Macmillan, 1996).

81. Mark R. Beissinger, "How Nationalisms Spread: Eastern Europe Adrift the Tides and Cycles of Nationalist Contention," *Social Research* 63 (Spring 1996): 97–146, esp. 111; Paul Lawrence, *Nationalism: History and Theory* (Harlow, UK: Pearson Longman, 2005), 80; E. J. Hobsbawm, *Nations and Nationalism Since 1780: Programme, Myth, Reality*, 2nd ed. (Cambridge, UK: Cambridge University Press, 1992), 166–167. See also Van Young, "Revolution and Imagined Communities"; Breuilly, *Nationalism and the State*, esp. 35.

CHAPTER 4

1. William L. Yancey, Pierre Rost, and A. Dudley Mann to Earl Russell, August 14, 1861, Records of the Confederate States of America, LOC.

2. Benedict Anderson, *Imagined Communities: Reflections on the Origin and Spread of Nationalism*, 2nd ed. (London: Verso, 1991); Eric Hobsbawm and Terence Ranger, eds., *The Invention of Tradition* (Cambridge, UK: Cambridge University Press, 1983); Homi K. Bhabha, ed., *Nation and Narration* (New York: Routledge, 1990).

3. Most recent historians of Confederate nationalism have, to a greater or lesser degree, been influenced by the "constructionist" approach. This is most notable in Ian Binnington, "'They Have Made a Nation': Confederates and the Creation of Confederate Nationalism" (PhD diss., University of Illinois, 2004).

4. John Breuilly, *Nationalism and the State*, 2nd ed. (Manchester: Manchester University Press, 1993), 69–70.

5. *Richmond Enquirer*, May 3, 1861; J. Quitman Moore, "The Belligerents," *De Bow's Review* 31, no. 1 (July 1861): 69; Grace B. Elmore Papers, Vol. 3: Memoir, February 6, 1861, SHC.

6. *Montgomery Advertiser*, March 27, 1861; David Levy Yulee to Joseph Finegan, January 5, 1861, VHS, Mss2 Y912a; William Henry Trescot to Howell Cobb, January 14, 1861, William Henry Trescot Papers, USC. See also Francis Pickens to Jefferson Davis, January 23, 1861, in Jefferson Davis, *The Papers of Jefferson Davis*, ed. Lynda Laswell Crist, vol. 7, *1861* (Baton Rouge: Louisiana State University Press, 1992).

7. H. Timrod, "Ode on the Meeting of the Southern Congress," broadside poem, USC; Robert E. Bonner, *Colors and Blood: Flag Passions of the Confederate South* (Princeton, NJ: Princeton University Press, 2002), 34.

8. This and the following paragraphs are based on research in the Records of the Confederate States of America, LOC; James M. Mason Papers, LOC; Henry Hotze Papers, LOC; Howard Jones, *Blue and Gray Diplomacy: A History of Union and Confederate Foreign Relations* (Chapel Hill: University of North Carolina Press, 2010); Charles M. Hubbard, *The Burden of Confederate Diplomacy* (Knoxville: University of Tennessee Press, 1998).

9. R. M. T. Hunter to John Slidell, September 23, 1861, Records of the Confederate States of America, LOC.

10. Robert E. May, *The Union, the Confederacy, and the Atlantic Rim* (West Lafayette, IN: Purdue University Press, 1995), 16; Robert Toombs to William L. Yancey et al., March 16, 1861, in James D. Richardson, ed., *A Compilation of the Messages and Papers of the Confederacy* (Nashville, TN: United States Publishing Company, 1906), 2, no. 5; *Richmond Examiner*, October 3, 1861.

11. William M. Browne to John Quintero, September 3, 1861, Records of the Confederate States of America, LOC.

12. Joseph Smith to Henry Gourdin, June 7, 1861, Henry Gourdin Papers, LOC; William Gregory to James M. Mason, July 27, 1861, James M. Mason Papers, LOC.

13. Gregory to Mason, July 27, 1861; L. C. Brown to Major Hubbard, undated [ca. January 1861], Brown-Ewell Family Papers, FHS; William Yancey and A. Dudley Mann to Robert Toombs, May 21, 1861, Records of the Confederate States, LOC; Kinley J. Brauer, "The Slavery Problem in the Diplomacy of the American Civil War," *Pacific Historical Review* 46, no. 3 (August 1977): 439–469.

14. A key theme of Anderson, *Imagined Communities*, is the importance of printed literature in promoting a sense of shared national identity even among people who have never actually encountered each other. On literature and Confederate nationalism, see Anne Sarah Rubin, *A Shattered Nation: The Rise and Fall of the Confederacy, 1861–1868* (Chapel Hill: University of North Carolina Press, 2005), 25–30; Binnington, "'They Have Made a Nation,'" 141–182; and, for the most thorough treatment, Michael Bernath, *Confederate Minds: The Struggle for Intellectual Independence in the Civil War South* (Chapel Hill: University of North Carolina Press, 2010).

15. "A National Song," *Richmond Enquirer*, May 14, 1861.

16. "Editorial Miscellany." *De Bow's Review* 30, no. 3 (March 1861): 384; *Charleston Mercury*, May 16, 1861.

17. *Charleston Courier*, editorial, July 2, 1861.

18. "Disenthralment of Southern Literature," *De Bow's Review* 31, no. 4–5 (October–November 1861): 347–361 (quotation at 361). On postcolonial anxiety as a characteristic of antebellum southern culture, see Michael O'Brien, *Conjectures of Order: Intellectual Life and the American South, 1810–1860* (Chapel Hill: University of North Carolina Press, 2004).

19. George Fitzhugh, "Hayti and the Monroe Doctrine," *De Bow's Review* 31, no. 2 (August 1861): 136.

20. J. Quitman Moore, "The Belligerents," *De Bow's Review* 31, no. 1 (July 1861): 69–77 (quotation at 74); "The Conflict of Northern and Southern Races," *De Bow's Review* 31, no. 4–5 (October–November 1861): 391–395 (quotation at 393); excerpt from *Richmond Examiner*, *Charleston Mercury*, April 30, 1861; Robert E. Bonner, "Roundheaded Cavaliers? The Context and Limits of a Confederate Racial Project," *Civil War History* 48, no. 1 (2002): 34–59; Ritchie Devon Watson, Jr., *Normans and Saxons: Southern Race Mythology and the Intellectual History of the American Civil War* (Baton Rouge: Louisiana State University Press, 2008); James M. McPherson, *Is Blood Thicker than Water? Crises of Nationalism in the Modern World* (New York: Vintage Books, 1998). Watson and McPherson give more weight to the prominence and importance of this theme than is warranted. For a useful corrective, see Don H. Doyle, *Nations Divided: America, Italy, and the Southern Question* (Athens, GA: University of Georgia Press, 2002), 80.

21. Roland Jones to Dabney Jones, February 27, 1861, Roland Jones Letters, ADAH.

22. See Linda Colley, *Britons: Forging the Nation: 1707–1837* (New Haven, CT: Yale University Press, 1992); Susan-Mary Grant, *North over South: Northern Nationalism and American Identity in the Antebellum Era* (Lawrence: University Press of Kansas, 2000); Joshua Searle-White, *The Psychology of Nationalism* (New York: Palgrave, 2001).

23. "The Decay of Nations," *Charleston Mercury*, May 16, 1861.

24. "Volunteer Forces," *Montgomery Advertiser*, April 18, 1861; see also *Richmond Examiner*, editorial, July 2, 1861. Interestingly, though perhaps not surprisingly, northern men thought of themselves as the more manly men, in contrast to the fiery secessionists to the South, who were so passionate as to be feminine. Michael Kimmel, *Manhood in America: A Cultural History* (New York: Free Press, 1996), 28; Reid Mitchell, "Soldiering, Manhood, and Coming of Age: A Northern Volunteer," in *Divided Houses: Gender and the Civil War*, ed. Catherine Clinton and Nina Silber (New York: Oxford University Press, 1992), 43–54.

25. George Fitzhugh, "The Women of the South," *De Bow's Review* 31, no. 2 (August 1861): 147–154 (quotation at 153); "Education of Southern Women," *De Bow's Review* 31, no. 4–5 (October–November 1861): 381–390 (quotation at 387).

26. Susan Cornwall Diary, January 31, 1861, SHC.

27. Paul D. Escott, *After Secession: Jefferson Davis and the Failure of Confederate Nationalism* (Baton Rouge: Louisiana State University Press, 1978), 35–38.

28. Speech of Alexander H. Stephens, March 21, 1861, reprinted in *The Civil War Archive: The History of the Civil War in Documents*, ed. Henry Steele Commager, revised by Erik Bruun (New York: Black Dog & Leventhal, 2000), 566–567. For a twentieth-century historian's belief that commitment to white supremacy defined the South, see Ulrich B. Phillips, "The Central Theme of Southern History," *American Historical Review* 34, no. 1 (October 1928): 30–43.

29. *Richmond Examiner*, editorial, March 14, 1861.

30. Robert Smith, *An Address to the Citizens of Alabama on the Constitution and Laws of the Confederate States of America by the Hon. Robert H. Smith, at Temperance Hall, on the 30th March, 1861* (Mobile, AL: Mobile Daily Register Print 1861), 11; "Serenade to Hon. Louis T. Wigfall," *Charleston Mercury*, April 4, 1861; "A Parallel," *Charleston Courier*, July 4, 1861. On the constitution as a basis of Confederate nationalism, see Binnington, "They Have Made a Nation," 48–95.

31. M. E. Huger to William Porcher Miles, February 7, 1861; William Porcher Miles Papers, SHC. On flags and Confederate nationalism, see Bonner, *Colors and Blood*, esp. 39–66.

32. John Pelham to sister, March 19, 1861, John Pelham Papers, ADAH.

33. Sarah Lois Wadley Diary, July 28, 1861, November 15, 1861, Sarah Lois Wadley Papers, SHC. As Richard McCaslin has shown, Robert E. Lee became known as a sort of second Washington. But in the first year or so of the Confederacy's existence, before Lee attained prominence, it was Davis who held that unofficial

title. McCaslin, *Lee in the Shadow of Washington* (Baton Rouge: Louisiana State University Press, 2001).

34. Susan Cornwall Diary, February 4, 1861, SHC.

35. Susan Cornwall Diary, February 22, 1861, SHC; *Richmond Enquirer*, May 7, 1861.

36. Letter from "Virginius," *Richmond Examiner*, July 11, 1861. For many more examples from throughout the Civil War, see James M. McPherson, *For Cause and Comrades: Why Men Fought in the Civil War* (New York: Oxford University Press, 1997), 105; Robert E. Bonner, *Mastering America: Southern Slaveholders and the Crisis of American Nationhood* (Cambridge, UK: Cambridge University Press, 2009); Drew Gilpin Faust, *The Creation of Confederate Nationalism: Ideology and Identity in the Civil War South* (Baton Rouge: Louisiana State University Press, 1988), 14, 27; Anne Sarah Rubin, "Seventy-six and Sixty-one: Confederates Remember the American Revolution," in *Where These Memories Grow: History, Memory, and Southern Identity*, ed. W. Fitzhugh Brundage (Chapel Hill: University of North Carolina Press, 2000).

37. G. Ward Hubbs, ed., *Voices from Company D: Diaries by the Greensboro Guards, Fifth Alabama Infantry Regiment, Army of Northern Virginia* (Athens, GA: University of Georgia Press, 2003), 11; "Fourth of July," *Charleston Courier*, July 6, 1861. Back in 1849, the *Vicksburg Whig* had predicted, "Beyond the existence of this Union, there will be no Fourth of July!" ("The Fourth," July 3, 1849). For Confederates' varied attitudes toward the Fourth of July, see Paul Quigley, "Independence Day Dilemmas in the American South, 1848–1865," *Journal of Southern History* 75, no. 2 (May 2009): 235–266.

38. Alexander Watkins Terrell, *Oration Delivered on the Fourth Day of July, 1861, at the Capitol, Austin, Texas* (Austin, TX: Printed by J. Marshall at "Gazette" Office, 1861), 14, 17.

39. "The Fourth of July," *Mobile Register*, July 2; "The Fourth of July at Shreveport," *Mobile Register*, July 4, 1861; Fletcher M. Green, "Listen to the Eagle Scream: One Hundred Years of the Fourth of July in North Carolina (1776–1876)," *North Carolina Historical Review* 31 (1954): 295–320, 529–549.

40. Dick Simpson to Caroline Virginia Taliaferro Miller, July 4, 1861, in *"Far, Far From Home": The Wartime Letters of Dick and Tally Simpson, Third South Carolina Volunteers*, ed. Guy R. Everson and Edward H. Simpson, Jr. (New York: Oxford University Press, 1994), 23; "The Glorious Fourth," *Mobile Register*, July 4, 1861.

41. Although the American Revolution was clearly compatible with slavery—after all, many of the revolutionary generation themselves had been slaveholders—it seemed increasingly less so through the course of the nineteenth century as the second, natural-rights-promoting paragraph of the Declaration assumed greater prominence. Union victory in the Civil War would complete this shift. See Pauline Maier, *American Scripture: Making the Declaration of Independence* (New

York: Random House, 1997), esp. 175–202; David Armitage, *The Declaration of Independence: A Global History* (Cambridge, MA: Harvard University Press, 2007), 63–102; Garry Wills, *Inventing America: Jefferson's Declaration of Independence* (Garden City, NY: Doubleday, 1978).

42. "Journal of the Whig Association," SCHS "*Richmond Examiner*, editorial, July 5, 1861; "A Parallel," *Charleston Courier*, July 4, 1861.

43. Letter from "Personne," *Charleston Courier*, July 6, 1861; Sarah Lois Wadley Diary, July 7, 1861, Sarah Lois Wadley Papers, SHC.

44. Sarah Lois Wadley Diary, October 26, 1860, February 16, 1861, Sarah Lois Wadley Papers, SHC.

45. William Proctor Gould Diary, September 6, 1861, ADAH.

46. Helen W. Swift to Anna Mercur, March 16, 1861, June 4, 1861, Anna Mercur Letters, SHC.

47. John J. Crittenden to Lt. Col. George B. Crittenden, April 30, 1861, John J. Crittenden Papers, FHS; Susan Fishback to Susan Grigsby, July 8, 1861, September 5, 1861, Grigsby Family Papers, FHS. William Freehling has demonstrated the importance of white border-state southerners to the outcome of the Civil War, and the more general significance of intra-southern divisions, in *The South versus the South: How Anti-Confederate Southerners Shaped the Course of the Civil War* (New York: Oxford University Press, 2001).

48. Samuella Hart Curd Diary, July 4, 1861, October 28, 1861, July 17, 1861, July 19, 1861, October 18, 1861, VHS.

49. L. P. Yandell to sister, April 22, 1861, L. P. Yandell to father, December 23, 1860, April 22, 1861, April 24, 1861, April 26, 1861, Yandell Family Papers, FHS. See also Amy Murrell Taylor, *The Divided Family in Civil War America* (Chapel Hill: University of North Carolina Press, 2005); Stephen W. Berry, *House of Abraham: Lincoln and the Todds; A Family Divided by War* (Boston: Houghton Mifflin, 2007).

50. John C. Pegram to father, July 5, 1861, July 16, 1861, August 30, 1861, Pegram Family Papers, VHS.

51. John C. Pegram to father, August 30, 1861; John C. Pegram to mother, October 22, 1861, Pegram Family Papers.

52. John C. Pegram to mother, January 4, 1862, Pegram Family Papers.

53. Daniel W. Hamilton, "The Confederate Sequestration Act," *Civil War History* 52 (2006): 373–408 (quotations at 380); Brian R. Dirck, "Posterity's Blush: Civil Liberties, Property Rights, and Property Confiscation in the Confederacy," *Civil War History* 48 (2003): 237–256, esp. 243.

54. See Stephen V. Ash, *When the Yankees Came: Conflict and Chaos in the Occupied South, 1861–1865* (Chapel Hill: University of North Carolina Press, 1995).

55. See William L. Yancey and A. Dudley Mann to Robert Toombs, July 15, 1861, Records of the Confederate States of America, LOC. In 1862, the British Secretary of War wrote a cabinet memo explaining that international law required

that a new entrant in the family of nations "should have a Government of its own, receiving the habitual obedience of its people," and that those people should feel no "habits of obedience" for their old government (Howard Jones, *Blue and Gray Diplomacy*, 267–9).

56. "List of Political and State Prisoners, for Governor Harris," Isham G. Harris Papers, LOC.

57. Petition to governor, May 12, 1861, John Quincy Adams Nadenbousch Papers, VHS.

58. H. C. Kendrick to brother, July 18, 1861, and to father, August 8, 1861, H. C. Kendrick Papers, SHC. See also David Blight, "No Desperate Hero: Manhood and Freedom in a Union Soldier's Experience," in Clinton and Silber, *Divided Houses*, 58; William L. Barney, *The Making of a Confederate: Walter Lenoir's Civil War* (Oxford: Oxford University Press, 2008).

59. H. C. Kendrick to sister, November 15, 1861, H. C. Kendrick Papers, SHC.

60. "The Duty Which the Soldier Owes to His Country," *Richmond Enquirer*, June 4, 1861; *Richmond Examiner*, July 18, 1861.

61. "Our Cause," *Montgomery Advertiser*, March 25, 1861.

62. "National Morality," *Mobile Register and Advertiser*, July 7, 1861. As Anthony D. Smith has shown, many nations that have conceived of themselves as "chosen peoples" have characterized that status as a two-way, almost contractual agreement between themselves and God: in return for God's continued favor, they have the obligation to comport themselves in morally upright ways. Smith, *Chosen Peoples: Sacred Sources of National Identity* (New York: Oxford University Press, 2004), esp. 51.

63. *Montgomery Advertiser*, editorial, March 20, 1861; *Richmond Examiner*, editorial, May 30, 1861; Cotton Planters' Convention quoted in *De Bow's Review*, 31, no. 1 (July 1861): 103. For comparisons, see Lawrence R. Samuel, *Pledging Allegiance: American Identity and the Bond Drive of World War II* (Washington, DC: Smithsonian Institution Press, 1997); Melinda Lawson, *Patriot Fires: Forging a New American Nationalism in the Civil War North* (Lawrence: University Press of Kansas, 2002), chap. 2.

64. Waddy Butler to Lucy Wood, April 25, 1861, Lucy W. Butler Papers, SHC.

65. W. Gilmore Simms, "Oh, the Sweet South," *Southern Literary Messenger* (January 1861): 5; Beth Baron, "The Construction of National Honour in Egypt," *Gender and History* 5, no. 2 (1993): 244–255; Andrew Parker et al., eds., *Nationalisms and Sexualities* (New York: Routledge, 1992); Joane Nagel, "Masculinity and Nationalism: Gender and Sexuality in the Making of Nations," *Ethnic and Racial Studies* 21, no. 2 (March 1998): 242–269; Karen Hagemann, "A Valorous *Volk* Family: The Nation, the Military, and the Gender Order in Prussia in the Time of the Anti-Napoleonic Wars, 1806–15," in *Gendered Nations: Nationalisms and Gender Order in the Long Nineteenth Century*, ed. Ida Blom, Catherine Hall, and Karen Hagemann (Oxford: Berg, 2000), 179–205. Southern men also represented

individual southern states as women in need of protection. In a speech in Richmond, for example, L. Q. C. Lamar praised Virginia, often described as the "mother" of the other southern states, for "raising a majestic arm to press back the foe that dare attempt to force her daughters into an unnatural and unwilling Union" (speech reprinted in the *Richmond Enquirer*, June 4, 1861). See also John Collins M'Cabe, "Maryland, Our Mother," *Southern Literary Messenger* 33 (December 1861): 411.

66. William Gilmore Simms to William Gilmore Simms, Jr., November 7, 1861, in *The Letters of William Gilmore Simms*, vol. 4, ed. Mary C. Simms Oliphant, Alfred Taylor Odell, and T. C. Duncan Eaves (Columbia: University of South Carolina Press, 1955), 379.

67. "The Southern War Song," *Richmond Enquirer*, May 28, 1861; "North Carolina. A Call to Arms," broadside poem, available online, http://docsouth.unc.edu/call/call.html. For perceptions of the Civil War as test of manhood, see Stephen W. Berry II, *All That Makes a Man: Love and Ambition in the Civil War South* (New York: Oxford University Press, 2003); Leann Whites, *The Civil War as a Crisis in Gender: Augusta, Georgia, 1860–1890* (Athens, GA: University of Georgia Press, 1995); Gerald F. Linderman, *Embattled Courage: The Experience of Combat in the American Civil War* (New York: Free Press, 1987); Rubin, *Shattered Nation*, 24; McPherson, *For Cause and Comrades*, 21–22.

68. Jefferson Davis, speech at Montgomery, Alabama, February 16, 1861, in *Jefferson Davis: The Essential Writings*, ed. William J. Cooper, Jr. (New York: Modern Library, 2003), 197. Feminist scholars have criticized Benedict Anderson's *Imagined Communities* for following the assumption of male nationalists in a variety of times and places that the "deep, horizontal comradeship" of nationalism is an all-male affair (Parker et. al., *Nationalisms and Sexualities*, 5).

69. For a similar argument, applied to one young Confederate couple, see Lesley J. Gordon, "Courting Nationalism: The Wartime Letters of Bobbie Mitchell and Nettie Fondren," in *Inside the Confederate Nation: Essays in Honor of Emory M. Thomas*, ed. Lesley J. Gordon and John C. Inscoe (Baton Rouge: Louisiana State University Press, 2005), 188–208.

70. Elizabeth R. Varon, *We Mean to Be Counted: Women and Politics in Antebellum Virginia* (Chapel Hill: University of North Carolina Press, 1998).

71. Lucy Wood to Waddy Butler, January 21, 1861, Lucy W. Butler Papers, SHC. On white southern women during the secession crisis and the early Confederacy, see Drew Gilpin Faust, *Mothers of Invention: Women of the Slaveholding South in the American Civil War* (New York: Random House, 1996); Faust, "Altars of Sacrifice: Confederate Women and the Narrative of War," in Clinton and Silber, *Divided Houses*, 171–199; Laura Edwards, *Scarlett Doesn't Live Here Anymore: Southern Women in the Civil War Era* (Urbana: University of Illinois Press, 2000); George C. Rable, *Civil Wars: Women and the Crisis of Southern Nationalism* (Urbana: University of Illinois Press, 1989).

72. James G. Hudson, "Diary of the Canebrake Rifle Guards," May 1, 1861, ADAH.

73. Ladies Volunteer Aid Society of the Pine Hills, Minutes, July 11, 1861, DU.

74. Diary of Lucy Wood, April 16, 1861, April 17, 1861, May 2, 1861, May 7, 1861, May 24, 1861, June 15, 1861, SHC. As Linda Colley has shown, British women participated in nationalism in similar ways during the Napoleonic Wars. (Colley, *Britons*, 261.)

75. Diary of Lucy Wood, April 16, 1861, June 8, 1861, September 26, 1861, SHC.

76. Margaret Josephine Gillis Diary, April 28, 1861, May 5, 1861, June 16, 1861, July 29, 1861, ADAH.

77. Margaret Josephine Gillis Diary, February 24, 1861, ADAH; LeeAnn Whites, "The Civil War as a Crisis in Gender," in Clinton and Silber, *Divided Houses*, 14; George Rable, "'Missing in Action': Women of the Confederacy," in Clinton and Silber, *Divided Houses*, 135; Faust, *Mothers of Invention*, 14–15.

78. Margaret M. Storey, *Loyalty and Loss: Alabama's Unionists in the Civil War and Reconstruction* (Baton Rouge: Louisiana State University Press, 2004), 42.

CHAPTER 5

1. Public letter from William Henry Trescot to J. R. Ingersoll, printed in *The Record*, August 27, 1863, copy in the William Henry Trescot Papers, USC; quotations at 99, 102, 104. The "rivers of blood" image has been used in different ways by statesmen from Thomas Jefferson to Winston Churchill. See Peter Onuf and Nicholas Greenwood Onuf, *Nations, Markets, and War: Modern History and the American Civil War* (Charlottesville: University of Virginia Press, 2006), epilogue.

2. I follow historians such as Drew Gilpin Faust, Gary W. Gallagher, Robert E. Bonner, and Jason Phillips in approaching Confederate nationalism from the perspective of the war years themselves rather than from the distorting perspective of after the Confederacy's defeat: Faust, *The Creation of Confederate Nationalism: Ideology and Identity in the Civil War South* (Baton Rouge: Louisiana State University Press, 1988), 1–7; Gallagher, *The Confederate War: How Popular Will, Nationalism, and Military Strategy Could Not Stave Off Defeat* (Cambridge, MA: Harvard University Press, 1997), 3–7; Bonner, *Mastering America: Southern Slaveholders and the Crisis of American Nationhood* (Cambridge, UK: Cambridge University Press, 2009); Phillips, *Diehard Rebels: The Confederate Culture of Invincibility* (Athens, GA: University of Georgia Press, 2007).

3. Emory M. Thomas, *The Confederacy as a Revolutionary Experience* (Englewood Cliffs, NJ: Prentice Hall, 1970); Bonner, *Mastering America*; Richard F. Bensel, *Yankee Leviathan: The Origins of Central State Authority in America, 1859–1877* (Cambridge, UK: Cambridge University Press, 1991); Eugene D. Genovese, "King Solomon's Dilemma—and the Confederacy's," *Southern Cultures* 10, no.

4 (Winter 2004): 55–75; Drew Gilpin Faust, "'The Dread Voice of Uncertainty': Naming the Dead in the American Civil War," *Southern Cultures* 11, no. 2 (Summer 2005): 7–32; Rod Andrew, "The Essential Nationalism of the People: Georgia's Confederate Congressional Election of 1863," in *Inside the Confederate Nation: Essays in Honor of Emory M. Thomas*, ed. Lesley J. Gordon and John C. Inscoe (Baton Rouge: Louisiana State University Press, 2005), 128–146; Stephanie McCurry, *Confederate Reckoning: Power and Politics in the Civil War South* (Cambridge, MA: Harvard University Press, 2010).

4. Bruce D. Porter, *War and the Rise of the State: The Military Foundations of Modern Politics* (New York: Free Press, 1994); C. A. Bayly, *The Birth of the Modern World, 1780–1914: Global Connections and Comparisons* (Malden, MA: Blackwell, 2004), 199–243; Thomas Bender, *A Nation Among Nations: America's Place in World History* (New York: Hill & Wang, 2006), 116–181; Miguel Angel Centeno, *Blood and Debt: War and the Nation-State in Latin America* (University Park: Pennsylvania State University Press, 2002); John Brewer, *The Sinews of Power: War, Money, and the English State, 1688–1783* (New York: Knopf, 1989); Linda Colley, *Britons: Forging the Nation: 1707–1837* (New Haven, CT: Yale University Press, 1992); Barbara Ehrenreich, *Blood Rites: Origins and History of the Passions of War* (New York: Metropolitan Books, 1997); eds. John L. Comaroff and Paul C. Stern, eds., *Perspectives on Nationalism and War* (London: Gordon & Breach, 1995); George L. Mosse, *Fallen Soldiers: Reshaping the Memory of the World Wars* (New York: Oxford University Press, 1990); Don Higginbotham, "War and State Formation in Revolutionary America," in *Empire and Nation: The American Revolution in the Atlantic World*, ed. Elija H. Gould and Peter S. Onuf (Baltimore: Johns Hopkins University Press, 2005), 54–71; Charles Royster, "Founding a Nation in Blood: Military Conflict and American Nationality," in *Arms and Independence: The Military Character of the American Revolution*, ed. Ronald Hoffman and Peter J. Albert (Charlottesville: University Press of Virginia, 1984), 25–49.

5. Diary of Lucy Wood, January, 1862, Lucy W. Butler Papers, SHC.

6. Davis's inaugural address is reprinted in Davis, *Jefferson Davis: The Essential Writings*, ed. William J. Cooper, Jr. (New York: Modern Library, 2003), 224–229. See Anne Sarah Rubin, "Seventy-six and Sixty-one: Confederates Remember the American Revolution," in *Where These Memories Grow: History, Memory, and Southern Identity*, edited by W. Fitzhugh Brundage (Chapel Hill: University of North Carolina Press, 2000), 85–105; Richard McCaslin, *Lee in the Shadow of Washington* (Baton Rouge: Louisiana State University Press, 2001).

7. G. Ward Hubbs, ed., *Voices from Company D: Diaries by the Greensboro Guards, Fifth Alabama Infantry Regiment, Army of Northern Virginia* (Athens, GA: University of Georgia Press, 2003), 147; Sarah Lois Wadley Diary, February 22, 1864, SHC.

8. "The So-Called United States," *Richmond Examiner*, August 21, 1862.

9. Levi Branson, *First Book in Composition, Applying the Principles of Grammar to the Art of Composing: Also, Giving Full Directions for Punctuation; Especially Designed for the Use of Southern Schools* (Raleigh, NC: Branson, Farrar, 1863), 117–118. Perhaps we should not make too much of this; many Confederate textbooks were only very hastily revised versions of United States editions, and perhaps this Fourth of July section slipped under the radar. See George C. Rable, *The Confederate Republic: A Revolution against Politics* (Chapel Hill: University of North Carolina Press, 1994), 179–183.

10. Edward O. Guerrant, *Bluegrass Confederate: The Headquarters Diary of Edward O. Guerrant*, ed. William C. Davis and Meredith L. Swentor (Baton Rouge: Louisiana State University Press, 1999), 115, 301–302.

11. Edmund Ruffin, *The Diary of Edmund Ruffin*, vol. 2, ed. William Kauffman Scarborough (Baton Rouge: Louisiana State University Press, 1977), 366–367.

12. *Charleston Mercury*, editorial, July 4, 1862; Anita Dwyer Withers Diary, July 4, 1862, SHC; James Johnson Kirkpatrick Diary, July 4, 1862, in *The 16th Mississippi Infantry: Civil War Letters and Reminiscences*, ed. Robert G. Evans (Jackson: University Press of Mississippi, 2002), 90; Ann McCoy to Lois Richardson Davis, July 3, 1864, Lois Richardson Davis Papers, DU.

13. John W. Wood, *Union and Secession in Mississippi* (Memphis, TN: Saunders, Parrish & Whitmore, printers, 1863), in *Southern Unionist Pamphlets and the Civil War* ed. Jon L. Wakleyn (Columbia: University of Missouri Press, 1999), 120–147, quotations at 146, 147. For unionists' feelings toward the U.S. flag, see also Stephen V. Ash, *When the Yankees Came: Conflict and Chaos in the Occupied South, 1861–1865* (Chapel Hill: University of North Carolina Press, 1995), 108–109. For other efforts to align the legacy of 1776 with the unionist cause, see Margaret M. Storey, *Loyalty and Loss: Alabama's Unionists in the Civil War and Reconstruction* (Baton Rouge: Louisiana State University Press, 2004); Noel C. Fisher, "Definitions of Victory: East Tennessee Unionists in the Civil War and Reconstruction," in *Guerrillas, Unionists, and Violence on the Confederate Home Front*, ed. Daniel E. Sutherland (Fayetteville: University of Arkansas Press, 1999), 95.

14. Margaret Nourse Diary, July 4, 1862, "Tuesday" [ca. June 10, 1862], May 26, 1862, VHS.

15. Robert J. Breckinridge, *The Civil War: Its Nature and End* (Cincinnati, OH: Published at the Office of the Danville Review, 1861), 670. See also Daniel E. Sutherland, "Introduction: The Desperate Side of War," and "The Absence of Violence: Confederates and Unionists in Culpeper County," both in Sutherland, *Guerrillas, Unionists, and Violence*, 3–15, 75–87; and Fisher, "Definitions of Victory," esp. 95.

16. Herschel V. Johnson to A. E. Cochran, October 25, 1862 and Johnson to "Several Gentlemen in Middle Georgia," September 25, 1864, newspaper clipping, both in Herschel V. Johnson Papers, DU.

17. Henry St. Paul believed that the Confederacy should have done more to differ-
    entiate its name, its flag, and so on, from the United States: Henry St. Paul, *Our
    Home and Foreign Policy* (Mobile, AL: Printed at the Office of the Daily Register
    and Advertiser, 1863), 9.

18. *Richmond Examiner*, editorial, September 5, 1861; "The War—the Yankee Race,"
    Richmond Examiner, April 24, 1862; *Richmond Examiner*, editorial, December
    16, 1862.

19. G. W. Archer, "Awake!—Arise!," in *War Poetry of the South*, ed. William Gilmore
    Simms (New York: Richardson & Company, 1866), 362–364; Lucy Johnston
    Ambler Diary, July 27, 1863, Ambler-Brown Family Papers, DU; George W.
    Davis to Rebecca Pitchford Davis, July 7, 1863, Rebecca Pitchford Davis Papers,
    SHC. See also Anne Sarah Rubin, *Shattered Nation: The Rise and Fall of the Con-
    federacy, 1861–1868* (Chapel Hill: University of North Carolina Press, 2005),
    86–100; and Bruce Cauthen, "Confederate and Afrikaner Nationalism: Myth,
    Identity, and Gender in Comparative Perspective," PhD diss., University of Lon-
    don, 1999," 123–129; Colley, *Britons*.

20. Robert Kean, diary entry, June 7, 1863, in Kean, *Inside the Confederate Govern-
    ment: The Diary of Robert Garlick Hill Kean*, ed. Edward Younger (New York:
    Oxford University Press, 1957), 69–71. Atrocity stories filled southern newspa-
    pers, diaries, and letters. For a few examples, see Sarah Lois Wadley Diary, July
    22, 1861, SHC; William Bobo, *The Confederate* (Mobile, AL: S. H. Goetzel, 1863);
    Richmond Enquirer, July 4, 1862. Jason Phillips has argued that there were two
    major types of anti-Yankee image—the "inept" and the "barbaric"—the latter of
    which grew more predominant as the war progressed. Jason Phillips, *Diehard
    Rebels*, 40–75.

21. "A Yankee Letter—The Skulls of the 'Rebels,'" *Richmond Examiner*, July 1,
    1862.

22. Lucy Wood Diary, June 7, 1861, in Lucy W. Butler Papers, SHC; Davis, *Essential
    Writings*, 225. As Linda Colley has shown, a similar process took place during
    the American Revolution. Colonists disseminated stories of British atrocities in
    print, increasing perceptions of the dissimilarity of the two sides by portraying
    the British as subhuman invaders. In both cases, this was an effective technique
    for quickly separating from former compatriots who otherwise might not have
    seemed so different at all. And the fact that Britain and the North used non-
    white troops meant that in both cases would-be separatists also used race to
    underline the "otherness" of the would-be unifiers. Linda Colley, *Captives: The
    Story of Britain's Pursuit of Empire and How Its Soldiers and Civilians Were Held
    Captive by the Dream of Global Supremacy, 1600–1850* (New York: Pantheon
    Books, 2002), 222–232.

23. Abstract of proclamation, September 4, 1862, in Davis, *The Papers of Jefferson
    Davis*, ed. Lynda Caswell Christ, vol. 8, *1862* (Baton Rouge: Louisiana State Uni-
    versity Press, 1995), 377.

24. "Yankee Outrages," *Charleston Courier*, July 2, 1862; *Montgomery Advertiser*, October 11, 1864. As Jason Phillips has argued, Confederate culture often represented the Yankee as a threat to all three pillars of southern manhood: the control of white women, African Americans, and land (Jason Phillips, *Diehard Rebels*). For instructive comparisons, see Karen Hagemann, "Of 'Manly Valor' and 'German Honor': Nation, War, and Masculinity in the Age of the Prussian Uprising against Napoleon," *Central European History* 30 (1997): 187–220; Joane Nagel, "Masculinity and Nationalism: Gender and Sexuality in the Making of Nations," *Ethnic and Racial Studies* 21, no. 2 (March 1998): 242–269.

25. Jefferson Davis, speech to congress, November 18, 1861, in Davis, *Papers*, 7:416–417; Jefferson Davis, proclamation, *Richmond Examiner*, August 18, 1863. "Outranges in Mississippi," *Richmond Examiner*, August 18, 1863.

26. "To the Friends of the Cause of the Confederate States," printed circular, Columbia, May 31, 1864, Mary Amarinthia Snowden Papers, USC; *Address to Christians Throughout the World* (Richmond, 1863), 6; *Richmond Examiner*, editorial, July 24, 1862.

27. Judah P. Benjamin to John Slidell, January 8, 1864, Benjamin to Henry Hotze, January 9, 1864, John Slidell to Judah Benjamin, July 25, 1862, all in Records of the Confederate States of America, LOC.

28. *Richmond Enquirer*, March 16, 1863, quoted in Faust, *Creation of Confederate Nationalism*, 13; Robert E. May, *The Union, the Confederacy, and the Atlantic Rim* (West Lafayette, IN: Purdue University Press, 1995), 16–17; St. Paul, *Our Home and Foreign Policy*. On the diplomatic consequences for the American Civil War, see Gregory Louis Mattson, "Pariah Diplomacy: The Slavery Issue in Confederate Foreign Relations" (PhD diss., University of Southern Mississippi, 1999); John Kutolowski, "The Effect of the Polish Insurrection of 1863 on American Civil War Diplomacy," *Historian* 27 (1965): 560–577. An English correspondent of James M. Mason suggested the formation of a European Congress "to settle both the Polish and American Questions, at the same time." Hilton Kay to James Mason, June 13, 1863, James M. Mason Papers, LOC.

29. To be sure, Union emancipation policy was at first met with mixed feelings among Europeans—many of whom agreed with southern critics that this was a desperate, inhumane tactic designed to foment race war in the South. But ultimately the recasting of the war as one between proslavery and emancipation further impeded Confederate diplomatic efforts.

30. The importance of the humanitarian argument can be tracked in the Records of the Confederate States, LOC, and the James M. Mason Papers, LOC.

31. The standard work on Confederate conscription remains Albert Burton Moore, *Conscription and Conflict in the Confederacy* (New York: Macmillan, 1924).

32. Karen Hagemann, "A Valorous *Volk* Family: The Nation, the Military, and the Gender Order in Prussia in the Time of the Anti-Napoleonic Wars, 1806–15," in

Ida Blom, Catherine Hall, and Karen Hagemann, *Gendered Nations: Nationalisms and Gender Order in the Long Nineteenth Century* (Oxford: Berg, 2000), 179–205; Jorn Leonhard, "Nation-States and Wars," in *What is a Nation? Europe 1789–1914*, ed. Timothy Baycroft and Mark Hewitson (Oxford: Oxford University Press, 2006), 231–254; Centeno, *Blood and Debt*, 220–221.

33. George Gordon, *Speech of Hon. George A. Gordon, of Chatham, on the Constitutionality of the Conscription Laws: Passed by the Congress of the Confederate States, Delivered in the Senate of Georgia, on Tuesday, 9th of December, 1862* (Atlanta, GA: Printed at the Office of the Daily Intelligencer, 1862), 13. Opposition to conscription is emphasized in Moore, *Conscription and Conflict*. See also Forrest McDonald, *States' Rights and the Union: Imperium in Imperio* (Lawrence: University Press of Kansas, 2000), 204 ff.; W. Buck Yearns, *The Confederate Congress* (Athens, GA: University of Georgia Press, 1960), 65–66; Richard E. Beringer et al., *Why the South Lost the Civil War* (Athens, GA: University of Georgia Press, 1986), 223–226.

34. Emory M. Thomas, *The Confederate Nation: 1861–1865* (New York: Harper & Row, 1979), 260. This potential power, according to Richard Bensel, represented a fundamental difference in the Union and Confederacy's central authority during the war. Bensel, *Yankee Leviathan*, 130. On Confederate state formation, see also John Majewski, *Modernizing a Slave Economy: The Economic Vision of the Confederate Nation* (Chapel Hill: University of North Carolina Press, 2009).

35. John M. Sacher, "'A Very Disagreeable Business': Confederate Conscription in Louisiana," *Civil War History* 53 (2007): 141–169. More generally, see Ash, *When the Yankees Came*.

36. John Hedrick to Benjamin S. Hedrick, June 20, 1862, Benjamin S. Hedrick Papers, SHC. For more on the "question of sovereignty" in coastal North Carolina, see Wayne K. Durrill, *War of Another Kind: A Southern Community in the Great Rebellion* (New York: Oxford University Press, 1990), chap. 4.

37. John Hedrick to Benjamin S. Hedrick, June 20, 1862, July 27, 1862, August 24, 1862, Benjamin S. Hedrick Papers, SHC.

38. Jubal Early to Robert Young Conrad, January 27, 1864, Holmes Conrad Papers, VHS.

39. William Blair, *Virginia's Private War: Feeding Body and Soul in the Confederacy, 1861–1865* (New York: Oxford University Press, 1998).

40. Thomas H. Haughton to Captain Pearson, June 29, 1864, and July 14, 1864, in Confederate States of America, Bureau of Conscription, 7th North Carolina Congressional District Records, SHC.

41. A similar fusing occurred in response to reports of rape of Serbian women by ethnic Albanians in the 1980s. According to Wendy Bracewell, "a narrative of threatened masculinity . . . reinforced by a more general narrative of gender crisis, offered militarism as a way of winning back both individual manliness

and national dignity." By the mid 1980s, Serbs had even made "nationalist rape" a separate and more serious offense than conventional rape, illuminating the fusion of nationalism and sexuality. Bracewell, "Rape in Kosovo: Masculinity and Serbian Nationalism," *Nations and Nationalism* 6, no. 4 (October 2000): 567.

42. Robert E. Bonner, *Colors and Blood: Flag Passions of the Confederate South* (Princeton, NJ: Princeton University Press, 2002), 110–114.

43. A. J. Requier, "Our Faith in '61"; Paul Hamilton Hayne, "My Mother-Land"; Alexander B. Meek, "Wouldst Thou Have me Love Thee"; all in Simms, *War Poetry of the South*, 58–60, 117–123, 61–62. Meek's poem is strikingly similar to his Mexican War ode "The Fields of Mexico," which appeared in his collection *Songs and Poems of the South* (Mobile, AL: S. H. Goetzel & Co., 1857), 9–12. This similarity is a perfect example of how wartime nationalism drew on prewar tropes.

44. Diary entries, September 1, 1861, September 9, 1865, Elizabeth Collier Diary, SHC. See also entry for January 4, 1865, Grace Elmore Diary, SHC.

45. Harry Lewis to mother, May 15, 1863, Harry Lewis Papers, SCHS. See Stephen W. Berry II, *All That Makes a Man: Love and Ambition in the Civil War South* (New York: Oxford University Press, 2003).

46. Private O. Goddin to Gov. Vance, February 27, 1863, in *North Carolina Civil War Documentary*, ed. W. Buck Yearns and John G. Barrett (Chapel Hill: University of North Carolina Press, 1980), 97–99. For more on different kinds of tensions and connections between family and nation, see Aaron Sheehan-Dean, *Why Confederates Fought: Family and Nation in Civil War Virginia* (Chapel Hill: University of North Carolina Press, 2007), and Chandra Manning, *What This Cruel War was Over: Soldiers, Slavery, and the Civil War* (New York: Knopf, 2007).

47. Confederate States of America, Bureau of Conscription, 7th North Carolina Congressional District Records, SHC; Paul D. Escott, *After Secession: Jefferson Davis and the Failure of Confederate Nationalism* (Baton Rouge: Louisiana State University Press, 1978), 135–167; McCurry, *Confederate Reckoning*; Blair, *Virginia's Private War*, 5, passim; Victoria Bynum, "'War within a War': Women's Participation in the Revolt of the North Carolina Piedmont, 1863–1865," *Frontiers* 9 (1987): 43–49. Blair shows that local communities initially attempted to deal with the economic problems caused by mobilization, but they were quickly overwhelmed and *had* to turn to state and national governments for support.

48. McCurry, *Confederate Reckoning*; Laura Edwards, *Scarlett Doesn't Live Here Anymore: Southern Women in the Civil War Era* (Urbana: University of Illinois Press, 2000), 93; Rable, *Civil Wars*, 73–90.

49. D. K. McRae, *On Love of Country: An Address Delivered Before the Young Ladies of the Clio Society of Oxford Female College, June 2nd, 1862* (Raleigh, NC: Strother

and Marcom, 1864), 6–7. The year 1862 in the title is a misprint; it should read 1864.

50. *The Education of Teachers in the South* (Lynchburg, VA: Virginian Power-Press Book and Job Office, 1864), 3, 15.

51. Women's involvement in public-private partnerships was fairly common in the nineteenth-century United States. See Brian Balogh, *A Government Out of Sight: The Mystery of National Authority in Nineteenth-Century America* (Cambridge, UK: Cambridge University Press, 2009).

52. From Mississippi and Alabama Citizens to Jefferson Davis, October 13, 1862, in Davis, *Papers*, vol. 7; Caroline Howard Gilman to her children, March 27, 1863, Caroline Howard Gilman Papers, SCHS; copy of letter from Stephen R. Mallory to Richard Yeadon, February 27, 1864, Mary Amarinthia Snowden Papers, USC. The limitations of the transformation are illustrated by the fact that Mallory sent the letter to Yeadon rather than to the "noble women" themselves. According to Linda Kerber, a similar ambiguity characterized female citizenship claims during the revolutionary era: although women were denied the formal status of male citizens, they were clearly crucial members of the newly United States. Kerber, "May All Our Citizens be Soldiers and All Our Soldiers Citizens: The Ambiguities of Female Citizenship in the New Nation," in *Women, Militarism, and War: Essays in History, Politics, and Social Theory*, ed. Jean Bethke Elshtain and Sheila Tobias (Savage, MD: Rowman and Littlefield, 1990): 89–103.

53. Mary Amarinthia Snowden Papers, USC.

54. See Elizabeth R. Varon, *We Mean to Be Counted: White Women and Politics in Antebellum Virginia* (Chapel Hill: University of North Carolina Press, 1998).

55. Entry for May 13, 1865, Sarah Lois Wadley diary; Lou [Haillee?] to Amelia, ca. 1865, Benjamin H. Teague Papers, USC.

56. McCurry, *Confederate Reckoning*; Bruce C. Levine, *Confederate Emancipation: Southern Plans to Free and Arm Slaves During the Civil War* (New York: Oxford University Press, 2006).

57. John Thurman to Sallie Ecklin Thurman, March 17, 1862, May 24, 1862, John Thurman and Sallie Ecklin Thurman Papers, SHC.

58. John Thurman to Sallie Ecklin Thurman, February 20, 1865, March 6, 1865, John Thurman and Sallie Ecklin Thurman Papers, SHC.

59. See Wakelyn, *Southern Unionist Pamphlets*.

60. On the negative image of "speculators," see Faust, *Creation of Confederate Nationalism*, 41–57.

61. Sutherland, *Guerrillas, Unionists, and Violence*. Herschel Johnson distinguished between nationalism and political dissent, writing that "independance is not Good Government. It is simply, separate nationality." Johnson to A. E. Cochran, October 8, 1862, Johnson Papers, DU.

62. Davis, *Essential Writings*, 229. See also Rubin, *Shattered Nation*, 50–52; Blair, *Virginia's Private War*; Judkin Browning, "Removing the Mask of Nationality: Unionism, Racism, and Federal Military Occupation in North Carolina, 1862–1865," *Journal of Southern History* 71, no. 3 (Aug 2005): 589–620; Sheehan-Dean, *Why Confederates Fought*; Jacqueline Glass Campbell, *When Sherman Marched North from the Sea: Resistance on the Confederate Home Front* (Chapel Hill: University of North Carolina Press, 2003).

63. Ernest Renan, "What Is a Nation?" in *Nation and Narration*, ed. Homi K. Bhabha (New York: Routledge, 1990), 19.

64. Joshua Searle-White, *The Psychology of Nationalism* (New York: Palgrave, 2001), esp. 94.

65. Anthony D. Smith, *Chosen Peoples: Sacred Sources of National Identity* (Oxford: Oxford University Press, 2004), 219. See also Lloyd Kramer, *Nationalism: Political Cultures in Europe and America, 1775–1865* (New York: Twayne, 1998), 77–83; Mosse, *Fallen Soldiers*.

66. On Civil War Americans' attitudes toward death, see Drew Gilpin Faust, *This Republic of Suffering: Death and the American Civil War* (New York: Knopf, 2008); Mark S. Schantz, *Awaiting the Heavenly Country: The Civil War and America's Culture of Death* (Ithaca, NY: Cornell University Press, 2008).

67. Palmer speech reprinted in the *Bellville (TX) Countryman*, July 10, 1861; J. Quitman Moore, "The Belligerents," *De Bow's Review* 31, no. 1 (July 1861): 70.

68. M. A. Jennings, "Cleburne," in Simms, *War Poetry of the South*, 280–281; Sarah Lois Wadley Diary, April 13, 1862, SHC; "The Battle of Richmond," *Charleston Mercury*, July 7, 1862. See also McRae, *On Love of Country*, 5, 14.

69. James L. Petigru to Carey, July 4, 1862, James L. Petigru Papers, LOC.

70. Diary entry, October 28, 1861, Lucy Wood Diary, Lucy W. Butler Papers, SHC (Wood was Lucy W. Butler's maiden name); John Lewis to mother, June 10, 1864 (misdated as 1863), Lewis Papers, SHC.

71. Thomas's letter quoted in Rebecca Pitchford Davis to Burwell, December 20, 1863, Rebecca Pitchford Davis Papers, SHC.

72. Obituary, *Raleigh Christian Advocate*, November 25, 1864, in Rebecca Pitchford Davis Papers, SHC.

73. Stacey Jean Klein, "Wielding the Pen: Margaret Preston, Confederate Nationalist Literature, and the Expansion of a Woman's Place in the South," *Civil War History* 49, no. 3 (September 2003): 221–234. For a similar example, see Connie Lester, "Lucy Virginia French: Out of the Bitterness of My Heart," in *The Human Tradition in Civil War and Reconstruction*, ed. Steven E. Woodworth (Wilmington, DE: Scholarly Resources, 2000).

74. Richard E. Jaques to Lute, June 13, 1864, Richard E. Jaques Letters, DU.

75. Captain William E. Tysinger Broadside, VHS; obituary of J. Beverley Stanard, *Richmond Examiner*, July 7, 1864; Benjamin M. Palmer, *Address Delivered at the*

Funeral of General Maxcy Gregg, in the Presbyterian Church, Columbia, SC, December 20, 1862 (Columbia, SC: Southern Guardian Steam-Power Press, 1863), 7–8. Palmer viewed Gregg's sacrifice as being for the state of South Carolina as much as for the Confederacy as a whole, but the two objects of allegiance seemed to be complementary rather than conflicting.

76. Diary entry, July 28, 1863, Kate D. Foster Diary, DU. See also John T. Wood to Lola (his wife), May 5, 1862, John Taylor Wood Papers, SHC.

77. Drew Gilpin Faust has also recognized the blurring of religious and nationalist justifications of death sacrifice (Faust, *This Republic of Suffering*, esp. 189.) See also Bonner, *Mastering America*, 241–251. On Confederates' religion more generally, see Jason Phillips, *Diehard Confederates* (Athens, GA: University of Georgia Press, 2007), 9–39.

78. Diary entry, December 23, 1861, Elmore Diary; *Patriotic Prayer for the Southern Cause*, VHS; Henry H. Tucker, *God in the War: A Sermon Delivered Before the Legislature of Georgia, in the Capitol at Milledgeville, on Friday, November 15, 1861, Being a Day Set Apart for Fasting, Humiliation and Prayer, by His Excellency the President of the Confederate States* (Milledgeville, GA: Boughton, Nisbet & Barnes, State Printers, 1861).

79. John Paris, *A Sermon: Preached Before Brig.-gen. Hoke's Brigade, at Kinston, N.C., on the 28th of February, 1864, Upon the Death of Twenty-two Men, Who Had Been Executed in the Presence of the Brigade for the Crime of Desertion* (Greensborough, NC: A. W. Ingold & Co., 1864), 12.

80. George F. Pierce, *The Word of God a Nation's Life: A Sermon Preached Before the Bible Convention of the Confederate States, Augusta, Georgia, March 19th, 1862* (Augusta, GA: Constitutionalist, 1862), 5, 10, 11; Anthony D. Smith, *Chosen Peoples*, esp. 51, 94; Cauthen, "Confederate and Afrikaner Nationalism," 46–56.

81. H. C. Kendrick to mother and father, March 9, 1863, H. C. Kendrick Papers, SHC; Thomas Davis to Rebecca Pitchford Davis, September 16, 1864, Rebecca Pitchford Davis Papers, SHC. On religion in the Confederate armies, see Drew Gilpin Faust, "Christian Soldiers: The Meaning of Revivalism in the Confederate Army," *Journal of Southern History* 53, no. 1 (1987): 63–90.

82. John Hendricks Kinyoun to wife, July 10, 1864, John H. Kinyoun Papers, SHC; letters from John W. Hudson, February 28, 1862; James Hancock, March 1, 1862, in Davis, *Papers*, vol. 8; "Circular [on Sabbath Mails]," Batesville, MS, January 4, 1862, Rare Book Collection, University of North Carolina at Chapel Hill; "To the People of the Southern Confederacy," broadside, VHS. See also Herschel V. Johnson to A. E. Cochran, November 16, 1861, Johnson Papers, DU. On calls to reform slavery, see Faust, *Creation of Confederate Nationalism*.

83. See especially Beringer et al., *Why the South Lost*.

84. Faust, *Creation of Confederate Nationalism*, chap. 3.

85. L. J. Morgan Letter (to sister), June 8, 1864, ADAH; Charles Fenton James to Emma James, February 13, 1865, Charles Fenton James Letters, VHS.

86. Walter Lenoir to Rufus Lenoir, February 20, 1862, Lenoir Family Papers, SHC; William L. Barney, *The Making of a Confederate: Walter Lenoir's Civil War* (Oxford: Oxford University Press, 2008).

87. William Bingham to Walter Lenoir, December 1, 1863, Lenoir Family Papers, SHC.

88. Collier diary, April 11, 1862, July 3, 1862; *Richmond Examiner*, editorial, March 6, 1862.

89. Kate D. Foster Diary, July 30, 1863, DU; H. C. Kendrick to parents, January 6, 1863, H. C. Kendrick Papers, SHC. As Kurt Berends has observed, "both Christianity and nationalism posit a role for violence in salvation." Kurt O. Berends, "Confederate Sacrifice and the 'Redemption' of the South," in *Religion in the American South: Protestants and Others in History and Culture*, ed. Beth Barton Schweiger and Donald G. Mathews (Chapel Hill: University of North Carolina Press, 2004), 99–123, quotation at 109. See also Mitchell Snay, *The Gospel of Disunion: Religion and Separatism in the Antebellum South* (1993; Chapel Hill: University of North Carolina Press, 1997).

90. For Paraguay, China, and other contemporaneous examples, see Bender, *Nation among Nations*.

91. Paris, *Sermon*, 12; Elliott quoted in Charles Reagan Wilson, *Baptized in Blood: The Religion of the Lost Cause* (Athens, GA: University of Georgia Press, 1980), 5. Wilson shows that a belief that the Confederacy had been "baptized in blood" went on to underpin the "civil religion" of the Lost Cause after 1865.

CONCLUSION

1. David W. Blight, *Race and Reunion: The Civil War in American Memory* (Cambridge, MA: Harvard University Press, 2001); Gaines M. Foster, *Ghosts of the Confederacy: Defeat, the Lost Cause, and the Emergence of the New South* (New York: Oxford University Press, 1987); Charles Reagan Wilson, *Baptized in Blood: The Religion of the Lost Cause* (Athens, GA: University of Georgia Press, 1980); W. Fitzhugh Brundage, *The Southern Past: A Clash of Race and Memory* (Cambridge, MA: Harvard University Press, 2005).

Bibliography

MANUSCRIPT SOURCES

Alabama Department of Archives and History, Montgomery, Alabama

J. Minerva Abercrombie Letter
Curry Family Papers
Margaret Josephine Gillis Diary
William Proctor Gould Diary
James G. Hudson Diary
Roland Jones Letters
E. Lewis Letter
L. J. Morgan Letter
John Pelham Papers
C. A. Ryder, Mobile Rifles Diary
Senter Family Papers
William Lowndes Yancey Papers

Filson Historical Society, Louisville, Kentucky

Bodley Family Papers
Brown-Ewell Family Papers
Clark-Strater-Watson Family Papers
Cox Family Journal
Reuben Durrett Papers
Green Family Papers
Grigsby Family Papers
Kentucky Confederate Provisional Government Records
Preston Family Papers

Secession Calling Card
Henry L. Stone Papers
Tucker Family Papers
Uncle Billy Letter
William L. Yancey Letter
Yandell Family Papers

Library of Congress, Manuscript Department, Washington, D.C.

William G. Brownlow Papers
John J. Crittenden Papers
George Eustis Papers
Henry Gourdin Papers
Isham G. Harris Papers
Henry Hotze Papers
Duncan F. Kenner Papers
James M. Mason Papers
James L. Petigru Papers
Records of the Confederate States of America
William C. Rives Papers
John Newton Waddel Diary
William Henry Trescot Papers
Louis T. Wigfall Family Papers

Rare Book, Manuscript, and Special Collections Library, Perkins Library,
Duke University, Durham, North Carolina

Ambler-Brown Family Papers
George Booker Papers
Lois Richardson Davis Papers
Jasper Davis Papers
Kate D. Foster Diary
Great Britain, Consulate, Savannah, Papers
Henry W. Hilliard Papers
Richard E. Jaques Letters
Herschel V. Johnson Papers
John Hendricks Kinyoun Papers
Ladies Volunteer Aid Society of the Pine Hills, Minutes
Alexander Beaufort Meek Papers
Minutes of the Proceedings of the Greenville Ladies Association
Nathaniel Niles Papers
Ellen E. Peirce Papers

Nathaniel Beverley Tucker Papers
W. M. Willcox Papers
James M. Wright Collection

South Carolina Historical Society, Charleston, South Carolina

Barnwell Family Papers
Chesnut Family Papers
R. Y. Dwight Scrapbook
Caroline Howard Gilman Papers
Journal of the Whig Association
Nelson Mitchell Papers
Robert Barnwell Rhett Papers
Southern Rights Association of St. John's Berkeley and St. Stephen's Papers
Stuart Family Papers
Henry Pinckney Walker Papers

South Caroliniana Library, University of South Carolina, Columbia,
South Carolina

Lewis Malone Ayer Papers
Milledge Luke Bonham Papers
Preston Brooks Papers
Constitution of Minute Men, for the Defence of Southern Rights
Ann Pamela Cunningham Papers
William Henry Gist Papers
Paul Hamilton Hayne Papers
Minute Men, Saluda Association, Minutes, 1860
Robert Barnwell Rhett Papers
Charles Carroll Simms Collection
Mary Amarinthia Snowden Papers
William Henry Trescot Papers

Southern Historical Collection, Wilson Library, University of North Carolina,
Chapel Hill, North Carolina

Mary Ann Albinson Papers
James Lusk Alcorn Papers
Mary Jeffreys Bethell Diary
Thomas Bragg Diary
Lucy Wood Butler Papers
Kate S. Carney Diary

Elizabeth Collier Diary

Confederate States of America, Bureau of Conscription, 7th North Carolina Congressional District Records

Susan Cornwall Diary

Dabney Cosby Papers

Allen Turner Davidson Papers

Rebecca Pitchford Davis Papers

Wilse Dial Letter

Grace B. Elmore Papers

David Gavin Diary

Charles Iverson Graves Papers

Percy Spain Hartwell Diary

Benjamin Sherwood Hedrick Papers

William H. Holcombe Papers

H. C. Kendrick Papers

Lenoir Family Papers

Harry Lewis Papers

Christopher G. Memminger Papers

Anna Mercur Papers

William Porcher Miles Papers

James G. Ramsay Papers

Robert Barnwell Rhett Papers

Joseph Sams Papers

Whitemarsh Seabrook Papers

James H. Stanley Papers

John Thurman and Sallie Ecklin Thurman Papers

Sarah Lois Wadley Diary

Williamson Whitehead Diary

Anita Dwyer Withers Diary

John Taylor Wood Papers

Benjamin C. Yancey Papers

Virginia Historical Society, Richmond, Virginia

Aylett Family Papers

John N. Cadwallader Papers

Holmes Conrad Papers

Robert Young Conrad Papers

Stapleton Crutchfield Speech

Samuella Hart Curd Diary

Hunter Family Papers

Charles Fenton James Letters

Larue Family Papers

John Letcher Papers

Lunsford Lindsay Lomax Letter

Daniel H. London Papers

Josiah Staunton Moore Papers

John Quincy Adams Nadenbousch Papers

Margaret Nourse Diary

Pegram Family Papers

Record of the Organization and Transactions of the Central Southern Rights Association of Virginia

Edmund Ruffin Papers

George P. C. Rumbough Speech

Rutherfoord Family Papers

Elliott L. Story Diary

Captain William E. Tysinger Broadside

J. L. Valentine Petition

Frederick E. Wimberly Speech

David Levy Yulee Letter

PERIODICALS

Bellville (TX) Countryman, 1861–65.

Brownlow's Knoxville Whig, 1848–65.

Charleston Courier, 1860–63.

Charleston Mercury, 1855–56, 1861–64.

Columbus (GA) Enquirer, 1848–63.

De Bow's Review, 1851–61.

Montgomery Advertiser, 1861.

Mobile Daily Register, 1851–62.

Richmond Enquirer, 1848–64.

Richmond Examiner, 1861–64.

Richmond Whig, 1849–61.

Rising Sun (Newberry, SC), 1858.

Russell's Magazine, 1857–58.

Southern Literary Messenger, 1848–64.

Southern Quarterly Review, 1848–64.

Texas Republican (Marshall, TX), 1849–61.

Vicksburg Whig, 1848–56.

PUBLISHED PRIMARY SOURCES

Address to Christians throughout the World. Richmond, 1863.

Avery, William Waightstill. *Address Delivered before the Two Literary Societies of the University of North Carolina, June 4, 1851.* Raleigh, NC: William W. Holden, 1851.

Ayer, Lewis M. *An Address on the Question of Separate State Secession, to the People of Barnwell District*. Charleston, SC: Steam-Power Press of Walker & James, 1851.

———. *Patriotism and State Sovereignty: An Oration, Delivered before the Two Societies of the South-Carolina College, on the Fourth of December, 1858*. Charleston, SC: Printed by A. J. Burke, 1859.

———. *Southern Rights and the Cuban Question: An Address, Delivered at Whippy Swamp, on the Fourth of July, 1855*. Charleston, SC: A. J. Burke, 1855.

Barbour, B. Johnson. *An Address Delivered before the Literary Societies of the Virginia Military Institute, at Lexington, on the 4th of July, 1854*. Richmond, VA: Macfarlane & Fergusson, 1854.

Belz, Herman, ed. *The Webster-Hayne Debate on the Nature of the Union: Selected Documents*. Indianapolis: Liberty Fund, 2000.

Bobo, William. *The Confederate*. Mobile, AL: S. H. Goetzel, 1863.

Branson, Levi. *First Book in Composition, Applying the Principles of Grammar to the Art of Composing: Also, Giving Full Directions for Punctuation; Especially Designed for the Use of Southern Schools*. Raleigh, NC: Branson, Farrar, 1863.

Breckinridge, Robert J. *The Civil War: Its Nature and End*. Cincinnati, OH: Published at the Office of the Danville Review, 1861.

———. *Discourse of Dr. R. J. Breckinridge, Delivered on the Day of National Humiliation, January 4, 1861*. Lexington, KY, 1861.

Brown, Albert Gallatin. 1863. *State of the Country: Speech of Hon. A. G. Brown, of Mississippi, in the Confederate Senate, December 24, 1863*. Available online, http://docsouth.unc.edu/imls/browna/menu.html.

Calhoun, John C. *The Papers of John C. Calhoun*. Edited by Clyde N. Wilson. 28 vols. Columbia: University of South Carolina Press, 1959–2003.

Carroll, Bartholomew R. *"The Claims of Historical Studies upon the Youth of Our Country": An Oration Delivered before the Polytechnic and Calliopean Societies, of the Citadel Academy, at their Annual Commencement, April 8th, 1859*. Charleston, SC: Walker, Evans & Co., 1859.

Carroll, Bartholomew, and B. F. Porter. *Speeches of Hon. B. F. Porter, and B. R. Carroll, Esq., Delivered before the Association of the Friends of Irish Independence, in Charleston, So. Ca., on Wednesday Evening, May 31st, 1848*. Charleston, SC: Burges, James & Paxton, Printers, 1848.

Caruthers, E. W. *A Discourse Delivered at the Alamance Academy, July 4th, 1848*. Greensborough, NC: Printed by Swaim and Sherwood, 1848.

Cherry, Conrad, ed. *God's New Israel: Religious Interpretations of American Destiny*. Rev. ed. Chapel Hill: University of North Carolina Press, 1998.

Cheves, Langdon. *Speech of Hon. Langdon Cheves, in the Southern Convention, at Nashville, Tennessee, November 14, 1850*. N.p.: Southern Rights Association, 1850.

City Celebration of the Anniversary of the National Independence, at Lafayette Square, New Orleans, LA, July 4th, 1864. New Orleans: Printed at the Era Steam Book and Job Office, 1864.

Clark, William L., Jr., *Importance of Integrity of National Character: An Oration, Delivered by Invitation of the Citizens of Winchester, Virginia, in the Old Lutheran Church, July 4, 1853.* Winchester, VA: Printed by Senseney & Coffroth, 1853.

Coit, J. C. *A Discourse upon Governments, Divine and Human: Prepared by Appointment of the Presbytery of Harmony, and Delivered before That Body During Its Sessions in Indiantown Church, Williamsburg District, S.C., April, 1853.* Columbia, SC: Printed by T. F. Greneker, 1853.

Commager, Henry Steele, ed. *The Civil War Archive: The History of the Civil War in Documents.* Revised by Erik Bruun. New York: Black Dog & Leventhal, 2000.

Comrades of the Southern Cross: Constitution of the Southern Cross, adopted August 28th, 1863. Macon, GA: Burke, Boykin, 1863.

Craik, James. *The Union: National and State Sovereignty Alike Essential to American Liberty: A Discourse Delivered in the Hall of the House of Representatives at the Capitol in Frankfort, Ky., December 19, 1859.* Louisville, KY: Morton & Griswold, 1860.

Cumming, Kate. *The Journal of Kate Cumming: A Confederate Nurse, 1862–1865.* Edited by Harwell, Richard. Savannah, GA: Beehive, 1975.

Curry, Jabez L. M. *Perils and Duty of the South: Substance of a Speech Delivered by Jabez L. M. Curry, in Talladega, Alabama, November 26, 1860.* N.p.: Printed by Lemuel Towers, 1860.

Dabney, Robert L. *The Christian's Best Motive for Patriotism: A Sermon, Preached in the College Church, Hampden Sidney, VA, on the 1st of November, 1860, a General Fast Day, Appointed by the Synod of Virginia, to Pray for Escape from National Convulsions.* Richmond, VA: Chas. H. Wynne, Printer, 1860.

Davis, Jefferson. *Jefferson Davis: The Essential Writings.* Edited by William J. Cooper, Jr. New York: Modern Library, 2003.

———. *The Papers of Jefferson Davis.* Edited by Lynda Laswell Crist. 12 vols. Baton Rouge: Louisiana State University Press, 1971–.

Dawson, Andrew H. H. *An Oration on the Origin, Purposes and Claims of the Ladies' Mt. Vernon Association.* Savannah, GA: E. J. Purse, Printer, 1858.

Dumond, Dwight L., ed. *Southern Editorials on Secession.* New York: Century Co., 1931.

Dunwody, Charles A. *Address of Charles A. Dunwody, before the Citizens of Roswell and the Roswell Guards, July 4, A.D. 1860.* Marietta, GA: Statesman Book and Job Office Print, 1860.

The Education of Teachers in the South. Lynchburg, VA: Virginian Power-Press Book and Job Office, 1864.

Evans, Robert G., ed. *The 16th Mississippi Infantry: Civil War Letters and Reminiscences.* Jackson: University Press of Mississippi, 2002.

Everson, Guy R., and Edward H. Simpson, Jr., eds. *"Far, Far From Home": The War-time Letters of Dick and Tally Simpson, Third South Carolina Volunteers*. New York: Oxford University Press, 1994.

Fitzhugh, George. *Cannibals All! Or, Slaves without Masters*. Edited by C. Vann Wood-ward. Cambridge, MA: Belknap Press of Harvard University Press, 1960.

Freehling, William, ed. *The Nullification Era: A Documentary Record*. New York: Harper & Row, 1967.

Gadsden, Christopher P. *Duty to God not to be Overlooked in Duty to the State: A Ser-mon, Preached at St. Luke's Church, Charleston, S.C., on the Twenty-Third Sunday after Trinity, November 11, 1860*. Charleston, SC: Steam-Power Presses of Evans and Cogswell, 1860.

Gilman, Samuel, and William D. Porter. *Proceedings of the Semi-Centennial Celebra-tion of the Washington Light Infantry, 22d and 23d February, 1857*. Charleston, SC: Walker and Evans, 1857.

Gordon, George. *Speech of Hon. George A. Gordon, of Chatham, on the Constitutional-ity of the Conscription Laws: Passed by the Congress of the Confederate States, Deliv-ered in the Senate of Georgia, on Tuesday, 9th of December, 1862*. Atlanta, GA: Printed at the Office of the Daily Intelligencer, 1862.

Grayson, William J. *The Hireling and the Slave, Chicora, and Other Poems*. Charleston, SC: McCarter & Co., 1856.

———. *Letter to His Excellency Whitemarsh B. Seabrook, Governor of the State of South-Carolina, on the Dissolution of the Union*. Charleston, SC: A. E. Miller, 1850.

Guerrant, Edward O. *Bluegrass Confederate: The Headquarters Diary of Edward O. Guerrant*. Edited by William C. Davis and Meredith L. Swentor. Baton Rouge: Louisiana State University Press, 1999.

Hammond, James H. *Selections from the Letters and Speeches of the Hon. James H. Hammond*. Edited by Clyde N. Wilson. Spartanburg, SC: Reprint Company, 1978. First published 1866 by J. F. Trow and Co., Printers.

Hanckel, Thomas M. *Government, and the Right of Revolution: An Oration, Delivered before the '76 Association, and Cincinnati Society, on Monday, July 4th, 1859, by Thos. M. Hanckel, Esq., a Member of the '76 Association*. Charleston, SC: Printed by A. J. Burke, 1859.

Handy, Isaac W. K. *Our National Sins: A Sermon, Delivered in the First Presbyterian Church, Portsmouth, VA, on the Day of Fasting, Humiliation, and Prayer, January 4, 1861*. Portsmouth, VA: Printed at the Office of the Daily and Weekly Transcript, 1861.

Hilliard, Henry W. *The Spirit of Liberty: An Oration Delivered before the Literary Soci-eties of the University of Virginia on the 27th July, 1859*. Montgomery, AL: Barrett & Wimbish, 1860.

Holcombe, James P. *Sketches of the Political Issues and Controversies of the Revolution: A Discourse, Delivered before the Virginia Historical Society, at their Ninth Annual Meeting, January 17, 1856*. Richmond, VA: Published by the Society, 1856.

Holden, W. W. *Oration Delivered in the City of Raleigh, North Carolina, July 4th, 1856.* Raleigh, NC: Holden & Wilson, "Standard" Office, 1856.

Holmes, George F. *The Virginia Colony; Or the Relation of the English Colonial Settlements in America to the General History of the Civilized World: An Address Delivered at the Annual Meeting of the Virginia Historical Society, at Richmond, December 15, 1859.* Richmond, VA: Chas. H. Wynne, Printer, 1860.

Hubbs, G. Ward, ed., *Voices from Company D: Diaries by the Greensboro Guards, Fifth Alabama Infantry Regiment, Army of Northern Virginia.* Athens, GA: University of Georgia Press, 2003.

Jacobs, Ferdinand. *The Committing of Our Cause to God: A Sermon Preached in the Second Presbyterian Church, Charleston, S.C., on Friday, the 6th of December; A Day of Fasting, Humiliation, and Prayer, Appointed by the Legislature of South Carolina, in View of the State of Our Federal Relations.* Charleston, SC: A. J. Burke, 1850.

Kean, Robert Garlick Hill. *Inside the Confederate Government: The Diary of Robert Garlick Hill Kean.* Edited by Edward Younger. New York: Oxford University Press, 1957.

Landis, Robert W. *The Duty and Obligations of American Citizens in Relation to the Union: An Oration Pronounced in Somerset, Kentucky, on February 22, 1860.* Somerset, KY: White & Barron, 1860.

Lanneau, Fleetwood. *Oration Delivered before the Cincinnati, and the '76 Association, July 4, 1857.* Charleston, SC: Steam Power Press of Walker, Evans & Co., 1857.

Lauter, Paul, Richard Yarborough, and Juan Bruce-Novoa, eds. *The Heath Anthology of American Literature.* 2nd ed. 2 vols. Lexington, MA: Heath, 1994.

Lochrane, O. A. *An Oration, Delivered before the Hibernian and Irish Union Societies of Savannah, on the 18th March, 1850.* Savannah, GA, G. N. Nichols, 1850.

London, Daniel H. *Speech of Daniel H. London on the Commercial, Agricultural & Intellectual Independence of Virginia and the South, Delivered in the Hall of the House of Delegates on the Night of the 5th January 1860; and his Letter to Joseph Segar, Esq, Respecting the Pilot Laws.* Richmond, VA: Printed at Enquirer Book and Job Office, 1860.

Lyon, Theodoric C. *Do the Times Demand a Southern Confederacy? The Constitutionality, Rightfulnesss & Expediency of Secession.* Columbus, MS: privately printed, 1861.

McCrady, John. *"Home Education a Necessity of the South": An Oration Delivered before the Chrestomathic Society of the College of Charleston, on Friday March 2d, 1860.* Charleston, SC: Steam Power Presses of Walker, Evans, & Co., 1860.

———. *A System of Independent Research, the Chief Educational Want of the South: An Address Delivered before the Society of the Alumni of the College of Charleston, at the Inauguration of the Charleston College Library.* Charleston, SC: Printed by A. J. Burke, 1856.

McCulloh, Anthony. *An Oration Delivered before the Oglethorpe Light Infantry, at Woodhome Near Savannah.* Savannah, GA: Purse's Print, 1856.

McRae, D. K. *On Love of Country: An Address Delivered before the Young Ladies of the Clio Society of Oxford Female College, June 2nd, 1862.* Raleigh, NC: Strother and Marcom, 1864.

Meek, Alexander Beaufort. *Americanism in Literature: an Oration before the Phi Kappa and Demosthenian Societies of the University of Georgia, at Athens, August 8, 1844.* Charleston, SC: Burges and James, Printers, 1844.

Meek, A. B. *Songs and Poems of the South.* Mobile, AL: S. H. Goetzel & Co., 1857.

Mikell, William E. *Oration Delivered before the Washington Light Infantry on their Fifty-Second Anniversary, at the Institute Hall, February 22, 1859.* Charleston, SC: Steam Power Press of Walker, Evans & Co., 1859.

Miles, William Porcher. *Oration Delivered before the Fourth of July Association.* Charleston, SC: James S. Burges, 1849.

Miller, Henry W. *Address Delivered before the Philanthropic and Dialectic Societies of the University of North Carolina, June 3, 1857.* Raleigh, NC: Holden & Wilson, 1857.

Mitchel, John. *The Last Conquest of Ireland (Perhaps).* Edited by Patrick Maume. Dublin: University College Dublin Press, 2005.

Mitchell, Nelson. *Oration, Delivered before the Fourth of July Association, by Nelson Mitchell, Esq., on the Fourth of July, 1848.* Charleston, SC: James S. Burges, 1849.

Morgan, Sarah. *The Civil War Diary of a Southern Woman.* Edited by Charles East. New York: Simon & Schuster, 1991.

Nicholas, S. S. *South Carolina, Disunion, and a Mississippi Valley Confederacy.* Louisville, KY, 1860.

Nisbet, Eugenius Aristides. *Address on the Seventy-third Anniversary of American Independence (July 4th., 1849): Delivered at the Request of a Committee on Behalf of the Citizens of Macon.* Macon, GA: Rose, 1849.

Palmer, Benjamin M. *Address Delivered at the Funeral of General Maxcy Gregg, in the Presbyterian Church, Columbia, S.C., December 20, 1862.* Columbia, SC: Southern Guardian Steam-Power Press, 1863.

———. *Influence of Religious Belief upon National Character: An Oration Delivered before the Demosthenian and Phi Kappa Societies of the University of Georgia, August 7, 1845.* Athens, GA: Printed at the Banner Office, 1845.

———. *The South: Her Peril and Duty.* In Wakelyn, *Southern Pamphlets on Secession,* 63–77.

Paris, John. *A Sermon: Preached before Brig.-gen. Hoke's Brigade, at Kinston, N.C., on the 28th of February, 1864, upon the Death of Twenty-two Men, Who Had Been Executed in the Presence of the Brigade for the Crime of Desertion.* Greensborough, NC: A. W. Ingold & Co., 1864.

Petherbridge, Rev. C. W. *Christian Warriors.* Richmond, VA: Soldiers' Tract Association, n.d.

Pettigrew, James Johnston. *Notes on Spain and the Spaniards, in the Summer of 1859, with a Glance at Sardinia: By a Carolinian.* Charleston, SC: Steam-Power Presses of Evans & Cogswell, 1861.

Pierce, George F. *The Word of God a Nation's Life: A Sermon Preached before the Bible Convention of the Confederate States, Augusta, Georgia, March 19th, 1862.* Augusta, GA: Constitutionalist, 1862.

Pinckney, Henry L., Jr. *An Oration Delivered on the Fourth of July 1851, before the '76 and Cincinnati Societies.* Charleston, SC: Printed by A. E. Miller, 1851.

Porcher, Frederick A. *An Oration Delivered before the Inhabitants of Pineville, So. Ca., on Monday, July 4, 1831, the 56th Anniversary of the Declaration of American Independence.* Charleston, SC: Printed by J. S. Burges, 1831.

Porter, David H. *Religion and the State: A Discourse Delivered in the First Presbyterian Church, Savannah, Georgia, July 4th, 1858.* Savannah, GA: Power Press of John M. Cooper & Co., 1858.

Porter, William D. *State Pride: An Oration Delivered before the Calliopean and Polytechnic Societies of the State Military School, at Charleston, on the 5th April, 1860.* Charleston, SC: Walker, Evans, & Co., 1860.

Pratt, N. A. *Perils of a Dissolution of the Union: A Discourse, Delivered in the Presbyterian Church, of Roswell, on the Day of Public Thanksgiving, November 20, 1856.* Atlanta: C. R. Hanleiter, & Co., Printers, 1856.

Pressley, Benjamin C. *Reasons for the Dissolution of the Union, Being a Reply to the Letter of the Hon. W. J. Grayson, and to his Answer to One of the People.* Charleston, SC: A. J. Burke, 1850.

Pringle, W. Alston. *Oration Delivered before the Fourth of July Association, at the Hibernian Hall, July Fourth, 1850.* Charleston, SC: Steam-Power Press of Walker & James, 1850.

The Proceedings and Address of the Central Southern Rights Association of Virginia, to the Citizens of Virginia, Adopted January 10, 1851. Richmond, VA: Printed by Ritchies and Dunnavant, 1851.

Proceedings of the Meeting of Delegates from the Southern Rights Associations of South Carolina, held at Charleston, May 1851. Columbia, SC: Printed by Johnson & Cavis, 1851.

Ramsay, J. G. *Duty of Literary Men to Their Country: An Address Delivered before the Alumni of Davidson College, North Carolina.* Salisbury, NC: Bruner & James, 1849.

———. *Love of Country: An Address Delivered before the Ciceronian and Platonic Societies of the United Baptist Institute, Taylorsville, N.C., May 31, 1860.* Salisbury, NC: J. J. Bruner, Printer, 1860.

Ransom, Matt W. *Address Delivered before the Dialectic and Philanthropic Societies of the University of North Carolina, June 4, 1856.* Raleigh, NC: "Carolina Cultivator" Office, 1856.

The Reconciliation of the Unfortunate Quarrel between "Charlie of the South," and his Brother Jonathan, "Away down East": A Dialogue—in One Act. 2nd ed. Charleston, SC, 1848.

Reese, George, ed. *Proceedings of the Virginia State Convention of 1861, February 13–May 1.* 4 vols. Richmond: Virginia State Library, 1965.

Richardson, James D., ed. *A Compilation of the Messages and Papers of the Confederacy.* 2 vols. Nashville, TN: United States Publishing Company, 1906.

Richardson, John Peter. *Oration, Delivered in Clarendon, on the Fourth of July, 1851.* Columbia, SC: Printed at the South Carolinian Office, 1851.

Rives, W. C. *Discourse on the Uses and Importance of History: Illustrated by a Comparison of the French and American Revolutions; Delivered before the Historical Department of the Society of Alumni of the University of Virginia, 29th June 1847.* Richmond, VA: Printed by Shepherd and Colin, 1847.

Robertson, James I., Jr., ed. *Soldier of Southwestern Virginia: The Civil War Letters of Captain John Preston Sheffey.* Baton Rouge: Louisiana State University Press, 2004.

Ross, D. Barton *The Southern Speaker, or Sixth Reader: Containing, in Great Variety, the Masterpieces of Oratory in Prose, Poetry, and Dialogue.* New Orleans: J. B. Steel, 1856.

Ruffin, Edmund. *Anticipations of the Future, to Serve as Lessons for the Present Time, in the Form of Extracts from Letters from an English Resident in the United States, to the London Times, from 1864 to 1870.* Richmond, VA: J. W. Randolph, 1860.

———. *The Diary of Edmund Ruffin.* Edited by William Kauffman Scarborough. 3 vols. Baton Rouge: Louisiana State University Press, 1972–1989.

Russell, William Howard. *My Diary North and South.* Edited by Eugene H. Berwanger. Baton Rouge: Louisiana State University Press, 2001.

Rutherfoord, John C. *Speech of John C. Rutherfoord, of Goochland, in the House of Delegates of Virginia, 21 February, 1860, in Favor of the Proposed Conference of Southern States.* Richmond, VA: Wm. H. Clemmitt, Printer, 1860.

Simms, William Gilmore. *Areytos, or Songs and Ballads of the South, with other Poems.* Charleston, SC: Russell & Jones, 1860.

———. *The Letters of William Gilmore Simms.* Edited by Mary C. Simms Oliphant, Alfred Taylor Odell, and T. C. Duncan Eaves. 6 vols. Columbia: University of South Carolina Press, 1952–82.

———. *Poems, Descriptive, Dramatic, Legendary, and Contemplative.* 2 vols. Charleston, SC: John Russell, 1853.

———. *Self-Development: An Oration, Delivered before the Literary Societies of Oglethorpe University, Georgia; November 10, 1847.* Milledgeville, GA: Published by the Thalian Society, 1847.

———. *The Simms Reader: Selections from the Writings of William Gilmore Simms.* Edited by John Caldwell Guilds. Publications of the Southern Texts Society. Charlottesville: University Press of Virginia, 2001.

———. *The Social Principle: The True Source of National Permanence: An Oration, delivered before the Erosophic Society of the University of Alabama, December 13, 1842.* Reprinted from 1843 edition, with a preface by David Moltke-Hansen. Columbia: Southern Studies Program, University of South Carolina, 1980.

———. *The Sources of American Independence: An Oration, on the Sixty-Ninth Anniversary of American Independence, Delivered at Aiken, South-Carolina, before the Town Council and Citizens Thereof.* Aiken, SC: Published by Council, 1844.

————, ed. *War Poetry of the South*. New York: Richardson & Company, 1866.

Smith, Robert. *An Address to the Citizens of Alabama on the Constitution and Laws of the Confederate States of America by the Hon. Robert H. Smith, at Temperance Hall, on the 30th March, 1861*. Mobile, AL: Mobile Daily Register Print 1861.

Smith, Whitefoord. *God, the Refuge of His People, Delivered before the General Assembly of South Carolina, on Friday, December 6 1850, being a Day of Fasting, Humiliation, and Prayer*. Columbia, SC: Printed by A. S. Johnson, 1850.

[Smythe, James M.] *Ethel Somers; or, The Fate of the Union*. Augusta, GA: H. D. Norrell, 1857.

Sparrow, William. *The Nation's Privileges, and Their Preservation: A Sermon Preached on the Day of Our National Anniversary, 1852, in Christ Church, Alexandria, Va.* Philadelphia: T. K. and P. G. Collins, 1852.

St. Paul, Henry. *Our Home and Foreign Policy*. Mobile, AL: Printed at the Office of the Daily Register and Advertiser, 1863.

Taggart, Charles M. *The Moral Mission of Our Country: Two Discourses Delivered before the Unitarian Christians, of Charleston, S.C. on Sunday, July 3d*. Charleston, SC: Steam Power-Press of Walker & James, 1853.

Terrell, Alexander Watkins. *Oration Delivered on the Fourth Day of July, 1861, at the Capitol, Austin, Texas*. Austin, TX: Printed by J. Marshall at "Gazette" Office, 1861.

Trescot, William H. *The Diplomacy of the Revolution: An Historical Study*. New York: D. Appleton & Co., 1852.

————. *Oration Delivered before the Beaufort Volunteer Artillery, on July 4th, 1850*. Charleston, SC: Press of Walker & James, 1850.

————. "Oration Delivered before the South-Carolina Historical Society, Thursday, May 19, 1859." In *Collections of the South Carolina Historical Society*, 3:9–10. Charleston, SC: South Carolina Historical Society, 1859.

————. *Oration Delivered before the Washington Light Infantry on the 22d February 1847*. Charleston, SC: Printed by Walter & Burke, 1847.

————. *The Position and Course of the South*. Charleston, SC: Walker & James, 1850.

Tucker, Henry H. *God in the War: A Sermon Delivered before the Legislature of Georgia, in the Capitol at Milledgeville, on Friday, November 15, 1861, Being a Day Set Apart for Fasting, Humiliation and Prayer, by His Excellency the President of the Confederate States*. Milledgeville, GA: Boughton, Nisbet & Barnes, State Printers, 1861.

Tucker, Nathaniel Beverly. *The Partisan Leader: A Tale of the Future*. Edited by C. Hugh Holman. Chapel Hill: University of North Carolina Press, 1971.

————. *Prescience: A Speech, Delivered by Hon, Beverly Tucker, of Virginia, in the Southern Convention, Held at Nashville, Tenn., April 13th, 1850*. Richmond, VA: West & Johnson, 1862.

Voorhees, D. W. *The American Citizen: An Address Delivered by Hon. D. W. Voorhees, of Indiana, before the Literary Societies of the University of Virginia, July 4th, 1860*. Terre Haute, IN: R. H. Simpson & Co. Printers, 1860.

Wakelyn, Jon L., ed. *Southern Pamphlets on Secession, November 1860–April 1861.* Chapel Hill: University of North Carolina Press, 1996.

———, ed. *Southern Unionist Pamphlets and the Civil War.* Columbia: University of Missouri Press, 1999.

Wallace, Daniel. *The Political Life and Services of the Hon. R. Barnwell Rhett, of South Carolina, by "A Cotemporary" (the Late Hon. Daniel Wallace): Also, His Speech at Grahamville, South Carolina, July 4th, 1859.* N.p.; microfilmed by SCHS.

Ward, John E. *Address Delivered before the Georgia Historical Society, on its Nineteenth Anniversary, February 12, 1858, by John E. Ward.* Savannah, GA: George N. Nichols, Printer, 1858.

Webster, Noah. *An American Dictionary of the English Language.* Unabridged. Pictorial Edition, Philadelphia: J. B. Lippincott & Co., 1859.

Woodward, C. Vann. ed. *Mary Chesnut's Civil War.* New Haven, CT: Yale University Press, 1981.

Wright, Joshua G. *An Oration: Delivered in the Methodist Episcopal Church, Wilmington, N. C. on the Fourth of July, A.D. 1851.* Wilmington, NC: Printed at the "Herald" Book and Job Office, 1851.

Yearns, W. Buck, and John G. Barrett. *North Carolina Civil War Documentary.* Chapel Hill: University of North Carolina Press, 1980.

Yellott, Coleman. *Oration Delivered by Coleman Yellott, Esq., of Baltimore, at the Celebration at St. Timothy's Hall, Baltimore County, Maryland, July 5th, 1852.* Baltimore: Jos. Robinson, 1852.

SECONDARY SOURCES

Anderson, Benedict. *Imagined Communities: Reflections on the Origin and Spread of Nationalism.* 2nd ed. London: Verso, 1991.

Appelbaum, Diana Karter. *The Glorious Fourth: An American Holiday, an American History.* New York: Facts on File, 1989.

Appleby, Joyce, Lynn Hunt, and Margaret Jacob, *Telling the Truth about History.* New York: Norton, 1994.

Armitage, David. *The Declaration of Independence: A Global History.* Cambridge, MA: Harvard University Press, 2007.

Armstrong, John. *Nations before Nationalism.* Chapel Hill: University of North Carolina Press, 1982.

Ash, Stephen V. *When the Yankees Came: Conflict and Chaos in the Occupied South, 1861–1865.* Chapel Hill: University of North Carolina Press, 1995.

Ashworth, John. *Slavery, Capitalism, and Politics in the Antebellum Republic.* Vol. 1, *Commerce and Compromise, 1820–1850.* Cambridge, UK: Cambridge University Press, 1995.

Ayers, Edward L. *In the Presence of Mine Enemies: War in the Heart of America, 1859–1863.* New York: Norton, 2003.

———. *What Caused The Civil War? Reflections on the South and Southern History.* New York: Norton, 2005.

Ayers, Edward L., Patricia Nelson Limerick, Stephen Nissenbaum, and Peter S. Onuf. *All Over the Map: Rethinking American Regions.* Baltimore: Johns Hopkins University Press, 1996.

Baker, Thomas N. "National History in the Age of Michelet, Macaulay, and Bancroft." In *A Companion to Western Historical Thought,* edited by Lloyd Kramer and Sarah Maza, 185–204. Malden, MA: Blackwell, 2002.

Bailyn, Bernard. *The Ideological Origins of the American Revolution.* Rev. ed. Cambridge, MA: Belknap Press of Harvard University Press, 1992.

Balibar, Etienne, and Immanuel Maurice Wallerstein. *Race, Nation, Class: Ambiguous Identities.* London: Verso, 1991.

Balogh, Brian. *A Government Out of Sight: The Mystery of National Authority in Nineteenth-Century America.* Cambridge, UK: Cambridge University Press, 2009.

Barney, William L. *The Making of a Confederate: Walter Lenoir's Civil War.* Oxford: Oxford University Press, 2008.

———. *The Road to Secession: A New Perspective on the Old South.* New York: Praeger, 1972.

———. *The Secessionist Impulse: Alabama and Mississippi in 1860.* Rev ed. Tuscaloosa: University of Alabama Press, 2004. First published 1974 by Princeton University Press.

Barnwell, John. *Love of Order: South Carolina's First Secession Crisis.* Chapel Hill: University of North Carolina Press, 1982.

Baron, Beth. "The Construction of National Honour in Egypt." *Gender and History* 5, no. 2 (1993): 244–255.

Baycroft, Timothy, and Mark Hewitson, eds. *What Is a Nation? Europe 1789–1914.* Oxford: Oxford University Press, 2006.

Bayly, C. A. *The Birth of the Modern World, 1780–1914: Global Connections and Comparisons.* Malden, MA: Blackwell, 2004.

———. *Origins of Nationality in South Asia: Patriotism and Ethical Government in the Making of Modern India.* New Delhi: Oxford University Press, 1998.

Bayly, C. A., and Eugenio F. Biagini, eds. *Giuseppe Mazzini and the Globalisation of Democratic Nationalism, 1830–1920.* Oxford: Oxford University Press for the British Academy, 2008.

Beissinger, Mark R. "How Nationalisms Spread: Eastern Europe Adrift the Tides and Cycles of Nationalist Contention." *Social Research* 63 (Spring 1996): 97–146.

Bellah, Robert N. "Civil Religion in America." *Daedalus* 96 (1967): 1–21.

Bender, Thomas. *A Nation among Nations: America's Place in World History.* New York: Hill & Wang, 2006.

Bensel, Richard F. *Yankee Leviathan: The Origins of Central State Authority in America, 1859–1877.* Cambridge, UK: Cambridge University Press, 1991.

Berends, Kurt O. "Confederate Sacrifice and the 'Redemption' of the South." In *Religion in the American South: Protestants and Others in History and Culture*, edited by Beth Barton Schweiger and Donald G. Mathews, 99–123. Chapel Hill: University of North Carolina Press, 2004.

Berger, Stefan. "National Movements." In *A Companion to Nineteenth Century Europe, 1789–1914*, edited by Stefan Berger, 178–192. Malden, MA: Blackwell, 2006.

Berger, Stefan, Mark Donovan, and Kevin Passmore, eds. *Writing National Histories: Western Europe since 1800*. London: Routledge, 1999.

Beringer, Richard E., Herman Hattaway, Archer Jones, and William N. Still, Jr. *Why the South Lost the Civil War*. Athens, GA: University of Georgia Press, 1986.

Bernath, Michael. *Confederate Minds: The Struggle for Intellectual Independence in the Civil War South*. Chapel Hill: University of North Carolina Press, 2010.

Berry, Stephen W., II. *All That Makes a Man: Love and Ambition in the Civil War South*. New York: Oxford University Press, 2003.

———. *House of Abraham: Lincoln and the Todds; A Family Divided by War*. Boston: Houghton Mifflin, 2007.

Bhabha, Homi K., ed. *Nation and Narration*. New York: Routledge, 1990.

Billig, Michael. *Banal Nationalism*. London: Sage, 1995.

Binkley, Robert C. *Realism and Nationalism, 1852–1871*. New York: Harper & Brothers, 1935.

Binnington, Ian. "'They Have Made a Nation': Confederates and the Creation of Confederate Nationalism." PhD diss., University of Illinois, 2004.

Blair, William. *Virginia's Private War: Feeding Body and Soul in the Confederacy, 1861–1865*. New York: Oxford University Press, 1998.

Blight, David. "No Desperate Hero: Manhood and Freedom in a Union Soldier's Experience." In Clinton and Silber, *Divided Houses*, 55–75.

———. *Race and Reunion: The Civil War in American Memory*. Cambridge, MA: Harvard University Press, 2001.

Blom, Ida, Catherine Hall, and Karen Hagemann, eds. *Gendered Nations: Nationalisms and Gender Order in the Long Nineteenth Century*. Oxford: Berg, 2000.

Bonner, Robert E. *Colors and Blood: Flag Passions of the Confederate South*. Princeton, NJ: Princeton University Press, 2002.

———. *Mastering America: Southern Slaveholders and the Crisis of American Nationhood*. Cambridge, UK: Cambridge University Press, 2009.

———. "Roundheaded Cavaliers? The Context and Limits of a Confederate Racial Project." *Civil War History* 48, no. 1 (2002): 34–59.

Boyce, D. George. *Nationalism in Ireland*. 2nd ed. London: Routledge, 1991.

Bracewell, Wendy. "Rape in Kosovo: Masculinity and Serbian Nationalism." *Nations and Nationalism* 6, no. 4 (October 2000): 563–590.

Bradburn, Douglas. *The Citizenship Revolution: Politics and the Creation of the American Union, 1774–1804*. Charlottesville: University of Virginia Press, 2009.

Brauer, Kinley J. "The Slavery Problem in the Diplomacy of the American Civil War." *Pacific Historical Review* 46, no. 3 (August 1977): 439–469.

Breen, T. H. *The Marketplace of Revolution: How Consumer Politics Shaped American Independence.* New York: Oxford University Press, 2004.

Breuilly, John. *The Formation of the First German Nation-State, 1800–1871.* Basingstoke, UK: Macmillan, 1996.

———. "Historians and the Nation." In *History and Historians in the Twentieth Century,* edited by Peter Burke, 55–87. Oxford: Oxford University Press, 2002.

———. *Nationalism and the State.* 2nd ed. Manchester: Manchester University Press, 1993.

Brewer, John. *The Sinews of Power: War, Money, and the English State, 1688–1783.* New York: Knopf, 1989.

Britton, James C. "The Decline and Fall of Nations in Antebellum Southern Thought: A Study of Southern Historical Consciousness." PhD diss., University of North Carolina, 1988.

Browning, Judkin. "Removing the Mask of Nationality: Unionism, Racism, and Federal Military Occupation in North Carolina, 1862–1865." *Journal of Southern History* 71, no. 3 (August 2005): 589–620.

Rogers M. Smith, "The 'American Creed' and American Identity: The Limits of Liberal Citizenship in the United States." *Western Political Quarterly* 41 (1988): 225–251.

———. *Citizenship and Nationhood in France and Germany.* Cambridge, MA: Harvard University Press, 1992.

Brundage, W. Fitzhugh. *The Southern Past: A Clash of Race and Memory.* Cambridge, MA: Harvard University Press, 2005.

Budd, John. "Henry Timrod: Poetic Voice of Southern Nationalism." *Southern Studies* 20 (1981): 437–446.

Bynum, Victoria. *Unruly Women: The Politics of Social and Sexual Control in the Old South.* Chapel Hill: University of North Carolina Press, 1992.

———. "'War within a War': Women's Participation in the Revolt of the North Carolina Piedmont, 1863–1865." *Frontiers* 9 (1987): 43–49.

Campbell, Jacqueline Glass. *When Sherman Marched North from the Sea: Resistance on the Confederate Home Front.* Chapel Hill: University of North Carolina Press, 2003.

Carmichael, Peter. *The Last Generation: Young Virginians in Peace, War, and Reunion.* Chapel Hill: University of North Carolina Press, 2005.

Carpenter, Jesse T. *The South as a Conscious Minority, 1789–1861.* Edited by John McCardell. Columbia: University of South Carolina Press, 1990. First printed 1930 by the New York University Press.

Cauthen, Bruce. "Confederate and Afrikaner Nationalism: Myth, Identity, and Gender in Comparative Perspective." PhD diss., University of London, 1999.

———. "Covenant and Continuity: Ethno-Symbolism and the Myth of Divine Election." *Nations and Nationalism* 10, no. 1 (January 2004): 24–25.

Centeno, Miguel Angel. *Blood and Debt: War and the Nation-State in Latin America.* University Park: Pennsylvania State University Press, 2002.

Channing, Steven A. *Crisis of Fear: Secession in Carolina.* New York: Norton, 1974.

Chasteen, John Charles. *Americanos: Latin America's Struggle for Independence.* New York: Oxford University Press, 2008.

Cheng, Eileen Ka-May. *The Plain and Noble Garb of Truth: Nationalism and Impartiality in American Historical Writing, 1784–1860.* Athens, GA: University of Georgia Press, 2008.

Clinton, Catherine, and Nina Silber, eds. *Divided Houses: Gender and the Civil War.* New York: Oxford University Press, 1992.

Cobb, James C. *Away Down South: A History of Southern Identity.* New York: Oxford University Press, 2005.

Cohen, Lester H. *The Revolutionary Histories: Contemporary Narratives of the American Revolution.* Ithaca, NY: Cornell University Press, 1980.

Colbourn, Trevor. *The Lamp of Experience: Whig History and the Intellectual Origins of the American Revolution.* Indianapolis: Liberty Fund, 1998. First published 1965 by University of North Carolina Press.

Colley, Linda. *Britons: Forging the Nation: 1707–1837.* New Haven, CT: Yale University Press, 1992.

———. *Captives: The Story of Britain's Pursuit of Empire and How Its Soldiers and Civilians Were Held Captive by the Dream of Global Supremacy, 1600–1850.* New York: Pantheon Books, 2002.

Comaroff, John L., and Paul C. Stern, eds. *Perspectives on Nationalism and War.* London: Gordon & Breach, 1995.

Coulter, E. Merton "What the South Has Done about Its History." *Journal of Southern History* 2 (1936): 3–28.

Craven, Avery. *Edmund Ruffin, Southerner: A Study in Secession.* Baton Rouge: Louisiana State University Press, 1991. First published 1932 by Appleton.

———. *The Growth of Southern Nationalism, 1848–1861.* A History of the South 6. Baton Rouge: Louisiana State University Press, 1953.

Crofts, Daniel. *Reluctant Confederates: Upper South Unionists in the Secession Crisis.* Chapel Hill: University of North Carolina Press, 1989.

Current-Garcia, Eugene. "Southern Literary Criticism and the Sectional Dilemma." *Journal of Southern History* 15 (1949): 325–341.

Curti, Merle. *The Roots of American Loyalty.* New York: Columbia University Press, 1946.

Dal Lago, Enrico. *Agrarian Elites: American Slaveholders and Southern Italian Landowners, 1815–1861.* Baton Rouge: Louisiana State University Press, 2005.

Davis, William C. *Rhett: The Turbulent Life and Times of a Fire-Eater.* Columbia: University of South Carolina Press, 2001.

Day, Graham, and Andrew Thompson. *Theorizing Nationalism.* Basingstoke, UK: Palgrave Macmillan, 2004.

Deák, István. *Lawful Revolution: Louis Kossuth and the Hungarians, 1848–1849.* London: Phoenix, 2001.

Degler, Carl. "One among Many: The United States and National Unification," in *Lincoln, the War President,* edited by Gabor S. Boritt, 91–119. New York: Oxford University Press, 1992.

Dennis, Matthew. *Red, White, and Blue Letter Days: An American Calendar.* Ithaca, NY: Cornell University Press, 2002.

Dew, Charles B. *Apostles of Disunion: Southern Secession Commissioners and the Causes of the Civil War.* Charlottesville: University Press of Virginia, 2001.

Dirck, Brian R. "Posterity's Blush: Civil Liberties, Property Rights, and Property Confiscation in the Confederacy." *Civil War History* 48 (2003): 237–256.

Doyle, Don H. *Nations Divided: America, Italy, and the Southern Question.* Athens, GA: University of Georgia Press, 2002.

———, ed. *Secession as an International Phenomenon.* Athens, GA: University of Georgia Press, 2010.

Doyle, Don H., and Marco Antonio Pamplona, eds. *Nationalism in the New World.* Athens, GA: University of Georgia Press, 2006.

Durrill, Wayne K. "Ritual, Community and War: Local Flag Presentation Ceremonies and Disunity in the Early Confederacy." *Journal of Social History* 39 (2006): 1105–1122.

———. *War of Another Kind: A Southern Community in the Great Rebellion.* New York: Oxford University Press, 1990.

Edwards, Laura. *Gendered Strife and Confusion: The Political Culture of Reconstruction.* Urbana: University of Illinois Press, 1997.

———. *Scarlett Doesn't Live Here Anymore: Southern Women in the Civil War Era.* Urbana: University of Illinois Press, 2000.

Ehrenreich, Barbara. *Blood Rites: Origins and History of the Passions of War.* New York: Metropolitan Books, 1997.

Escott, Paul D. *After Secession: Jefferson Davis and the Failure of Confederate Nationalism.* Baton Rouge: Louisiana State University Press, 1978.

Etcheson, Nicole. *Bleeding Kansas: Contested Liberty in the Civil War Era.* Lawrence: University Press of Kansas, 2004.

Ezell, John S. "A Southern Education for Southrons." *Journal of Southern History* 17, no. 3 (August 1951): 303–327.

Fahs, Alice. *The Imagined Civil War: Popular Literature of the North and South, 1861–1865.* Chapel Hill: University of North Carolina Press, 2001.

Faust, Drew Gilpin. "Altars of Sacrifice: Confederate Women and the Narrative of War." In Clinton and Silber, *Divided Houses,* 171–199.

———. "Christian Soldiers: The Meaning of Revivalism in the Confederate Army." *Journal of Southern History* 53, no. 1 (1987): 63–90.

———. *The Creation of Confederate Nationalism: Ideology and Identity in the Civil War South.* Baton Rouge: Louisiana State University Press, 1988.

———. "'The Dread Voice of Uncertainty': Naming the Dead in the American Civil War." *Southern Cultures* 11, no. 2 (Summer 2005): 7–32.

———, ed. *The Ideology of Slavery: Proslavery Thought in the Antebellum South, 1830–1860*. Baton Rouge: Louisiana State University Press, 1981.

———. *James Henry Hammond and the Old South: A Design for Mastery*. Baton Rouge: Louisiana State University Press, 1982.

———. *Mothers of Invention: Women of the Slaveholding South in the American Civil War*. New York: Random House, 1996.

———. *A Sacred Circle: The Dilemma of the Intellectual in the Old South, 1840–1860*. Baltimore: Johns Hopkins University Press, 1977.

———. *This Republic of Suffering: Death and the American Civil War*. New York: Knopf, 2008.

Fehrenbacher, Don E. *The Slaveholding Republic: An Account of the United States Government's Relations to Slavery*. New York: Oxford University Press, 2001.

Ford, Lacy K., Jr. *Origins of Southern Radicalism: The South Carolina Upcountry, 1800–1860*. New York: Oxford University Press, 1988.

Forgie, George B. *Patricide in the House Divided: A Psychological Interpretation of Lincoln and His Age*. New York: Norton, 1979.

Fought, Leigh. *Southern Womanhood and Slavery: A Biography of Louisa S. McCord, 1810–1879*. Columbia: University of Missouri Press, 2003.

Foster, Gaines M. *Ghosts of the Confederacy: Defeat, the Lost Cause, and the Emergence of the New South*. New York: Oxford University Press, 1987.

Fox-Genovese, Elizabeth. *Within the Plantation Household: Black and White Women of the Old South*. Chapel Hill: University of North Carolina Press, 1988.

Fox-Genovese, Elizabeth, and Eugene D. Genovese. *The Mind of the Master Class: History and Faith in the Southern Slaveholders' Worldview*. Cambridge, UK: Cambridge University Press, 2005.

Franklin, John Hope. "The North, the South, and the American Revolution." *Journal of American History* 62 (1975): 5–23.

Fredrickson, George M. *The Black Image in the White Mind: The Debate on Afro-American Character and Destiny, 1817–1914*. New York: Harper & Row, 1971.

———. "The Historical Construction of Race and Citizenship in the United States." In *Diverse Nations: Explorations in the History of Racial and Ethnic Pluralism*, 21–38. Boulder, CO: Paradigm, 2008.

———. *White Supremacy: A Comparative Study in American and South African History*. New York: Oxford University Press, 1981.

Freehling, William W. *Prelude to Civil War: The Nullification Controversy in South Carolina, 1816–1836*. New York: Harper & Row, 1966.

———. *The Road to Disunion*. 2 vols. New York: Oxford University Press, 1990–2007.

———. *The South versus the South: How Anti-Confederate Southerners Shaped the Course of the Civil War*. New York: Oxford University Press, 2001.

Friend, Craig Thompson, and Lorri Glover, eds. *Southern Manhood: Perspectives on Masculinity in the Old South.* Athens, GA: University of Georgia Press, 2004.

Gallagher, Gary W. *The Confederate War: How Popular Will, Nationalism, and Military Strategy Could Not Stave Off Defeat.* Cambridge, MA: Harvard University Press, 1997.

———. "Disaffection, Persistence, and Nation: Some Directions in Recent Scholarship on the Confederacy." *Civil War History* 55, no. 3 (2009): 329–353

Gellner, Ernest. *Nations and Nationalism.* Oxford: Blackwell, 1983.

Genovese, Eugene D. "King Solomon's Dilemma—and the Confederacy's." *Southern Cultures* 10, no. 4 (Winter 2004): 55–75.

———. *The Political Economy of Slavery: Studies in the Economy and Society of the Slave South.* New York: Random House, 1965.

———. *The Slaveholders' Dilemma: Freedom and Progress in Southern Conservative Thought, 1820–1860.* Columbia: University of South Carolina Press, 1995.

———. *The World the Slaveholders Made: Two Essays in Interpretation.* New York: Random House, 1969.

Gerstle, Gary. *American Crucible: Race and Nation in the Twentieth Century.* Princeton, NJ: Princeton University Press, 2001.

Gleeson, David T. *The Irish in the South, 1815–1877.* Chapel Hill: University of North Carolina Press, 2001.

Gordon, Lesley J., and John C. Inscoe, eds. *Inside the Confederate Nation: Essays in Honor of Emory M. Thomas.* Baton Rouge: Louisiana State University Press, 2005.

Grant, Susan-Mary. "Americans Forging a New Nation, 1860–1916." In Doyle and Pamplona, *Nationalism in the New World,* , 80–98.

———. "'The Charter of its Birthright': The Civil War and American Nationalism." *Nations and Nationalism* 4, no. 2 (1998): 163–185.

———. *North over South: Northern Nationalism and American Identity in the Antebellum Era.* Lawrence: University Press of Kansas, 2000.

Green, Abigail. *Fatherlands: State-Building and Nationhood in Nineteenth-Century Germany.* Cambridge, UK: Cambridge University Press, 2001.

Green, Fletcher M. "Listen to the Eagle Scream: One Hundred Years of the Fourth of July in North Carolina (1776–1876)." *North Carolina Historical Review* 31 (1954): 295–320, 529–549.

Greenberg, Kenneth. *Masters and Statesman: The Political Culture of American Slavery.* New Studies in American Intellectual and Cultural History. Baltimore: Johns Hopkins University Press, 1985.

Greenfeld, Liah. *Nationalism: Five Roads to Modernity.* Cambridge, MA: Harvard University Press, 1992.

Guterl, Matthew Pratt. *American Mediterranean: Southern Slaveholders in the Age of Emancipation.* Cambridge, MA: Harvard University Press, 2008.

Guyatt, Nicholas. *Providence and the Invention of the United States, 1607–1876.* New York: Cambridge University Press, 2007.

Hagemann, Karen. "Of 'Manly Valor' and 'German Honor': Nation, War, and Masculinity in the Age of the Prussian Uprising Against Napoleon." *Central European History* 30 (1997): 187–220.

Hahn, Steven. *A Nation under Our Feet: Black Political Struggles in the Rural South from Slavery to the Great Migration.* Cambridge, MA: Harvard University Press, 2003.

———. *The Roots of Southern Populism: Yeoman Farmers and the Transformation of the Georgia Upcountry, 1850–1890.* New York: Oxford University Press, 1983.

Hall, Catherine, Jane Lewis, Keith McClelland, and Jane Rendall, eds. "Special Issue on Gender, Nationalisms and National Identities." Special issue, *Gender and History* 5, no. 2 (Summer 1993).

Hamilton, Daniel W. "The Confederate Sequestration Act." *Civil War History* 52 (2006): 373–408.

Hay, Robert Pettus. "Freedom's Jubilee: One Hundred Years of the Fourth of July, 1776–1876." PhD diss., University of Kentucky, 1967.

Hayes, Carlton. *Essays on Nationalism.* New York: Russell & Russell, 1966. First published 1926 by Macmillan.

Hechter, Michael. *Containing Nationalism.* New York: Oxford University Press, 2000.

———. *Internal Colonialism: The Celtic Fringe in British National Development, 1536–1966.* Berkeley: University of California Press, 1975.

Heidler, David S. *Pulling the Temple Down: The Fire-Eaters and the Destruction of the Union.* Mechanicsburg, PA: Stackpole Books, 1994.

Helgerson, Richard. *Forms of Nationhood: The Elizabethan Writing of England.* Chicago: University of Chicago Press, 1995.

Higginbotham, Don. "War and State Formation in Revolutionary America." In *Empire and Nation: The American Revolution in the Atlantic World*, edited by Elija H. Gould and Peter S. Onuf, 54–71. Baltimore: Johns Hopkins University Press, 2005.

Hobsbawm, E. J. *Nations and Nationalism since 1780: Programme, Myth, Reality.* 2nd ed. Cambridge, UK: Cambridge University Press, 1992.

Hobsbawm, Eric, and Terence Ranger, eds. *The Invention of Tradition.* Cambridge, UK: Cambridge University Press, 1983.

Holt, Michael F. *The Political Crisis of the 1850s.* New York: Norton, 1983. First published 1978 by Wiley.

Horsman, Reginald. *Race and Manifest Destiny: The Origins of American Racial Anglo-Saxonism.* Cambridge, MA: Harvard University Press, 1981.

Hubbard, Charles M. *The Burden of Confederate Diplomacy.* Knoxville: University of Tennessee Press, 1998.

Huff, A. V., Jr. "The Eagle and the Vulture: Changing Attitudes Toward Nationalism in Fourth of July Orations Delivered in Charleston, 1778–1860." *South Atlantic Quarterly* 73 (1974): 10–22.

Hunt, Michael H. *Ideology and U.S. Foreign Policy*. New Haven, CT: Yale University Press, 1987.

Hutchinson, John. *The Dynamics of Cultural Nationalism: The Gaelic Revival and the Creation of the Irish Nation State*. London: Allen & Unwin, 1987.

Huysseune, Michael. "Masculinity and Secessionism in Italy: An Assessment." *Nations and Nationalism* 6, no. 4 (October 2000): 591–610.

Inscoe, John C., and Robert C. Kenzer, eds. *Enemies of the Country: New Perspectives on Unionists in the Civil War South*. Athens, GA: University of Georgia Press, 2001.

James, Joseph Ralph, Jr. "The Transformation of the Fourth of July in South Carolina, 1850 to 1919." MA thesis, Louisiana State University, 1987.

Jones, H. G., ed. *Historical Consciousness in the Early Republic: The Origins of State Historical Societies, Museums, and Collections, 1791–1861*. North Caroliniana Society Imprints 25. Chapel Hill, NC: North Caroliniana Society and North Carolina Collection, 1995.

Jones, Howard. *Blue and Gray Diplomacy: A History of Union and Confederate Foreign Relations*. Chapel Hill: University of North Carolina Press, 2010.

Kammen, Michael. *A Season of Youth: The American Revolution and the Historical Imagination*. Ithaca, NY: Cornell University Press, 1978.

Kandiyoti, Deniz, ed. "The Awkward Relationship: Gender and Nationalism." Special issue, *Nations and Nationalism* 6, no. 4 (October 2000).

Kedourie, Elie. *Nationalism*. 4th ed. Oxford: Blackwell, 1993.

Kerber, Linda K. "May All Our Citizens be Soldiers and All Our Soldiers Citizens: The Ambiguities of Female Citizenship in the New Nation." In *Women, Militarism, and War: Essays in History, Politics, and Social Theory*, edited by Jean Bethke Elshtain and Sheila Tobias, 89–103. Savage, MD: Rowman & Littlefield, 1990.

———. "The Meanings of Citizenship." *Journal of American History* 84, no. 3 (December 1997): 833–854.

———. *Women of the Republic: Intellect and Ideology in Revolutionary America*. Chapel Hill: University of North Carolina Press, 1980.

Kersh, Rogan. *Dreams of a More Perfect Union*. Ithaca, NY: Cornell University Press, 2001.

Kettner, James H. *The Development of American Citizenship, 1608–1870*. Chapel Hill: University of North Carolina Press, 1978.

Kimmel, Michael. *Manhood in America: A Cultural History*. New York: Free Press, 1996.

Klein, Stacey Jean. "Wielding the Pen: Margaret Preston, Confederate Nationalist Literature, and the Expansion of a Woman's Place in the South." *Civil War History* 49, no. 3 (September 2003): 221–234.

Kohn, Hans. *American Nationalism: An Interpretive Essay*. New York: Macmillan, 1957.

———. *Prophets and Peoples: Studies in Nineteenth Century Nationalism*. New York: Macmillan, 1946.

Kolchin, Peter. "The South and the World." *Journal of Southern History* 75, no. 3 (August 2009): 565–581.

———. *Unfree Labor: American Slavery and Russian Serfdom.* Cambridge, MA: Belknap Press of the Harvard University Press, 1987.

Kornprobst, Markus. "Episteme, Nation-Builders and National Identity: The Re-Construction of Irishness." *Nations and Nationalism* 11, no. 3 (July 2005): 403–421.

Kramer, Lloyd. *Nationalism: Political Cultures in Europe and America, 1775–1865.* Studies in Intellectual and Cultural History. New York: Twayne, 1998.

Kutolowski, John. "The Effect of the Polish Insurrection of 1863 on American Civil War Diplomacy." *Historian* 27 (1965): 560–577.

Lawrence, Paul. *Nationalism: History and Theory.* Harlow, UK: Pearson Longman, 2005.

Lawson, Melinda. *Patriot Fires: Forging a New American Nationalism in the Civil War North.* Lawrence: University Press of Kansas, 2002.

Leerssen, Joep. *National Thought in Europe: A Cultural History.* Amsterdam: Amsterdam University Press, 2006.

Lepore, Jill. *A is for American: Letters and Other Characters in the Newly United States.* New York: Knopf, 2002.

———. *In the Name of War: King Philip's War and the Origins of American Identity.* New York: Random House, 1998.

Lester, Connie. "Lucy Virginia French: Out of the Bitterness of My Heart." In *The Human Tradition in Civil War and Reconstruction,* edited by Steven E. Woodworth. Wilmington, DE: Scholarly Resources, 2000.

Levine, Bruce. *Confederate Emancipation: Southern Plans to Free and Arm Slaves During the Civil War.* New York: Oxford University Press, 2006.

Linderman, Gerald F. *Embattled Courage: The Experience of Combat in the American Civil War.* New York: Free Press, 1987.

Link, William A. *Roots of Secession: Slavery and Politics in Antebellum Virginia.* Chapel Hill: University of North Carolina Press, 2003.

Maier, Pauline. *American Scripture: Making the Declaration of Independence.* New York: Random House, 1997.

Majewski, John. *Modernizing a Slave Economy: The Economic Vision of the Confederate Nation.* Chapel Hill: University of North Carolina Press, 2009.

Manning, Chandra. *What This Cruel War was Over: Soldiers, Slavery, and the Civil War.* New York: Knopf, 2007.

Marraro, Howard Rosario. *American Opinion on the Unification of Italy, 1846–1861.* New York: Columbia University Press, 1932.

Mattson, Gregory Louis. "Pariah Diplomacy: The Slavery Issue in Confederate Foreign Relations." PhD diss., University of Southern Mississippi, 1999.

Maxwell, Alexander. "Multiple Nationalism: National Concepts in Nineteenth-Century Hungary and Benedict Anderson's Imagined Communities." *Nationalism and Ethnic Politics* 11 (2005): 385–414.

May, Robert E. "Psychobiography and Secession: The Southern Radical as Maladjusted 'Outsider.'" *Civil War History* 34 (1988): 46–69.

———. *The Southern Dream of a Caribbean Empire, 1854–1861*. Rev. ed. Gainesville: University Press of Florida, 2002.

———. *The Union, the Confederacy, and the Atlantic Rim*. West Lafayette, IN: Purdue University Press, 1995.

McCardell, John. *The Idea of a Southern Nation: Southern Nationalists and Southern Nationalism, 1830–1860*. New York: Norton, 1979.

McCaslin, Richard. *Lee in the Shadow of Washington*. Baton Rouge: Louisiana State University Press, 2001.

McCurry, Stephanie. *Confederate Reckoning: Power and Politics in the Civil War South*. Cambridge, MA: Harvard University Press, 2010.

———. *Masters of Small Worlds: Yeoman Households, Gender Relations, and the Political Culture of the Antebellum South Carolina Low Country*. New York: Oxford University Press, 1995.

McDaniel, W. Caleb. "Repealing Unions: American Abolitionists, Irish Repeal, and the Origins of Garrisonian Disunionism." *Journal of the Early Republic* 28 (2008): 243–269.

McDonald, Forrest. *States' Rights and the Union: Imperium in Imperio*. Lawrence: University Press of Kansas, 2000.

McGovern, Bryan P. *John Mitchel: Irish Nationalist, Southern Secessionist*. Knoxville: University of Tennessee Press, 2009.

McKenzie, Robert Tracy. "Contesting Secession: Parson Brownlow and the Rhetoric of Proslavery Unionism, 1860–1861." *Civil War History* 48 (2002): 294–312.

McPherson, James M. "Antebellum Southern Exceptionalism: A New Look at an Old Question." *Civil War History* 29 (1983): 230–244. Reprinted in *Civil War History* 50 (2004): 418–433

———. *For Cause and Comrades: Why Men Fought in the Civil War*. New York: Oxford University Press, 1997.

———. *Is Blood Thicker than Water? Crises of Nationalism in the Modern World*. New York: Vintage Books, 1998.

Miller, Randall M., Harry S. Stout, and Charles Reagan Wilson, eds. *Religion and the American Civil War*. New York: Oxford University Press, 1998.

Mitchell, Reid. "Soldiering, Manhood, and Coming of Age: A Northern Volunteer." In Clinton and Silber, *Divided Houses*, 43–54.

Moore, Albert Burton. *Conscription and Conflict in the Confederacy*. New York: Macmillan, 1924.

Morgan, Edmund. *American Slavery, American Freedom: The Ordeal of Colonial Virginia*. New York: Norton, 1975.

Morrison, Michael A. "American Reaction to European Revolutions, 1848–1852: Sectionalism, Memory, and the Revolutionary Heritage." *Civil War History* 49, no. 2 (2003): 111–132.

Morton, Graeme. *Unionist-Nationalism: Governing Urban Scotland, 1830–1860.* East Linton, UK: Tuckwell, 1999.

Mosse, George L. *Fallen Soldiers: Reshaping the Memory of the World Wars.* New York: Oxford University Press, 1990.

———. *Nationalism and Sexuality: Respectability and Abnormal Sexuality in Modern Europe.* New York: Fertig, 1985.

Mueller-Vollmer, Kurt. "The Discourse of a National Literature in the Early Republic, 1785–1846." In *Negotiations of America's National Identity,* edited by Roland Hagenbuchle and Josef Raab in cooperation with Marietta Messmer, 1:280–295. Tübingen, Germany: Stauffenburg Verlag, 2000.

Murrin, John M. "A Roof without Walls: The Dilemma of American National Identity." In *Beyond Confederation: Origins of the Constitution and American National Identity,* edited by Richard R. Beeman, Stephen Botein, and Edward C. Carter III, 333–348. Chapel Hill: University of North Carolina Press, 1987.

Nagel, Joane. "Masculinity and Nationalism: Gender and Sexuality in the Making of Nations." *Ethnic and Racial Studies* 21, no. 2 (March 1998): 242–269.

Nagel, Paul C. *One Nation Indivisible: The Union in American Thought, 1776–1861.* New York: Oxford University Press, 1964.

———. *This Sacred Trust: American Nationality, 1798–1898.* New York: Oxford University Press, 1971.

O'Brien, Michael. *Conjectures of Order: Intellectual Life and the American South, 1810–1860.* 2 vols. Chapel Hill: University of North Carolina Press, 2004.

———. *Rethinking the South: Essays in Intellectual History.* Baltimore: Johns Hopkins University Press, 1988.

O'Leary, Cecilia Elizabeth. *To Die for: The Paradox of American Patriotism.* Princeton, N.J.: Princeton University Press, 2000.

Olsberg, R. Nicholas. "A Government of Class and Race: William Henry Trescot and the South Carolina Chivalry." PhD diss., University of South Carolina, 1972.

Olsen, Christopher J. *Political Culture and Secession in Mississippi: Masculinity, Honor, and the Antiparty Tradition, 1830–1860.* New York: Oxford University Press, 2000.

Onuf, Peter S. *Jefferson's Empire: The Language of American Nationhood.* Charlottesville: University Press of Virginia, 2000.

Onuf, Peter, and Nicholas Greenwood Onuf. *Nations, Markets, and War: Modern History and the American Civil War.* Charlottesville: University of Virginia Press, 2006.

Osterweis, Rollin G. *Romanticism and Nationalism in the Old South.* Baton Rouge: Louisiana State University Press, 1967. First published 1949 by Yale University Press.

Owens, Harry P., and James J. Cooke, eds. *The Old South in the Crucible of War.* Jackson: University Press of Mississippi, 1983.

Parish, Peter J. "An Exception to Most of the Rules: What Made American Nationalism Different in the Mid-Nineteenth Century?" *Prologue: Quarterly of the National Archives,* 27, no. 3 (Fall 1995): 219–229.

Parker, Andrew, Mary Russo, Doris Sommer, and Patricia Yaeger, eds. *Nationalisms and Sexualities*. New York: Routledge, 1992.

Persons, Stow. "The Cyclical Theory of History in Eighteenth Century America." *American Quarterly* 6 (1954): 147–163.

Pessen, Edward. "How Different from Each Other Were the Antebellum North and South?" *American Historical Review* 85 (1980): 1119–1149.

Peterson, Merrill D. *The Jefferson Image in the American Mind*. New York: Oxford University Press, 1960.

———. *John Brown: The Legend Revisited*. Charlottesville: University of Virginia Press, 2002.

Pflanze, Otto. "Nationalism in Europe, 1848–1871." *Review of Politics* 28 (April 1966): 129–143.

Phillips, Jason. *Diehard Rebels: The Confederate Culture of Invincibility*. Athens, GA: University of Georgia Press, 2007.

Phillips, Ulrich B. "The Central Theme of Southern History." *American Historical Review* 34, no. 1 (October 1928): 30–43.

Pocock, J. G. A. *The Machiavellian Moment: Florentine Political Thought and the Atlantic Republican Tradition*. Princeton, NJ: Princeton University Press, 1975.

Porter, Bruce D. *War and the Rise of the State: The Military Foundations of Modern Politics*. New York: Free Press, 1994.

Potter, David M. "The Civil War." In *The Comparative Approach to American History*, edited by C. Vann Woodward, 135–145. New York: Oxford University Press, 1968.

———. "The Historian's Use of Nationalism and Vice Versa." In *The South and the Sectional Conflict*, 34–83. Baton Rouge: Louisiana State University Press, 1968.

———. *The Impending Crisis, 1848–1861*. Completed and edited by Don E. Fehrenbacher. New American Nation Series. New York: Harper & Row, 1976.

Quigley, Paul. "Secessionists in an Age of Secession: The Slave South in Transatlantic Perspective." In *Secession as an International Phenomenon*, ed. Doyle, 151–173.

Quigley, Paul. "Independence Day Dilemmas in the American South, 1848–1865." *Journal of Southern History* 75, no. 2 (May 2009): 235–266.

———. "'That History is Truly the Life of Nations': History and Southern Nationalism in Antebellum South Carolina." *South Carolina Historical Magazine* 106, no. 1 (January 2005): 7–33.

Rable, George C. *Civil Wars: Women and the Crisis of Southern Nationalism*. Urbana: University of Illinois Press, 1989.

———. *The Confederate Republic: A Revolution against Politics*. Chapel Hill: University of North Carolina Press, 1994.

———. "'Missing in Action': Women of the Confederacy." In Clinton and Silber, *Divided Houses*, 134–146.

Reed, John Shelton. *The Enduring South: Subcultural Persistence in Mass Cultural Society*. Chapel Hill: University of North Carolina Press, 1986. First published 1972 by Lexington Books.

Reicher, Stephen, and Nick Hopkins. *Self and Nation: Categorization, Contestation and Mobilization*. London: Sage, 2001.

Renan, Ernest. "What Is a Nation?" In Bhabha, *Nation and Narration*, 8–22.

Riall, Lucy. *Garibaldi: Invention of a Hero*. New Haven, CT: Yale University Press, 2007.

———. *Risorgimento: The History of Italy from Napoleon to Nation-State*. New York: Palgrave Macmillan, 2009.

Roberts, Giselle. *The Confederate Belle*. Columbia: University of Missouri Press, 2003.

———. "Our Cause: Southern Women and Confederate Nationalism in Mississippi and Louisiana." *Journal of Mississippi History* 62 (Summer 2000).

Roberts, Timothy M. *Distant Revolutions: 1848 and the Challenge to American Exceptionalism*. Charlottesville: University of Virginia Press, 2009.

Rodgers, Daniel T. "Republicanism: The Career of a Concept." *Journal of American History* 79, no. 1 (June 1992): 11–38.

Rose, Sonya O. "Sex, Citizenship, and the Nation in World War II Britain." *American Historical Review* 103, no. 4 (1998): 1147–1176.

Ross, Dorothy. "'Are We a Nation?' The Conjuncture of Nationhood and Race in the United States, 1850–1876." *Modern Intellectual History* 2 (2005): 327–360.

———. "Historical Consciousness in Nineteenth-Century America." *American Historical Review* 89 (1984): 909–928.

Rossiter, Clinton. *The American Quest, 1790–1860: An Emerging Nation in Search of Identity, Unity, and Modernity*. New York: Harcourt Brace Jovanovich, 1971.

Royster, Charles. *The Destructive War: William Tecumseh, Stonewall Jackson, and the Americans*. New York: Knopf, 1991.

———. "Founding a Nation in Blood: Military Conflict and American Nationality." In *Arms and Independence: The Military Character of the American Revolution*, edited by Ronald Hoffman and Peter J. Albert, 25–49. Charlottesville: University Press of Virginia, 1984.

Rubin, Anne Sarah. "Seventy-six and Sixty-one: Confederates Remember the American Revolution." In *Where These Memories Grow: History, Memory, and Southern Identity*, edited by W. Fitzhugh Brundage, 85–105. Chapel Hill: University of North Carolina Press, 2000.

———. *A Shattered Nation: The Rise and Fall of the Confederacy, 1861–1868*. Chapel Hill: University of North Carolina Press, 2005.

Rugemer, Edward Bartlett. *The Problem of Emancipation: The Caribbean Roots of the American Civil War*. Baton Rouge: Louisiana State University Press, 2008.

Sacher, John M. "'A Very Disagreeable Business': Confederate Conscription in Louisiana." *Civil War History* 53 (2007): 141–169.

Samuel, Lawrence R. *Pledging Allegiance: American Identity and the Bond Drive of World War II*. Washington, DC: Smithsonian Institution Press, 1997.

Scarborough, William Kauffman. *Masters of the Big House: Elite Slaveholders of the Mid-Nineteenth-Century South*. Baton Rouge: Louisiana State University Press, 2003.

Schantz, Mark S. *Awaiting the Heavenly Country: The Civil War and America's Culture of Death*. Ithaca, NY: Cornell University Press, 2008.

Scheckel, Susan. *The Insistence of the Indian: Race and Nationalism in Nineteenth-Century American Culture*. Princeton, NJ: Princeton University Press, 1998.

Schoen, Brian. *The Fragile Fabric of Union: Cotton, Federal Politics, and the Global Origins of the Civil War*. Baltimore: Johns Hopkins University Press, 2009.

Schultz, Diane. *The Most Glorious Fourth: Vicksburg and Gettysburg, July 4, 1863*. New York: Norton, 2002.

Skurnowicz, Joan S. *Romantic Nationalism and Liberalism: Joachim Lelewel and the Polish National Idea*. Boulder, CO: East European Monographs, 1981.

Searle-White, Joshua. *The Psychology of Nationalism*. New York: Palgrave, 2001.

Sedgwick, Eve Kosofsky. "Nationalisms and Sexualities in the Age of Wilde," in Parker et al., *Nationalisms and Sexualities*, 235–245.

Sheehan-Dean, Aaron. *Why Confederates Fought: Family and Nation in Civil War Virginia*. Chapel Hill: University of North Carolina Press, 2007.

Siegel, Frederick F. *The Roots of Southern Distinctiveness: Tobacco and Society in Danville, Virginia, 1780–1865*. Chapel Hill: University of North Carolina Press, 1987.

Silber, Nina. *The Romance of Reunion: Northerners and the South, 1865–1900*. Chapel Hill: University of North Carolina Press, 1993.

Sinha, Manisha. *The Counterrevolution of Secession: Politics and Ideology in Antebellum South Carolina*. Chapel Hill: University of North Carolina Press, 2000.

Smith, Anthony D. *Chosen Peoples: Sacred Sources of National Identity*. Oxford: Oxford University Press, 2004.

———. *The Nation in History: Historiographical Debates about Ethnicity and Nationalism*. Menahem Stern Jerusalem Lectures. Hanover, NH: University Press of New England, 2000.

Smith, Dennis Mack. *Mazzini*. New Haven, CT: Yale University Press, 1994.

Smith, Rogers M. *Civic Ideals: Conflicting Visions of Citizenship in U.S. History*. New Haven, CT: Yale University Press, 1997.

Snay, Mitchell. *The Gospel of Disunion: Religion and Separatism in the Antebellum South*. Chapel Hill: University of North Carolina Press, 1997. First published 1993 by Cambridge University Press.

Spencer, Donald S. *Louis Kossuth and Young America: A Study of Sectionalism and Foreign Policy, 1848–1852*. Columbia: University of Missouri Press, 1977.

Steele, Brian. "Thomas Jefferson's Gender Frontier." *Journal of American History* 95, no. 1 (June 2008): 17–42.

Stern, Paul C. "Why do People Sacrifice for their Nations?" In Comaroff and Stern, *Perspectives on Nationalism and War*, 99–121.

Storey, Margaret M. "Civil War Unionists and the Political Culture of Loyalty in Alabama, 1861–1861." *Journal of Southern History* 69 (February 2003): 71–106.

———. *Loyalty and Loss: Alabama's Unionists in the Civil War and Reconstruction.*
Baton Rouge: Louisiana State University Press, 2004.

Sutherland, Daniel E., ed. *Guerrillas, Unionists, and Violence on the Confederate Home
Front.* Fayetteville: University of Arkansas Press, 1999.

Taylor, Amy Murrell. *The Divided Family in Civil War America.* Chapel Hill: University of North Carolina Press, 2005.

Taylor, William R. *Cavalier and Yankee: The Old South and American National Character.* Cambridge, MA: Harvard University Press, 1979.

Thomas, Emory M. *The Confederacy as a Revolutionary Experience.* Englewood Cliffs,
NJ: Prentice Hall, 1970.

———. *The Confederate Nation: 1861–1865.* New York: Harper & Row, 1979.

Thornton, J. Mills. *Politics and Power in a Slave Society: Alabama, 1800–1860.* Baton
Rouge: Louisiana State University Press, 1978.

Towers, Frank. "The Origins of the Antimodern South: Romantic Nationalism and
the Secession Movement in the American South." In *Secession as an International
Phenomenon,* ed. Doyle, 174–192.

Travers, Len. *Celebrating the Fourth: Independence Day and the Rites of Nationalism in
the Early Republic.* Amherst: University of Massachusetts Press, 1997.

Tuveson, Ernest Lee. *Redeemer Nation: The Idea of America's Millennial Role.* Chicago:
University of Chicago Press, 1968.

Van Young, Eric. "Revolution and Imagined Communities in Mexico, 1810–1821." In
Doyle and Pamplona, *Nationalism in the New World,* 184–207.

Varon, Elizabeth R. *Disunion! The Coming of the American Civil War, 1789–1859.*
Chapel Hill: University of North Carolina Press, 2008.

———. *We Mean to Be Counted: White Women and Politics in Antebellum Virginia.*
Chapel Hill: University of North Carolina Press, 1998.

Wakelyn, Jon L. *The Politics of a Literary Man: William Gilmore Simms.* Westport, CT:
Greenwood, 1973.

Waldstreicher, David. *In the Midst of Perpetual Fetes: The Making of American Nationalism, 1776–1820.* Chapel Hill: University of North Carolina Press, 1997.

Walther, Eric H. *The Fire-Eaters.* Baton Rouge: Louisiana State University Press, 1992.

———. *William Lowndes Yancey and the Coming of the American Civil War.* Chapel
Hill: University of North Carolina Press, 2006.

Watson, Harry L. "Conflict and Collaboration: Yeomen, Slaveholders, and Politics in
the Antebellum South." *Social History* 10 (1985): 273–298.

———. *Liberty and Power: The Politics of Jacksonian America.* New York: Hill & Wang,
1990.

Watson, Ritchie Devon, Jr. *Normans and Saxons: Southern Race Mythology and the
Intellectual History of the American Civil War.* Baton Rouge: Louisiana State University Press, 2008.

West, Stephen A. "Minute Men, Yeomen, and the Mobilization for Secession in the South Carolina Upcountry." *Journal of Southern History* 71, no. 1 (February 2005): 75–104.

Whitehead, Annie, Clara Connolly, Erica Carter, Helen Crowley, eds. "Nationalisms and National Identities." Special issue, *Feminist Review* 44 (Summer 1993).

Whites, Leann. *The Civil War as a Crisis in Gender: Augusta, Georgia, 1860–1890.* Athens, GA: University of Georgia Press, 1995.

———. "The Civil War as a Crisis in Gender." In Clinton and Silber, *Divided Houses,* 3–21.

Wiebe, Robert H. *Who We Are: A History of Popular Nationalism.* Princeton, NJ: Princeton University Press, 2002.

Williams, Colin, ed. *National Separatism.* Cardiff: University of Wales Press, 1982.

Wills, Garry. *Inventing America: Jefferson's Declaration of Independence.* Garden City, NY: Doubleday, 1978.

Wilson, Charles Reagan. *Baptized in Blood: The Religion of the Lost Cause.* Athens, GA: University of Georgia Press, 1980.

Wiltse, Charles M. "A Critical Southerner: John C. Calhoun on the Revolutions of 1848." *Journal of Southern History* 15 (1949): 299–310.

Wyatt-Brown, Bertram. *Hearts of Darkness: Wellsprings of a Southern Literary Tradition.* Baton Rouge: Louisiana State University Press, 2003.

———. *The Shaping of Southern Culture: Honor, Grace, and War, 1760s–1880s.* Chapel Hill: University of North Carolina Press, 2001.

———. *Southern Honor: Ethics and Behavior in the Old South.* New York: Oxford University Press, 1982.

Yearns, W. Buck. *The Confederate Congress.* Athens, GA: University of Georgia Press, 1960.

Zacek, Joseph Frederick. *Palacký: The Historian as Scholar and Nationalist.* The Hague: Mouton, 1970.

Zelinsky, Wilbur. *Nation into State: The Shifting Symbolic Foundations of American Nationalism.* Chapel Hill: University of North Carolina Press, 1988.

Index

CPSIA information can be obtained at www.ICGtesting.com
Printed in the USA
BVOW05s1544180914

367405BV00001B/1/P